HISTORICAL GAZETTEER
1785-1888

and

DIRECTORY, 1887-1888

of

Tioga County
New York

VOLUME TWO

DIRECTORY, 1887-1888

Compiled and Edited by

W. B. Gay

HERITAGE BOOKS
2008

HERITAGE BOOKS
AN IMPRINT OF HERITAGE BOOKS, INC.

Books, CDs, and more—Worldwide

For our listing of thousands of titles see our website
at
www.HeritageBooks.com

A Facsimile Reprint
Published 2008 by
HERITAGE BOOKS, INC.
Publishing Division
100 Railroad Ave. #104
Westminster, Maryland 21157

Originally published: W. B. Gay & Co.
The Syracuse Journal Company
Printers and Binders
Syracuse, New York
1887

— Publisher's Notice —
In reprints such as this, it is often not possible to remove blemishes from the original. We feel the contents of this book warrant its reissue despite these blemishes and hope you will agree and read it with pleasure.

International Standard Book Numbers
Paperbound: 978-0-7884-4894-2
Clothbound: 978-0-7884-7460-6

PART SECOND.

DIRECTORY

—OF—

TIOGA COUNTY, NEW YORK.

1887--'88.

COMPILED AND PUBLISHED

—BY—

W. B. GAY & CO.

PERMANENT OFFICE   -   -   -   SYRACUSE, N. Y.

"He that hath much to do, will do something wrong, and of that wrong must suffer the consequences; and if it were possible that he should always act rightly, yet when such numbers are to judge of his conduct, the bad will censure and obstruct him by malevolence, and the good sometimes by mistake."—SAMUEL JOHNSON.

SYRACUSE, N. Y.:
THE SYRACUSE JOURNAL COMPANY, PRINTERS AND BINDERS.
1887.

E. H. HOUSE'S
—IS THE PLACE TO BUY—
Coal, Wood, Lumber or Shingles.

SOUTHERN CENTRAL COAL YARD,
229 McMaster Street,   Owego, N. Y.

Owego Cruciform Casket Company.

Manufacturers of and dealers in all kinds of Lumber and Building Material. Planing and Matching, Re-sawing, Scroll Sawing, Bracket Sawing, Shaping and Turning of every description.

Doors, Sash and Blinds on hand and extra and odd sizes furnished at short notice.

French Glass of all sizes kept in stock, and Sash Doors and Windows glazed.

Flooring, Ceiling, Siding and Mouldings furnished in any quantity, large or small.

SHINGLES AND LATH.

All kinds of lumber in the rough or dressed kept constantly on hand.
Bee-hive and Honey-box material furnished to order.
Lumber taken in exchange for work.
Manufacturers of Hall's Celebrated Combined Sheathing and Lath, send for circulars and sample. Also manufacturers of all kinds of fine Cloth Covered Caskets, and dealers in fine finished wood Caskets and Coffins, and all kinds of

UNDERTAKER'S SUPPLIES.

Agents for Utopia, the "Triumph" Embalming Fluid of the age, and all kinds of Embalmer's Supplies.

All orders filled with accuracy and dispatch.

Send for illustrated album of styles and price list, and give us a trial.

OWEGO CRUCIFORM CASKET CO.,
OWEGO, TIOGA CO., N. Y.

Factory and Office, 42, 44 and 46 Delphine St.

STARKEY & WINTERS, Wholesale and Retail Druggists, Owego.

DIRECTORY
OF
TIOGA COUNTY, NEW YORK.

EXPLANATIONS.

Directory is arranged as follows:—
1—Name of individual or firm.
2—Postoffice address in parenthesis if different from the name of town.
3—The figures following the letter r indicate the number of the road on which the party resides, and will be found by reference to the map in the back part of this work. Where no road number is given the party is suppossd to reside in the village.
4—Business or occupation.
5—A star (*) placed before a name indicates an advertiser in this work.
6—Figures placed after the occupation of a farmer indicate the number of acres owned or leased
7—Names in CAPITALS are those who have kindly given their patronage to the work, and without whose aid its publication would have been impossible.

☞ **For additional names, changes and corrections, see Errata.**

ABBREVIATIONS.—Ab., above; ave., avenue; bds., boards; bet., between; cor., corner; E., east; emp., employee; fac. op., factory operative; h., house; manuf., manufacturer; Mfg., manufacturing; N., north; n., near; opp., opposite; prop., proprietor; reg., registered as applied to live stock; regt., regiment; S., south; supt., superintendent; W., west.
The word *street* is implied.

BARTON.

WAVERLY VILLAGE.*

(Postoffice address is Waverly, unless otherwise designated in parenthesis.)

Ackerly Nathaniel, clerk L. V. R. R. freight office, h 47 Waverly.
ACKLEY & BAILEY, (P. R. A. and J. B. B.) props. Tioga Hotel, Fulton cor. Elizabeth.
ACKLEY PERRIN R., (Ackley & Bailey) h S. Waverly.

---

* For the sake of convenience we print the directory of the incorporated village of Waverly separate from the balance of the town of Barton.
STARKEY & WINTERS, promptly fill Mail and Telephone Orders.

Akins Jane, dressmaker, 118 Clark, bds. do.
Albertson Charles, milk depot and creamery, h 5 Orange.
Albertson Clarence, milk dealer, bds. 5 Orange.
Albertson Daniel, retired, h 11 Orange.
Aldrich Samuel, emp. Novelty Works, h 344 Broad.
Aldrich Vernie, emp. Novelty Works, h 344 Broad.
ALLEN ADOLPHUS G., (Allen & Campbell) also att'y at law, over 203 Broad, h 8 Park Place.
Allen D. Wellington, att'y at law, bds. 8 Park Place.
Allen Elizabeth G., widow Peleg, h 33 Waverly.
Allen Louis S., clerk, bds. 33 Waverly.
Allen William H., resident, h 321 Broad.
American House, (A. P. Head, prop.) 260 Broad.
Andre Jacob, retired, bds. 19 Chemung.
Angell Edward J., market gardener, h 472 Chemung.
Angell James E., market gardener 470 Chemung, h do.
Angell Mary L., green-house, 472 Chemung.
Aplin Eliza, widow James, h 29 Waverly.
Atkins William, retired, h 120 Clark.
Atwater Dewitt C., livery and boarding stable, Clark, and farmer 200, h 139 Clark.
Atwater Lewis D., teller, First National Bank, bds. 139 Clark.
Atwood Mary S., widow Rev. William, bds. Pennsylvania ave.
Atwood William W., station agent D. L. & W. R. R., h 50 Fulton.
BAILEY JOHN B., (Ackley & Bailey) bds. Tioga Hotel.
Baker Mary T. Mrs., millinery, 143 Waverly, h do.
Baker Melvin J., carpenter, h 143 Waverly.
Baldwin Albert B., boots and shoes, 6 Fulton, h 300 Chemung cor. Fulton.
Baldwin Francis H., retired, h 300 Chemung.
BALDWIN HUGH J., lumber, also builder and jobber, Broad n. Pennsylvania ave., h 320 Pennsylvania ave.
Ball John M. Rev., retired Baptist clergyman, h. 8 Pine.
Barber Clara A., preceptress academy, bds. 11 Broad.
BARNES & MILLER, (B. D. B. and L. C. M.) groceries and provisions, 277 Broad.
BARNES BENJAMIN D., (Barnes & Miller) bds. Seely's Hotel.
Barnes John C., mason, h 10 Elm.
Barnum & Personius, (S. D. B. and D. V. P.) seed, hay and grain, 264 Broad.
Barnum Hervey J., printer, bds. 166 Clark.
Barnum John W., book-keeper, h 166 Clark.
Barnum Lillian, book-keeper, 264 Broad, bds. Bradford.
Barnum Smith D., (Barnum & Personius) h Bradford.
Barr John, upholsterer, h over 251 Broad.
Barr John C., cabinet maker, Elizabeth, h Chemung.
Barrington Michael, laborer, h Erie.
BARROWS ABRAM H., (Wilcox & Barrows) h 120 Waverly.
Barton Alfred, clerk, h Clark.
Barton Charles, emp. pipe foundry, h 102 Waverly.
Bassett Henry, carpenter, h Orange.
Bassett James, clerk, bds. over 226 Broad.
Bauer Andrew M., painter, h 30 Broad.
Baxter Robert J., machinist, h 12 Providence.
Beach Arthur N., telegraph operator, bds. Christie House.

Beach Eliza J., physician, 208 Pennsylvania ave., h do.
Beams Horace E., emp. Swift & Co., h 28 Clark.
Beardslee Edson E., drayman, h 2 Ithaca.
Beardslee Mary Mrs., dressmaker, 2 Ithaca, h do.
Beekman Emma, dressmaker, 127 Chemung, bds. do.
Beekman Sarah A., widow Isaac, h 127 Chemung.
Bell Minor, emp. Novelty Works, h 25 Providence.
Belles William, emp. Thatcher & Co., h 427 Chemung.
Bellis Jacob, emp. Novelty Works, bds. 111 Howard.
Beman John, hack stable, and prop. transfer line, Clark, bds. Tioga Hotel.
Beman Merritt, h Loder, refused to give information.
Bennet Stephen, druggist, and sporting goods, Broad, h 5 Clark.
Bennett Alanson, night watch, h off Lincoln.
Bennett Alfred, retired, h 128 Chemung.
Bennett Frank, teamster, bds. 17 Providence.
Bennett Sophia, widow Amos, h rear 32 Fulton.
Bentley Abram W., livery, Broad, h 23 do.
Bentley John L., liveryman, Broad, bds. 23 do.
Berry Ira L., traveling salesman, h 106 Fulton.
Betowski W. Leon, merchant tailor, 123 Broad, h 10 Johnson.
Bill Mary, widow, h 343 Broad.
Bingham Jefferson, grocer, h 337 Broad.
Bissett William H., laborer, bds. Lyman ave.
Bixby Fred, telegraph operator, bds. 47 Fulton.
Bixby Harrison, h 446 Chemung.
Blizzard Edward, messenger, bds. 131 Fulton.
Blizzard George S., drayman, h 131 Fulton.
Blossom Amanda, dressmaker, bds. 16 Chemung.
Blossom Jason B., contractor and builder, 16 Chemung, h do.
Boda & Dimmock, (W. H. B. and C. S. D.) meat market, 231 Broad.
Boda William H., (Boda & Dimmock) h 32 Pine.
Bodle John D., carpenter, bds. 411 Chemung.
BOGART HENRY, engineer, h 8 Tioga.
Boggs Charles, porter, Hotel Warford, bds. do.
Boggs George, laborer, bds. 401 Chemung.
Bonfoey Hubert R., clerk L. V. R. R. freight office, h over 237 Broad.
Bonnell Benjamin W., clerk Erie freight office, h 122 Clark.
Boorom Chauncey D., carpenter, h Chemung.
Borland William, laborer, h 43 Orange.
Bostwick Silas W., painter and paper-hanger, Waverly, h do.
Botrand Sylvester, brakeman, h 139 Howard.
Bowen George Rev., rector Grace Church, h 400 Chemung.
Bowen George H., cutter, bds. 400 Chemung.
Bowen James, clerk postoffice, bds. 400 Chemung.
Bowen Mary I., clerk, bds. 400 Chemung cor. Waverly.
Boyd Harry C., cigar packer, h Fulton.
Bradley Julian A., machinist, h 22 Johnson.
Bradley William H., resident, h Loder.
*BRAY JAMES B., editor and prop. *Free Press*, also job printing, 15 Fulton, h 17 do.
Brewster Curtis, variety store, Broad, h 308 Pennsylvania ave.
Brewster Elliot S., carpenter, h Fulton.
Brewster Harvey C., emp. Erie depot, h 180 Clark.

BARTON—WAVERLY VILLAGE.

Brewster M. Lewis, emp. Erie R. R., h 10 Pine.
Brewster Newton C., teacher of penmanship, h E. Waverly.
Brewster Rosanna, widow George, h 180 Clark.
Briley ——, widow ——. milliner over 151 Broad, h do.
Bristol Nathan S., clerk L. V. R. R. freight office, h 108 Waverly.
Brockitt George H., brakeman, h Spring.
BROOKS CHARLES C., insurance, over 201 Broad, h 106 Pennsylvania.
Brooks Charles E., chief of police, bds. 106 Pennsylvania ave.
Brooks Charles W., clerk, h 13 Orange.
Brooks Lizzie D., dress and cloak maker, 12 Waverly, h do.
Brougham Mary C., resident, h 501 Chemung.
BROWN CHARLES E., pianos, organs and sewing machines, 267 Broad, h 125 Lincoln cor. Hickory.
Brown Charles E., emp R. R. shops, Sayre, h Lyman ave.
BROWN DOWLINGTON J., tea store, 261 Broad, h 29 Orange.
Brown Ella, teacher, bds. 11 Broad.
Brown Jacob M., clerk, bds. 29 Orange.
Brown Merle A. J., clerk, bds. Lincoln cor. Hickory.
Brown Orilla, widow Jesse, h 39 Broad.
BRUSTER GEORGE C., art and ladies furnishing goods, 232 Broad, h Pennsylvania ave.
Buck Abbie B., widow Josiah T., h 206 Chemung.
Buck George, resident, h 130 Howard.
Buck Michael B., brakeman, bds. Loder.
Buckbee Augusta, widow Enos, h 119 Clark.
Buckley Nellie, widow Bradford, h 466 Chemung.
Buley James D., retired, h 35 Fulton.
Buley Joseph M., town collector, and sexton Presbyterian Church, h 112 Chemung.
Buley Joseph M., Jr., messenger, W. U. Tel. office, bds. 112 Chemung.
Buley Judd E., book-keeper for H. J. Baldwin, bds. 35 Fulton.
Buley Lewis J. Q., clerk, bds. 112 Chemung.
BUNN ALBERT R., boots and shoes, 219 Broad, h 121 Waverly.
Bunnell D. Ann, widow William, bds. 43 Waverly.
Burgess Lizzie T., teacher, bds. 505 Chemung.
Burke Mrs., widow ——, h Erie.
Bush Abram, passenger conductor, G. I. & S. R. R , room over 265 Broad.
Bush Laura S., (H. M. Wilcox & Co.) widow J. G., h 25 Waverly.
Butts Henry S., manuf. patent medicines, h 204 Pennsylvania ave.
Cadwell Lorenzo, retired, h 123 Chemung.
Cahill Michael, foreman repair shop, Erie R. R., h 57 Broad.
Cahill Michael J., clerk, bds. 57 Broad.
Cain Daniel W., laborer, h 33 Waverly.
Callahan John, laborer, h 121 Erie.
Camp Carrie Mrs., resident, h Clark.
Campbell Abram F., carpenter, h Clark.
Campbell Clarence C., coal dealer at East Waverly, h 8 Park Place.
Campbell Emery J., resident, h 420 Chemung.
Campbell Frank J., clerk, L. V. R. R. freight office, h 48 Fulton.
Campbell William, car inspector, h 111 Lincoln.
Canall Charles W., cigarmaker, bds. 135 Chemung.
Caney Phœbe A., laundress, h Hickory.
Careau Frances, dressmaker, bds. 43 Orange.

Carey Daniel G., patent medicine manuf., Broad, h 421 Chemung.
Carey Erastus, laborer, h Hickory.
Carey Rebecca C., widow William J., bds. 45 Orange.
Carey Samuel C., traveling salesman, bds. 421 Chemung.
Carmody Thomas F., saloon, Fulton h do.
Carmoody Simon, assistant train dispatcher, Erie R. R., bds. Warford House.
Carpenter Harrison W., laborer, h. 109 Lincoln.
Carpenter Lou A., widow Stephen, resident, bds. 33 Fulton.
Carr & Teachman, (C. S. C. & I. P. T.,) meat market 119 Broad.
Carr Clark S., (Carr & Teachman) h 34 Broad.
Carr Robert, brakeman, h 236 Broad.
Carroll John, station agent Erie depot, h 110 Fulton.
Case Angeline E., widow John, h 111 Howard.
Case Cornelius, carpenter, h 125 Howard.
Case George W., carpenter, h 47 Orange.
Case Irving, painter, bds. 125 Howard.
Case James, foreman Novelty works, h 24 Loder.
Chaffee Charles F., drug clerk, h 113 Park ave.
Chaffee Daniel, switchman, h 12 Loder.
Chaffee Ellen A., widow William A., h 5 Lincoln.
Chaffee Myrtie M., dressmaker, bds. 5 Lincoln.
Chall John, building mover, h 29 Broad.
Chamberlain Edward, drayman, h Pine.
Chambers Catharine, widow Thomas, bds. 15 Loder.
Chatam Myron, clerk, bds. Waverly.
Christie House, W. H. Goldsmith, prop., Fulton, opp. Erie depot.
Christie John M., retired, h. 27 Fulton.
Clark Benjaman B., retired, h 200 Penn. ave.
CLARK CHARLES H., bakery and confectionery, 121 Broad, h Pleasant.
CLARK JAMES A., hardware, stoves, etc., 217 Broad, h 316 Penn. ave.
Clark Lyman W., painter, h over 234 Broad.
Clark Warren M., foreman Sayre Butter Package Company, h 116 Waverly.
Clarke & Ralyea, (F. H. C. & W. H. R.) cigars and tobacco, 275 Broad.
Clarke Floyd H., (Clarke & Ralyea) h Chemung.
Clawsey James, laborer, h Erie.
Clemens Charles H., emp. pipe foundry, h 330 Broad.
Clohessy Michael J., clerk, h Pitney.
Cobb Adolphus, locomotive engineer, bds. Warford House.
Cochran Frisby M., engineer, h 123 Clark.
Coffee John, laborer, h 112 Howard.
Cole Archie, cigarmaker, bds 104 Waverly.
Cole Charles, porter Commercial Hotel, bds. do.
Cole Mary, widow James, h 135 Howard.
Cole Minnie E., widow Edmond C., h 104 Waverly.
Coleman Gabriel, farmer, h 24 Park Place.
Colemam Jacob S., carpenter, h 24 Park Place.
Coleman Samuel, blacksmith, bds. 437 Chemung.
Collins Michael, switchman, h Broad.
Commercial Hotel, D. S. Kennedy, prop., Fulton cor. Elizabeth.
Compton Eugene, harness maker, h over 151 Broad.
Compton James E., miller, h 140 Waverly.
Compton Richard W., shoemaker, Erie, h do.
Comstock A. B. Mrs., art teacher, 126 Waverly.

Comstock Alphonso B., photographer over 208 Broad, h 126 Waverly.
Cone Betsey, widow John, h 3 Tioga.
Congdon Lynn, emp. Novelty works, h 337 Broad.
Conklin Levi K., emp. wheel foundry, h. 318 Broad.
Conley Michael, brakeman, bds. 381 Broad.
Cooper Daniel H. Rev., pastor Baptist church, h 13 Tioga.
Cooper Seymour R., sewing machines, 18 Johnson, h. do.
Corby Allen W., emp. Toy shop.
Corby Ezekiel, teamster, h 17 Providence.
Corey William A., carpenter, h 310 Penn. ave.
Cortright Lewis, switchman, h 131 Chemung.
Cortright Mrs., h 16 Loder.
Corwin Lewis, shoemaker, Broad, h Pine.
Corwin Oliver B., butter, salt, and grass seed, 270 Broad, h Fulton.
Coryell Vincent M., retired, h 20 Park ave.
Costello John, blacksmith, bds. 147 Howard.
Courtwright William H., emp. S. A. Genung, h Fulton.
Cowen William C., conductor, h 105 Clark.
Cramer John, locomotive engineer, h 202 Howard.
Crandall Charles M., manuf. Crandall's building blocks, toys and games, Broad n Spaulding, h. Howard.
Crandall Jesse M., book-keeper for C. M. Crandall, bds. Howard.
Criddle James, resident, h 8 Providence.
Crispin Charles E., photographer, bds. over 241 Broad.
Crogger George, barber, h over 283 Broad.
Crowley Jerry, laborer, h 219 Howard.
Cummings Edward, retired, h 33 Orange.
Curran Andrew, laborer, h 223 Erie.
Curran Catharine M., widow Thaddeus, bds. 159 Clark.
Curran Floyd, clerk, h 110 Howard.
Curran Merritt D., brakeman, h 2 Ithaca.
Curran Thomas, resident, h 121 Erie.
Curran William, emp. Erie R. R., h 18 Broad.
Curtis Frederick, barkeeper, h 416 Chemung.
Curtis Levi, miller, h 100 Penn. ave.
DAILEY WILLIAM E., mason, 1 Spring, h do.
Daily Harriet B., widow Peter, h 118 Clark.
Daily John, musician, h 14 Johnson.
Dalton Thomas, laborer, h 39 Broad.
Dalton William, brakeman, h 413 Chemung.
Darling Dexter H., clerk 202 Front, rooms do.
Davenport Frank L., laborer, bds. Chemung cor. Orchard.
Davenport Jacob, teamster, h 413 Chemung.
Davis Samuel S., emp. Novelty Works, h 26 Elm.
Dearborn Charles, conductor Lehigh Valley R. R., h Chemung.
Dearborn Mack, conductor, h 118 Clark.
Debabery Augustus, peanut vender, Broad n Loder.
DECKER ABRAM I., supervisor, also prop. Decker tannery, h Chemung.
Decker Andrew J., carpenter, h 18 Orange.
Decker Jefferson, laborer, h 45 Orange.
Decker John, emp. Decker's tannery, h 19 Clark.
Decker Seely, laborer, h 135 Howard.
DeForest Charles, supt. poor, h 114 Waverly.

Deitrich Lewis, watchman, bds. 381 Broad.
Delaney David C., emp. Erie Ex. Co., bds. 16 Providence.
Delaney Dewitt C., sewing machines, bds. Spaulding.
Delaney John, brakeman, h 113 Erie.
Delany Daisy, clerk, h Fulton.
Delany John, night watch Lehigh Valley R. R. office, h Fulton.
Delany Josie E., millinery, 211 Broad, h 47 Fulton.
Delany William E., freight agent D., L. & W. depot, h 47 Fulton.
Demorest Clarence L., boots and shoes, 247 Broad, h 7 Tioga.
Demorest Elmer, traveling salesman, h 44 Waverly.
Demorest Polly B., widow Leonard, h 7 Tioga.
Denn Alfred W., resident, bds. 22 Elm.
Denn Almira, resident, h 20 Elm.
Denn Angeline, widow Alfred, h 22 Elm.
Denton Mary, resident, bds. 6 Park Place.
Deuel Amos E., harness maker, 250 Broad, h Lincoln.
Deuel Amos E., Jr., postal clerk, h 108 Lincoln.
Deuel John T., manager for A. E. Deuel, bds. 108 Lincoln.
Devine Michael J., clerk, h 244 Broad.
Deyo William S., emp. Mills & O'Brien, h Broad.
Dick Andrew, carpenter, h Elm.
Dickson Jane, widow Charles, h 337 Broad.
Dilamarter John, laborer, h Chemung cor. Tioga.
Dimmick Franklin, retired, h 107 Chemung.
Dimmock Charles S., (Boda & Dimmock) h 192 Clark.
Dingee John T., florist, 116 Lincoln, h do.
Dingman Edward, mason, bds. Hotel Warford.
Dinmore Joseph V., resident, h 128 Clark.
Doane Emmett A., carpenter, bds. 138 Chemung.
Doane Gabriel P., contractor and builder, 138 Chemung, h do.
Dobell William, emp. Novelty Works, h over 151 Broad.
Dodge Ira G., lumber dealer, bds. 9 Providence.
Donnelly Owen, shoemaker, 218 Erie, h do.
Donovan Frank, brakeman, bds. 22 Park Place.
Dorsett & Faulkner, (S. C. D. and J. E. F.) meat market, 215 Broad.
Dorsett Samuel C., (Dorsett & Faulkner) h 105 Waverly.
Dorsey Albert B., emp. pipe foundry, h 232 Erie.
Douglass John, night clerk Tioga Hotel, bds. do.
Dove Burr, emp. Novelty Works, bds. 18 Chemung.
Dove Fred, cigarmaker, bds. 18 Chemung.
Dove Maria, widow Samuel, h 18 Chemung.
Downs Thomas, blacksmith, h Broad.
Draper Eli S., emp. Bottling Works, h 24 Clark.
Driscoll Mary, widow Jeremiah, bds. 105 Chemung.
Drobnyk Joseph F., cutter, h 125 Fulton.
DuBois Joseph, retired, h 22 Waverly.
Dunham James J., wagonmaker, Broad n Pennsylvania ave., h do.
Dunn Charles A., emp. pipe foundry, bds. Christie House.
Dunn Peter F., porter, bds. Broad n Loder.
Dunning Charity, widow William, h 138 Waverly.
Dunning Jacob P., retired, bds. Warford House.
Dunning Julia C., widow Jacob, bds. 47 Waverly.
Durfey Almira, widow Lyman, bds. 301 Chemung.

Durfey Edson B., miller, h Broad n Johnson.
Durfey Riton, resident. bds. 301 Chemung.
EATON AMBROSE P., att'y at law, Exchange blk., Main, h at Smithboro.
Edgcomb Leroy, resident, h 13 Lincoln.
Edmiston Thomas P., car inspector, h 48 Waverly.
Eichenberg Edward J., baker and confectioner, Athens, Pa., h Cadwell.
Eichenberg James, laborer, h 18 Chemung.
Eisenhart George H., cigarmaker, h 38 Pine.
Ellis Dell C., widow Fred F., h over 263 Broad.
Ellis Elizabeth, widow Joseph, h 313 Broad.
Ellis Henrietta, widow Joseph H., bds. 108 Waverly.
Ellis Lodesca, widow Cyrus J., h 229 Broad.
Ellis Hiram, clerk, h 117 Fulton.
ELLIS J. ADDISON, carpenter, h 23 Lincoln.
ELLIS SEELE H., art goods, 229 Broad, h do.
Ellis Sidney E., manager clothing store. 230 Broad, h over do.
ELMER HOWARD, prest. First Nat. Bank, h Pennsylvania ave.
Elsbree Eugene C., watchman, h 20 Providence.
Emery Bartholomew W., emp. Novelty Works, h 330 Broad.
Emmerson William E., clerk, h Center.
Englebreck John, harness maker and boarding-house, 21 Waverly.
ENGLEMAN GUS, variety store, 131 Broad, h 118 Chemung.
English David W., barber, 127 1-2 Broad.
Enos Truman E., book-keeper Citizens Bank, bds. 10 Park Place.
Enwright John, machinist, h 17 Johnson.
Evans Henry L., laborer, h Clinton ave., cor. Pine.
Everett Elijah H., clerk, h 338 Broad.
Excelsior Mutual Benefit Association, (C. C Brooks, prest.; C. E. Pendleton treas.; L. C. Corey, secy.) over 201 Broad.
FAIRCHILD & THOMAS, (Murray F. & Holly W. T.) fire, life and accident insurance, over First National Bank.
Fairchild Anna, clerk, bds. Bradford.
Fairchild Mary E., book-keeper Fairchild & Thomas, bds Bradford,
FAIRCHILD MURRAY, (Fairchild & Thomas) bds. Tioga House.
Falsey Margarett C., teacher, bds. Clark.
Falsey Mary, clerk, bds. Clark.
Falsey Michael, furniture finisher, h Clark.
Falsey Sarah A., dressmaker, Clark, bds. do.
FARLEY & SANDERS, (W. C. F. & C. H. S.) groceries, crockery, and provisions, 231 Broad.
FARLEY WILLIAM C., (Farley & Sanders) h 10 Broad.
Farrel John, emp. toy factory, bds. 329 Broad.
Farrell Mary A., widow Daniel, bds. 130 Lincoln.
Farricy Mary, widow Dennis, h Chemung cor. Erie R. R.
Faulkner John E., (Dorsett & Faulkner) h 4 Chemung.
Ferguson Hartwell M. & Co., (Edwin W. Horton) tobacco and cigars, 200 Broad.
Furguson Hartwell M., (H. M. Furguson & Co.) h 133 Chemung.
Fern Julius E., candy maker, h over 249 Broad.
Fessenden Harvey C., clerk, h Clark.
Fessenden Harvey G., undertaker, h 121 Clark.
Floyd Elizabeth, widow Harvey, M., bds. 42 Waverly.

FLOYD JACOB B., att'y at law, Exchange bldg., Broad, h 42 Waverly cor. Tioga.
Flynn John, laborer, Chemung.
Flynn Michael, blacksmith. bds. 381 Broad.
FIRST NATIONAL BANK OF WAVERLY, (Howard Elmer, prest.; N. S. Johnson, vice-prest.; F. E. Lyford, cashier; P. L. Lang, asst. cashier.) Broad cor. Fulton.
Fish George W., retired, h 295 Chemung.
Fish John B., telegraph operator, h Providence.
Fisher Alton A., clerk, bds. 100 Chemung.
Fisher George O., emp. Novelty Works, h 100 Chemung.
Fitzgeral Michael, laborer, h 378 Broad.
Follett Phoebe A., widow Sluman, h 50 Waverly.
Follett Sophia H., Mrs., resident, 32 Park ave.
Fosburg Ellen A., widow James, laundress, h 170 Clark.
Fralick Abram, machinist, h 113 Waverly.
Fralick Ransom, machinist, bds. 113 Waverly.
Frauenthal Isedore E., fruits and oysters, 244 Broad, bds. Tioga.
French George H., station baggage agent, Erie R. R., h 12 Tioga.
French Carrie, dressmaker, 314 Broad, h do.
French Hiram G., clerk, h 12 Tioga.
French Rachel, resident, bds. 12 Tioga.
French William T., clerk, h 4 Lincoln.
*FREE PRESS, James B. Bray, prop., 15 Fulton.
Freestone George S., (Parsons & Freestone) bds. 47 Fulton.
Frink Frederick, supt., Toy works, bds. Tioga Hotel.
Frisbie Chauncey M., book-keeper, 203 Broad, h. Chemung.
Fritcher Elsa M., widow James, h 301 Chemung.
Frost Minnie, clerk, bds. Erie.
Frost Thomas, laborer, h 211 Erie.
Fuller Mrs., widow, h 107 Howard.
Gallagher Patrick, car inspector, h 57 Broad.
Galloway Emory H., emp. L. V. R. R., h 21 Johnson.
Ganther Jacob, emp. L. V. R. R., h 25 Providence.
Gardner Elizabeth B., widow Levi, h 446 Chemung.
Gardner William H., resident, bds. 446 Chemung.
Gas Light Co. of Waverly, (William F. Warner, prest.; Henry G. Merriam, secy. and treas.) office Waverly, over Merriam Bros.
Gee Lucy, widow William, bds. 14 Broad.
GENUNG GEORGE D., editor *The Waverly Advocate*, h 105 Pine.
Genung Reuben H., emp. Novelty Works, bds. 155 Waverly.
GENUNG SALMON A., wood dealer, h Fulton.
GENUNG SHERMAN A., contractor and builder, sash, doors, blinds, etc., Fulton, h 12 Pleasant.
Gerould B. & Co., (J. H. Shoemaker) groceries and provisions, 111 Broad.
Gerould Beebe, (B. Gerould & Co.) h 41 Fulton.
Gibbons Hannah, widow Sylvester, h 246 Broad.
Gibbons James S., groceries and provisions, 546 Broad, h do.
Gibson Robert W., barber, over 213 Broad, h do.
Gilbert Elliot R., switchman, h 142 Clark.
GLEASON WILLIAM H., switchman, h 19 Elm.
Goade Richard J., machinist, h 27 Clark.
Goble Abner, carpenter, h 411 Chemung.

Goble Mary E., widow Smith, h 16 Providence.
Goff G. Halsey, manager Swift's Chicago dressed beef icing station, h 315 Broad.
Golden John, laborer, bds. Broad.
Golden Patrick, laborer, h Broad.
Goldsmith William H., prop. Christie House, Fulton, h do.
Gore Harry W., drug clerk, h 7 Athens.
Gorman Edward, emp. Erie R. R., h 10 Clark.
Gorman John, brakeman, h 345 Broad.
Gorman Michael, fireman, h 233 Erie.
Gormon Patrick, laborer, h 233 Erie.
Gorski Samuel, tailor, h 21 Chemung.
Goulden Charles F., law student, bds. Bradford.
Grace Bertha, teacher, bds. Blizard.
Grace Joseph, lumberman, h Blizard.
Grace Patrick J., carpenter, h 15 Loder.
Grafft George H., justice of the peace, over 214 Broad, h Main.
Gray Ann, widow Arthur, bds 22 Waverly.
Gray Dewitt C., coal, wood, lime and cement, Erie, h 124 Clark.
Green Edward, resident, h 28 Waverly.
Green Frederick C., clerk Christie House, bds. do.
Green Jesse, clerk, bds. 28 Waverly.
Green John P., retired, h 28 Broad.
Greer Fred, brakeman, bds. 127 Chemung.
Greer Henry C., fireman, h 314 Broad.
Gregory Charles W., painter, h 12 Broad.
Gridley Henry N., engineer, h 6 Tioga.
Griswold Frank, emp. Novelty Works, bds. 111 Howard.
Groesbeck Cornelius V., emp. U. S. express company, h 5 Broad.
Guyer James E., coal, lime and cement, also carriages, sleighs and farming implements, Clark, h 115 Waverly.
Hagadorn Henry, teaming and livery, 2 Broad, h do.
Hagadorn James C., liveryman, bds. 2 Broad.
Haight Guy C., bar-keeper 12 Fulton, h Broad.
Hair Daniel, emp. gas works, bds. Erie.
Hair John, emp. gas works, h Erie.
HALL & LYON, (S. C. H. & G. F. L.) novelty furniture works, 356 Broad.
Hall Eli R., tin-smith, h 13 Broad.
Hall Eugene A., baker, h Chemung.
Hall G. Munson, brakeman, rear 110 Chemung.
HALL STEPHEN C., (Hall & Lyon) h 33 Park ave.
Hallet & Son, (H. & H. W.) groceries, crockery and provisions, 245 Broad.
Hallet Harry W., (Hallet & Son) bds. 4 Tioga.
Hallet Hatfield, (Hallet & Son) h 4 Tioga.
Hallett Clarence W., painter, h 72 Fulton.
Hallett DeKalb, painter, bds. 72 Fulton.
Hallett Joseph E., insurance, 409 Chemung, h do.
Hamilton Simeon V., retired, h 120 Lincoln.
Hammond Charles, laborer, h 401 Chemung.
Hancock Irving, barber, over 225 Broad, h do.
Hancock Mary, widow Jeremiah, nurse, h Moore cor. Fulton.
HANFORD & LORD, (M. F. H. & L. F. L.) groceries, provisions and bakers, 222 Broad.

Hanford Edward S., asst. postmaster and town clerk, bds. Warford House.
HANFORD MAURICE F., (Hanford & Lord) h 14 Main.
Hanford Noah, emp. Novelty Works, h Lincoln.
Hanley Matthew, resident, h 235 Erie.
Hanna Charles G., emp. Erie express, h 129 Waverly.
Hanna James A., carpenter, h 139 Howard.
Hanrehan Michael, switchman, bds. 147 Howard.
Harden Oscar, clerk, bds. 29 Providence cor. Spaulding.
Harding Adney, carpenter, h 5 Providence.
Harding Jabez B., train dispatcher, L. V. R. R., h 14 Waverly.
Harding John, car inspector, h 216 Howard.
Harnden Daniel D., physician and surgeon, 7 Waverly, h do.
Harnden Rufus S., physician and surgeon, 31 Fulton, h 33 do.
Harrigan John J., engineer, h 103 Chemung.
Harris Elisha T., resident, bds. 31 Broad.
Harris Emeline E., widow Daniel N., resident, h. 31 Broad.
Harris George R., jeweler, 2 Fulton, bds. 31 Broad.
Harris Thomas, laborer, h 216 Erie.
Harsh Andrew, mason, bds. 333 Broad.
Harsh Cornelius, mason, h 333 Broad.
Harsh Harriet, widow Charles M., h 442 Chemung.
Hart Brothers, (Willard K., & Irving S.) groceries and provisions, 205 Broad.
Hart Irving S., (Hart Bros.) h 18 Maple.
Hart Willard K., (Hart Bros.) h 18 Maple.
Havens John, painter, h over 224 Broad.
Hawley Chauncey, emp. Toy factory, bds. 329 Broad.
Haworth John C., lamp lighter, h Moore.
Haworth Thomas W., printer, bds. Moore.
Hayes Fred B., (H. H. Hayes & Son) bds. 107 Fulton.
Hayes H. H. & Son, (Fred B.) drugs and medicines, 236 Broad.
Hayes Henry H., (H. H. Hayes & Son) h 107 Fulton.
Hayes John, emp. Novelty Works, bds. Broad.
Hayes Mary Mrs., resident, h Broad.
Hayes William, emp. Novelty Works, h Broad.
HAYWOOD CHARLES M., marble and granite cemetery works, 107 Broad, residence at Owego.
Head Anson P., prop. American House.
Head Richard, saloon and restaurant, 252 Broad, h do.
Hemstreet Anthony, resident, h 469 Chemung.
Hemstreet Gertrude, h 501 Chemung.
Hemstreet Ida M., clerk, bds. Chemung.
Henessy William, car inspector, h 27 Orange.
Henry Edward, barber, over 219 Broad, h do.
Hern Bert J., clerk, bds. 159 Clark.
Hern John, groceries and provisions, 117 Broad, h 159 Clark.
Herrick Hugh T., book-keeper over 201 Broad, h 411 Chemung.
Hess Charles, carpenter, h 75 Fulton.
Hess Nirum J., contractor and builder, Fulton, h do.
Hesser Abram, emp. L. V. R. R., h 26 Lincoln.
Hewitt Henry, carpenter, h 32 Fulton.
Hickey John, resident, h 381 Broad.
Higbee Allison B., clerk, h over 218 Broad.
Higgins Edward M., tanner, h 23 Orange.

Higgins Edward W., brakeman, bds. 23 Orange.
Higgins Gilbert C., conductor, bds 23 Orange.
Higgins John J., engeneer, bds 23 Orange.
Higgins Mary, book-keeper, bds. 23 Orange.
Higgins Theresa, dressmaker, bds. 23 Orange.
Higgins William P., fireman, bds. 23 Orange.
Hildebrand Andrew, boots and shoes, 225 Broad, h 112 Clark.
Hill Erastus, carpenter and builder, h 10 Park Place.
Hill George W., shoemaker under 127 Broad, h 22 Loder.
Hill Henry, shoemaker Broad, h 22 Loder.
Hine Lucy A., widow Harrison, h 318 Broad.
Hinman Eliza A., widow Henry, boarding-house, 114 Chemung.
Hinman Helen, widow James, bds. 329 Broad.
Hinman Helen M., clerk, h 114 Chemung.
Hinman Sarah W., widow Charles, bds. 11 Providence.
Hinman Truman, retired, h 36 Broad.
Hinman William E., painter and paper-hanger, bds. 114 Chemung.
Hilton Willard M., physician and surgeon, Pennsylvania ave., h do.
Hoadley Miles S., conductor, h 104 Fulton.
Hoban John W., 255 Broad, h do.
Hoban William, clerk, bds. over 255 Broad.
Hoff I. P. & C., (William D. Hoff) jewelers, 202 Broad.
Hoff Ives P., (I. P. Hoff & Co.) h Fulton.
Hoff William D., (I. P. Hoff & Co.) h Pennsylvania ave.
Hogan Hugh, track walker, h Erie.
Holbert Emmet J., retired, h 9 Park ave.
Holland Phebe, widow Henry, h 229 Erie.
Holmes John A., traveling salesman, h Moore cor. Fulton.
Hoover John F., painter, h Fulton.
Hopkins James J., engineer, h 101 Chemung.
Hopkins William, emp. Novelty Works, bds. 16 Providence.
Horton Edwin W., (H. M. Ferguson & Co.) bds. 135 Chemung.
Horton Emma E. Mrs., fruit and confectionery, 210 Broad, h do.
Horton George, emp. Axel Works, bds. 330 Broad.
Horton James F., manager for Mrs. Emma Horton, h 210 Broad.
Horton Mary E., widow Daniel D., bds. Chemung cor. Orchard.
Horton Sarah, resident, bds. 3 Athens.
Horton William H., gardener, h 135 Chemung.
Hotalen Mordecai, carpenter, h 30 Orange.
Hotalen Peter, carpenter, h 6 Lincoln.
Hotalen Randall, drayman, h 139 Lincoln.
HOTEL WARFORD, (Wadsworth & Kelsey, prop's.) Broad cor. Fulton.
House Frank B., emp. Novelty Works, h Clark.
Hovey J. Fred, train dispatcher, L. V. R. R., h 128 Lincoln.
Hoyt Adeline, widow John L, resident, h 8 Orchard.
Hoyt C. Chester, switchman, h 8 Broad.
Hoyt Jehiel G., teamster, h 142 Clark.
Hoyt John H., employed in Sayre, bds. 8 Orchard.
Hubbell Nelson, station agent, h off Lincoln.
Hubbell William, teamster, bds. 17 Providence.
Hugg Lyman D., traveling salesman, h 106 Chemung.
Hugg Willis P., clerk, bds. 106 Chemung.
Huggins Carrie C., teacher, bds 2 Athens.

Huggins Elizabeth H., widow James A., h 2 Athens.
Hull Phillip M., teacher, h 18 Elm.
Hulse William H., butcher, h Ulster.
Hyatt Jonah G., inventor and patentee Hyatt's door carrier, h Waverly.
Ichenberg John, retired, bds. 129 Clark.
Inman William F., resident, h 400 Chemung.
ISLEY & SONS, stone cutters, and masons, dealers in curbing and flagging, 36 Waverly.
ISLEY JAMES, (Isley & Sons) 36 Waverly, h do.
ISLEY WALTER, (Isley & Sons) bds. 36 Waverly.
ISLEY WILLIAM R., (Isley & Sons) bds. 36 Waverly.
Jarvis Mary, widow Alva, h 6 Elm.
Jenkins Celia Mrs., resident, h 310 Pennsylvania ave.
Johnson Benjamin F., traveling salesman, h Pine.
Johnson Nathan S., vice-prest. First Nat. Bank, h Chemung.
Johnson Parmenas A., physician, 14 Pennsylvania ave., h do.
Johnson Solomon C., retired, bds. Pine.
JOHNSON WILLIAM E., physician and surgeon, 8 Waverly, h 44 Park ave.
Jones Charles W., book-keeper, h Chemung.
Jones James, bartender, bds. 125 Broad.
Jones John R., butter dealer, 268 Broad, h 19 Park ave.
Jones William H. W., book-keeper, 268 Broad, bds. 19 Park ave.
Jordan Charles S., saloon, 259 Broad, h do.
Kane John, laborer, h 225 Erie.
Kane John, butcher, h 132 Lincoln.
Kane Michael, brakeman, bds. Warford House.
Kaneir John, laborer, bds. Chemung cor. Broad.
Kaneir Patrick, laborer, h Chemung cor. Broad.
Kase John E., furniture finisher, h 39 Fulton.
Keefe John, emp. Erie R. R., bds. 19 Loder.
Keeler Faank W., foreman *Waverly Advocate*, h Pennsylvania ave.
Keeler George L., clerk, h Athens cor. Tioga.
Keeler Thomas, painter and paper-hanger, Broad, h Lyman ave.
Keller Charles, laborer, bds. 381 Broad.
Kelly Thomas, mason, h Erie.
Kelly Viola D., music teacher, bds. Elizabeth.
KELSEY CHARLES D., (Wadsworth & Kelsey) bds. Hotel Warford.
Kelsey William H., clerk, Hotel Warford, bds. do.
Kemp Milner, clerk, h 51 Waverly.
Kennedy Daniel A., clerk, h 12 Johnson.
Kennedy Duncan S., propr. Commercial Hotel, h do.
Kennedy Edward, turner, bds, 329 Broad.
Kennedy James, retired, h 12 Johnson.
Kennedy James H., clerk, bds. 12 Johnson.
Kennedy Michael W., cashier Erie freight office, bds. 12 Johnson.
Kenney Michael J., machinist, h 147 Howard.
Kenney William E., conductor, h 101 Spalding.
Kenrick James, emp. L. V. R. R., h 134 Howard.
Kenyon James A., retired, h 314 Pennsylvania ave.
Kilmer Clarence, emp. Novelty Works, bds. 25 Orange.
Kilmer John, clerk, h 25 Orange.
Kingsbury Frank A., clerk, h Lincoln.
Kinney Anna, widow Henry C., h 3 Providence.

Kinney F. Eloise, telephone operator, h 114 Clark.
Kinney Greeley, resident, h 322 Broad.
Kinney Horace, book-keeper Citizens Bank, bds. Howard.
Kinney H. Wall, clerk L. V. R. R. Ft. office, bds. Tioga House.
Kinney Juliet T., widow Newton, h 114 Clark.
Kinney Margaret, widow Daniel, h 113 Erie.
Kinney Michael, laborer, h 218 Howard.
Kinney Miles L., clerk, bds. 114 Clark.
Kinney Perley H., retired, h 134 Waverly.
Kinney Simon, depot police, h 40 Fulton.
Kinsman & Young, (J. E. K. & J. F. Y.) blacksmiths, 3 Pennsylvania ave.
Kinsman Fred, clerk, h Waverly.
Kinsman John E., (Kinsman & Young) h 10 Lincoln.
KLINE ALBERT, clerk, h over 253 Broad.
Knapp Charles, teamster, bds. 10 Park ave.
Knapp Charles S., watchmaker, bds. Waverly.
Knapp David D., jeweler, optician and engraver, 211 Broad, h 49 Waverly.
Knapp Harry W., clerk, bds. Read.
KNAPP JOSEPH W., dry goods, 203 Broad, h Read.
Kniffin Daniel R., clerk, h over 235 Broad.
Knight Henry C., resident, h 125 Waverly.
Krist Frederick, emp. Novelty Works, bds. 22 Park Place.
Krist Joseph, emp. Novelty Works, h 22 Park Place.
La Barre Jehiel T., carpenter, h 329 Broad.
Laine Henry T., emp. L. V. R. R., h 325 Broad.
Lambkin Russell, emp. Novelty Works, h 33 Fulton.
La Mont Phebe, resident, h 44 Broad.
Lane Irene A., widow Lewis, h Pine.
Lang Percy L., asst. cashier First Nat. Bank, h. 105 Chemung.
Langheed John H., emp. Atwater's Livery, h 127 Chemung.
Lantz George W., clerk, 138 Clark.
Lappla Philip H., wood carver, h 16 Park Place.
Lariew H. Porter, agent Elmira oil company, h Loder.
Larnard Asoeph S., confectionery and cigars, 3 Elizabeth, h do.
LARNARD A. WARREN, contractor and builder, Lyman ave. h do.
Larnard George H., clerk, bds. 3 Elizabeth.
Larnard Theo R., carpenter, h 129 Lincoln.
LASSLY ELIJAH M., livery and feed stable, Clark n Broad, h 141 Waverly.
Lathrop Frederick M., emp. L. V. R. R., h 8 Athens.
Lathrop Helen, widow Simon, h 8 Athens.
Lawrence Charles, stationery engineer, bds. 330 Broad.
Layman J. Lewellyn, emp. R. R. shop, Sayre, h 19 Clark.
Leavitt Clara W., widow Harry, bds. Lincoln.
Lehigh Valley R. R. Freight Office, Bert Hayden, agent, Fulton cor. Erie.
Lemon Israel G., fire and life insurance, over 245 Broad, h 17 Orange.
LEMON JAMES, foundry and machine shop and manuf. land rollers, Broad, h 8 Park ave.
Lenox Frank B., brakeman, bds. 263 Broad.
Lenox George F., baggageman, h 101 Broad.
LENT CLARENCE A., contractor and builder, Lincoln cor. Spring.
Lent W. Nelson, apiarist, bds. Lincoln.
Lester Albert J., clerk L. V. R. R. Ft. office, h 6 Athens.
Lewis John H., resident, h Pine.

Lewis Walter H., resident, h 17 Park Place.
Linden Hugh, emp. pipe foundry, bds. Christie House.
Lindsey Frances A. Mrs., laundress, h Pine.
Lindsey Grant W., cigar maker h over 336 Broad.
Lindsey William, carpenter, h 31 Clark.
Lindsley Parks, steward Tioga Hotel, bds. do.
Lockerby George, brakeman, h Elm.
Lockerby Wallace H., barber 12 Fulton, h Broad cor. Pine.
Lockwood George, tinner, bds. Warford House.
LORD LOUIS F., (Hanford & Lord) h 16 Main.
Lott John, car inspector, h Lyman ave.
Lowman Everette H., postal clerk, bds. 473 Chemung.
Lowman Harriet C., widow Hovey E., resident, h 473 Chemung.
Lowman Nathan B., clerk L. V. R. R. Ft. office, h 473 Chemung.
Lubars Anna D., widow John F., bds. 11 Lincoln.
Luce John G., book-keeper First Nat. Bank, h 22 E. Main.
Luce Joseph D., machinist, h Loder.
LUM DANIEL J., insurance, Waverly, h do.
Lum Mattie C., teacher, bds. Waverly.
LYFORD FREDERICK E., cashire First Nat. Bank, h 21 Park Place.
LYMAN MOSES, resident, h Waverly.
Lynch James, clerk, bds. Loder.
Lynch Rose A., millinery over 232 Broad, h do.
Lyon ———, farmer, h 111 Park ave.
LYON GEORGE F., (Hall & Lyon) h Fulton.
Lyons Charles T., physician and surgeon, retired, h 204 Chemung.
Lyons Smith E., clerk, h 29 Waverly.
Mack Mary Mrs., resident, h Broad.
Mahoney John, shoemaker, Broad, h 105 Chemung.
Mandeville Emmet, painter, bds. 16 Providence.
Mandeville Henry D., fireman, h Pine.
Mandeville Mahlon H., jeweler over 228 Broad, h 111 Fulton.
Manners Vincent C., clerk, bds. 11 Broad.
MANNING ELWIN W., manager for Mrs. E. W. Manning, 249 Broad, h 103 Waverly.
MANNING E. W. MRS., millinery of all kinds, 249 Broad, h 103 Waverly.
Manning Gurdon G., justice of the peace, over 206 Broad, h 37 Clark.
Maroney Daniel, railroad conductor, h 140 Howard.
Moseley George E., laborer. h 210 Howard.
Masonic Hall, Thomas Salisbury, janitor, Manners Block, Broad.
Masterson Julius C., retired, bds. 21 Johnson.
Maxwell Emily A., widow Albert P., h 18 Providence.
Maxwell Frank B., conductor, h Clark.
McArdle Bernard, blacksmith, 302 Broad, h Clinton ave.
McCarthy Daniel, engineer, h 19 Loder.
McCarthy James, laborer, h Erie.
McDonald Amanda, widow Alexander, h 422 Chemung.
McDonald David, baggageman, h 41 Waverly.
McDonald Duncan, retired, h 40 Waverly.
McDONALD DUNCAN, locomotive engineer, h Chemung.
McDONALD DUNCAN J., news and variety store, 247 Broad, h 422 Chemung.
McDonald Eliza, widow Morris, h 14 Clark.

McDonald Nellie, book-keeper Mills & O'Brian, h Howard cor. Spaulding.
McDonald Owen, laborer, h 201 Howard.
McDonald Owen, Jr., laborer, h 201 Howard.
McDonald Patrick, bar-tender Tioga House, bds. do.
McDONALD SARAH A. MRS., tailoring and gents' furnishing goods, 265 Broad, h Chemung.
McDonald Wellington, clerk, bds. Warford House.
McDonough Patrick, bds. 345 Broad.
McElwain Alexander, shoemaker, h 5 Chemung.
McElwain Margarett, widow Robert, h 5 Chemung.
McEwen William, emp. Novelty Works, h 155 Waverly.
McGuffie Matthew, clerk U. S. Ex. Co., h Loder.
McHale Patrick J., emp. L. V. R. R., h 19 Johnson.
McINTYRE ALBERT J., mason, Lincoln, h do.
McKerrow William, car inspector, h 111 Lincoln.
McKibbin Henry, emp. Novelty Works, bds. 18 Orange.
McMahon John, brakeman, bds. Commercial Hotel.
McNanara George, cigarmaker, h over 219 Broad.
McNeirney John, laborer, h 376 Broad.
McPherson Nancy, widow, Alexander, bds. 34 Broad.
McShane Edward Rev., pastor St. James church, h 103 Clark.
Mead Charles A., carpenter, h Spring.
Mead Eadie W., photographer, bds. 10 Providence.
Mead Joseph, traveling salesman, h 12 Pine.
Mead Montgomery, photographer, h 10 Providence.
Mead Tabitha J. Mrs., photographer over 204 Broad, h 10 Providence.
Meeker Mrs., widow John, h 24 Providence.
Melvin Emma Miss, laundress, h 2 Pennsylvania ave.
Mercereau & Co., (John and Henry) cigar manuf. Broad cor. Penn. ave.
Mercereau Henry C., (Mercereau & Co.) h 4 Park Place.
Mercereau Henry, (Mercereau & Co.) h Maple.
Mercereau John, (Mercereau & Co.) h Maple.
Mercereau John D., (Mercereau & Co.) h 15 Park Place.
MERRIAM BROS., (H. G. & C. E.) hardware, 235 Broad and 3 Waverly.
MERRIAM CHARLES E., (Merriam Bros.) Broad, h 414 Chemung.
Merriam Frank W., book-keeper 356 Broad, bds. 414 Chemung.
MERRIAM HENRY G., (Merriam Bros.) h 13 Park ave.
Merrill Arthur T., emp. R. R. shops Sayre, h 10 Tioga.
Merrill Elisha B., retired, h 22 Lincoln.
Merrill Lena E., emp. Toy Shop, bds. 10 Tioga.
Merrill Luke T., retired, h 109 Clark.
Miller Cassandra B., dressmaker 482 Chemung, h do.
Miller Charles, drayman, h 15 Johnson.
Miller Charles W., tinsmith, h 108 Howard.
Miller Edmund, retired, h 23 Fulton.
Miller Emma Mrs., resident, h 26 Waverly.
MILLER LOUIS C., (Barnes & Miller) h 15 Johnson.
Miller Samuel W., meat market, 248 Broad, h 482 Chemung.
MILLS & O'BRIAN, (T. M. & M. D. O'B.) bottling works, Elizabeth.
Mills Charles L., farmer 30, h 113 Chemung.
MILLS THEODORE, (Mills & O'Brian) h 25 Clark.
Mills Thomas, cabinet maker, h 103 Spaulding.

STARKEY & WINTERS, Wholesale and Retail Druggists, Owego.

Millspaugh Paul, clerk, bds. 109 Waverly.
Mink George R., cigarmaker, h 10 Athens.
Minick Benjamin F., retired, bds. 2 Orchard.
Minnick I. H. Mrs., dressmaker 28 Loder, h do.
Minnick Isaac H., machinist, h 28 Loder.
Minnick Robert F., clerk, bds 28 Loder.
Mitchell Thomas S., machinist, h 3 Athens.
MIX JAMES F., carpenter, R. R. shops Sayre, h 159 Waverly.
Moelich Julius, machinist, h 217 Howard.
Monyhan Johanna, widow John, h 138 Howard.
Monyhan John, blacksmith, h 138 Howard.
Monyhan Patrick, blacksmith, bds. 138 Howard.
Morgan William, fireman, h 316 Broad.
Moore Lemuel C., carpenter, h 129 Howard.
Morgan David, painter, 51 Waverly, h do.
MORGAN FREDERICK S., mason, Clark, h do.
Morgan George B., mason, h 16 Johnson.
Morgan George Mrs., milliner, 16 Johnson, h do.
MORGAN JOHN W., mason contractor, h 112 Lincoln.
Morley Dwight, saloon and billiards, 6 Waverly, h do.
Morris Charles, emp. Novelty Works, bds. 16 Providence.
Mosier Hiram W., carpenter, h Pine.
Moore Lemuel C., carpenter, h 22 Maple.
Moore William E., farmer, h 105 Park ave.
Mott Amasa S., tailor over 222 Broad, h 28 Park ave.
Mott William N., tailor over 222 Broad, h 28 Park ave.
Mullock Albert, (Mullock Bros.) h Elm.
Mullock Bros., (Corwin & Albert) drugs and medicines, 229 Broad.
Mullock Corwin, (Mullock Bros.) h 131 Waverly.
Mullock Gabriel L., (Ornamental Sign Company) h 135 Waverly.
MULOCK LEWIS W., retired, h 135 Waverly.
Muncey Adolph, emp. L. V. R. R., bds. Loder.
Muncey Alfred, carpenter, h Loder.
Munn Frank E., (Sager & Munn) h 106 Waverly.
Murdoch Charles, foreman Erie transfer, rooms Campbell Block, Broad.
Murdoch Eliza N., (E. N. Murdoch & Co.) h 123 Waverly.
Murdoch E. N. & Co., (J. K. Murdoch) fancy goods, 222 Broad.
Murdoch John K., (E. N. Murdoch & Co.) also agent U. S. Ex. Co., h 123 Waverly.
Murray George S., clerk, bds. Pine.
Murray Harriet E., widow Thomas J., resident, h Pine.
Murray Hattie C., dressmaker, bds. Pine.
Murray Isaac C., baker, h Pine.
Murray Jacob, retired, h Chemung.
Murray Mary L., dressmaker, Pine, bds do.
Murry George S., clerk, h 114 Pine.
Myer John M., retired, h 16 Elm.
Myer Samuel S., laborer, bds. 16 Elm.
Myers Charles K., tobacconist and gunsmith, 201 Broad, h 168 Clark.
Myers David W., carpenter, h 196 Clark.
Myers Edward D., clerk, bds. 115 Clark.
Myers George L., baker, bds. 115 Clark.

STARKEY & WINTERS, Druggists. Owego. Close Prices to Dealers.

Myers Leonard D., constable and deputy sheriff, h 115 Clark.
Nelson Elmer, dentist, over 251 Broad, h Bradford.
Nelson James, mason, h 146 Waverly.
Nelson Myron H., conductor, h 123 Fulton.
Nelson Phineas, harness and trunks, 127 Broad, h Clark.
Nevins James P., clerk, bds. 37 Clark.
Newland Charles, clerk, bds. Clark.
Newland Edward H., traveling salesman, h Clark.
Newell Frank M., (Newell Mfg. Co.) h Clark.
Newell Stephen H., traveling salesman, h 30 Fulton.
Nichols Eben, carpenter, h 11 Pine.
NICHOLS HURLEY L., tobacco and cigars, 213 Broad, h Pine.
Nichols Leonard H., bartender, bds. over 209 Broad.
NOBLE ALBERT C., (Noble & Noble) h Elizabeth.
*NOBLE & NOBLE, (W. H. & A. C.) publishers *Weekly Tribune*, Elizabeth.
Noble Mary B., widow Dr. Carlton M., bds. Elizabeth.
NOBLE WILLIAM H., (Noble & Noble) h Elizabeth.
Nolan James, blacksmith, h 12 Providence.
Noonan Mortice, laborer, h 220 Erie.
North W. Edward, carpenter, h 140 Clark.
Northup Emery H., clerk, h Pitney.
O'Brian Edward, brakeman, bds. 12 Providence.
O'Brian James, retired, bds. 36 Fulton.
O'BRIAN MICHAEL D., (Mills & O'Brian) h 36 Fulton.
O'Brien Thomas, brakeman, h 27 Park Place.
O'Farrell Edward J., clerk, h Fulton.
Olney Caleb B., retired, h 16 Broad.
Orange Emily H., widow George W., h 206 Chemung.
Ornamental Sign Company, (G. L. Mullock & S. C. Smith) Broad.
Osterhout Katie, dressmaker, 23 Broad, bds do.
Owen Hannah, widow William P., resident, h 40 Fulton.
Owen Ithiel P., painter, h 343 Broad.
Palmer Kate, widow Luman, h 24 Lincoln.
Parks Albert E., painter, h 29 Providence.
Parks James R., retired, h 11 Lincoln.
Parks Ned L., emp. pipe foundry, h Erie cor. Pennsylvania ave.
Parshall Luther, real estate, h 464 Chemung.
Parshall Ransom, retired, h 12 Elm.
Parsons & Freestone, (James F. P. & George S. F.) groceries and provisions, 207 Broad.
Parsons Fred K., fireman, h 31 Orange.
Parsons James F., (Parsons & Freestone) h Loder.
Paul James M., emp. M. Lyman and farmer 54, h Moore.
Payne Frederick Y., traveling salesman, h 6 Park Place.
Payne Sarah, widow Hiram, h 204 Chemung.
Pearman Julia M., resident, h 140 Clark.
Pease David, marble cutter, h 120 Chemung.
Peironnet Emma V., widow John S., resident, h 26 Waverly.
Pendell Charles D., emp. Toy Shop, bds. 143 Lincoln.
Pendell John Lyman, emp. Toy Shop, bds. 143 Lincoln.
Pendell John R. Rev., (Bap.) h 144 Lincoln.
Pendell Mary E. O., music teacher, bds. 143 Lincoln.
Pendleton Charles E., ex-cashier Home Savings Bank, bds. 106 Penn. ave.

Penney Eleanor, widow Nelson F., resident, h 308 Pennsylvania ave.
Pepper Frank, laborer, h 49 Orange.
Perkins Edward F., clerk, h Broad.
Perkins Frank A., clerk, bds. Broad cor. Chemung.
PERKINS FRED C., clothing, hats, caps and gents' furnishing goods, 208 Main, h 70 Fulton.
Perkins La Fayette, traveling salesman, 1 Broad.
Perry Hanson, emp. Sniffen & Scott, h Clark.
Personius Daniel V., (Barnum & Personius) 12 Clinton ave.
Persons E. Delos, groceries, crockery and provisions, 206 Broad, h 38 Clark.
Phillips Frank W., plumber, h Chemung.
Phillips Harry E., clerk 251 Broad, h at Sayre.
Phillips John W., painter and paper-hanger, bds Chemung.
Phillips Thomas J., (Phillips & Curtis) h 45 Waverly.
Piatt Susan, widow John, bds. 443 Chemung.
Pierce Alonzo E., emp. Erie R. R., h 108 Chemung.
Pierce Amelia M., widow John H., resident, bds. 126 Waverly.
Pierce Henry G., commercial traveler, h 323 Broad.
Pierce Josiah, retired, h 106 Chemung.
Pike George, clerk, bds. 36 Pine.
Pike Grove N., meat market, 109 Broad, h 36 Pine.
PILGRIM FREDERICK, bakery and confectionery, 241 Broad, h do.
Polleys Ellen D., widow William, h 112 Waverly.
Polleys Harriet, compositor, bds. 112 Waverly.
Poole Eva M., milliner, bds. 6 Tioga.
Post Henry W., butcher, h Providence.
Post John C., laborer, h 70 Fulton.
Powers Frank, brakeman, h 111 Erie.
Powers John, shoemaker, h 130 Lincoln.
Powell Levi J., saloon and restaurant, h 115 Howard.
Price George, brakeman, h Broad n Pennsylvania ave.
Price Nathaniel W., retired, h 5 Pine.
Price N. W. Mrs., carpet weaver, 5 Pine h do.
Price Willis H., carpenter, h Blizard.
PUFF & WILLIAMS, (M. F. P. & A. D. W.) meat market, Fulton.
PUFF MYRON F., (Puff & Williams) h Pleasant.
Purdy Charles E., saloon, 125 Broad, h do.
Quick Adeline L., resident, bds. 113 Fulton.
Quick Alvin, emp. L. V. R. R., bds. 16 Providence.
Quick Fannie C., emp. Toy Factory, bds. 113 Fulton.
Quick Mary, widow Stephen C., resident, h 113 Fulton.
Quick Minnie Mrs., private school, 3 Athens, h do.
Quick Susan A., emp. Toy Factory, bds. 113 Fulton.
Quigley Michael, groceries and provisions, 263 Broad, h Loder.
Quimby Elmer, blacksmith, Broad, bds. 34 do.
Race Jabez W., resident, h Waverly.
Racklyeft John, boots and shoes, 267 Broad, h 36 Broad.
Ralyea William H., (Clark & Ralyea) h Fulton.
Randolph Byron F., conductor, h 132 Clark.
Reckhow Sarah A., widow Isaac, resident, h 21 Pennsylvania ave.
Reese Elias, night watchman, h Fulton.
Reeve James I., retired, h 27 Park avenue.
Reigeluth Conrad, drug clerk, bds. 164 Clark.

Reigeluth John J., tinsmith, h Clinton ave.
Reigeluth Louisa, dressmaker, bds. 164 Clark.
Reigeluth Mary, widow Jacob, h 164 Clark.
Rew Samuel, barber, bds. Warford House.
Reynolds James, blacksmith, bds. Broad.
Reynolds Johanna, widow John, h Broad.
Rezeau Harry G., saloon 209 Broad, h do.
Rezeau Joseph O., saloon 209 Broad, h do.
Richardson Isaac, barkeeper, h Waverly.
Riggs George W., carpenter, h 9 Pine.
RIKER JAMES, author and librarian, h 23 Park ave.
Ritz Joseph, shoemaker, bds. Christie House.
Robbins Harry E., jeweler, h 36 Broad.
Robinson Jesse, painter, h 9 Orange.
Rodhlof John, saloon, 273 Broad, h do.
ROGERS CHARLES H., contractor and builder, 413 Chemung, h do.
Rogers Edwin E., clerk L. V. R. R. Ft. office, h 125 Chemung.
Rogers Irvin H., clerk L. V. R. R. Ft. office, h Pleasant.
Rogers William T., retired, h 28 Lincoln.
Rolfe Cornelius J., brakeman, bds. 15 Providence.
Rolfe Peter B., teamster, h 15 Providence.
Rolfe Willet W., butcher, bds. 15 Providence.
Rood Horace W., brakeman, h 125 Erie.
Root Hubert A., emp. R. R. shops Sayre, h 133 Lincoln.
Rose David A., pattern maker, h 7 Loder.
Rosecrants Abram, laborer, bds. 39 Broad.
Ross Frank, carpenter and builder, 10 Pine, h do.
Rowland Bert K., clerk, bds. 13 Waverly.
Rowland John R., wines and liquors, also carriages and wagons, also Burle's patent egg preserver, 242 Broad, h 13 Waverly.
Rowland Kate A., teacher, bds. Pennsylvania ave. n Broad.
Rowland William A., carpenter and builder, h Pennsylvania ave. n Broad.
Ruher Louis, machinist, h over 271 Broad.
Ryan Bridget, widow Michael, h Broad.
Ryan Conrad, laborer, h Erie cor. Pennsylvania ave.
Ryan Dennis, telegraph lineman, h Erie cor. Pennsylvania ave.
Ryan Jeremiah, town collector, bds. 10 Broad.
Ryan John, railroad emp., rooms over 265 Broad.
Ryan Thomas B., ass't yard master Erie R. R., h 7 Pennsylvania ave.
Sager & Munn, (T. A. S. and F. E. Munn) groceries, crockery and provisions, 234 Broad.
Sager Alvin D., clerk, h 104 Waverly.
Sager Thaddeus A., (Sager & Munn) h 119 Fulton.
Salisbury Thomas L., painter, 130 Waverly, h do.
Salonsky Isaac, clothing and gents' furnishings, 224 Broad, h do.
SANDERS CHARLES H., (Farley & Sanders) h Fulton.
Sanders Hiram E., policeman, h 103 Howard.
Sargeant James C., emp. freight house, h 28 Orange.
Sargeant J. C. Mrs., dressmaker, 28 Orange, h do.
Sawyer Charles H., farmer 280, h 474 Chemung.
Sawyer Fannie, widow Moses, h 109 Waverly.
Sawyer Frederick A., cashier Citizens Bank, h 474 Chemung.
Sawyer Fred H., emp. Novelty Company, h 2 Orchard.

Sawyer Hugh T., clerk L. V. R. R. freight office, h 109 Waverly.
SAWYER J. THEODORE, president Citizens Bank, h 451 Chemung.
Sawyer Julina, widow John L., h 451 Chemung.
Sawyer Mary, widow James M., resident, h 25 Park Place.
SAYRE BUTTER PACKAGE CO., (R. D. and H. C. Van Deuzer, and T. F. Page) Factoryville, Main.
Scanlan Bartholomew, emp. L. V. freight house, h 9 Loder.
Scanlon Martin, telegraph operator, bds. Pennsylvania ave. n Broad.
Schutt William H., clerk, h 10 Orange.
Schutte Magdalena, widow Rudolph, h 115 Howard.
Schutte Rudolph, Jr., clerk, bds. 115 Howard.
Scott Charles E., Loyal Sock coal, 256 Broad, h 7 Athens.
Scott Robert, clerk, bds. Pennsylvania ave.
Scott Robert H., (Sniffen & Scott) h 20 Park ave.
Seacord John, contractor and builder, 27 Lincoln, h do.
Sedgwick William, retired jeweler, h 127 Clark.
Seely Charles, saloon and restaurant, 129 Broad.
Seely Edmund, boarding, 12 Park ave.
Seely Frederick, bartender, bds. 129 Broad.
SEELY WILLIAM F., groceries, crockery and provisions, 257 Broad, h 107 Pennsylvania ave.
Shaehan Michael, saloon, also prop. Tioga Bottling Works, Broad cor. Loder.
Shannessy Patrick, emp. Erie R. R., h 127 Erie.
Sharpe Arminda, widow William, h 11 Broad.
Shaw Hulda J., dress and cloak maker, 9 Waverly, h do.
Shaw Robert R., poor-master, h 11 Johnson.
SHEAR JOHN C., prop. Waverly Steam Flouring Mill, 300 Broad, h 101 Park ave.
Sheeler Edward P., night clerk U. S. Ex. Co., h Fulton.
Shehan Patrick, resident, h 375 Broad.
Sheldon Mary B., widow Charles H., resident, h 20 Park ave.
Shelp Charles F., lumber, h 131 Lincoln.
Shepard William Mrs., resident, bds. Warford House.
SHERMAN CHARLES W., mason, 428 Chemung, h do.
Sherry Hiram I., horse dealer, h 6 Pine.
Sherry J. Robert, veterinary surgeon, bds. 6 Pine.
Sherwood William, emp. pipe foundry, h 343 Broad.
Shipman Charles H., conductor, h 43 Waverly.
Shoemaker Jabez H., (B. Gerould & Co.) h Broad.
SHOEMAKER JUDGE F., att'y at law, over 214 Broad, h 505 Chemung.
Shoemaker Samuel O., emp. U. S. express company, h 156 Clark.
Shook William, commercial traveler, h 18 Pennsylvania ave.
Shriver Christina, widow Henry, h 9 Elm.
Shulenburg Sarah, dress and cloak maker, 304 Chemung.
Simmers E. Louisa, widow John W., resident, 116 Chemung.
Simmons Edward W., clerk, h 11 Johnson.
Simmons Frederick C., clerk, bds. 71 Fulton.
Simmons John H., cabinet maker, h 27 Providence.
Simmons Silas W., retired, h 71 Fulton.
Simmons William R., groceries and provisions, 269 Broad, h Howard.
Simpson Elliot B., blacksmith, bds. 437 Chemung.
Simpson Isaac D., blacksmith, cor. Penn. ave. and Broad, h 437 Chemung.
SIMPSON WILLIAM H., blacksmith, 301 Broad, h 439 Chemung.

Simcoe Eli, contractor and builder, Orange, h 15 do.
Skellenger Charles, meat cutter, bds. 36 Pine.
SLAUGHTER & VAN ATTA, (S. W. S. and J. C. Van A.) drugs, medicines and wall paper, 233 Broad.
SLAUGHTER S. W., (Slaughter & Van Atta) also vice-prest. Citizens Bank, h 408 Chemung.
Slawson Andrew A., postmaster, undertaking and furniture, 223 Broad, h 443 Chemung.
Slawson Jeremiah M., musical merchandise and sewing machines, 202 Broad, h 32 Waverly.
Sligh Susan Mrs., resident, bds. 10 Athens.
Sliney Charles, laborer, rooms 33 Waverly.
Sliney Charles H., book-keeper Erie R. R. Co., associate press correspondent, bds. Warford House.
Sliney William H., yard master Erie R. R., bds. Warford House.
Slocum Olney, clerk, bds. Orange.
Smead Edward, baker, bds. 34 Broad.
Smeaton Mary A., teacher, bds. 152 Clark.
SMEATON THOMAS, mason contractor, 152 Clark.
Smith Augustus W., emp. Novelty Works, h 28 Orange.
Smith Bros. & Co., (W. J., M. O. and H. G. S.) picture mouldings, frames, etc., over 207 Broad.
Smith Charles O., (Smith Bros.) 19 Chemung.
Smith Clayton A., foreman *Free Press* office, bds. 17 Fulton.
Smith Daniel S., baker, h 21 Fulton.
Smith D. S. Mrs., dressmaker, 21 Fulton, h do.
Smith Edwin S., resident, h 37 Waverly.
Smith Floyd, emp. Erie R. R., bds. 141 Waverly.
Smith Fred E., clerk L. V. R. R. freight office, h 70 Broad.
Smith Fred F., tinsmith, bds. 184 Clark.
Smith Henry G., (Smith Bros. & Co.) h in Candor.
Smith John L., laborer, h 184 Clark.
Smith Mary K., widow Hanford, h 37 Waverly.
Smith Merritt W., blacksmith, h 40 Broad.
Smith Minor O., (Smith Bros. & Co.) h 15 Chemung.
Smith Olin A., emp. livery, and farmer 50, h 157 Clark.
Smith S. Charles, sign writing, Broad cor. Pine, h 9 Orange.
Smith Willis J., (Smith Bros. & Co.) bds. Fulton.
Smith W. M. Adelbert, laborer, bds. 37 Waverly.
Smitt Antoni B., merchant tailor, 10 Fulton, h 125 do.
Snell Patrick, laborer, h Erie.
Sniffen & Scott, (H. S. and R. H. S.) grain, coal, seeds, wool, wagons and farm implements, Broad n Loder.
Sniffen Henry H., (Sniffen & Scott) bds. Tioga House.
Snook Frederick M., dentist, over 231 Broad, h 13 Pennsylvania ave.
Snyder De LaFayette, resident, h 119 Clark.
Somers Maurice, laborer, h 204 Howard.
Space Henry, traveling salesman, bds. over 267 Broad.
Space Jennie L., widow John A., dressmaker, over 267 Broad, h do.
Spaulding William H., police justice, h 113 Clark.
Speh Charles Prof., teacher of music, French and German.
Spencer Charles F., boots and shoes, 226 Broad, h 445 Chemung.
Spencer C. I. Mrs., resident, 104 Lincoln.

BARTON—WAVERLY VILLAGE.

Spencer George M., emp. Swift's ice-house, h Broad n Pennsylvania ave.
Sproul Andrew, railroad conductor, h 5 Spaulding.
Sproul Herbert L., clerk, bds. 5 Spaulding.
Stalker Albert, emp. Novelty Works, h Broad.
Stanley Belle, art teacher, 101 Pennsylvania ave., bds. Broad.
Stanley Clark M., dentist, h Cadwell.
Stark Somers J., railroad conductor, h 203 Howard.
Steele Edward J., telegraph operator, bds. Warford House.
Stevenson William, clerk, h 244 Broad.
Stevenson William R., locomotive engineer, h 21 Providence.
Steward Malvina, widow Loren G., bds. 2 Ithaca.
Stewart William H., retired, h 13 Park Place.
Stone George P., machinist, bds. 12 Pennsylvania ave.
Stone James R., retired, h 105 Park ave.
Stone William P., resident, h 12 Pennsylvania ave.
Stout Ernest A., book-keeper, 235 Broad, h over do.
STOWELL HOLLIS L., dry goods, 237 Broad, h 405 Chemung.
Strange Matthew, laborer, h 4 Broad.
Strouse Huldah, widow Neal, dressmaker over 218 Broad, h do.
Suiter Sophia, widow Robert, bds. 28 Loder.
Sullivan Anna, dressmaker, 105 Chemung, bds. do.
Sullivan Etta, dressmaker, 315 Broad, h do.
Sullivan Hannah, dressmaker, 315 Broad, h do.
Sullivan Mary, dressmaker, 315 Broad, h do.
Sullivan Michael, emp. Erie R. R., h 26 Providence.
Sullivan Michael, track foreman, bds. 9 Loder.
Sutton Augustus, barber, bds. Warford House.
Sutton Clarence M., emp. Novelty Works, bds. 466 Chemung.
Sutton Ernest, emp. Toy works, h 101 Pennsylvania ave.
Sutton Frank M., cabinet maker, h 466 Chemung.
Swaig Henry, porter Tioga Hotel, bds. do.
SWAIN LESTER, groceries, provisions and restaurant, Fulton, h do.
Swain William H., book-keeper, 251 Broad, h 117 Howard.
SWEET WESLEY, furniture and undertaking, 243 Broad, h 10 Park ave.
Taladay Frederick, carpenter, bds. 5 Providence.
Tannery Harriet, widow James B., resident, 423 Chemung.
TANNERY IDA Miss, millinery, over 233 Broad, h 243 Chemung.
Tannery Mary, widow, h 17 Clark.
Taylor John L., pastor 1st Presbyterian church, h 11 Park Place.
Teachman Isaac P., (Carr & Teachman) h 30 Chemung.
Telephone Exchange, (F. E. Smith, of Elmira, Mgr.) over First Nat. Bank.
Terry Edward H., mason, h 5 Pennsylvania ave.
Terry Edward H., Jr., shipping clerk, 275 Broad, bds. 5 Pennsylvania ave.
Terry Edward H. Mrs., dressmaker, 5 Pennsylvania ave., h do.
Terry Fred S., city baggage express, bds. 160 Clark.
Terry Ira M., carpenter, h Broad.
Terry John, retired, h Hickory.
Terry Orrin T., clerk, bds. 5 Pennsylvania ave.
Terry T. Jefferson, car inspector, h 160 Clark.
Terry Walter T., car inspector, h 160 Clark.
Tew William E., real estate and insurance, over 214 Broad, h do.
Thatcher Harris C., manager The W. S. Thatcher Co., h 12 Park Place.
Thatcher Helen, widow Walter S., woven wire mattresses, h 12 Park Place.

Thayer Roma B., emp. Novelty Works, h 313 Broad.
THE CITIZENS BANK, (J. T. Sawyer, pres't, S. W. Slaughter, vice-pres't, F. A. Sawyer, cashier) 214 Broad.
*THE WAVERLY ADVOCATE, (Edgar L. Vincent, pub., and George D. Genung, editor, weekly) 4 Elizabeth.
The W S. Thatcher Co., (Harry C. Thatcher, Mgr.) manuf. woven wire mattresses, Fulton.
THOMAS HOLLY W., (Fairchild & Thomas) h 14 S. Main.
Thompson Abner, brakeman, bds. Commercial Hotel.
Thompson Abram J., clerk, h 144 Waverly.
Thompson Guy M., emp. Novelty Works, bds. 144 Waverly.
Thompson Sadie, teacher, bds. 3 Providence.
Thompson William E., butcher, h 8 Pine.
Thrall Emery, R. R. conductor, h. 348 Broad.
Tillman David B., book-keeper, bds. over 253 Broad.
Tillman Moses, carpenter, h over 253 Broad.
Tilton Edson A., clerk, bds. 111 Howard.
Tilton Ira, clerk, bds. 111 Broad.
Tilton Isaac S., clerk, bds. 111 Howard.
Tioga Bottling Works, Michael Shaehan, prop., Broad cor. Loder.
TIOGA HOTEL, Ackley & Bailey, proprs., Fulton Cor. Elizabeth.
Tioga Laundry, George B. Witter, prop., 113 Broad.
Tobin James, section foreman, Erie R. R., h. 119 Erie.
Toppen Henry, painter, 114 Waverly, h do.
Towner Jane, tailoress, h 9 Waverly.
Tozer John F., livery stable, Fulton, opp. Opera House, h 30 Waverly.
Tozer Lavina, widow Charles P., h 129 Waverly.
Tracy Edward G., drugs, and wall paper, 228 Broad, h Fulton cor. Chemung.
Tracy John L., books, stationery and newsroom, 204 Broad, h 3 Orange.
Travis Landes L., locomotive engineer, h 10 Spalding.
Travis Littleton, coachman, h 401 Chemung.
Troutman Jacob, brakeman, h 30 Broad.
Tucker John T., physician and surgeon, over 224 Broad, h do.
Turner Amelia, widow Joseph, h 144 Howard.
Turner Edward, locomotive engineer, h 20 Park Place.
Turney William E, confectioner, 239 Broad, h 130 Clark.
Tuthill Caroline A., teacher, bds. Waverly.
Tuthill Charles E., clerk, h 124 Waverly.
Tuthill Elvira, widow Jacob G., h Waverly.
Twist Michael, mason, bds. 381 Broad.
Tyrrell Augustus, physician, over 222 Broad, h do.
United States Ex. Co., J. K. Murdoch, agt., 8 Fulton.
Unger Solomon, clothing and gents' furnishings, 230 Broad, h in Elmira.
Unger Adolph, clothing and merchant tailor, 221 Broad, h Fulton.
Updike Archibald, market gardener, h 85 Clark.
Updike Frank A., carpenter, h Clinton ave.
Utter John, architect, h 120 Howard.
Vail Alonzo V. C., lumber dealer, h 128 Waverly.
Vail Daniel, resident, h 121 Howard.
Vail Merton W., painter, h 309 Pennsylvania ave.
Vail Michael, brakeman, bds. Warford House.
Vail Michael, switchman, bds. over 263 Broad.
VanAmburgh Abdial B., wagon shop 304 Broad, h 133 Howard.

BARTON—WAVERLY VILLAGE.

VanAtta Azariah, contractor and builder, 111 Pennsylvania ave., h do.
VanAtta Clarence, clerk, h 109 Fulton.
VanAtta E. Clair, clerk, h 9 Tioga.
VanAtta Edwin H., drug clerk, bds. 5 Park ave.
VAN ATTA JOHN C., (Slaughter & VanAtta) h 5 Park ave.
VanCleft Mary J., dressmaker, bds. 139 Waverly.
VanCleft Sarah A., widow Benjamin O., h 139 Waverly.
VanCleft Wells, laborer, h Hickory.
VAN DERLIP CHARLES T., D. D. S., dentist, preservation of the natural teeth a specialty, over 201 Broad, h Cadwell.
VanDerlip Sisters, (Mary and Elizabeth) dressmakers, h 24 Park ave.
VanDermark Edward, porter, Tioga Hotel, bds. do.
VanDermark Mrs., widow Albert, bds. 14 Pennsylvania ave.
VanDeuzer Annie, teacher, bds. 468 Chemung.
VanDeuzer Dell, emp. pipe foundry, h over 263 Broad.
VAN DEUZER HOWARD C., (Sayre Butter Package Co.) bds. Tioga Hotel.
VanDeuzer Richard, mechanic, bds. over 263 Broad.
VanDeuzer Richard D., (Sayre Butter Package Co.) h 468 Chemung.
Van Gaasbeck, clerk, Christie House, bds. do.
VanGaasbeck Josephine, widow John, h 132 Chemung.
VanGorden Harry M., sexton of cemetery, h 38 Pine.
VanGorden Mary E., dressmaker, bds. 38 Pine.
VanVelsor & Co., (Alexander Zoltowski) merchant tailors, 212 Broad.
VanVelsor George B., (VanVelsor & Co.) h 117 Waverly.
VanVelsor Jane, widow Benjamin, bds. 117 Waverly.
Vaughn William, retired, h 16 Park ave.
Vibbert Charles M., contractor and builder, h 148 Waverly.
VINCENT EDGAR L., publisher *The Waverly Advocate*, h Clark.
Voorheirs Barbara, widow Sherman, h Blizard.
Voorheirs Stephen, cigar maker, bds. Blizard.
Vreeland Isaac S., M. D., physician and surgeon, over 229 Broad, h Pennsylvania ave.
WADSWORTH SAMUEL H., (Wadsworth & Kelsey) Hotel Warford.
WADSWORTH & KELSEY, props. Hotel Warford, Broad cor. Fulton.
Waldo George F., retired, h 101 Pennsylvania ave.
WALKER EDWARD E., (T. S. Walker & Son) h 306 Pennsylvania ave.
Walker Eliza, resident, bds. 6 Elm.
WALKER HOWARD S., clerk, bds. Waverly.
WALKER LEANDER, groceries and provisions, 253 Broad, h Waverly.
Walker N. Dell, widow George H., resident, h. 102 Lincoln.
WALKER T. S. & SON, (Edward E.) groceries and provisions, 250 and 252 Broad.
WALKER THADDEUS S., (T. S. Walker & Son) h r 60.
WALLACE ALFRED H., carpenter, h 150 Waverly.
Wallace Grandsville, porter, Tioga Hotel, bds. do.
Wallace William A., emp. Novelty Works, bds. 150 Waverly.
Walsh Maggie, milliner, bds. over 232 Broad.
Walton S. Lincoln, tanner, h 73 Fulton.
Ward Amrose, emp. planing mill, h 37 Orange.
Ward John E., resident.
Ward Mary, widow Hugh, h Loder.
Ware Walter, inventor, h 27 Park ave.

Warner Anna P., resident, bds. 11 Park ave.
WARNER WILLIAM F., lawyer, also pres't Waverly Gas Light Co., Waverly, h 11 Providence.
Warren James, emp. wheel foundry, h Erie.
Waters Edward T., marble cutter, h Erie.
WATROUS BROS., (William L., and estate of Addison) dry goods, cloaks, and carpets, 227 Broad.
WATROUS WILLIAM L., (Watrous Bros.) h 14 Park Place.
Watson John, mason, h 102 Waverly.
WAVERLY CASH STORE., (Barnes & Miller, props.) groceries and provisions, 277 Broad.
Waverly Opera House, C. Mullock, manager. Fulton.
Waverly Steam Flouring Mills, John C. Shear, prop., 300 Broad.
*WAVERLY TRIBUNE, (weekly) Noble & Noble, publishers, Elizabeth.
Weatherly Leonora, widow Perry, h 44 Waverly.
WEBB HENRY A., prop. Webb's Dining Hall, 216 Broad, h do.
WEBB'S DINING HALL, Henry A. Webb, prop., 216 Broad.
Welch John, laborer, h Erie.
Weller Charles M., baggageman, h 105 Howard.
WELLER G. FRED, resident, h 188 Clark.
Wells Elizabeth S., widow Rev. Daniel, bds. 414 Chemung.
Welsh John, moulder, h Loder.
Welsh Julia, widow James, h Loder.
Welton Anna E., widow Lyman, h Chemung.
Welton Warner, laborer, h Pine.
West George P., retired, h 21 Orange.
Westbrook Calvin T., drayman, h 7 Broad.
Wheat Mark M., laborer, h Pine.
Whitaker Henry, engineer, h 19 Lincoln.
Whitaker Horace, street commissioner, h 435 Chemung.
Whitaker Richard, mechanic and green-house, h 102 Howard.
Whitaker William D., railroad conductor, h Providence n Pennsylvania ave.
White Horton, emp. pipe works, h 10 Tioga.
White James, bar-keeper, h Broad.
White Jerome, laborer, h 430 Chemung.
White Mary, widow Patrick h 354 Broad.
Wickham Joseph D., invalid, h 105 Howard.
Wiesmer Sarah, widow George, resident, h 101 Broad.
WILCOX & BARROWS, (W. W. W. and A. H. B.) meat market, 271 Broad.
Wilcox George S., retired, h 40 Park ave.
Wilcox H. M. & Co., (L. S. Bush) dry goods, 218 Broad.
Wilcox Howard M., (H. M. Wilcox & Co.) h 25 Waverly.
Wilcox Silas E., resident, h over 269 Broad.
WILCOX WYATT W., (Wilcox & Barrows) h 40 Park ave.
Wilkinson Margaret, widow George D., resident, h 19 Broad.
WILLIAMS ADELBERT D., (Puff & Williams) h Loder.
Williams Addie, dressmaker, 20 Clark, h do.
Williams Ann, resident, h 3 Tioga.
Williams Daniel, painter, bds. 20 Clark.
Williams John F., laborer, h 18 Chemung.
Williams Mary E., widow Gabriel, h 20 Clark.

STARKEY & WINTERS, Wholesale and Retail Druggists, Owego.

Williams Mastin L., retired, h 129 Clark.
Wilson Alosco H., expressman, 24 Waverly.
Wilson George W., locomotive engineer, h 349 Broad.
Winnie William U., laborer, h 23 Clark.
Witter George B., prop. Tioga Laundry, 113 Broad, h do.
Woodburn James L., barber, Fulton, h do.
Wolcott Ira M., resident, bds. over 259 Broad.
Wolcott Maria, widow Silas, h 444 Chemung.
Wolcott Park, clerk, h Chemung.
Wolcott Raymond, clerk, h 444 Chemung.
Wolcott Tompkins S., bartender, h over 259 Broad.
Wood Hiram C., R. R. signal tender, h 110 Chemung.
Woodruff Emma C., widow Dr. Jacob D., resident, 7 Tioga.
Woodruff James O. Rev., pastor M. E. church, h 53 Waverly.
Woodworth William H., laborer, h 26 Providence.
Wright Daniel, lumberman, h 24 Clark.
Wright Festus A., emp. J. T. Sawyer, h 451 Chemung.
Young Henry H., tanner, h 196 Clark.
Young John F., (Kinsman & Young) h 6 Providence.
Ziegler Benjamin F., cigar maker and tobacconist, Johnson, h 141 Fulton.
Zeigler William R., conductor, h Hickory.
Zoltowski Alexander, (VanVelsor & Co.) h 7 Chemung.
Zoltowski Anthony, tailor, bds. 7 Chemung.

BARTON

OUTSIDE WAVERLY VILLAGE.

(For explanations, etc., see page 3, part second.)

(Postoffice address is Barton, unless otherwise designated in parenthesis.)

Ackley Alexander W., (Lockwood) r 2, prop. saw-mill and farmer 1,400.
Ackley Charles E., (Lockwood) r 16, sawyer and farmer.
Ackley Francis, (Factoryville) r 47, laborer.
Ackley Samuel, (Lockwood) farm laborer.
Adell Fayette G., laborer.
Akins J. Frank, (Lockwood) r 48, farmer 58.
Akins Rebecca, (Lockwood) r 47, widow George, resident.
Albright Adam, (North Barton) r 34, prop. threshing machine and farmer 76.
Albright Hiram C., r 40, resident.
Albright Isaac D., r 40, prop. steam thresher and farmer 120.
Albright Joseph, r 27, farmer.
Albright Joseph A., (North Barton) r 34, farmer.
Albright Sarah, (Factoryville) r 42, widow Josiah, farm 50.
Allen David, (Factoryville) r 65, farmer.
ALLEN JOHN, (Waverly) r 60, prop. Cayuta Dairy milk route and farmer.
ANDRE ABRAM T., (Lockwood) lumber dealer and contractor, h Main.
Andre Isaac J., (Factoryville) laborer.
Andre John, (Lockwood) r 29, apiarist 16 swarms.
Andrew George, (Factoryville) laborer, h Owego.

STARKEY & WINTERS, Druggists, Owego. Close Prices to Dealers.

Andrus Mary D., Lockwood) r 1, widow Thomas, farm 44.
Andrus Richard, (Lockwood) commissioner of highways and farmer 60.
Arhart Henry, (Factoryville) brakeman, bds. Jackson House.
Armstrong Joseph, retired, h Spencer.
Atchison Thomas, r 38, farmer.
Averil Miles D., (Waverly) r 65, farmer, leases of Horace Taylor 5.
Baker Alonzo, (Lockwood) r 28, farmer 50.
Ball Isaac, (Factoryville) laborer, h 533, Chemung.
Ball William N., (Factoryville) resident, h 521 Chemung.
Bandfield Ira, (Waverly) off r 65, farmer 90.
Bandfield Ira E., (Waverly) off r 65, farmer with his father Ira.
Barden Charles, (Halsey Valley) r 25, farmer.
Barden Edward, (Halsey Valley) r 25, farmer.
Barden Ira, (Halsey Valley) r 9, laborer.
Barden Simon, (Halsey Valley) r 23, farmer.
Barden Zalmon, r 39, farmer 45.
Barker Abigail, (Factoryville) widow John, resident, Main.
Barnes Christopher, (North Barton) r 17, farmer.
BARNUM ELI, (North Barton) r 4, farmer 114.
Barr John C., Jr., (Waverly) carpenter, h Chemung.
Barton Tip, r 53, laborer.
Bartron Albin, r 53, watchman.
Bartron Frank, r 54, farmer with his father Joseph.
BARTRON JACOB, r 54, farmer with his father Joseph.
Bartron Pernando, r 53, laborer.
Bartron Joseph, r 54, farmer 80.
Beams Marvin, r 41, farmer.
Beers Lyman, (Factoryville) laborer, h Charles.
Bellis William, (Factoryville) emp. Thatcher's mattress shop, h Orchard.
Bellis Marietta, (North Barton) r 35, widow Charles, resident.
Bellis Philip, (North Barton) r 35, farmer.
Bennett Emma, (Factoryville) widow David, resident, h Owego.
Bennett Lou, (Factoryville) cook, bds. Owego.
Bensley DeWitt C., justice of the peace and pension attorney, Spencer, h do.
BENSLEY ELLIOTT L., off r 55, farmer 200.
Bensley John H., teacher, bds. Spencer.
Bensley Lucina P., r 55, widow Daniel, resident.
Bensley William, poormaster, h Spencer.
Bensley William H., R. R. section hand, bds. Spencer.
Bentley George, off r 39, peddler.
BESEMER DANIEL V., (North Barton) r 18, apiarist 60 swarms and farmer 310.
Besemer George D., (North Barton) r 18, farmer.
Besemer James, (Lockwood) r 32, farmer 50.
BINGHAM BROTHERS, (Lockwood) (G. W. & E. J. B.) flour and feed, saw, lath and planing-mill, and general merchandise.
BINGHAM EDMUND J., (Lockwood) (Bingham Bros.) h Main.
BINGHAM GEORGE W., (Bingham Bros.) (Lockwood) h Main.
Bingham John, (Lockwood) r 1, farmer 27.
BOGART GEORGE W., r 40, farmer 80.
Bogart G. Fred, r 40, farmer with his father George W.
Bogart James, (Waverly) r 60, farmer 47.
Bogart John S., (Waverly) prop. saw-mill and farmer 40.

Bogart Joseph V., (Reniff) r 1, farmer 124.
Bogart Lawrence, (Factoryville) r 60, farmer.
Bogart Nathaniel V., (Waverly) r 47, farmer 130.
BOGART PETER V., (Lockwood) lumbering and farmer 65, h Main.
Bogart William, r 41, farmer.
Bowman Catharine, (Waverly) r 62, widow Absalom, resident.
Bowman Emmet, (Waverly) r 62, farmer 65, and leases of Catharine Bowman 60, and on shares with Mrs. La Mont 15.
Boyce Frank, (Factoryville) conductor, h Ithaca.
Boyce Genevieve, (Factoryville) boarding-house, Ithaca.
Boyce Lyman, (Halsey Valley) r 8, blacksmith.
Brant Mary B., (Waverly) widow Luke S., resident, h Orchard.
Brewster Harvey E., (Factoryville) r 69, farm laborer.
Brewster Henry C., (Factoryville) r 69, farm laborer.
Brewster John E., (North Barton) r 19, farmer 200.
Brink Albert J., (Factoryville) r 64, farmer.
Brink Charles, (Waverly) r 59, farmer, leases of Jacob Brink 80.
BROCK GEORGE D., (Lockwood) (A. V. C. Vail & Co.) postmaster, h Main.
BROOKS AUGUSTUS, (Lockwood) prop. turning, scroll-sawing and wagon shop, contractor and builder, and manuf. church seats.
Brown Avery, (North Barton) r 11, farmer.
Brown Charles, (Lockwood) r 2, farmer 50.
Brown Ezra, (Waverly) r 47, farmer 150.
Brown Francis, (North Barton) r 19, farmer 120.
Brown George, (Halsey Valley) r 23, farmer.
Brown Marshall, (North Barton) r 19, farmer, with his father Francis.
Brown Shubel C., (North Barton) r 4, farmer 100.
Bruster Ainslee, (Lockwood) off r 2, farmer 175.
Bruster Daniel, (North Barton) r 19, farmer 100.
Bruster Elwood, (North Barton) r 17, farmer.
Bruster Nathaniel M., (North Barton) r 17, farmer, on shares with O. M. Bruster 150.
Bruster Oliver M., (Waverly) r 49, farmer 25.
BUCK LYMAN, (Waverly) r 65, school-trustee, prop. Buck's farm, dairy milk route, and farmer 100.
Bunce Louisa, (Factoryville) widow John, resident, bds. Main.
Bunnell Henry, (Waverly) r 48½, farmer 145.
BURKE OSCAR F., (Waverly) r 60, carpenter, and farmer 6.
Burt Israel, (Waverly) retired, bds. Orchard.
Callahan Fanny, (Factoryville) widow John, resident.
Campbell Emerson, (Waverly) r 62½, farmer, leases of John Murray 100.
Canfield Amos, (Waverly) r 62, farmer 150.
CANFIELD EZRA, (Lockwood) r 46, physician and surgeon.
Carey Benjamin, (Waverly) teamster, h Main, E. Waverly.
Carey Clarissa J., widow David N., resident.
Carey Irving R., (Factoryville) laborer, h Chemung.
Carey John, R. R. section foreman, h Spencer.
Carey Samuel, r 36 farmer.
Carlisle John, (Halsey Valley) r 22, laborer.
Cary Ezra, r 66, farmer 145.
Cary Leonard, (Halsey Valley) r 25, farmer.
Cary William E., (Wright & Cary) h Spencer.

Case Isaac, (Factoryville) resident, h Owego.
Cashaday Horace, (Halsey Valley) r 12, farmer.
Casterline Coe, (Factoryville) carpenter, h Owego.
Cater William, (Waverly) laborer, h Owego.
CAYUTA CREAMERY, (Factoryville) (Schuyler & Harding, props.) near depot.
Central House, (Factoryville) F. D. Tooker, prop., Main cor. Ithaca.
Cheney Armenia, (Waverly) r 59, widow John, resident.
Church Franklin L., (Lockwood) r 46, apiarist 23 swarms, and farmer, leases of J. C. Lyons 500.
Church Walsteen A., (Lockwood) farmer with his father Franklin L.
Clark Mary, (Lockwood) r 2, farm 50.
Clarke Harmon, r $54\frac{1}{2}$, school trustee, and farmer 75.
Clawson Harmon, r 40, farmer, leases of Jeremiah Bogart 80.
Clearwater Amanda, (Factoryville) r 60, widow Stephen, resident.
Clock Clarence E., (Factoryville) postmaster and station agent, h Ithaca.
COLEMAN CHARLES H., (Lockwood) r 1, prop. turning, scroll-sawing, wagon and blacksmith shop, also dealer in wagons, sleighs and agricultural implements.
Coleman Eliza J., widow William D., resident.
Coleman George, (Waverly) r 43, farmer 50.
Coleman Jedediah D., live stock dealer, h Main.
Coleman John B., postmaster and bridge carpenter, Main, h do.
Coleman Joshua, r $54\frac{1}{2}$, farmer 45.
Coleman Sadie L., deputy postmaster, bds. Main.
Collins Cornelius, (Lockwood) r 31, farmer 100.
Collins Emeline, (Factoryville) r 60, widow Samuel, resident.
Combs Clarence, (Factoryville) r 68, farm laborer.
Combs George, (Factoryville) farm laborer, h Chemung.
Conklin Emmet, (Factoryville) r 67, laborer.
Conklin Julia, (Waverly) widow Timothy, laundress, h Main.
Cook Daniel, r 55, physician and surgeon.
Cooley Fred L., (North Barton) r 17, farmer.
Cooley Harvey L., (Factoryville) retired, h Main.
Cooley Hattie J., (North Barton) r 17, dressmaker.
Cooley Robert, (Lockwood) r 32, farmer.
Cooley Robert R., (North Barton) r 17, farmer 50.
Corey Leonel C., (Factoryville) telegraph operator, h Ithaca.
Corey William, (Factoryville) resident, h Ithaca.
Cornell Alanson, stationery engineer, h Spencer.
Cornell Daniel B., clerk, bds. Main.
Cornell William, general merchant, and prop. of feed and saw-mill, Main, h do.
Cornish Marvin J., (Factoryville) laborer, h Ithaca.
Cortright Abram, (North Barton) r 11, farmer.
Courtwright David J., (Factoryvllle) r 42, farmer on shares with M. Sawyer.
Courtwright Martin V. B., carpenter and joiner, h Spencer.
Cowles Adelbert C., (Waverly) r 60, small fruit grower.
Cowles Caleb, (Waverly) r 60, orchard 150 trees and small fruit grower.
Crandall Alfonzo, (Halsey Valley) r 5, farmer.
Crans Ard F., (Factoryville) r 60, blacksmith.
Crans Eliza, (Lockwood) r 1, resident.
CRANS FRANK, (Lockwood) r 1, apiarist 56 swarms, and farmer.
Crisfield Ellsworth E., (North Barton) r 4, farmer with his father John.

Crisfield George B., (North Barton) r 15, farmer, on shares with C. C. Hedges 145.
Crisfield John, (North Barton) r 4, farmer 180.
Cronin Bartholomew, (Lockwood) R. R. section foreman, bds. Gilbert House.
Cronin Michael, (Factoryville) R. R. section foreman, h Charles.
Crotsley George, r 41, farmer, with his father Lewis.
Crotsley Lewis. r 41, farmer 200.
Cumber Solomon, r 41, farmer.
Curran David, (Waverly) r 49½, farmer.
Curran Floyd, (Waverly) r 62, clerk.
Curran Horace H., (Waverly) r 60, mason.
Curran John J., (Waverly) r 60, mason.
Curtis Samuel, (Factoryville) conductor, h near depot.
Dalton James, laborer, h Spencer.
Damon Edward F., (Waverly) r 62½, farmer.
Daniels Mary E., (Waverly) widow Javan, tailoress, h Main, E. Waverly.
Davenport Albert, (North Barton) r 18, farmer.
Davenport Alonzo, farm laborer, h Main.
Davenport Andrew, laborer, h Railroad.
Davenport Charles A., laborer, h Railroad.
Davenport David, r 39, retired.
Davenport George, r 39, farmer 73.
Davenport Leslie, (Factoryville) emp. Sayre Butter Package Co., bds. Chemung.
Davenport Miles, r 39, carpenter.
DAVIS MARY M. Miss, (Lockwood) r 46, resident.
DECKER TANNERY, Abram I. Decker, prop., Main, E. Waverly.
Dewandler Henry, (Waverly) r 60, farm laborer.
Dewey George, (Lockwood) r 31, farm laborer.
DeWitt William M., (Factoryville) r 60, teaming.
Deyo Isaac, Jr., (Factoryville) r 60, farm laborer.
Dickerson Orson, r 34, farmer 80.
Dillon Martin, (Reniff) foreman Reniff mills.
Dingman William E., (Waverly) laborer, h Chemung.
Doane William B., (Waverly) r 62½, farmer, on shares with J. Murray 100.
Dollason Frances H., (Factoryville) widow Austin A., dressmaker, Main.
Doney Abner, (Lockwood) carpenter, h Church.
Doty Asa, (Factoryville) r 18, farmer 55.
Doud Augustus, (Waverly) retired, h Main.
Doyle Jacob, r 40, farmer 102.
Doyle John, r 40, farmer 8.
Drake Andrew J., off r 66, farmer 200.
Drake Betsey, (Halsey Valley) r 23, farm 100.
Drake Ezra, (Halsey Valley) r 22, farmer.
Drake George C., (Waverly) r 62, carpenter.
Drake James H., (Halsey Valley) r 23, farmer.
Drake Jedediah, r 37, farmer.
Drake Nathaniel, (Lockwood) laborer.
Drake Susan, off r 66, widow Elsworth, resident.
Draper Spencer J., (Factoryville) laborer, h Owego.
Drogan John, (Factoryville) emp. Sayre freight house, h Charles.
Dunn John, (Factoryville) laborer, h Main.
Dunn John, Jr., (Factoryville) laborer, bds. Main.

BARTON—OUTSIDE WAVERLY.

Dunn Kate, (Factoryville) r 65, house-keeper.
EATON AMBROSE C., (Factoryville) (D. H. E. & SON) h Main.
EATON DAVID H., (Factoryville) (D. H. E. & Son) h Main.
EATON D. H. & SON, (Factoryville) tin and hardware, manufrs. of Eaton's refrigerator butter packages.
Edgarton Willis, (Lockwood) r 46, blacksmith.
Edgcomb George G., (Factoryville) r 47, apiarist 30 swarms, and farmer 155.
Edgcomb Gilbert, (Factoryville) r 60, farmer with his mother Lucinda.
Edgcomb Lucinda, (Factoryville) r 60, widow Hobart, farm 140.
Edgcomb Lucy, (Waverly) r 60, widow Gilbert, resident.
Edwards Aaron, (Halsey Valley) r 9, farmer 45.
Edwards George F., (Halsey Valley) r 9, farmer.
Ellas A. Clark, wagon-maker, Main, h do.
Ellas Orrin, retired, h Main.
Ellas Sarah Ann, resident, h Main.
Elliott William B., (Factoryville) retired, h Chemung.
Ellis Charles B., (Waverly) off r 49, farmer 100.
ELLIS GILBERT S., (Waverly) r 64, commissioner of highways, auctioneer and farmer 35.
Ellis Ira D., (Factoryville) r 64, farmer 44.
Ellis Jesse, (Factoryville) r 59, farmer 87.
Ellis John, (Factoryville) r 65, farmer.
Ellis John, (Factoryville) painter, bds. Ithaca.
Ellis Lewis B., (Waverly) r 49, farmer 77.
Ellis Sela, (Factoryville) r 60, farmer 135.
Ellis Thaddeus W., (Factoryville) r 64, farmer 170.
Ellis William T., (Factoryville) r 65, farmer.
Ellison John, (Lockwood) r 28, farmer 50.
Ellison Samuel W., (Lockwood) r 29, farmer 118.
Ellison Susan, (Lockwood) r 29, widow Samuel, resident.
Ellison William B., (North Barton) r 16, farmer 62.
Elson Julius, r 40, farmer.
Elwell Orlando, (Reniff) r 1, sawyer and carpenter.
Evans Ziba, Rev., (Lockwood) pastor M. E. church, h Main cor. Church.
Evarts Andrew J., (Factoryville) general merchant, Main, h do.
Evelin Henry, (North Barton) r 4, farmer, leases of Dr. Vosburgh.
Evelyn Christopher, (North Barton) r 11, farmer 36.
Evenden Eliza, (North Barton) r 2, widow Robert, farm 50.
Evenden William, (North Barton) r 2, farmer.
Evens Richard E., (Waverly) laborer, h Orchard.
Fiester Jacob, retired farmer, h Main.
Filkins Cornelius, (Factoryville) carpenter, h near depot.
Finch Amasa, (Factoryville) wagon and sleigh manuf., Main, h do.
Finch Cynthia, (Factoryville) resident, bds. Main.
Finch Wilbur F., (Factoryville) postal clerk, h Main.
Fisher Douglass T., (Halsey Valley) r 21, farmer.
Fisk Willis J., (Lockwood) r 1, watch repairer and miller.
FLECKENSTINE JACOB W., (Waverly) r 60, prop. Iron Bridge stone quarry.
Fleming Oscar, (Lockwood) r 45, farmer, leases of Mrs. S. Davis 96.
Follett Harriet, (Lockwood) r 45, widow Cyrus, farm 120.
Foote Gilbert E., (Waverly) off r 46, assessor and farmer 150.
Forbes Henry S., (Waverly) r 64, farmer on shares with G. B. Pennell 100.

Forbes Hester, (Waverly) r 64, widow Archibald, resident.
Forman Edward M., r 55, farmer 100.
Forman Miles, prop. Temperance Hotel, Main.
Forsyth Edward, (Halsey Valley) r 8, farmer.
Forsyth Frederick, (Halsey Valley) r 8, farmer.
Foster Eli, (Waverly) r 47, farmer 50.
Foster Katie, (Halsey Valley) r 9, widow Daniel, resident.
Foster Shalor S., (Waverly) r 47, farmer with his father Eli.
Frisbie Charles F., (North Barton) r 14, farmer.
Frisbie Frederick, (Halsey Valley) r 8, farmer.
Frisbie William R., (North Barton) r 14, farmer 250.
Fuller Celinda, (Factoryville) widow Richard, resident, h Charles.
Fuller F. Adelbert, (Factoryville) laborer, h Charles.
Furman William A., (Reniff) r 1, farmer 35.
Garrison William R., (Factoryville) brakeman, h Charles.
Gee William, (Halsey Valley) r 21, farmer.
Genung Alva E., (Waverly) r 18, farmer 70.
Genung Harvey, (North Barton) r 27, farmer.
Genung Lydia L., (Waverly) r 18, widow Nathaniel, farm 80.
Genung William W., (Waverly) r 18, farmer.
Georgia George, (Lockwood) r 29, farmer.
Gilbert House, (Lockwood) Mrs. Eva J. Gilbert, prop., Main, opp. depot.
Gilbert Laton, (Lockwood) Gilbert House, Main.
Giles Joseph W., (Halsey Valley) r 22, farmer.
Gillan Benjamin R., (Factoryville) blacksmith, h Main.
Gillan William, (Factoryville) fireman, h Main.
Gillett Albert, (Reniff) r 1, emp. Reniff mills.
GILLETT & DECKER CREAMERY CO., (Reniff) W. E. Gillett, and A. I. Decker, props., near R. R.
Gillett Morris H., (Reniff) r 1, head sawyer Reniff mills.
Gillett Nathan R., (Reniff) retired.
GILLETT WILLIS E., (Reniff) (Gillett & Decker Co.) postmaster, general merchant, prop. Reniff Mills, and farmer 147, and in Chemung county 372, and in Tennessee 150.
Giltner Dexter E., (Waverly) carpenter, h Ithaca.
Giltner Ezra A., r 39, farmer 175.
Giltner Francis, r 39, farmer.
Giltner Wesley, r 54½, farmer 30.
Giltner William, off r 38, farmer.
Golden George M., (Lockwood) r 31, farmer 180.
Golden Isaac, (North Barton) r 33, farmer.
Goodwin Mrs., (Halsey Valley) r 9, widow Floyd, resident.
Gorton George, (North Barton) r 19, farmer 30.
Gorton Nathan, r 54, farmer 10.
Gould John, (Halsey Valley) r 23, farmer.
Grafft George H., (Waverly) justice of the peace, h Main, E. Waverly.
Gregory Franklin, (Lockwood) r 2, farmer, on shares with Dr. Hollenback 175.
Green Edward L., (Factoryville) express messenger, h Charles.
Green William H., r 54, farmer, on shares with H. A. Hollenback 224.
Greer Jane A., (Factoryville) widow Thomas, resident, h Ithaca.
Gridley Charles E., (Factoryville) (T. E. Gridley & Son) h Main.
Gridley T. E. & Son, (C. E. G.) (Factoryville) general store, Main.
Gridley Thomas E., (Factoryville) (T. E. Gridley & Son) h Main.

HAGADORN DEWITT C., (Lockwood) station and express agent, and telegraph operator, also dealer in coal, lime and cement, fence posts and R. R. ties.
Haley Michael, (Factoryville) off r 60, laborer.
Hallett John, (Waverly) r 62, painter.
Hallett William, (Waverly) off r 62, retired.
Hamilton Simeon, (Waverly) off r 60, carpenter.
Hammond Gordon S., (Waverly) r 49, farmer, on shares with J. C. Lyons 160.
Hanford Clark, (Factoryville) apiarist and shoemaker.
Hanford Julia A., (Factoryville) widow Noah, resident, bds. Main.
HANFORD MAURICE F., (Waverly) (Hanford & Lord) h Main, E. Waverly.
HANNA CHARLES F., (Factoryville) r 66, prop. saw-mill, and farmer 60.
Hanna George E., (Factoryville) brakeman, bds. Main.
Hanna George I., (Waverly) farmer 130.
Hanna G. Quigg, (Factoryville) resident, h Main.
Hanna Ira, r 55, farmer 100.
Hanna Lorentes J., (Factoryville) butcher, h Main.
Hanna Selah S., (Factoryville) farmer.
Hardenstine John L., (Waverly) painter.
Harding Amos, (Waverly) r 49, painter.
Harding Benjamin J., (Factoryville) r 59, farmer 54.
HARDING CHARLES E., (Factoryville) carpenter, h Ithaca.
Harding Charles H., (Waverly) r 59, farmer, leases of Ira Harding estate 80.
Harding Cornelius, (Waverly) r 48, farmer.
Harding Cynthia S., (Waverly) r 59, widow Ira, resident.
Harding Elliot, (Waverly) r 59, farmer.
HARDING FRANK W., r 52, farmer 90.
HARDING HORACE T., (Factoryville) (Schuyler & Harding) r 60, farmer 23½, and in Chemung county 150.
Harding James B., (Waverly) r 59, teacher, and farmer 54.
Harding James N., (Factoryville) retired, bds. Ithaca.
Harding James O., (Factoryville) emp. Sayre Butter Package Company, bds. Ithaca.
Harding Nancy H., r 52, widow John, resident.
Harding Samuel T., teacher, bds. Spencer.
Harding William, (Factoryville) (Schuyler & Harding) h Owego.
Harford A. Jackson, (Reniff) off r 1, farmer.
Harford George B., (Factoryville) teaming, h Main.
Harford Lewis, (Reniff) off r 1, farmer.
HARFORD TUNIS I., (Reniff) r 1, school trustee and farmer 60, a member of the 161st Regt., N. Y. Vols.
Harris George V., (Factoryville) carpenter, h Main.
Hart Edward C., (Waverly) r 60, emp. Novelty Works.
Hazen Fred, r 41, farm laborer.
Hedges Charles C., (North Barton) r 15, farmer 145.
Hedges Christopher, (VanEttenville, Chem. Co.) r 1, lumberman and farmer.
Hedges Laura M., (Lockwood) widow John B., resident.
Hess Adelbert, (Halsey Valley) r 12, farmer.
Hess Fred, (Halsey Valley) r 20, farmer.
Hess George, (Halsey Valley) r 7, farmer.
Hess Jacob, (Halsey Valley) r 20, farmer 60.
Hess Sylvester N., (North Barton) r 11, farmer.

Hill Ira G., (Factoryville) r 60, retired.
HILL JOHN G., (Factoryville) r 68, farmer 78.
Hill Albert L.. (Factoryville) laborer, bds. Ithaca.
Hills Charles M., (Factoryville) book-agent, bds. Ithaca.
Hollenback Harry A., r 54, farmer 224.
Hollenback John W., traveling salesman, h Spencer.
Hollenback M. Hunter, retired, h Spencer.
Holt Charles B., r 53, apiarist 40 swarms, and farmer 500.
Holt Herbert, (Halsey Valley) r 5, farmer 100.
Holt Herman B., r 53, farmer.
Hooker Nelson, (North Barton) r 27, farmer, leases of George Besemer.
Hoover Martin, (Factoryville) r 65, laborer.
Hoover William, r 41, prop. steam thresher, and farmer.
Hopkins Henry, school trustee, and farmer 48.
Hopkins John Q., r 68, farmer, on shares with S. Hanna 100.
Hopkins Stephen, (Waverly) r 62, retired.
Hopkins Stephen, Jr., (Waverly) r 62, manager Electric Light Co.
Horton Beverly P., farmer 25.
Howe John W.. (Waverly) off r 49, farmer, on shares with C. B. Ellis 100.
Hoyt Edmund H., (North Barton) r 14, postmaster, and farmer 60.
Hoyt Joseph N., (Waverly) r 60, milk dealer.
Hoyt Sylvanus H., (North Barton) r 11 cor. 14, farmer 50.
Hubbell Cassius M., (North Barton) r 17, farmer, with his father Volney.
Hubbell Melissa H., widow David C., resident, bds. Charles.
Hubbell Volney, (North Barton) r 17, peach orchard 1,100 trees, and farmer 105.
Hulett John, (Factoryville) r 59, farmer 97.
Hulett Milo, (Halsey Valley) r 9, retired.
Hulett N. Tallmadge, (Factoryville) r 59, farmer with his father John.
Hulett Theophilus, r 11, district clerk, and farmer 35.
Hyatt Alanson (Lockwood) broom-maker, h Church.
Ilette Lewis, (Factoryville) retired, h Main.
Jackson Amos, (Factoryville) prop. Jackson House, Main.
Jackson House, (Factoryville) A. Jackson, prop., Main.
Jarvis Stephen, (Waverly) off r 65, farmer.
Jennings Daniel, (Waverly) r 68, teaming.
Jewell Levi, (Halsey Valley) r 9, farmer.
Johnson Arthur A., r 40, farmer on shares with C. B. Holt 200.
Johnson Cyrus, (Factoryville) r 60, farmer 53.
Johnson Edmund J., prop. Johnson House, Main.
JOHNSON HERBERT L., (Factoryville) r 67, farmer, leases of T. W. Ellis 183.
Johnson House, (E. J. Johnson, prop.) Main.
Johnson Lucinda, (Factoryville) r 60, widow Thomas F., resident.
Johnson Philetus B., (Waverly) r 62½, farmer 50.
Jones Benjamin S., (Waverly) r 65, farmer for Mrs. Sophia Howard.
Jones Edward, (Factoryville) laborer, h Main,
Jones Eugene C., (Factoryville) laborer.
Jones George, (Factoryville) off r 60, mason.
Jones William N., (Factoryville) brakeman, h Main.
Joyce F. Delphine, (Factoryville) r 60, widow Michael, resident.
Kain Edward M., station agent, express agent and telegraph operator, also coal dealer, bds. Spencer cor. Main.

Kane James F., blacksmith, bds. Main.
Kaulback John H., (Waverly) leather finisher, bds. Main, E. Waverly.
Kaulback John J., (Waverly) supt. Decker Tannery, h Main, E. Waverly.
Keeler Thomas, (Waverly) r 49, farm laborer.
Kelley Fred L., (Reniff) r 1, farmer with his father Lutheran.
Kelley Lutheran, (Reniff) r 1, apiarist 14 swarms, and farmer 130.
Kellogg Joseph, (Lockwood) off r 47, resident.
Kelsey Horace, Rev., r 37, (Bapt.) retired.
Ketcham Avery, (Lockwood) r 33, farmer.
Ketchem Ida, widow Lewis, resident.
King Clayton G., (Waverly) r 47, farmer.
King Henry, (Halsey Valley) r 21, farmer.
King John W., r 52, farmer on shares with A. J. Van Atta 103.
King Le Grand, (Lockwood) r 45, farmer 300.
King Salmon D., r 38, farmer 200.
King Sarah M., (Waverly) r 47, widow George, resident.
King Sheffield, (Lockwood) r 15, farmer.
King Warren J., (Lockwood) r 16, farmer 80.
Kingsworth Leonard, (North Barton) r 32, farmer 150.
Kinney John, off r 39, farmer 8.
Kirk Frederick H., (Factoryville) r 60, quarryman.
Kishpaugh George, (North Barton) r 16, farm laborer.
Kishpaugh Jonas, (Halsey Valley) r 26, farmer 100.
Kline Mazie A., (Waverly) r 62½ teacher.
Kline Wesley B., (Waverly) r 62½, farmer, leases of J. Beuly 170.
Knapp Azel, (Waverly) r 59, farmer 150.
Knapp Jerome B., (Waverly) r 59, farmer.
Kreamer Lot S., (Waverly) conductor, h Main, E. Waverly.
Lambert John L., (North Barton) r. 4, farmer.
LA MONT MARY C., (Factoryville) widow Allen, farm 95.
Lauderback George, r 39, farmer 30.
Lauderback Henry, r 39, farmer 30.
Laughlin Theodore, (Waverly) r 44, farmer on shares with C. Sawyer.
Lawheed Joseph S., (Factoryville) r 47 tanner.
Lawrence James C., (Factoryville) brakeman, h Charles.
Lee Henry B., (Factoryville) r 49, farm laborer.
Lee Ira H., (Factoryville) r 48½, district clerk and farmer 131.
Lee James, (North Barton) r 3, farmer.
Leonard Charles, r 55, blacksmith.
Lewis Harrison, (Waverly) r 59, farmer 53.
Liddle Richard, (Factoryville) retired farmer, h Owego.
LORD LOUIS F., (Hanford & Lord, Waverly) h Main, E. Waverly.
Lott George W., (Van Ettenville, Chem. Co.) prop. saw-mill and farmer 500.
Lott Live Oak, (Van Ettenville, Chem. Co.) r 1, lumberman and farmer.
Lubars Theodore H., (Waverly) stationary engineer, h Main, E. Waverly.
Luce Chauncey, (North Barton) r 11, farmer.
Luce John, (Waverly) resident, h Main, E. Waverly.
Lynch Uriah, (Halsey Valley) r 6, farmer.
Lyon Alonzo, (Waverly) painter and paper-hanger, h Chemung.
Lyons Henry, (Lockwood) r 46 retired farmer.
Lyons John, (Lockwood) r 1, farmer 300.
Lyons Jonathan C., (Factoryville) retired farmer, h Ithaca.
Lyons Nelson H., (Factoryville) farmer 35, h Ithaca.

STARKEY & WINTERS, Wholesale and Retail Druggists, Owego.

Maloy I. Shepard, (Waverly) janitor High school, h Orchard.
Manderville Benjamin F., (Waverly) r 60, emp. Sayre shops and farmer 28.
Manning Betsey, (Waverly) widow Job, resident, bds. Main.
MANNING ELI D., (Halsey Valley) r 9, apiarist and farmer 46.
Manning Fred B., (Halsey Valley) r 9, feed and cidar-mill, and turning shop.
Manning John, (Halsey Valley) r 9, farmer 50.
Manning John, r 39, farmer 145.
Manning Judson, (Halsey Valley) r 9 cooper.
Manning Reuben C., (Waverly) farmer, h Main.
Mansfield Charles S., r 40, farmer on shares with J. Doyle.
Mapes Milton C., (Factoryville) blacksmith, Main, h do.
Masterton Samuel, r 41, farmer.
Masterson Urial, (Halsey Valley) r 19, farmer 15.
McCarthy Florence, (Factoryville) conductor, h Ithaca.
Mead Elizabeth, (Factoryville) r 60, widow Jacob W., resident.
Mead George H., (Factoryville) r 60, farm laborer.
Mead Judson, (Factoryville) r 60, farm laborer.
Mead Wallace, (Waverly) r 60, laborer.
Merrill A. Jackson, (Factoryville) r 59, farmer 40.
Merrill Sutherland T., (Factoryville) r 59, farmer with his father A. Jackson.
Metzker John W., (Factoryville) student, bds. Spring.
Millage Jacob A., (Factoryville) laborer, h Ball.
Millard Royal J., (Lockwood) teamster, h Main.
Millen Alonzo P., r 55, farmer on shares with C. Sawyer 96.
Miller Catharine E., (Lockwood) widow Gilbert M. L, resident, h Main.
Miller Henry, R. R. section hand, bds. Johnson House.
Miller James, (Factoryville) emp. Novelty Works, h Main.
Miller John, (Factoryville) brakeman, bds. Main.
Mills Adolphus, (Waverly) r 59, farmer.
Mills William G., (Waverly) r 59, farmer 120.
Monroe Charles, r 55, farmer.
Morse Asa, (Lockwood) off r 1, laborer.
Murray William W., (Factoryville) blacksmith, h Main.
Myers Peter, (Lockwood) r 32, farmer, leases of M. L. Williams.
New John T., (Factoryville) farm laborer, h Charles.
Newkirk Diantha (Factoryville) widow Ezra, resident, h Owego.
Nichols Charles H., (Lockwood) farm laborer.
Nichols Chauncey S., (North Barton) r 18, farmer 83.
Nichols Harriet A., (North Barton) r 18, widow Robert T., resident.
Nichols Harvey L., (Waverly) r 49, farm laborer.
Northrup Isaac D., (Waverly) r 62, farmer, leases of J. Kennedy 160.
Northrup William C., (Waverly) r 62, farmer with his father Isaac D.
Osborn John, (Factoryville) stationary engineer, h Ithaca.
Park Alvira, r 55, widow John, resident.
Park Daniel, r 55, farmer 100.
Park John J., r 55, farmer 65.
Parker Charles P., (Factoryville) r 48½, carpenter, and farmer 30.
Parks Joel, painter, h Spencer.
Parry Chauncey, r 39, farmer 15.
Partridge Sarah, (Factoryville) widow Abram, bds. Main.
Peck Luther Rev., pastor M. E. church, h Spencer.
Pembleton Charles, (Factoryville) r 69, farmer 124.
Pennell Gershem B., (Factoryville) retired farmer.

STARKEY & WINTERS, Druggists. Owego. Close Prices to Dealers.

Peters Frederick J., (Waverly) clerk, h Main, E. Waverly.
Peterson Charles, (Waverly) r 62½, farm laborer.
Petty Nathan D., laborer, h Main.
Phillips Nellie S., (Factoryville) widow Addison B., resident, h Main.
Piatt Charles, (Factoryville) r 60, laborer.
Pierce Mary A., (Factoryville) resident, bds. Main.
Poole Frank, (Halsey Valley) r 9, blacksmith, and farmer 100.
Poole George, (Halsey Valley) r 6, farmer.
Porter Zeal W., (Factoryville) r 48½, farmer.
Primrose James, r 55, laborer.
Quick Jay, (Halsey Valley) off r 12, farmer 50.
Raymond Augusta, (Factoryville) r 67, resident.
Raymond Isaac L., (Factoryville) r 67, farmer 500.
Raymond Rebecca, (Factoryville) r 67, resident.
Reed Eugene N., (North Barton) r 11, farmer.
Rezeau Henry G., (Waverly) r 62½, horse trainer and farmer.
Rezeau Joseph O., (Waverly) r 62½, farmer 60.
Rhodes Isaac, (Factoryville) carpenter, h 517 Chemung.
Richards Horace, (Waverly) r 57, school trustee, and farmer 100.
Rinker Frank, (Lockwood) r 29, farm laborer.
Robinson Frederick, (Factoryville) emp. Novelty Works, bds. Owego.
Robinson Leroy E., (Factoryville) teaming, h Owego.
Rockwell Charles M., (Factoryville) laborer, h Chemung.
Rolls Hosea H., (Waverly) r 64, farmer.
Root Frank L., (Halsey Valley) r 5, farmer 31.
Root Lester, (Halsey Valley) r 9, prop. bowling alley and pool-room.
Root Ransom R., shoemaker, Main, h North.
Ross Horace, (Lockwood) sawyer, bds. Main.
Ross John B., (Lockwood) lumberman.
Sabins Luther, (Factoryville) laborer, h Main.
Sager James, (Waverly) r 43, farmer 37.
Sager Marcus B., (Waverly) r 43, farmer 50.
Sager Philander A., (Halsey Valley) r 21, farmer.
Sager Simon, (Halsey Valley) r 25, farmer.
Salmon Franklin J., Rev., pastor Baptist church.
Saunders Charlotte, (Factoryville) r 69, widow Nathan, farm 50.
Saunders Mary W., (Factoryville) r 65, farm 83.
Saunders Nancy J., (Factoryville) r 65, resident.
Sawyer Moses E., (Factoryville) farmer, h Main.
Sawyer William A., (Factoryville) emp. Sayre shops, h Main.
SCHUYLER & HARDING, (Factoryville) props. Cayuta creamery, near depot.
Schuyler Ann, (Waverly) r 34, widow Philip C., farm.
Schuyler Arminda, (Lockwood) off r 47, resident.
SCHUYLER FORT A., (Factoryville) (Schuyler & Harding) highway commissioner, and farmer 300, h Main.
Schuyler John, (Lockwood) r 48, farmer, leases of J. Bogart 40.
Schuyler Norman, (Waverly) r 27½, farmer.
Schuyler Speer, (Halsey Valley) r 19, farmer.
Scott Mary, (Factoryville) r 65, widow Levi, house-keeper.
Scutt Horace, (Halsey Valley) r 21, farmer.
Seaman George, (Reniff) r 1, laborer.
Searles Cornelius, (Waverly) r 57, farmer 57.

Searles J. Nicholas, (Factoryville) r 68, sawyer.
Searles Truman, (Lockwood) farm laborer.
Searles Emanuel, (Factoryville) r 18, farmer 60.
Severn Lemuel, (North Barton) r 14, farmer 50.
Shackelton John, farmer 350, and in Illinois 200.
Shadrick Henry, (Halsey Valley) r 9, farmer.
Shahan Patrick, (Waverly) R. R. section foreman, h Broad.
Shahan Patrick, Jr., (Waverly) machinist, bds. Broad, E. Waverly.
Sharp Frederick, retired, h Railroad.
Shelp Mahala, (Factoryville) r 60, widow Freeman, farm 25.
Shepard Joseph, (Factoryville) resident, bds. Main.
Sherman James, (Waverly) r 64, mason.
Sherman J. Gideon, (Factoryville) r 52, farmer on shares with James Swartwood 72.
Sherman John H., (Waverly) r 64, mason.
Sherman John S., (Factoryville) r 65, farmer, leases 160.
Sherman S. Melinda, (Waverly) r 64, widow James W., resident.
Sherman Stephen, (Factoryville) r 52, retired.
Shipman Harvey D., (Waverly) r 18, school trustee, and farmer 100.
SHIPMAN PERLIE E., (Waverly) r 4, dressmaker.
Shipman Philip H., r 54, farmer 30.
SHIPMAN RUFUS T., (Waverly) r 43, apiarist 20 swarms and farmer 50.
Shipman Shaler B., (North Barton) r 34, farmer 130.
Shoemaker Aaron, r 41, farmer.
Shoemaker Henry, r 35, farmer 60.
Shoemaker Peggy A., (Factoryville) widow Daniel, resident, bds. Main.
Shores Elizabeth Mrs., (Waverly) resident, bds. Orchard.
Shorter Harriet, (Halsey Valley) r 22, widow Albert, resident.
Simons Charlotte W., (Waverly) r 47, widow Thomas, resident.
Skillings Giles, (Halsey Valley) r 9, carpenter.
Skillings James, L., (Halsey Valley) r 9, laborer.
SLITER JAMES M., (Waverly) r 49, farmer 128. Farm for sale.
Sliter J. Watson, (Factoryville) laborer, h Orchard.
Sliter Nicholas, (Factoryville) retired, bds. Orchard.
Sliter Phoebe, Mrs. (Factoryville) resident, bds. Orchard.
Sliter Warren, (Factoryville) painter, h Orchard.
Slutzer Louis, (Factoryville) track hand, bds. Jackson House.
Sly Jeffrey A., (Waverly) r 49, farmer 75.
Smith Asa M., (Factoryville) brakeman, h Spring.
Smith Charles B., (Waverly) r 64, retired.
Smith Charles G., (Waverly) r 49½, farmer.
Smith Daniel, (Waverly) r 44, farmer.
Smith Deborah A., (Factoryville) widow Joseph, resident, h Main.
Smith Emily, (Halsey Valley) r 9, widow David.
Smith Emmet W., (Waverly) r 60, emp. Novelty Works.
Smith Freeman D., (Waverly) r 50, farmer 15.
Smith George J., (Waverly) r 49½, resident.
Smith Hannah, (Factoryville) r 47, widow Jesse, resident.
Smith Hester, (Lockwood) r 28. widow Charles, farm 50.
SMITH JAMES H., (Factoryville) telegraph operator, bds. Spring.
Smith John, Jr., (North Barton) r 17, farmer 82.
Smith Lorenzo, (Waverly) r 49, farmer, leases of Mrs. Mary C. La Mont 120.
Smith Phoebe, (Waverly) r 50, widow Benjamin, resident.

SMITH RUSHTON, (Waverly) r 64, civil engineer and farmer 50.
Smith William E., (Waverly) r 49½, farmer on shares with G. Graff 130.
Solomon George, (Waverly) r 49, farmer 90.
SOLOMON JOHN V., (Waverly) r 69, carpenter and farmer 15.
Soper Will, (Lockwood) off r 48, farmer.
Southwick Warren, (Halsey Valley) r 20, farmer.
Spear Barney B., (Lockwood) r 46, farmer on shares with J. T. Sawyer 130.
Spear Samuel (North Barton) r 14, farmer on shares with Shubel Brown 100.
Squires Frederick S., (Factoryville) emp. Novelty Works, h Orchard.
Squires James P., (Factoryville) r 60, farmer 50.
Squires Miles E., (Factoryville) resident, h Orchard.
Squires Molbrow H., (Waverly) farmer.
Stalker Albert, (Factoryville) clerk h Main.
Stanton Mary E., (Factoryville) widow Simon, laundress, h Main.
Stebbins O. Harrison, (North Barton) r 17, farmer 50.
Stebbins William H., (Factoryville) driver, h 545 Chemung.
Stevens Allen, (Factoryville) blacksmith, h Main.
Stevens Samuel, (Lockwood) r 46, groceries and meat-market.
Stever James H., (Waverly) r 62, carpenter.
Stever Jeremiah A., (Lockwood) r 46, head sawyer Bingham's mills.
Steward Adam, (Lockwood) r 45, farmer 9,
Steward Catharine, r 39, widow William, resident.
Steward Horace A., (Waverly) r 69, farmer.
Stewart Augustus, (Halsey Valley) r 21, farmer.
Stewart Edgar S., (Factoryville) r 69, emp. Novelty Works.
Stewart Harriet, (Factoryville) widow George H., resident, bds. Main.
Stewart Jane A., (Waverly) r 18, resident.
Stewart Thomas E., (Factoryville) r 60, farm laborer.
Struble John, (Waverly) r 48½, farmer.
Stuart Cornelius C., (Lockwood) laborer.
Stuart Will E., painter, Main, h do.
Sutherland Edward J., (Factoryville) tinsmith, bds. Ithaca.
Sutherland Thomas, (Factoryville) stationary engineer, h Ithaca.
Swain Mary J., (Factoryville) r 60, widow Jacob, resident.
Swarthout Charles B., (Factoryville) carpenter, h Chemung.
Swartwood Darius E., r 41, emp. Sayre shops, and farmer 61.
Swartwood Ezekiel, r 53, farmer 6.
Swartwood James, r 53, retired.
Swartwood John P., r 67, farmer 120
Swartwood Mary Miss, r 53, resident.
Swartwood Parthema Miss, r 53, resident.
Swartwood William, r 41, retired.
Talcott Oscar, (Halsey Valley) r 25, farmer.
Taylor Chester, (Halsey Valley) r 9, laborer.
Taylor Daniel, (Halsey Valley) r 6 farmer.
Taylor Edwin, (Halsey Valley) r 6, farmer.
Taylor Elizabeth, (Halsey Valley) r 5, widow Eli, farm 100.
Taylor George, (Halsey Valley) r 9, farmer 24.
Taylor Orin, (Halsey Valley) r 6, farmer.
Temperance Hotel, (M. Forman, prop.) Main.
Terry William R., (Waverly) r 64, book agent.
Thayer Mary E. Mrs., (Factoryville) r 59, resident.
Thayer William, (Factoryville) r 65 farmer.

Thomas Aaron, (Lockwood) r 46, emp. Bingham's mills.
Thomas Charles, (Factoryville) emp. Pipe Works, bds. Jackson House.
Thomas George D., (Lockwood) r 46, fireman.
THOMAS HALLOWAY W., (Waverly) insurance, h Main, E. Waverly.
Thomas Lucy, (Factoryville) widow James, h Orchard.
Thrall C. Adelbert, (Lockwood) r 2, school trustee and farmer 100.
Thrall Sarah, (Waverly) r 49, widow Charles, resident.
Tilbery Edgar, r 39, farmer 72.
Tompkins Mary A., (Factoryville) widow Charles, dressmaker, h Ithaca.
Tompkins Samuel W., r 54½, farmer on shares with Elizabeth Coleman's estate 160.
Tooker Frederick D., (Factoryville) prop. Central House.
Tozer Almerin, (Factoryville) resident, h Ithaca.
Tozer Alonzo, (Waverly) r 60, farmer.
Tozer Edward A., (Waverly) r 60, farmer 47.
Tozer Harry H., (Waverly) r 60, farm laborer.
Tozer Henry, (Waverly) r 60, farmer 100.
Tozer James, (Lockwood) r 16, farmer.
Tozer Mary A., (Lockwood) r 16, widow William, farm 40.
Tubbs Irving D., (Lockwood) r 29, farmer on shares with A. Ackley 100.
Turnbull James, (Factoryville) moulder, bds. Central House.
Tuthill James N., (Factoryville) r 69, farmer.
Tuthill William L., (Waverly) r 62, farmer 150.
VAIL A. V. C. & CO., (G. D. Brock) (Lockwood) saw and planing mill and general merchandise, Main.
Vail A. V. C., (Lockwood) (A. V. C. Vail & Co.) farmer 350, residence in Waverly.
VanAtta ——, (Factoryville) r 60, gardener.
VanAtta Benjamin, farm laborer, h Spencer.
VanAtta Fanny J., r 52, widow Peter, resident.
VAN ATTA OSCAR H., r 52, master Tioga County Pomona Grange, district clerk, and farmer 75.
VAN BUREN EUGENE L., (Lockwood) r 46, farmer 75.
VanBuren Lorenzo, (Lockwood) r 1, farm laborer.
VanCleft Wells W., (Waverly) r 62, laborer.
VanDermark Frederick, (Factoryville) r 60, farmer on shares with William Shepard estate.
VanEtten Alfred, (North Barton) r 4, farmer.
VanEtten Elisha, (Halsey Valley) r 25, farmer.
VanEtten Richard, (Halsey Valley) r 26, farmer.
VanHorn Charles, (Waverly) r 57, farm laborer.
VanLuvin Alison, (Halsey Valley) r 5, farmer 46.
VanMarter F. Wesley, (Halsey Valley) r 12, farmer 65.
VanRiper ——, (Factoryville) r 65, farmer on shares with Mary Saunders 80.
VanTyle Arthur, (Lockwood) retired, bds. Main.
VanVleet Theodore, (Halsey Valley) r 5, farmer.
Varner John H., (Waverly) emp. freight yard, h Main, E. Waverly.
Vasbinder Harrison, (Halsey Valley) r 10, farmer.
Vasbinder James H., (Halsey Valley) r 9, resident.
Vastbinder Lewis, (Halsey Valley) r 8, farmer.
Vosburgh Everett, (Halsey Valley) r 9, farmer.
Vosburgh Henry P., (Halsey Valley) r 9, physician and surgeon.
Wakefield Martha M., (Factoryville) resident, bds. Ithaca.

Walden John N., (Halsey Valley) r 12, farmer 50.
Walden Leander, (Waverly) emp. Steam mill, h Orchard.
Walden Theodore, (Factoryville) r 69, farmer on shares with S. Ellis 135.
Walden Thomas, (Waverly) r 49, farmer 25.
Walker Edward H., (Waverly) farmer.
Walker Emmet, (Waverly) r 62, farmer 170.
WALKER LEANDER, (Waverly) r 62, grocery, Broad.
Walker Loren A., (Waverly) r 60, apiarist 40 swarms, and farmer 33.
Walker Richard, (Factoryville) off r 60, laborer.
WALKER THADDEUS S., (Waverly) (T. S. Walker & Son) r 60.
Warner John A., (Waverly) r 65, milk dealer.
WASHBURN GEORGE H., (Factoryville) r 65, farmer.
Watson John F., (Factoryville) resident, h Main.
Weed Cornelius E., (Lockwood) r 32, farmer 72.
Weed William F., (Lockwood) farmer with his father Cornelius E.
Weller Erastus, (Factoryville) r 42, farmer.
Weller William S., (Factoryville) r 60, brakeman.
Wells O. Eugene, (Reniff) foreman creamery.
Welton Eugene E., (Waverly) fireman, h Orchard.
West Samuel, (Lockwood) r 45, retired.
West Wilson, (Reniff) off r 1, farmer 126.
Westbrook Henry, (North Barton) r 17, farmer.
Westfall Harry, (Factoryville) carpenter, h Main.
Westfall John V., r 55, farmer 100.
Wheeler Grant, r 34, farmer.
Wheeler H. Samuel, retired, h Main.
Wheeler Isaac R., r 66, farmer.
Wheeler Nirum, (Factoryville) r 66, farm laborer.
Wheeler Philip H., (North Barton) r 32, farmer 63.
WHITAKER LEWIS, (Factoryville) r 59, farmer 102.
Whitaker William H., (Waverly) resident, h Orchard.
Whitmarsh Ira, Jr., r 39, R. R. section hand.
Wilbur Dennison, (Halsey Valley) r 7, farmer.
Wilbur Hiram, (Halsey Valley) r 6, farmer.
Wilcox Lyman, (Factoryville) retired, h Ithaca.
Wilkinson Charles S., (Waverly) r 65, school clerk, and farmer 175.
Wilkinson C. Raymond, (Waverly) r 65, commercial traveler.
Wilkinson Joseph G., (Waverly) r 68, retired.
Williams Alanson C. (Reniff) r 1, farmer 60.
Williams Justus A., (North Barton) r 28, farmer 10.
Williams Lucinda, (North Barton) r 17, widow Sylvester H., farm 46.
Williams Mastin, (Lockwood) r 28, farmer 40.
Williams Moses S., (Reniff) r 1, farmer on shares with Joseph Bogart.
Williams Winton T., (Waverly) r 47, farmer 70.
Willis Frank, (Lockwood) r 16, farm laborer.
Willis William, r 39, farmer 150.
Wood Eunice A., (Factoryville) widow Oliver P., resident, h Main.
WOOD JAMES C., (Factoryville) general merchant, also deputy post-master, Main, h do.
Woodard Henry, (Waverly) off r 62, farmer, leases of James Benley 100.
Worrick David A., (North Barton) r 17, farmer 50.
Worster Simon, (Factoryville) emp. Novelty Works, h Owego.

STARKEY & WINTERS, Wholesale and Retail Druggists, Owego.

Wright & Cary, (C. E. W. and W. E. C.) general merchants, Main.
Wright Charles E., (Wright & Cary) h Main.
Wright Miama, (Factoryville) r 59, widow Sylvenus, farm 40.
Yaple Amos S., r 39, carpenter.
Yaple Peter, r 57, farm laborer.
Yates Emily, (Factoryville) widow Thomas, resident.
Yates Jerome N., (Factoryville) mail carrier, bds. Main.
Yates Thomas P., (Factoryville) lumberman and farmer.

BERKSHIRE.

(*For explanations, etc., see page* 3, *part second.*)

(Postoffice address is Berkshire, unless otherwise designated in parenthesis.)

Akins Caroline P., r 21, widow Stephen, farm 140.
Akins Henry S., (Speedville, Tomp. Co.) r 18, saw and planing-mill, cheese-box factory, cider-mill, wood turner and manuf. potato crates.
Akins John P., r 21, farmer, works for Caroline P., 140.
Andrews Asa, r 3, farmer, leases of Walter Jewett 190.
Bailey Isaac B., r 28, sawyer.
Baker Clarence A., r 5, farmer, leases of Talcott Leonard 154.
Baker George W., r 11½, farmer.
Ball Asa, r 24, farmer 150.
Ball Caroline, widow of Anson, h Main.
Ball George P., produce buyer.
Ball Hannah E., widow of Alvah M., resident, h Main.
Ball John, prop. saw-mill and farmer 40.
Ball Robert H., farmer 140, h Main.
Ball Stephen L., farmer 88.
Ballard James O., (Ketchumville) r 28, farmer 39.
Ballou Alden, off r 23, farmer.
Ballou Nelson A., r 36, farmer 71.
Ballou Reuben, off r 23, farmer 97.
Bancroft William H., (Ketchumville) r 32, farmer 59.
Barr George A., farmer 50, h Glen.
Bates Otis L., r 10, farmer 75.
Bates Spencer, r 10, farmer.
Beebe Herman P., r 9, laborer.
Beebe Philo E., r 9, farmer 75.
Bennett Lucius M., laborer, h Glen.
Benton Charles W., r 17, manuf. of axe-helves, and farmer 45.
Benton Thomas J., r 17, painter and farmer.
BERKSHIRE FLOURING MILLS, Leet & Hollenbeck, proprs.
BERKSHIRE HOUSE, (Ira Crawford, prop.) livery connected.
Bidwell Elizabeth M., widow Hiram H., resident, h Main.
Bidwell Roxey A., widow Samuel C., resident, h Main.

STARKEY & WINTERS, properly fill Mail and Telephone Orders.

TOWN OF BERKSHIRE.

BLACKMAN ABRAM, dealer in live stock, and farmer 160, h Main.
Borthwick Joseph, (Jenksville) r 19, farmer 81.
Boyer Stephen H., (Speedsville, Tomp. Co.) r 18, farmer 400.
BRAINARD CHARLES E., r 27 cor. 26, dealer in the Deering mower, reaper and binder, wheel rakes, spring tooth harrows, sulky and land plows, wagons and carriages, also agent for arctic creamery, and farmer 220.
Briggs Thomas, r 38, laborer.
Brookins Charles E., (Ketchumville) r 33, laborer.
Brown Abraham, carpenter, and farmer with James Cumming 50, h Main.
Brown Edwin B., r 38, farmer.
Brown Frances C., r 38, farm 80.
Brown Myron, r 38, carpenter, and farmer 12.
Brown Robert C , r 38, breeder of horses, and farmer 130.
Brown Romeo W., r 38, laborer.
BUFFINGTON CALVIN A., general blacksmith, manuf. of carriages, beam knives, mill-stone picks, etc., Railroad h Main.
Bunnell Eddie E., r 9, farmer 60.
Bunnell Henry J., (Center Lisle) r 29, resident.
Bunnell John G., (Center Lisle) r 29, farmer 125.
Bunnell Nancy A., r 9, widow Charles A., farmer 63.
Burgess Joseph, r 23, painter, and farmer 6.
Bush Marcene, r 38, farmer 80, and leases of F. C. Brown 40.
Bushnell William, (Wilson Creek) r 34, laborer.
Bushnell William B., flour, feed, coal, salt, and fertilizers, Depot, and in Newark Valley, farm 50.
Cady Gershom, (Ketchumville) r 31, laborer.
Carmer Charles, off r 29, farmer 25.
Chappins Mark, Jr., r 21, farmer, leases of Mark Chappins, of Sheldrake, N. Y., 130.
Church Elijah C., r 30, farmer 48.
CHURCH ORRIS, r 29, stone mason, carpenter, and farmer 9, served in Co. E 76th Regt., N. Y. Vols.
Christler William, (Wilson Creek) r 35, farmer.
Clark Gershom W., (Ketchumville) r 28, farmer 125.
Clark Horatio, general merchant, and deputy post-master, Main, cor. Depot, h do.
Clark Sanford H., r 36, apiarist, and farmer 70.
Clark Silas H., r 36, laborer.
Coats Charles, r 27, farmer 105.
Coats Joseph, r 27, farmer 3.
Cole James E., (Jenksville) r 19, farmer, leases of L. Maria Keeny, of Dryden, 227.
Cole Leslie, r 11½, laborer.
Collins Ambrose H., farmer 15, h Main.
COLLINS JUNIUS, wool and produce dealer, real estate agent for lands in Nebraska, also associate justice and justice of peace, h Main.
Comstock George S., (Speedsville, Tomp. Co.) r 18, teacher.
Cortright Henry, r 28, farmer 30.
CORTRIGHT JOHN, (Maine, Broome Co.) farmer, leases of Henry Van-Tyle, of Maine, 66.
Cortright William, r 14, laborer.
Costillo John, r 6, leather roller.

TOWN OF BERKSHIRE. 47

Courtright Darius, (Wilson Creek) r 28, farmer 95.
Crapo Richard, (Ketchumville) r 28, laborer.
Crawford Eugene, farmer, leases of Ira Crawford, h Main.
CRAWFORD IRA, prop. of Berkshire Hotel and livery, also farmer 370, and in Harford, Cortland Co., 50.
Crawford Ira O., sawyer and carpenter, h Main.
Crawford James H., carpenter, h East.
Croft Harry, emp. hub factory, bds. Glen.
Cross James O., merchant tailor, Main.
CROSS LOUIS J., house and carriage painter, paper-hanging and decorating, also breeder of Clay horses; breaking colts a speciaity, h Mechanic.
CROSS SARAH B., (wife of Louis J.) all kinds of upholstering, h Mechanic.
Cullen Miles, r 6, emp. tannery.
Cummings James, retired farmer, h Glen.
Curtis A. V., widow Mark, h Main.
DALE JOHN, r 38, farmer 38.
Darbonnier Stephen, (Dewey & Darbonnier) h Elm.
DAVIDGE, HORTON & CO., (Mrs. E. Davidge, Lucien Horton and James Davidge) r 6, props. Berkshire tannery, and manufrs. of hemlock sole leather, also farmers 150.
DAVIDGE JAMES, r 6, (Davidge, Horton & Co., and Davidge, Landfield & Co., of Newark Valley).
Decker Gideon, r 11, resident.
Dermody Michael, emp. tannery, h Main.
DEWEY & DARBONNIER, (Chas. J. D., and Stephen D.) dealers in dry-goods, groceries, hardware, boots and shoes, clothing, &c., also farmers 12, Main.
DEWEY CHARLES J., (Dewey & Darbonnier) also justice of peace, h Main.
Dewey Dwight W., teacher, bds. Main.
Doney John J., r 30, laborer.
Doney William H., r 30, farmer 48.
Dorwin Charles H., r 6, book-keeper, and farmer 4.
Eastman Charles, r 13, farmer.
Eastman Leonard O., county school commissioner, and medical student, office in Court House, Owego, and at residence in Berkshire.
Eastman Nancy W., widow George W., resident, h Main.
EASTMAN RALPH D., physician and surgeon, farm 132, h Main.
Edwards Charles M., (Ketchumville) r 28, laborer.
Edwards Merritt P., (Ketchumville) r 28, farmer 50.
Eldred M. F., r 6, laborer.
ELDRIDGE EDWARD O., (E. O. E. & Co.) notary public, h. Main.
ELDRIDGE E. O. & CO., (Edward O. Eldridge and Mrs. Caroline Johnson) dealers in dry goods, groceries, and general merchandise, Main.
Eldridge Mary S., widow of Edward H., resident.
Ellis William, teamster, h Railroad.
Ellis William, (Speedsville, Tomp. Co.) r 18, laborer.
Eston Elmer, (Ketchumville) r 31, farmer, leases of R. T. Gates, of North Lancing, 107.
Evans Irving W., r 28, farmer 83.
Evans John J., (Ketchumville) r 33, farmer, leases of Marion Rich, of Newark Valley, 60.
Evans Mary H., (Jenksville) r 19 cor. 41, widow of Joel, farm 7.

TOWN OF BERKSHIRE.

Evans William S., (Jenksville) r 19 cor. 41, farmer.
Everett Henry C., r 9, farmer 145.
Fitch Arthur, (Wilson Creek) off r 28, laborer.
FORD ARTHUR J., r 15 cor. 17, farmer 104.
FORD GEORGE, r 22, carpenter, and farmer 55.
FORD JOHN R., postmaster and farmer 171, h Elm.
FORD MARCUS J., r 16, farmer 119 and leases of James Baird of Speedsville 200.
Ford Sarah W., r 3, widow Lebbeus, resident.
FORD WILLIAM W., r 3, dairy 10 cows, farmer 117.
Foster Amos, r 11, farmer.
Foster John L., r 11, farmer, leases of Ira Crawford 165.
Freeland Lewis A., (Newark Valley) r 40, farmer 115.
Gay Isaac W., physician and surgeon, farmer 90, h Main.
Gilbert Marvin C., r 14, laborer.
Gilbert Marvin C., Jr., r 14, farmer 14.
Goldstein Brothers, (Jacob & Samuel) clothing and gents' furnishing goods.
Gould Joel, (Ketchumville) r 28, farmer 137.
Griner John N., restaurant, Depot.
HAIGHT EDITH J., art teacher, h Glen.
Haight Mary, widow Samuel F., farm 25, h Glen.
Hamilton Elliott, r 6, boarding-house.
Hamilton Susanna, r 8, widow Charles, resident.
Hart Arthur L., (Speedsville, Tomp. Co.) r 18, carpenter and farmer.
Hart Colden N., (Wilson Creek) r 34, postmaster, also dealer in cigars and tobacco.
Hart Samuel L., (Speedsville, Tomp. Co.) r 18, prop. grist-mill, also carpenter and farmer 7.
HART SARAH E., (Speedsville, Tomp. Co.) r 18, wife of Samuel L., cloth and carpet weaving.
Hart Selim M., (Speedsville, Tomp. Co.) r 18, carpenter and cabinet maker.
Hartwell Levi, r 29, farmer 50.
Hartwell Willard R., (Ketchumville) r 28, farmer 105.
Harvey Andrew J., (Wilson Creek) r 36, farmer 47.
Harvey Martin V., (Wilson Creek) farmer 140.
HAY HENRY L., painter, h Railroad.
Hay Van Rensselaer, r 11, farmer.
Hayden John, (Speedsville, Tomp. Co.) r 17, farmer 78.
HAYDEN PATSEY W., carpenter and builder, h Glen.
Higgins & Rounsevell, (Speedsville, Tomp. Co.) (John H. & George B. R.) r 18, props. Speedsville creamery and cheese factory.
Higgins John, (Speedsville, Tomp. Co.) (Higgins & Rounsevell) r 18, agricultural implements and farmer 75.
Hill T. James, emp. Berkshire Hotel, Main.
Hillsinger Charles, r 26, farmer 50.
Hillsinger William, r 26, laborer.
Hinds Robert, emp. tannery, h Main.
Hitchcock Caroline, resident, Elm.
HOLCOMB J. WALLACE, dealer in drugs, patent medicine, groceries, paints and oils, etc.
Holland Frank, r 9, farmer 30.
Holland James J., (Wilson Creek) r 11, farmer 21.
HOLLENBECK J. ERVING, (Leet & Hollenbeck).

TOWN OF BERKSHIRE.

HORTON LUCIEN, (Davidge, Horton & Co., and Davidge, Landfield & Co., of Newark Valley, also Sherwood & Horton) r 6.
Hough Rev. Joel J., pastor of Congregational Church.
Houghtaling Burt, carriage maker, millwright and wood turner, Mechanic bds. Main.
HOUGHTALING WILLIAM M., wagon-maker and repairing, h Main.
Houk Daniel, (Wilson Creek) r 35, shoemaker, apiarist and farmer 8.
Howland Fred E., r 24, laborer.
Howland George E., r 24, laborer.
Howland Harper, resident, Main.
Hubbard Howard M., r 20, carpenter and farmer, leases of J. R. Ford 112, Served in Co. B, 109th N. Y. State Vol.
Humphrey Erastus E., (Speedsville, Tomp. Co.) r 19 cor. 17, wagon maker and farmer 10.
HUTCHINSON ORRIN, (Wilson Creek) r 34, dairy 25 cows, farmer 190.
Japhet Elijah, r 28, farmer 31.
Japhet George W., r 9, dairy 7 cows, and farmer 95.
Japhet Gilbert L., r 9, farmer.
JAPHET MILO G., prop. saw-mill and novelty works, also dealer in lumber, lath, shingles, etc., Railroad.
JENKS NATHANIEL J., (Jenksville) r 42, dairy 20 cows, and farmer 157.
Jewett Asahel, r 3, dairy 15 cows, and farmer 220.
JEWETT WALTER, (Speedsville, Tomp. Co.) r 3 cor. 1, supervisor 12th term, dairy 20 cows, and farmer 420.
JOHNSON CAROLINE, (E. O. Eldridge & Co.) widow Carlisle P., h Main.
Johnson Edward, r 6, leather roller.
Johnson Eugene F., r 6, fire, life and accident insurance, sugar orchard 300 trees, and farmer 220.
Johnson Frank H., retired, bds. Main.
Johnson Frederick C., r 6, clerk.
Johnson William C., (Ketchumville) r 28, laborer.
Judd John N., r 6, dealer in harnesses, carriages, sleighs and agricultural imp., also farmer 107.
Keeny Willoughby L., (Speedsville, Tomp. Co.) r 17, farmer 120.
Kenyon William H., (Wilson Creek) r 34, farmer 50 in Maine, Broome Co.
Keyes Benjamin I., r 6, farmer, leases of George Royce.
Keyser Henry, r 15, farmer 100.
Kimball & Stannard, (Connecticut) (John F. K. and Lorenzo J. S.) r 35, stationary steam threshing machine, horse breeders, and farmers 197, and in Newark 110.
Kingsbery Henry, r 14, farmer 20.
Lacy Thomas, r 11, farmer 62½.
Lamb Lewis W., r 14, laborer.
Lee Frank L., r 27, farmer.
LEET & HOLLENBECK, (T. E. L. and J. E. H.) props. Berkshire Flouring mills, and dealers in flour, meal, feed and bran, near Depot.
LEET FRANK E. (Leet & Hollenbeck.)
LEGG ERASMUS D., (Speedsville, Tomp. Co.) r 18, breeder of English hurdle race horses, and coach horses, Holstein cattle and Hampshire sheep, dairy 15 cows, and farmer 220, sugar orchard 1,000 trees.
Legg George W., (Speedsville, Tomp. Co.) r 18, farmer.
Legg Layton J., (Jenksville) off r 41, farmer 110.
Legg Louis P., retired farmer, h Main.

TOWN OF BERKSHIRE.

Legg Reuben T., (Speedsville, Tomp. Co.) r 18, carp. and cabinet maker.
Leonard Charles Talcott, r 6, dairy 15 cows, and farmer 260.
Leonard Eunice C., r 14, widow George F., resident, farm with Ransom 168.
Leonard Henry G., retired tanner, h Elm.
LEONARD J. WALDO, farmer 180, h Elm.
Leonard Ransom, r 14, farmer with Eunice C. 168.
Lynch Albert C., farmer, h Main.
Lynch Charles O., r 24, deputy sheriff.
Lynch Eugene F., dealer in produce, and farmer 200.
Lynch George W., clerk, h Main.
Lynch Theodore, dealer in beef and live stock, also farmer 165, h Main.
Manning Alexander D., dealer in butter and eggs, h Main.
Manning Arthur B., r 24, farmer 10.
Manning Charles S., r 24, farmer 140.
Marshall George, r 3, laborer.
Maynard George, (Speedsville, Tomp. Co.) r 18, farmer, leases of John Cross of Speedsville 90.
MAYOR CHARLES, (Theodore & Son) r 38 cor. 39.
MAYOR THEODORE & SON, (Theo & Charles) r 38 cor. 39, breeders and dealers in Holstein cattle, dairy 16 cows, and farmers 136, sugar orchard 300.
McCoy Oliver A., (Speedsville, Tomp. Co.) r 18, carpenter.
McMahon James, r 5, farmer 41.
McMahon Patrick, r 5, farmer 40.
Meeks Edmund, (Speedsville, Tomp. Co.) r 18, farmer 105.
Merithew Edgar A., (Connecticut) r 35, farmer, leases of Norman A. Prentice 68.
Myre Frank, r 6, laborer.
Nicholson Charles, r 36, farmer, leases of Robert E. Waldo 106.
Noiton Benjamin, (Ketchumville) r 28, farmer 50.
Northrup Frank L., (Speedsville, Tomp. Co.) r 18, carpenter and painter.
Northrup George W., (Speedsville, Tomp. Co.) r 18, retired physician.
Oaks Jerome, (Ketchumville) r 28, agt. mowers and reapers, and farmer 136.
Oliver Peter, (Speedsville, Tomp. Co.) r 19, farmer.
Olney Marvin M., emp. hub factory, served in Co. E. 76th N. Y. Vols., and Co. F. 5th N. Y. Cavalry, h Main.
Owen Jay, (Speedsville, Tomp. Co.)(M. A. & Bros.) r 18.
Owen M. A. & Brothers, (Speedsville, Tomp. Co.) (Mc A. and Jay) r 18, manuf. tubs, firkins and barrels.
Owen Mc A., (Speedsville, Tomp. Co.) (M. A. & Bro.) r 18.
Orton James, r 30, farmer 38.
Overacker John M., r 3, laborer.
Parke Anson, (Jenksville) r 42, laborer.
Palmer Robert, r 6, laborer.
Parsons George, r 26, dairy 50 cows, and farmer 750.
Parsons Jemima, widow Chauncey, resident, h Glen.
Parsons William C., (Ketchumville) r 33, farmer, leases of W. H. Jackson of Newark Valley 140.
PATCH EVELINE L., r 39, widow William J., administratrix of estate of William J., farm 230, and in Richford 210.
PATCH HENRY W., r 39, dealer in horses, and farmer, works the estate of William J. Patch 230, dairy 14 cows, sugar orchard 200, wool grower 35 head.

STARKEY & WINTERS, Wholesale and Retail Druggists, Owego.

Patch Robert C., telegraph operator, bds. Main.
Payne Charles H., laborer, h Railroad.
Payne Frederick H., r 24, postal clerk, and farmer 100.
Payne Henry A., carpenter, and farmer 250, h Main.
Phillips Elias M., r 38, farmer, leases of J. Watrous, of Cortland, 140.
Phillips Sophia L., (Speedsville, Tomp. Co.) r 18, widow of Asa E., resident.
Pierce John, (Ketchumville) r 28, farmer 30.
Pierce Sylvester, (Ketchumville) r 28, farmer 80.
Pittsley Clarence A., r 14, laborer.
Pittsley Oscar, r 26, laborer.
Pittsley Sewel, r 14, laborer.
POLLEY HIRAM, manuf. and dealer in harnesses, whips, robes and blankets, Main, h do.
PRATT MARSHALL D., carriage-maker, veterinary surgeon, and constable, h West.
Prentice Austin H., (Connecticut) r 32, dairy 14 cows, and farmer 47 in Newark Valley, and leases of George Walter 92.
Prentice Irving B., (Newark Valley) r 40, farmer 97.
PRENTICE NORMAN A., dealer in fresh and salt meats, fish, oysters, clams, poultry and veal calves, also farmer 68, Main, h do.
Prentice Will E., (Newark Valley) r 40, farmer 112.
Preston Jay R., (Jenksville) r 41, farmer, leases of Abram Blackman.
Quinliran Edward, r 6, emp. tannery.
Rightmire Elizabeth, widow William H., farm 30, h Glen.
Rightmire Nathan, r 3, farmer 140.
Rightmire Squire, retired carpenter, h Glen.
Rightmire William P., r 6, foreman tannery.
Roberts William D., r 7, farmer, leases of E. R. Adams, of Nanticoke, 200.
Robinson Frank G., r 3, farmer with Newell 180, dairy 19 cows.
Robinson Newell, r 3, farmer with Frank G. 180, dairy 19 cows.
ROCKEFELLER CHARLES H., barber and hair-dresser, livery stable and constable, Main.
Rockwell Frank, r 15, farmer, leases of H. A. Payne 209.
ROCKWELL PETER, r 36, farmer 130.
Rockwood James W., r 38, farmer 10.
Rounsevell George B., (Speedsville, Tomp. Co.) (Higgins & R.) r 18.
ROYCE AMELIA B., wife of George C., farmer 120, h Main.
Royce Frederick B., r 6, dairy 10 cows, farmer 141.
ROYCE GEORGE C., breeder and dealer in Clay horses, prop. stock horse Good Luck Clay, and farmer 120, h Main.
Royce John B., r 6, retired farmer 60, aged 92.
Sargent Orrin, (Wilson Creek) r 33, farmer 45.
Sargent Silas, (Wilson Creek) r 33, farmer.
Scott Charles & Edmund F., r 22 cor. 41, apiarists, 65 to 100 colonies, egg and poultry raising, dairy 15 cows, 70 sheep, sugar orchard 300 trees, and farmers 247.
Scudder George D., teamster, Main.
Seamans Samuel M., general blacksmith, Main.
Sears Quincy A., r 38, farmer 25.
Shaff James H., r 30, farmer 90.
Shaff John D., r 9, dairy 16 cows, farmer 125.
Shaff Joseph, r 9, farmer 5.

STARKEY & WINTERS, Druggists, Owego. Close Prices to Dealers.

TOWN OF BERKSHIRE.

Shaff William H., r 11, farmer 100.
Shaw William F., r 5, farmer, son of William T.
SHAW WILLIAM T., r 5, breeder of short-horn cattle, dairy 30 cows, 20 head young stock and farmer 265.
Shepard C. Burton, r 28, farmer 50.
Shepard James, r 3, apiarist, breeder of horses and farmer 100.
Shepard John, r 29 1-2, farmer 140.
Sherman Edward A., (Ketchumville) r 33, farmer 105.
Sherman James W., (Wilson Creek) r 27, carpenter, dairy 10 cows, sugar orchard 200 trees and farmer 72.
SHERWOOD & HORTON, (H. G. S. & C. S. H. of English Center, Pa.) manuf. of wagon hubs, opp. Depot.
SIMMONDS ALPHEUS, r 3, dairy 12 cows, farmer 135.
Simmonds Charilla, r 3, wife of Alpheus, farm 55.
Simmonds George A., r 3, farmer.
SIMMONS SYLVESTER, (Jenksville) r 41, farmer.
SIMMONS WILLIAM E., (Jenksville) r 41, dairy 12 cows, breeder of horses and farmer 133.
Skellinger Daniel J., (Speedsville, Tomp. Co.) r 3 cor. 18, cooper.
SMITH ARTHUR E., r 4, sugar orchard 200 trees, farmer 93.
Smith Edwin, farmer 50, h Elm.
Smith Emory J., stone and plaster mason, h Railroad.
Smith George M., r 3, threshing and farmer 100.
Smith Ira J., r 3, tanner.
Smith John, engineer hub factory, bds. Elm.
Smith Mary J., r 4, widow Ezekiel D., resident.
Snedaker George, r 38, tool-maker.
Snedaker John, r 38, manuf. of tanners' beam knives, mill-stone picks and edge tools, also farmer 19.
Snedaker William V., r 38, laborer.
Sparrow Frank, emp. hub factory, h Glen.
Spencer Charles D., r 11 1-2, farmer 105.
Stanton Elisha W., (Speedsville, Tomp. Co.) r 18, tin pedlar.
Stephens Andrew, r 13, farmer 30.
Summerville Grant, r 6, night watch, tannery.
Sykes George D., r 39, teacher and farmer.
Sykes Horatio W., r 39, dairy 10 cows, sugar orchard 100 trees, farmer 114.
Taylor John H., farmer, leases J. W. Leonard.
Thompson Charles, r 28, laborer.
Thompson Samuel, farm in Richford 80, h Depot.
Thorn Charles F., (Wilson Creek) r 35, farmer.
Thorn Susan M., (Wilson Creek) r 35, widow Henry M., farm 63.
Thuillard Hyppolite, r 21, dairy 11 cows, farmer 110.
Torrey Betsey B., resident, h Main.
Torrey Charles S., r 40, farmer.
Torrey John, r 40, dairy 10 cows, farmer 117.
Torrey Lewis S., r 41, farmer, leases of Lyman Baker, of Candor, 143.
Towslee Delos, r 38, farmer, leases of R. Brown 13.
Turner Luther M., (Wilson Creek) r 29, road commissioner, farmer 50.
Turner William J., r 38, laborer.
Tyler Sherman B., r 14, laborer.
WALDO ELIJAH B., (Williams & Waldo) station and express agent, also dealer in butter, eggs and poultry, h Williams.

Waldo Hannah B., widow Dr. Joseph T., resident, h Main.
Waldo Juliette, widow Dwight, h Elm.
WALDO ROBERT EMMET, r 36, dairy 12 cows, farmer 106.
Walker Erastus T., r 3, farmer 68.
Walter Joseph S., r 27 cor. 11, physician and surgeon, and farmer 200.
Watkins John F., r 9, laborer.
Wauvle James A., r 9, farmer 72.
Wavle Peter, r 29½, wool grower 47 head, dairy 18 cows, and farmer with J. Shepard 30.
Whitaker Charles E., (Wilson Creek) r 34, dairy 7 cows, sugar orchard 400 trees, farmer 40; served in Co. F, 144th N. Y. Vols.
Whiting Caroline, (Speedsville, Tomp. Co.) r 18, widow Samuel, farm 80.
Whiting Frank S., (Speedsville, Tomp. Co.) r 18, blacksmith and farmer.
WILLIAMS & WALDO, (M. A. W., E. B. W. and A. B. W.) apiarists, and dealers in honey and bee-keepers' supplies.
Williams Eugene L., (Wilson Creek) r 27, farmer, leases of Lewis Williams 100.
Williams George, apiarist, prop. saw-mill, and farmer 190.
Williams Harvey J., r 9, farmer 50.
Williams Lewis, farmer 98, h Railroad.
WILLIAMS MORRIS A., (Williams & Waldo) dealer in potatoes, h Depot.
WINSHIP EDGAR., r 9, dairy 12 cows, farmer 100.
Winship William, r 9, farmer.
Wiswell Jerome B., (Ketchumville) r 31, farmer 60.
WITTER F. A. & CO., (Fred W. Witter) dealers in hardware, cutlery and household furniture, agricultural implements, also horse blankets, whips, shingles, etc., Main, h do.
WITTER FRANK A., (F. A. W. & Co.) h Main.
WITTER FRED W., (F. A. W. & Co.) h Main.
Wooster Asher B., r 6, stationary engineer.
Wright William F., r 8, sawyer, and farmer 94.
VanDyke Egbert, blacksmith and mechanic.
VAN GORDER CHARLES B., engineer in hub factory.
VAN GORDER GEORGE, r 38, farmer.
VanNorman Don R., bridge carpenter, h Elm.
VanNorman Fred, brakeman, h Elm.
VanSusan Clause, r 13, farmer 54.
VanSusan Diedrick, r 8, laborer.
VanSusten Diedrick, r 6, laborer.
Young Edward W., carpenter, h Main.
Young David H., (Jenksville) r 44 cor. 43, farmer.
Youngs Morris, r 29, farmer 25.
Youngs Orson R., r 27, laborer.
YOUNGS PETER, r 29, farrier, dairy 6 cows, farmer 82.

CANDOR.

(For explanations, etc., see page 3, part second.)

(Postoffice address is Candor, unless otherwise designated in parenthesis.)

Abbey William, r 112, carpenter.
Adams Gaylord W., resident, bds. Spencer.
Adkin Arcelius, r 111, laborer.
Ahart George, emp. Woolen Mills, h Preston.
Ahlers Dederick G., cooper, h Gould.
Aignor William, farmer, h Kinney.
Allen Ben, farmer, h Kinney.
Allen Ben, Jr., laborer, h Main.
Allen Frank, (West Candor) r 109, farmer 54.
Allen Frank, laborer, h off Kinney.
Allen Frank G., r 57, farmer 130.
Allen Hiram, r 57, resident.
ALLEN HOUSE, Iddo Vergason, proprietor, Main.
Allen Increase, lumberman, h Kinney.
Allen James M., r 29, carpenter and farmer 32.
Allen John J., r 99, farmer 16.
Allen Judson K., farmer 100, h Owego.
Allen Matthew K., farmer 50, h Owego.
Allen William D., r 29, carpenter and farmer 10.
ANDERSON EDWIN S., (Owego) r 126, farmer 151.
Anderson Ezra L., r 46, farmer.
Anderson George M., (Owego) r 123, farmer.
Anderson Joel, (Owego) r 123, apiarist and farmer 111.
Anderson Leroy, r 46, farmer 75.
Anderson Myron, (Catatonk) r 116, farmer 100.
ANDERSON PHILANDER, (Owego) r 123, farmer 250.
Anderson Stephen, (Catatonk) r 116, farmer 139.
Anderson Sylvenus, (Owego) r 131, farmer 75.
Anderson Truman, (Catatonk) r 115, farmer 100.
Anderson Willis, (Owego) r 124, farmer 85, and leases of Philander Anderson, 200.
Andrews Charles H., (Owego) r 117, leases of D. W. Andrews, 100.
Andrews Dana H., (Owego) r 123, farmer 25, and leases of Philetus Andrews, 212.
Andrews David W., (Owego) r 118, farmer 200.
Andrews Elmer E., (Owego) r 118, school teacher and farmer.
Andrews Frank, (Flemingville) farmer with Charles Crane, leases of John M. Grimes, 120.
ANDREWS LEVI, (Owego) r 131, farmer 175.
Andrews Thomas, (Owego) r 131, farmer 103.
Andrews William H., general merchant, Front, h do.
Andrews William R., clerk, bds. Front.
Armitage Ann E., widow Alfred, h Owego.

STARKEY & WINTERS, Wholesale and Retail Druggists, Owego.

Armitage Claude, clerk, h Owego.
ASHLAND HOUSE, Frank J. Norton, prop., Main.
Ayers Willis, (Willseyville) r 30, carpenter.
BACON GEORGE G., r 65. music teacher, agent for mnsical instruments fruit grower, and manuf. vinegar.
Bacon Harvey, r 116 cor. 99, farmer 10.
Bacon John G., r 65, farmer 100.
Bailey Charity M., widow William, resident, bds. Main.
Baird James L., (Speedsville, Tomp. Co.) r 18, farmer 100.
Bakeman Isaac, r 54, farmer 15.
Baker Aaron, (Caroline Center, Tomp. Co.) r 12, with William L., lumberman and farmer 180.
Baker Jesse, r 71, farmer 30.
Baker Lyman, (Caroline Center, Tomp. Co.) r 12, farmer in Berkshire 145.
Baker William L., (Caroline Center, Tomp. Co.) r 12, with Aaron Baker lumberman and farmer 180.
Bangs Charles E., r 90, teacher, and farmer 4.
Bangs William L., r 90, farmer 100.
Banks Alanson, (Willseyville) r 31, farmer 90.
Banks Nathan J., (Willseyville) r 31, farmer.
BARAGER CHARLES F., senator 26th district, prop. Candor Woolen Mills, also lumber business in Chenango Co., h Main.
Barber Hiram, r 139, cooper.
Barber John J., (Willseyville) r 1, leases of John Foote 37.
Barber Washington, r 57, laborer.
Barden Robert S., r 24, carpenter, and farmer 97.
Barden William, (Strait's Corners) r 112, farmer, leases of B. Coursen 108.
Barker George, r 63, laborer.
Barnes Charles W., farmer with his father James D.
Barnes Hugh S., (Catatonk) r 130, farmer 95.
Barnes James D., lumberman, and farmer 100.
Barnes Thomas, (Catatonk) r 130, farmer 70.
Barnes William, r 104, farmer 100.
Barrett Elliott, (West Newark) r 49, farmer 250.
Barrett Justus, (Weltonville) r 82, farmer, leases of Theodore Cortright, of Owego, 40.
Barrett Sidney A., (Strait's Corners) r 139, farmer 35.
BARRETT VAN NESS, (Jenksville) r 50, farmer 225.
BARROTT AMMIEL W., (Weltonville) r 120, dealer in live stock and farm produce, breeder of Hambletonian and Messenger horses, farmer 120, and leases of Abel Galpin 60.
BARROTT SAMUEL R., (Weltonville) r 82, prop. of saw and grist-mill, and dealer in lumber, lath, meal and feed, farmer 500, also lumber yard, and two tenements at Athens, Pa.
Barrott Simeon W., (Weltonville) r 84, farmer 190.
BARROTT VAN NESS W., (Weltonville) r 84, carpenter, and farmer, leases of Simeon W. Barrott 75.
Barto William, (Weltonville) r 83, sawyer, and farmer 50.
Bateman Joseph, (Weltonville) r 120, laborer.
Bates James D., r 99, farmer 94.
Baylor Charles F., blacksmith, Main, h Bank.
Baylor Daniel H., blacksmith, h Kinney.

STARKEY & WINTERS, promptly fill Mail and Telephone Orders.

TOWN OF CANDOR.

Beadle Jared J., farmer.
Beebe Abram, prop. Candor grist-mill, Main, h do.
Beebe Clark, emp. Candor grist-mill, h Ithaca.
Beeley John, (Strait's Corners) r 136, farmer, leases of J. Dougherty 52.
Beers George H., (Catatonk) r 129, farmer 52.
Belden James P., r 38, farmer 220.
Benedict Archibald W., (Willseyville) r 30, farmer.
Benton James F., (Speedville, Tomp. Co.) r 13, farmer 55.
Best David, (Catatonk) r 115, farmer 186.
Best George, (Strait's Corners) r 142, farmer 100.
Best John J., (Catatonk) r 115, farmer 22.
Best Richard, r 112, laborer.
Bishop Charles E., (Jenksville) r 49, farmer, leases of I. W. Gay, of Berkshire 90.
Bishop James, fire and life insurance, Main, h do.
Blewer Fred A., (Weltonville) r 120, farmer 50.
Blewer Levi, (Weltonville) r 84, laborer.
Blewer M. Lamont, (Weltonville) r 85, farmer 45.
Blinn Burdette, (Wilseyville) r 20, laborer.
Blinn Charles, r 56, section hand.
Blinn Eli R., (Jenksville) r 24, farmer 85.
Blinn Elmer, r 44, farmer.
Blinn Lewis, r 44, farmer 94.
Blinn Samuel E., farmer 122.
Blinn Sherman P., r 29 farmer 100.
Blinn Thomas P., r 29, farmer 60.
Blodgett Charles O., (Weltonville) r 84, farmer, leases of S. R. Barrott 230.
Blow Minard, (Weltonville) r 85, farmer, leases of Jasper Galpin, 50.
Bogardus George M., (Willseyville) r 30, farmer.
Bogert Peter, farmer 84, h Owego.
Boget William, (Strait's Corners) r 137, farmer 112.
Bolton Clarence S., blacksmith and horseshoer, Main, h do.
Bolton Lewis, emp. L. A. Hart, h Main.
Booth & Williams, (E. A. B. & E. S. W.) general merchants, Front.
Booth Brothers, (J. F. & T. S.) r 56, manufs. and dealers in lumber, and farmers 300.
Booth Catharine, r 37, widow of Abel H., farmer with George D., 218.
Booth Dennis, r 37, retired farmer.
Booth Edwin A., (Booth & Williams) also prest. First Nat. Bank, h Main.
BOOTH FREEMAN, r 37, farmer 206.
Booth George D., r 37, farmer with Catharine 218.
BOOTH HORACE F., fire insurance, prest. board of Education, and prop. Candor Iron Works, Main, h do.
Booth Jesse F., (Booth Bros.) r 56.
Booth Mary, widow Horace, h Main.
Booth Orange, r 37 cor. 57, lumberman, and farmer 250.
Booth Theron S., (Booth Bros.) r 56.
Booth Wakefield, r 37, resident.
Borthwick Alexander, (Jenksville) r 50, farmer, leases of Isaac D. Van Scoy 128.
Bortle Lawrence R., r 45, laborer.
Boyd Andrew, r 69, farmer 30.
Boyd Benjamin, r 69, farmer 30.
Braman Jesse H., stone mason, h Bank.
Braman Norton M., farmer, works for Mrs. Terwilligar 200, h Owego.

Briggs Mary L., resident, bds. Foundry.
Brink Homer A., (Weltonville) r 85, farmer 81.
Brink James S., r 70, thresher, and farmer 40.
Brink Joseph, r 54, farmer 25.
Brink Laverne, emp. W. J. Milks, bds. Spencer.
Brink Marland, (Weltonville) r 84, farmer.
Brink Philemon, (Weltonville) r 81, farmer, leases of W. B. Thomas 40.
Brink Stephen I., off r 116, laborer.
Brooks George T., contractor and builder, h Owego.
Brown Frank J., (Willseyville) r 30, farmer, leases of Wakeman Smith 215.
BROWN FRANK W., (West Candor) r 61, station and Natl. express agt., and telegraph operator.
Brown Sarah J., widow Jeremiah F., dressmaker.
Brundage Lydia, widow Emmet, h Main.
Burch L. H. Rev. rector St. Mark's Church, h Main.
Burchard Dana D., (Owego) r 131, farmer 52.
Burchard Elias, (Flemingville) r 122, farmer.
Burchard Franklin, (Flemingville) r 122, farmer.
Burchard Jason, (Flemingville) r 122, farmer.
Burchard Nelson, (Owego) r 122, farmer 100.
Burleigh Alfred, r 56, laborer.
Burleigh Eben, r 39, carpenter.
Burleigh Hezekiah, r 39, farmer 44.
Burleigh Millard F., r 39, farmer 50.
Burrows James, foreman woolen mills, h Church.
Burt George, (Catatonk) r 133, farmer 138.
Burt Lincoln C., (Catatonk) r 133, farmer with George.
Bush Abram R., (Willseyville) r 30, dealer in groceries.
Bush Elizabeth B., widow Isaac L., resident, h Owego.
Butler Orrin, (Strait's Corners) r 108, farmer 100.
Candor Humboldt Tannery, (E. S. Estey & Sons, props.) Front.
CANDOR IRON WORKS, (H. F. Booth, prop.) Foundry.
CANDOR WOOLEN MILLS, (Charles F. Barager, prop.) manuf. horse blankets, Main.
Caple Adam, r 104, teacher of vocal music, farmer 172.
Capel Edward, (Owego) off r 131, laborer.
Capel George, (Owego) r 117, laborer.
Capel John, (Owego) off r 131, farmer 50.
Caple Elgin P., r 104, farmer.
Caple Philip, (Catatonk) r 129, farmer 52.
Caple Philip J., (Catatonk) r 129, farmer 50.
Card George, (Strait's Corners) r 136, farmer.
Card Timothy, r 104, laborer.
Carl Peter, carpenter, h Owego.
Carlan William, (Catatonk) r 114, farmer 100.
Carlin James, emp. Frank L. Heath, bds. Main.
Carpenter Eliza A., r 63, widow Norman L., farm 150.
Carpenter Harry L., (Weltonville) r 84, house painting and graining.
Carpenter Orby V., blacksmith, machinist, etc., R. R. ave., h do.
CARPENTER WILLIAM L., blacksmith, machinist and wagon maker, R. R. ave., h do.
Carroll Thomas, r 95, farmer, works for Eliza Carroll 57.
Cass Frank, (Strait's Corners) r 108, farmer 48, and with William 152.

TOWN OF CANDOR.

Cass Samuel, (Strait's Corners) r 108, farmer 107.
Cass William, (Strait's Corners) r 108, farmer 75, and with Frank Cass 152.
Casterline Romeo W., (Strait's Corners) r 138, general blacksmithing.
Chandler William, (Catatonk) r 127, farmer 46.
Chapman Amos C., farmer, h Owego.
Chapman Foster, (Catatonk) laborer.
Chapman George, emp. woolen mill, bds. Mountain ave.
Chapman John D., farm laborer, h Mountain ave.
Chapman Milford, emp. woolen mill, h Railroad.
Chidester Chauncey W., (Weltonville) r 120, physician and surgeon.
CHIDSEY GEORGE C., liveryman, h Main.
CHIDSEY JOHN R., postmaster, also dealer in hardware, stoves and peddlers' supplies, Front, h do.
Chidsey Leonard, butcher, h Owego.
Clark Alexander H., (Catatonk) r 114, farmer 126.
Clark Herbert, r 54, farmer 10.
Clarke Leroy, r 44, farmer, works for Hiram J. Clark 180.
Cleveland Charles r 29, laborer.
Cleveland George M., (Willseyville) r 1, millwright and farmer 7.
Cleveland Joseph. r 5, laborer.
Coggin Loama I., r 139, farmer, works for Mrs. L. T. Coggin 10.
Cogswell Mary J., widow Joel, resident, h Owego.
Cole Jennie Mrs., resident, h Academy.
Cole William J., retired, h Main.
Compton Amos, (Catatonk) r 127, laborer.
COMSTOCK WILLIAM I., (Jenksville) r 20, farmer 175.
Coney Stephen, (West Candor) r 107, farmer 10.
Conklin Catherine B., widow Ephraim, resident, h Church.
Conklin Christopher, farmer, h Church.
Conklin Levi, (Speedsville, Tomp. Co.) r 21, farmer 120.
Conklin Norman, farmer, h Church.
CONNELL THOMAS J., clerk Allen House, bds. do.
Conrad George, r 7, farmer 41.
Cook Ezra S., (Weltonville) r 82, laborer.
Cook John W., (Strait's Corners) r 142, farmer 70.
Cook Joseph, r 93, laborer.
Coon Alonzo H., (Strait's Corners) r 143, threshing and farmer with William I. 112.
Coon William I., (Strait's Corners) r 143, threshing and farmer with Alonzo H. 112.
Cooper & Thornton, (West Candor) (J. H. C. & C. H. T.) r 62, cider-mill and threshing machine.
Cooper Caroline J., widow Arnold N., resident, h Kinney.
Cooper Fred B., (Strait's Corners) r 128, general store.
COOPER JOHN H., (West Candor) r 62, market gardening, 5 1-2 acres.
Cornick William, r 136, laborer.
Cornish Albert A., r 95, boot and shoemaker, farmer 27.
Cortright Amos J., (Weltonville) r 120, farmer 70.
Cortright Charles H., (Weltonville) r 86, farmer 80.
Cortright Collins, (Weltonville) r 84, farmer 75.
Cortright Franklin, (Weltonville) r 84, stone mason, farmer 65.
Cortright George, (Weltonville) r 85, farmer 100.
Cortright James, r 40, resident.

TOWN OF CANDOR. 59

Cortright James, (Weltonville) r 84, retired.
Cortright James F., (Weltonville) r 120, retired farmer.
CORTRIGHT JOSEPH J., (Weltonville) r 86, carpenter and joiner, farmer 40.
Cortright Marion A., (Weltonville) r 84, laborer.
Cortright Samuel, (Weltonville) r 120, retired farmer 30.
Cortright William C., (Weltonville) r 85, farmer 40.
Coursen Bartley, (Strait's Corners) r 139, farmer 350.
Coursen John M., (Strait's Corners) r 139, farmer 72.
Coursen Thomas H., r 95, farmer 30.
Courtright Henry A., (West Newark) r 82, dealer in agricultural implements, and farmer 100.
COWLES JAMES C., r 91, building moving, mason and farmer 65.
Cowles J. Harvey, r 116, farmer 54.
Crance DeWitt C., resident, h Railroad.
Crance Mary, widow Abram, resident, h Railroad.
Crane Charles, (Flemingville) r 122, shoemaker.
Cranmer I. J., resident, h Pond.
Crine Llewellyn, r 12, student.
Crine Perkins S., r 12, farmer.
Crine Stephen D., r 12, dairy farmer 260.
Cronk Byron E. Rev., (Bapt.) commissioner of highways; also, contractor and builder.
Cronk William D., r 90, manufacturer of birch and sarsaparilla beer, and agt. for the Grand Union Tea Co.
Crum Lafayette, (West Candor) r 108, farmer 240.
Crum McDonough, farmer, h Spencer.
Cummings William W., r 58, farmer, leases of J. Tompkins, of Spencer, 200, and of Ezra Bostwick, of Cortland, 96.
Curtis Fred, farmer.
Curtis William, r 5, wagonmaker.
Custard Anson, (Weltonville) r 84, farmer 71.
Cutchee Ambrose, (Catatonk) r 133, tanner.
Daggett William, (Jenksville) r 51, farmer, leases of Elizabeth Fuller. 73.
Dames Joseph O., retired, h Preston.
Darmody Thomas, laborer, h Railroad ave.
Davis Frank, fireman.
Dean Josie, r 57, station and express agt.
Decker Oliver H. P., resident, bds. Owego.
Decker Samuel, r 98, teaming and farmer 90.
Decker William, r 119, laborer.
DeGraw John, tin and hardware, Main, h Ann cor. McCarty.
DENNIS ALFRED, r 53, farmer 264.
Dennis Fred M., r 53, laborer.
Dennis Lorena Mrs., resident, h Owego.
Dennis Marvin, r 54, farmer with Wesley 167.
Dennis Wesley, r 54, teacher and farmer with Marvin 167.
Dewey Daniel, (Strait's Corners) r 142, laborer.
Dewey Frank E., r 111, farmer 92.
Deyo Jacob, (Weltonville) r 86, farmer 67.
Dixon Henry S., silversmith, h Church.
DIXON JOHN C., physician and surgeon, Main, h do.
Dohs George, (Catatonk) r 133, night watchman in tannery.

Dohs Jacob, (Catatonk) r 133, farmer 12½.
Doty Delos A., r 28, farmer, leases of James Doty 78.
Doty Edward J., clerk, h Thompson.
Doty George L., farmer 25.
Doty James, r 26, farmer 275.
Doty John J., r 73, farmer, leases of Samuel Decker 90.
Doty John Mrs., resident, h Kinney.
Doughty Andrew J., (Speedsville, Tomp. Co.) r 19, farmer 11.
Doughty Epenetus, (Speedsville, Tomp. Co.) r 19, farmer 140 and in Caroline 110.
Douglass George, (Strait's Corners) r 139, farmer 132.
Douglass John, farmer, 148, h Owego.
Douglass Otis A., (Strait's Corners) r 139, farmer.
Douglass William, (Strait's Corners) r 141, farmer 105.
Downing Jay S., r 87, fruit grower and farmer 39.
Downing Kay M., r 70, farmer.
Downing Lincoln L., r 70, farmer.
DOWNING STOUGHTON S., r 70, fruit grower, and farmer 120.
Draper Cynthia P., (Catatonk) r 133, widow Ira, resident.
DRAPER MENZ V., (Catatonk) r 130, blacksmith, and farmer 70.
Drew George, (Catatonk) r 114, laborer.
Duel Smith, r 36, farmer 50.
Duff Alexander B., (Strait's Corners) r 139, farmer 94.
DU MOND DAVID, cider-mill, and grain thresher, Ashland, h Main.
Dykeman Orrin, r 57, refused to give information.
Dykeman Solonas, r 56, farmer 45.
Dykeman William H., farm laborer, h Owego.
Eastham Nathan, (Strait's Corners) r 142, lumberman, and farmer 231.
Eastham Thomas, (Strait's Corners) r 142, lumberman, and farmer.
Eastman Amos, (Willseyville) r 2, farmer 75, and works for his wife Rachael 150.
Eastman John N., (Willseyville) r 1, farmer 85, and leases of Barlow Sanford 130.
Eastman Morgan, (Willseyville) r 1, farmer.
Easton Zenas R., r 98, watchman, h and lot.
Eccleston David, painter, h R. R. ave.
EDMUNDS CALEB W., r 98, sawyer, and farmer 15.
Edwards Caroline Mrs., laundress, h Owego.
Eichenburgh George, r 56, sawyer.
Eiklor George I., r 8, carpenter and builder, blacksmithing, farmer 50.
Ellison John T., r 28, farmer, leases of Joel Starkweather 84.
Ellsworth Ervin A., salesman, h Owego.
Ellsworth Frederick, r 28, farmer 50.
Elmendorf Clarence, carpenter, bds. Main.
ELMENDORF CYRENUS, contractor and builder, h Main.
Elmendorf George E., (Strait's Corners) r 141, farmer 112, and leases of Abram White 70.
Elmendorf Jonathan, (Strait's Corners) r 141, resident.
Embody Jacob, wagon-maker, Spencer, h do.
Embody Jacob C., cartman, h Gould.
Emerson Charity, (Strait's Corners) r 128, widow James, carpet-weaving.
Emerson Chester, (Strait's Corners) r 137, farmer 56.
Emerson Frederick A., (Strait's Corners) r 137, farmer 50.
Emery Sarah, (Strait's Corners) r 109, widow Isaac, farm 75.

TOWN OF CANDOR.

Ervay Charles, (Willseyville) r 3, farmer, leases of Ira Hoose.
Evans Richard, (Strait's Corners) r 143, farmer 50.
Evans Stephen C., salesman, h Main.
Farley Daniel, (Speedsville, Tomp. Co.) r 13, farmer 83.
Farley Eli J., (Speedsville, Tomp. Co.) r 14, carpenter, and farmer 9.
Farley Ellyn, (Speedsville, Tomp. Co.) r 13, farmer 20.
Farley Martin, (Speedsville, Tomp. Co.) r 13, farmer 30.
Faurot Mary Mrs., emp. blanket factory, h Owego.
Fellows James, (Strait's Corners) r 143, farmer 82.
Ferris Elihu, r 35, farmer 60.
Ferris George, (West Candor) r 107, farmer 30.
Ferris James, (West Candor) r 107, farmer.
Ferris Oliver, (West Candor) r 107, farmer 40.
Ferris Richard R., r 35, farmer 61.
Ferris Sarah, (West Candor) r 107, widow Stephen, farm 25.
Ferris Theron W., r 35, farmer 50.
FESSENDEN DAVID S., (William L. & Son) cabinet-maker.
FESSENDEN WILLIAM L., (W. L. & Son) pastor Wesleyan Methodist church, Candor, and South Beecher hill and Spaulding hill.
FESSENDEN W. L. & SON, (William L. & David S.) manufs. and dealers in furniture, undertaking goods, etc., Owego, h do.
Fiebig Charles F., carriage painter, Main, h Owego.
Fiebig Frances Mrs., resident, bds. Owego.
Fiebig John P., traveling salesman, bds. Main.
FIELD RICHARD, mason, h Mountain ave.
Filcinger Gabriel, (Willseyville) r 1, resident.
FIRST NATIONAL BANK OF CANDOR, (E. A. Booth, prest., J. W. McCarty, vice-prest., J. Thompson, cash.) Main.
Fisher John W., groceries and provisions, Main, h do.
Fitch Chancy S., r 46, farmer 114.
Fitch Frank E., r 46, farmer.
Flack Thomas W., (Catatonk) r 133, carpenter.
Fogarty John J., r 41, laborer.
Foot Sheldon W., r 103, resident.
Foot William, r 103, farmer 50.
Ford Nelson, laborer, h Owego.
Forsyth George, retired, h Humeston.
Foster Charles, (Jenksville) r 20, farmer 128.
Foster Charles H., laborer.
Foster Cyrus A., cooper, h Main.
FOSTER JONAS S., (Jenksville) r 20, farmer 178.
Foster Richard, (Jenksville) r 20, farmer.
Fredenburg Henry, (Catatonk) r 115, farmer, leases of Frank Whitmarsh, of Owego, 30.
Fronk Fred, (Catatonk) r 134 cor. 115, carpenter and farmer 30.
Frost John O., furniture dealer and undertaker, Main, h do.
Fuller Alvah, teamster, h Main.
Fuller Elizabeth, (Jenksville) r 51, widow Robert, farm 73.
Fuller George B., resident, bds. Kinney.
Fuller Gritman E., (Weltonville) r 78, farmer.
Fuller Jacob C., r 29, farmer 112.
Fuller Marvin, laborer, h Kinney.
Fuller Radaker, r 52, lumberman and farmer 96.

FULLER SAMUEL G., r 52, teacher and farmer 27.
Fuller Willard, r 54, farmer 25.
Gaige Henry, r 116, farmer 20.
Gaige James E., (Owego) r 118, farmer 50.
Gaige Thomas, (Owego) r 132, farmer 90.
Galpin Abel F., (Weltonville) r 84, farmer 60.
Galpin Catharine W., (Weltonville) r 85, widow Samuel, resident.
Galpin Edward, (Weltonville) r 85, carpenter and farmer 87.
Galpin George F., (Weltonville) r 74, with W. A. Mead and S. F. Galpin, steam threshing, hay pressing and sawing.
Galpin James T., (Weltonville) r 85, farmer 80.
Galpin Jasper, (Weltonville) r 85, farmer 95.
GALPIN JERUSHA, (Weltonville) r 53, widow Elisha, farm 58.
Galpin Luzern, (Weltonville) r 85, farmer 60.
Galpin Mary J., (Weltonville) r 53, wife of Taylor L., farm 52.
Galpin Myron E., (Weltonville) r 53, farmer.
Galpin Nelson, (Weltonville) r 78, farmer 91.
Galpin Robert C., (Weltonville) r 84, farmer 76.
Galpin Sidney F., (Weltonville) r 73, with W. A. Mead and G. F. Galpin, steam threshing, and farmer, leases ot Jasper Galpin 51.
Galpin Taylor L., (Weltonville) r 53, farmer.
Galpin Wayland, (Weltonville) r 85, farmer 60.
Gardner Charles, r 99, farmer 146.
Gates Eugene O., farmer, Owego.
Gay Nathaniel, (Jenksville) r 24, laborer.
German Cyrus B., contractor and builder, h Young.
German Edward C., telegraph operator, bds. Young.
German Frederick E., carpenter, bds. Young.
Gibbons Frank, mason, h Bank.
GILLMAN ROBERT C., r 30, farmer, leases of T. VanVleet 170.
Gould Franklin, (Catatonk) r 131, resident.
Graham Andrew J., (Weltonville) shoemaker.
Gransbury Edward, r 102, carpenter.
Grant James M., r 46, canvasser and farmer 58.
GRIDLEY CHARLES F., (West Candor) r 62, postmaster and farmer 250.
Gridley Charles L., (West Candor) r 60, farmer.
Gridley Charles N., r 36, farmer, leases of Newton S. Gridley 120.
Gridley Demorn, r 63, carpenter.
Gridley Newton S., r 36, farmer 120.
GRIDLEY S. EGBERT, prop. planing mill, and farmer 250, h Owego.
Gridley William C., (West Candor) r 60, lime and plaster, and farmer 115.
GRIFFIN FRED G., (N. W. Griffin & Son) bds. Main.
Griffin Lewis, r 56, farmer 295.
GRIFFIN NEHEMIAH W., (N. W. Griffin & Son) h Main.
GRIFFIN N. W. & SON., (Fred G.) livery, draymen and express, Main.
Griffin Walter, laborer.
GRIMES JOHN M., (Flemingsville) r 121, retired M. E. clergyman and farmer 152.
Guiles Andrew, (Strait's Corners) r 142, laborer.
Hadden Stephen, r 139, farmer.
Haddock Eugene B., (Speedsville, Tomp. Co.) r 18, farmer, leases of S. Blackman 100.
Haddock John V., (Speedsville, Tomp. Co.) r 18, farmer.

TOWN OF CANDOR. 63

Hale Dorcas, widow John, h Kinney.
Hale Lester B., r 103, farmer 100.
Hale Samuel, r 103, farmer.
Hall Edward R., principal Candor Academy, bds. Allen House.
Hall Emeline, r 58, widow Lewis, resident.
Hall LaFayette, (Willseyville) r 1, farmer 2.
Hallett Charles, (Willseyville) r 1, farmer 25.
Hammond Burt, (Weltonville) r 120, farmer 58.
Hammond Seth, (Strait's Corners) r 139, farmer 91.
Hand Harold N., r 64, laborer.
Handy Fernando D., weaver, h Foundry.
Handy Hannah C., widow James, h Foundry.
Hanes Erastus, r 63, well drilling.
Harding Charles O., painter, h Kinney.
Harding Odell, painter, bds. Kinney.
Harding Sherman, carpenter, h Bank.
HARRIS ALGERNON J., physician and surgeon, Main, h do.
HARRIS CYNTHIA E., widow Dr. John J.; resident, Main.
Hart Edward D, r 29, farmer 25.
Hart George H., farmer 120, h Main.
Hart Janette, off r 36, widow William, farm 75.
Hart John N., r 88, farmer, leases of Charles Mead 76.
Hart Jonathan B., r 63 cor. 64, retired cabinet maker, and farmer 33.
HART LEWIS A., dealer in produce, agricultural implements and phosphates; also, farmer 370, Main, h do.
Hart Louisa, widow Abel, resident, h Owego.
Hart Norman, apiarist, and farmer 140, and leases of his brother Horace 50.
Hart Reuben, r 88, farmer with John N.
Hart Selah, retired farmer, h Main.
Hartwell Warren T., jeweler, Main, h do.
Hasbrouck Josephus, (Willseyville) (Hoose & Hasbrouck) r 30, farmer 200.
Haskell Theodore A., (Jenksville) r 49, farmer 50.
Haskins George, r 69, laborer.
Haskins James, laborer, h Mountain ave.
Hatch Malinda, widow Russell, resident, h Railroad.
Hatch Parker, (Weltonville) r 85, carpenter, and farmer 50.
Haynard Frink, r 97, farmer.
Hazen Daniel, (Strait's Corners) r 140, farmer 84.
Hazen Orlando L., (Strait's Corners) r 140, farmer 39, and works for Daniel Hazen 84.
Hazen William, laborer, h Pond.
Head Emmet, (Willseyville) r 32, farmer 100.
Head Isaac, (Willseyville) r 4. farmer 76.
Head Lewis, (Willseyville) r 1, laborer.
Head Thomas, r 29, laborer.
HEATH FRANK L., coal dealer, and station and express agent, h Main.
HEATH HENRY D., tin and hardware, stoves and agricultural implements, Main, h do.
Heath James H., (Willseyville) r 30, veterinary surgeon, and notary public, and farmer 6.
Hedges Daniel A., r 29, farmer 102.
Hedges Frank M., r 29, farmer.
Henderson Hiram, r 54, farmer 52.

TOWN OF CANDOR.

HENDERSON JESSE W., foreman Hulmboldt tannery.
Henderson Theodore, (Johnson & Henderson) r 78, farmer 65.
Hendrickson Burton, r 99, farmer 18.
Herdic Peter, (Strait's Corners) r 139, carpenter, and farmer 47.
Herrick Alfred W., (Catatonk) r 116, refused to give information.
Herrick Burt., (Weltonville) r 120, farmer.
Herrick Stephen H., off r 116, farmer 100.
Herrick Walter, (Weltonville) r 120, farmer 116.
Hevland James, molder, h Owego.
HEWITT JASPER W. REV., r 95, retired M. E. clergyman.
Hill Charles F., Jr., (Weltonville) r 86, laborer.
Hills Charles S., (Weltonville) r 77, farmer 150.
Hills H. George, (Weltonville) r 77, farmer.
Hines Eddie G., r 54, laborer.
Hines Jesse A., r 54, farmer 18.
Hoff Lewis R., grist and flouring-mill, Main, h Owego.
Holden Dallas, (Weltonville) r 120, wagon-maker and blacksmith, and farmer 30.
Hollenback Eugene B., farm laborer, h Academy.
Holenback David J., (Strait's Corners) r 136, farmer 147.
Holenback James, r 99, retired.
Holenback John J., (Strait's Corners) r 136, farmer, leases of D. J. H., 67.
Hollenback Michael D., r 119, laborer.
Holenback Willard D., (Strait's Corners) r 136, farmer, leases of D. J. H., 80.
Hollister Elsie, r 36, farm 18.
Hollister George H., (Willseyville) r 30, laborer.
Hollister Harvey A., r 36, farmer 73.
HOLLISTER WARREN L., livery, Main, h Railroad.
Holmes Frank, tinsmith, bds. Owego.
Holmes John, dealer in cattle and horses, and farmer 200, h Owego.
Holmes John, farmer for L. A. Hart, h Main.
Holmes Robert B., clerk, h Main.
Holmes Samuel, retired, h Bank.
Hoose & Hasbrouck, (Willseyville) (Ira & Josephus H.) proprietors steam saw-mill, and lumber dealers, opp. depot.
Hoose C. Frank, (Willseyville) r 3, farmer.
Hoose Charles W., (Willseyville) r 3, farmer 150, and in Caroline 60.
Hoose Ira, (Willseyville) (Hoose & Hasbrook) farmer 150.
Houck Israel, r 95, apiarist 50 colonies, market gardening, and farmer 29.
Houk George E , r 95, blacksmith and farmer 30.
House Willard E , D.D. S., dentist, Main, h do.
Hover Adelbert D., (Weltonville) r 77, farmer 41.
Hover Benjamin, (West Newark) r 49, farmer, 122.
Hover Charles F., (Weltonville) laborer.
Hover Court L., (Jenksville) r 52, farmer, leases of James Newman.
Hover George, r 73, farmer, leases of Henry Hover 30.
Hover George F., tanner, h Foundry.
Hover Henry, (Speedsville, Tomp. Co.) r 22, farmer 100.
Hover Henry, (Weltonville) r 84, resident, aged 96.
Hover Leander, r 88, blacksmith, and farmer, leases of Henry Hover 30.
Hover Lettie, widow Alonzo, resident, h Owego.
Hover L. Frederick, (Weltonville) r 77, laborer.
Hover Merritt L., (Weltonville) r 85, farmer, leases of Henry Hover, 2d, 55.

HOVER ROBERT E., farmer.
Hover Silas. (Weltonville) r 81, laborer.
Hover Solomon, farmer 160.
Hover William P., r 73, farmer 20.
Hover Wilman S., r 43, farmer.
Howard Alvah, (West Candor) r 106, farmer.
Howard Alvin, (West Candor) r 62, farmer.
Howard Edward L., (South Danby, Tomp. Co.) r 34, farmer 184.
Howard Darius P., r 118, farmer.
HOWARD HIRAM O., r 118, breeder of horses, and farmer 128, and leases of Loring P. Howard, of Spencer 115.
HOWARD HIRAM O., r 118, horse breeder, and farmer 128, and leases of L. P. Howard, of Spencer 115.
Howard Martha, widow Samuel, resident, h Railroad.
Howard Rhoda R., (Catatonk) off r 126, widow Charles C., farm 118.
Howard Truman F., r 38, farmer 65.
HOWE EPENETUS, farmer, h Main cor. Mill.
Howell William, (Willseyville) r 1, farmer 30.
Howes Oscar, carpenter, and farmer 30, h Owego.
Howland Dana, r 5, farmer, leases of C. R. Chidsey 40.
Howland Frederick, farmer 140, h Main.
Howland Wilber F., r 38, iron and brass moulder, and farmer 97.
Hoyt Adoniram, r 28, farmer 5.
Hoyt Cordelia, widow Emanuel, h Main.
Hoyt George T., r 88, farmer 50.
Hoyt S. Judson, r 28, farmer 88.
HUBBARD ALBERT C., farmer, h Owego.
Hubbard Frank E., salesman, bds. Owego.
Hubbard George N., r 116, dealer in hop-poles, farmer 10.
HUBBARD GEORGE W., r 98, clerk.
HUBBARD WILLIAM H., r 98, with John F., of Denver, Col., prop. saw and grist-mill, dealer in lumber, lath, and farmer 400.
Hubbard William J., (Willseyville) r 30, saloon.
HUFTALING JOHN, apiarist, and emp. Hulmboldt tannery, a member Co. C., 86th Regt, N. Y. Vols.
Hughes Frank, (West Candor) r 62, laborer.
Hull Daniel O., r 65, farmer, leases of N. T. Hull 95.
Hull Frederick E., farm laborer, bds. Owego.
Hull Justin, retired, h Owego.
Hull Lebbeus, r 63, resident.
HULL LEONARD, farmer, h Owego.
Hull Nathan T., r 65, farmer 95.
Hull Warren, r 63, laborer.
Hulslander Asa, (West Candor) r 105, farmer 90.
Hulslander Henry J., r 37, farmer 110.
Hulslander Sylvester, r 101, threshing machine and stump pulling, farmer 60.
Hulslander William S., r 102, threshing and farming.
Humiston John H., music teacher, bds. Main.
Humiston Morris, harness-maker, Railroad, h Main.
Humphrey James F., (Weltonville) r 85, farmer 30, and leases of C. L. Deyo 65.
Hunsinger John, (Strait's Corners) r 136, farmer 83.
Hunt Henry, (Strait's Corners) r 136, farmer 50.

5

TOWN OF CANDOR.

Hunt Willis S., r 94, farmer 45.
Hunt William W., retired physician, h Owego.
Hurd Edgar D., (Willseyville) r 1, farmer 35.
Hurd John, (Willseyville) r 1, farmer 75.
Hyatt Clark, (Catatonk) r 115, laborer.
Hyde Persis E., (Strait's Corners) r 109, wife of William B., farm 60.
Hyde Silas, (Strait's Corners) r 104, laborer.
Hyde William B., (Strait's Corners) r 109, farmer.
JACKSON DWIGHT P., baker, grocer and confectioner, Main, h do.
Jackson John E., emp. Dwight P. Jackson, bds. Main.
Jackson Laura, widow John, resident, h Main.
Jacobs Fred, r 28, farmer 12.
Jacobs Hiram C., (Weltonville) r 75, Baptist clergyman and farmer 50.
Jacobs James, r 25, farmer 140.
Jacobs John W., r 41, farmer 156.
Jennings Benjamin, (Willseyville) r 31, farmer 110.
Jennings Edwin, retired, h Owego.
Jennings James H., druggist, Front, h do.
Johnson Abram, (West Candor) r 62, laborer.
Johnson Albert L., printer, h Owego.
Johnson & Henderson, (Leonard A. J. & Theodore H.) manufs. whip, broom and pen-holders, clothes-dryers, ladies' novelty work-baskets and wire goods in general, Church.
Johnson Charles F., artist penman, h Church.
JOHNSON EUGENE, r 102, farmer.
Johnson George L., resident, bds. Church.
Johnson George W., r 102, carpenter and farmer, leases Daniel Johnson 200.
Johnson Harmon, (Strait's Corners) r 140, farmer 60.
Johnson Harrison T., r 119, farmer 37.
Johnson Irving L., r 101, farmer 36.
Johnson John, (Strait's Corners) r 140, farmer 60.
Johnson Leonard A., cabinet-maker, Church, h do.
Johnson Leroy N., r 102, pension agent and farmer.
JOHNSON MYRON M., clerk, h Bank.
Johnson Philo, emp. Hulmboldt tannery, h Bank.
Johnson Rhoda, widow Chester, farm 36.
JOHNSON SILAS W., r 88, dealer in fruit and berries of all kinds and farmer 62.
Johnson Ulysses S., medical student, bds. Owego.
Johnson Orange, r 45, farmer 44.
Jones Charles T., (Strait's Corners) r 137 cor. 134, farmer 130.
Jones Sidney W., (Strait's Corners) r 137 cor 134, farmer 25.
Jordan Elbert, laborer, h Railroad.
Jordan Milo, r 38, farmer, leases of James P. Belden 220.
Jordan Frank, r 5, farmer, leases of William Perry, of Spencer, 75.
Judd Philecta, widow William, farm 53.
Judd Henry A., resident, bds. Bank.
Kattell Harmon, r 90, farmer.
Kattell Marshall R., r 90, carpenter and farmer 150.
Keeler Ethelbert B., r 94, carpenter and mason.
Keeler Hiram, r 94, farmer 23.
KELSEY DORA G., r 95, farm with Laura A. and Sarah A. 160.

STARKEY & WINTERS, Wholesale and Retail Druggists, Owego.

TOWN OF CANDOR.

KELSEY LAURA A., r 95, farm with Dora G. and Sarah A. 160.
KELSEY SERAH A., r 95, farm with Laura A. and Dora G. 160.
Kelsey Woodbridge, r 95, farmer 112.
Kenyon John H., r 25, farmer 53 and leases of Spaulding Bros., of Cortland, 72, and of George Truman, of Owego, 60.
KETCHUM WILLIAM P., insurance, pension attorney and notary public, Kinney, h do.
Kies Chauncey, r 7, farmer 22½.
Kirk John, r 28, farmer 70.
Kirk Richard, r 63, blacksmith.
Knapp Burr D., (Weltonville) general merchant.
Knapp Ezekiel W., r 24, farmer 104.
Knapp Harmon, r 24, farmer.
Kortright Susan, widow Abram, h Main.
Krofft George W., r 98, laborer.
Krofft William, (Catatonk) laborer.
KROM ABRAM H., r 64, farmer 200.
Kyle Daniel Y., (Speedsville, Tomp. Co.) r 22, farmer 117 and at Willseyville 54.
Kyle Enos J., (Speedsville, Tomp. Co.) r 22, blacksmith and farmer.
Kyle Samuel F., (Catatonk) (S. F. Kyle & Co.) r 27, farmer 127 and leases of James A. Kyle, of Shenandoah, Iowa, 40.
Kyle S. F. & Co., (Catatonk) (Samuel F., K. and W. H. Bailey), r 127, baled hay, straw and potatoes.
Kyle Theron D., (Owego) r 117, fruit grower and farmer 92½, and leases of J. A. Kyle 92½.
Kyle Thomas, retired, h Church.
La Barre George, blacksmith, h Bank.
LaGrange Elijah, laborer, h Owego.
Lake Augustus, (Weltonville) r 85, retired.
Lake Ebin, r 53, resident.
Lake George H., (Weltonville) r 85, farmer 101.
Lamb John, (Catatonk) r 133, retired.
Lane Bert, r 28, farmer, leases of Howard Mead 196.
Lane George A., (Weltonville) r 74 cor. 70, farmer 50, and leases of Nancy Snow, of Caroline, 29.
Lane Ceorge W., (West Candor) farmer.
Lane Harmon S., (West Candor) r 63, laborer.
Lane James, r 58, laborer.
Lane James A., r 52, farmer 87, and leases of Julia Hull, of Brookton, 135.
Lane Lamont, (Flemingville) r 121, laborer.
Lane Levi, (Weltonville) r 74 cor 70, farmer.
Lane Stephen, (Strait's Corners) r 140, farmer 53.
Lane Walter, r 116, farmer 64.
Lanphier David H., r 37, lumberman and farmer 20.
Lanphier William H., (Weltonville) r 85, farmer 112.
LARCOM ADELBERT D., r 54, farmer 53.
Larcom Julian C., r 54, farmer.
Larkin Hugh, (Catatonk) off r 114, farmer 210.
Leach William S., (Weltonville) r 84, farmer 74.
Legg Bert E., (Jenksville), r 46, farmer 30.
Legg David J., (Jenksville), r 49, farmer 30.

STARKEY & WINTERS, promptly fill Mail and Telephone Orders.

TOWN OF CANDOR.

Legg George W., (Speedsville, Tomp. Co.) r 13 cor. 14, farmer 107.
Legg Leonard C., (Speedsville, Tomp. Co.) r 22, farmer 180.
Legg Otto L., (Speedsville, Tomp. Co.) r 13 cor. 14, farmer.
Legg Stillman J., shoemaker, Main, h Kinney.
Leet Julius C., (Speedsville, Tomp. Co.) r 22, carpenter.
Leet Samuel, (Speedsville, Tomp. Co.) carpenter and leader of Leets' orchestra, farmer 50.
Leonard Richard, (Slaterville, Tomp. Co.) r $5\frac{1}{2}$, farmer 50.
Lewis John A., r 95, sewing machine agt.
Lewis Theodore H., carpenter and farmer 56, h Owego.
Lewis Thomas N., r 63 cor. 64, farmer 88.
Lisk William P., laborer, h R. R. ave.
Little Charles E., r 116, farmer 82.
Little Mary E., dressmaker, h Preston.
Little Mattie, teacher, h Preston.
Little Nettie, teacher, h Preston.
Little Thomas B., r 116, farmer 70.
Little William L., lumber and bark, Main, h do.
Locey Charles E., music teacher, bds. Owego.
Locey Isaac B., retired merchanic, h Main.
Logan Thomas, r 102, engineer and farmer 70.
Loring Horace W., r 56, farmer 10.
LOUNSBURY DANIEL, r 111, farmer 193.
Lovejoy Aaron, farm laborer, h Owego.
Lovejoy George W., r 45, farmer 130.
Lovejoy Jerome, r $38\frac{1}{2}$, farmer 65.
Lovejoy Lucy A., widow Josiah, seamstress, h Foundry.
LOVEJOY LYMAN B., laborer, h Main.
LOVEJOY WILLARD A., tanner, h Royal.
Lyme Henry, r 58, farmer, leases of Mrs. N. Gridley 151.
Lynch Fred, farm laborer, bds. R. R. ave.
Lynch Ira, contractor and builder, h Royal.
Lynch Nathaniel, farmer, h Main.
Lynch Sylvester D., resident, h R. R. ave.
Manley Joseph N., (Strait's Corners) r 141, farmer, works for John Manley of Danby 100.
Manning Charles F., (South Danby, Tomp. Co.) r 31, farmer 50.
Manning Robert P., (South Danby, Tomp. Co.) r 31, carpenter, and farmer 72.
Markle David, r 91, brick and plaster mason, and farmer, works for Lucy Chidsey 22.
Markle Fred C., r 91, brick layer.
MASTEN GEORGE W., apiarist 80 colonies, and farmer 50.
Masten G. Wallace, farmer, leases of Simon Van Luven 116.
Masten J. Willis, r 119, farmer 50.
Mayo Charles H., (Willseyville) r 30, section hand.
Mayo Hanford, r 56, laborer.
Mayo Hiram, r 29, saw and shingle-mill, and farmer 50.
McCARTY & THOMPSON, (J. W. McC. & J. T.) general merchants, Main cor. Mill.
McCARTY JOHN W., (McCarty & Thompson) h Main.
McCoy Edwin, (Jenksville) r 49, dealer in live stock, and farmer 115.
McCully George, r 29, laborer.

TOWN OF CANDOR.   69

McIntire Charles F., (Catatonk) r 134, farmer, leases of S. Sacket of Towanda Pa., 36.
McIntyre Frank, r 91, well-boring, and farmer 50.
McIntyre John J., 116, farmer 30.
McIntyre William, (Catatonk) r 115, farmer 25.
McPhalan John, (Speedsville, Tomp. Co.) r 13, farmer 50.
Mead Alanson, (Weltonville) r 85, farmer 75.
Mead Amzi, (Weltonville) laborer.
MEAD ASA E., r 70, fruit grower, and farmer 100.
MEAD CHARLES, (Weltonville) r 75, dry goods, groceries, boots and shoes, tobacco, patent medicines, and farmer 80.
Mead David P., retired wagon-maker, h Spencer.
Mead Ebin H., (Jenksville) r 78, farmer 62.
Mead Edward, (Flemingville) r 119, farmer 100.
Mead Ezekiel, (Flemingville) r 119, farmer 160.
Mead Fayette, (Weltonville) r 76, farmer.
Mead John G., emp. W. J. Milks, h Bank.
Mead Josephus, farmer, h Owego.
Mead Joshua E., (Flemingville) r 119, retired.
Mead Mileden, (West Newark) r 81, farmer 113.
Mead Milton, (West Newark) r 81, laborer.
Mead Nathan, (Catatonk) off r 126, farmer, leases of Roba R. Howard 118.
Mead Newton T., (Weltonville) r 45, farmer 55.
Mead Russel B., (Jenksville) r 49, farmer.
Mead Russel J., (Weltonville) r 76, carpenter, and farmer 120.
MEAD WILLIS A., r 70, with Sidney and G. F. Galpin, steam threshing machine, hay pressing and sawing.
Meddaugh Preston, (Speedsville, Tomp. Co.) r 22, farmer, leases of L. C. Leonard 180.
Meier Frederick, r 42, farmer 45.
Merchant Gideon, r 37, sawyer, and overseer of George B. Pumpelly steam saw-mill.
Merchant Gideon, (Willseyville) r 32, carpenter.
Mericle Henry, farmer 91, h Main.
Merrick Abner, (Speedsville, Tomp. Co.) r 13, mason, and farmer 90.
Merrill Ann E., (Willseyville) widow M. Nelson, station and express agent.
Merrill Nellie, (Willseyville) telegraph operator.
Merritt Abram, r 69, farmer 23.
Middaugh Asa, (Strait's Corners) r 105, farmer 60.
Milks George, clerk Ashland House, bds. do.
MILKS WILLIAM J., veterinary surgeon, and meat market, Spencer, h do.
MILLER AUGUSTINE, (Weltonville) r 120, farmer 90.
Miller Fred, (Weltonville) r 120, dealer in live stock, and farmer.
Miller Daniel S., physician and surgeon, Main, h do.
Minor Christopher C., (Willseyville) r 30, general store.
Mix Emory C., (Willseyville) r 30, postmaster, and blacksmith.
Mix John C., (Willseyville) r 1, prop. threshing-machine, and farmer 74.
Mix Miles C., (Willseyville) r 30, blacksmith, and farmer 9.
Monell Samuel, (Willseyville) r 1, farmer 14.
Mooney Burt, tanner, h Church.
Mooney Esther, widow Thomas, h Church.
Moore Betsey D., widow John R., resident, h Church.
Moore Oscar, (Speedsville, Tomp. Co.) r 14, farmer 62.

MOREY ARCHIE E., 71, apiarist 90 colonies, and carpenter.
Morey Benjamin S., saloon and restaurant, and farmer 50, Main, h do.
MOREY EDWARD A., r 71, farmer 66.
Morrison James, r 88, farmer 32.
Morrison Wesley, r 116, farmer 25.
Munroe Henry, r 63, farmer 170.
Munroe James, r 63, farmer 140.
Munroe John H., (Willseyville) r 1, laborer.
Munroe Joshua, r 63, farmer.
Mustoe Martin, r 69, farmer 46.
Nelson Asa, (Catatonk) r 115, farmer 50.
Nelson Elmore, (West Candor) r 59, farmer.
Nelson Nathaniel, (Strait's Corners) off r 139, farmer.
Nelson Orville, r 24, farmer 120.
Newman Alonzo M., (Jenksville) r 78, farmer 130.
Newman James, (Jenksville) r 50, farmer 133.
Newman William T., (Flemingville) r 123, farmer in Owego 22.
Neuse James W., laborer, h Church.
Nickerson Lucy E., widow Amos, seamstress, h R. R. ave.
North James E., manuf. washing-machines and clothes wringers, h Main.
NORTON FRANK J., prop. Ashland House, Main.
O'Brien Thomas, (Willseyville) r 30, saloon and groceries.
O'Connell Daniel, (Catatonk) fireman for National Transit Co.
Oldfield Joel, r 102, farmer.
Oliver Allen D., r 40, fireman, and farmer 5.
Oltz Deborah, widow Henry, resident, h Pond.
Oltz Frances A., resident, bds. Pond.
Orcutt David, r 95, carpenter, and farmer 12.
Orcutt Elizabeth, (Catatonk) r 115, widow James E., farm 55.
Orcutt William C., gunsmith, clock and watch repairer and general jobbing, Owego, h do.
Ormsby Robert L., farm laborer, h Foundry.
Osborn Arthur, r 116, physician, M. E. clergyman and farmer 50.
Osburn William V., (Speedsville, Tomp. Co.) r 18, apiarist 100 colonies, carpenter, wagon repairing and farmer 25.
Ott George, (Catatonk) r 135, farmer 100.
OWEN ABEL C., (Strait's Corners) r 109, carpenter and farmer 95.
Owen Christopher, (Catatonk) r 130, farmer 76.
Owen George B., (Strait's Corners) r 108, farmer 50.
Owen Jerome D., r 114, farmer 108.
Owen William, r 29, general merchant and farmer 32.
Palmatier Charles W., emp. Hulmboldt tannery, h Humiston.
PARMELE FREDERICK, retired, h Main.
Parmele John C., justice of the peace, Main, h Owego.
Palmer George W., (Jenksville) r 20, farmer with J. D. 180.
Palmer Jasper, laborer.
Palmer John D., (Jenksville) r 20, farmer with G. W. 180.
Parsons M. Eva, teacher, bds. Owego.
Parsons Minnie R., teacher, bds. Owego.
Parsons William A., traveling salesman, h Owego.
Pass Peter, (Strait's Corners) r 108, farmer with Thomas W. 160.
Pass Thomas W., (Strait's Corners) r 108, farmer with Peter 160.
Patterson John, (Willseyville) r 1, section hand.

Payne William J., clerk.
Pealing Lanis F., farm laborer, h Owego.
Pearse Charles, r 29, farmer 5.
Perham Harlow C., wagon maker, h Church.
Perrine Daniel H., (Catatonk) r 134, brick and plaster mason and farmer 183.
Perrine Henry, (Catatonk) r 134, farmer, leases of P. Caple 100.
Perrine Joseph, (Strait's Corners) r 136, farmer 50.
Perry Elizabeth, widow Solomon, h Main.
Perry Emmet J., (Willseyville) r 1, farmer, leases of H. Durfee 40.
Personeus Chester, (Willseyville) r 1, farmer 80.
Personeus Cornelius B., r 116, tin peddler.
Personeus Erwin, r 28, farmer 62.
Personeus Ezra C., r 58, farmer, works for Charles Hill, of Danby, 180.
Personeus Ira, r 28, farmer 155.
Pesoneus Lucy, widow Chauncey, laundress, h Main.
PETERS CHARLES G., r 65, dealer in live stock and breeder of fine road horses and Jersey cattle, farmer 200.
Peters Richard, carpenter.
Phelps Asa, (Flemingville) r 121, farmer 97.
Phelps Herrick J., (Flemingville) r 121, farmer, leases of Jesse Phelps 100.
Phelps Sheldon, (Flemingville) r 121, farmer.
Phelps Samuel, (Weltonville) r 120, farmer, leases of Eliza Brink 100.
Pierce Albert, (Slaterville, Tomp. Co.) r 5½, farmer 70.
Palmatier John, emp. Woolen mills, h Mountain ave.
Pompelly George, prop. of saw-mill at Gridleyville, h Main.
Potter Henry P., farmer 100, h Spencer.
Potter Mary, widow Harvey, resident, Spencer.
Pultz Luther, (Owego) r 131, farmer 128.
Quick Fremont, (Speedsville, Tomp. Co.) r 13, farmer 25.
Quick Henry, (Catatonk), r 127, dairy 15 cows, farmer 112½.
Quick Philip E., (Catatonk) r 127, farmer.
QUIMBY ELMER E., blacksmith; special attention given to horse-shoeing, Owego, h do.
Quinn James, (Catatonk) r 133, tanner.
Quinn James, Jr., (Catatonk) r 133, leather finisher.
Quinn John, (Catatonk) r 133, tanner.
Quinn Thomas, (Catatonk) r 133, leather finisher.
Reasor James B., r 44, cooper and farmer 30.
Reese Henry E., (Weltonville) r 120, farmer.
Reynolds Franklin H., r 96, tin peddler.
Rice Heman, r 29, farmer 6.
Rice Lorenzo, r 29, farmer 79.
Rice Lorenzo A., (Catatonk) r 114, farmer, leases of J. M. Anderson 100.
Richardson Charles, (West Newark) r 80, farmer, works for Horace 150.
Richardson Henry H., (West Newark) r 49, farmer 90.
RICHARDSON HORACE, (West Newark) r 80, farmer 150.
Richardson Jerome, restaurant and farmer 63, Main, h Owego.
Riggs Oliver P., retired, h Owego.
Rightmire Cornelius S., (West Candor) r 59, laborer.
Roach Benny, laborer, h Humiston.
Robberts James E., laborer, h Young.
ROBBINS JOHN E., r 42, farmer 82.
ROBINSON ALDICE A., fire and life insurance, Main, h do.

Robinson Charles, (West Candor) r 59, farmer 30.
Robinson Edward J., (West Candor) r 59, farmer 50.
Robinson Harrison, (West Candor) r 59, farmer.
Robinson Luther B., painter and farmer.
Robinson Maria, r 116, widow Semour, h and lot.
Robinson Murtillow A., carpenter, h Foundry.
Robinson Philander, retired, h Main.
Rockwell Rufus, (Speedsville, Tomp. Co.) r 22, farmer 120.
Roe Emory D., r 63, farmer, leases of Irving Hart, of Waverly, 100.
ROE EUGENE F., r 5, apiarist and manuf. and dealer in apiarist supplies.
Roe Gamaliel, r 5, steam feed-mill and threshing machine, and farmer 140.
Roe George F., farm laborer, bds. Pond.
Roe Horace M., r 5, farmer.
Roe William F., r 25, apiarist, 115 colonies, and manuf. and dealer in apiarist supplies, carpenter and farmer 109.
Rolfe James K., r 88, farmer 50.
ROPER WILLIAM E., physician and surgeon, h Owego.
Rose Jacob P., laborer, h Main.
Rose Rodney S. Rev., retired M. E. Clergyman.
ROSS EDGAR D., r 58, farmer 100.
Ross Edmund, (Strait's Corners) r 141, farmer 44.
Ross Frank, (M. L. Ross & Son) h Spencer.
Ross Harry, (Willseyville) r 3, farmer 230.
Ross Lester Z., r 58, farmer 163.
Ross Milton L., (M. L. Ross & Son) also commercial traveler, also farmer 54. h Spencer.
Ross M. L. & Son, (Frank) druggists, Main.
Rowe Henry R., (Catatonk) r 133, telegraph operator for National Transit Co.
Royal Morris B., insurance and farmer 30, h Owego.
Ryan John, (Catatonk) r 133, laborer.
RYAN JOHN, lumber and hides, Mill, h Main.
Sabin Edgar D., r 65, farmer with M. E. Cowles, of Spencer, 125.
Sackett Lucy, widow Nathaniel L., resident, h Owego.
Sackett Mary, dressmaker, h Owego.
Sackett Nathaniel O., retired, h Main.
Sanford Harmon, (Willseyville) r 1 cor. 31, farmer, leases of Lewis Griffin 107.
Sarson John, (Willseyville) r 3, farmer 137.
Sarson John C. F., (Willseyville) r 3, house-painter.
Sarson Samuel T., (Willseyville) r 3, carpenter.
Sarson Thomas E., (Willseyville) r 3, works for John Sarson 137.
Sawyer Frank, (West Candor) r 61, deputy-postmaster, and farmer 46.
Sawyer Fred W., emp. D. L. & W. R. R., h Railroad.
Sawyer Ira, (West Candor) r 62, farmer 123.
Sawyer Luther, (West Candor) r 62, general merchant.
Scharf George W., tinsmith, h Preston.
Scofield Clarence H., r 63, well drilling.
Scofield Truman, (West Candor) r 62, dealer in live stock, and farmer 82.
Schooley Edmund, r 6, farmer 100.
Scott Elbert O., att'y and counselor at law, Main, bds. Allen House.
Seaman Joel, r 116, dealer in sheep and cattle, farmer 60.
SEAMAN LE GRAND, r 89, dealer in live stock, and farmer 75, and works for Amanda Gosen 80.

TOWN OF CANDOR. 73

Searles George M., carriage and sleigh manufactory, Main, h Railroad.
Sewell John, (Weltonville) r 78, carpenter, and farmer 55, and saw-mill with R. Fuller and Julia Hull.
Shaffer Joseph, (Catatonk) r 133, farmer with Wesley 50.
Shaffer Wesley, (Catatonk) r 133, farmer with Joseph 50.
Shaler Frederick, r 95, laborer.
Shaw James, (Flemingville) r 123, laborer.
Sheerer John D., peddler, h Church.
Sherman Elisha J., r 114, farmer 37.
Sherman James, laborer, h Mountain ave.
Shipman Charles, (Strait's Corners) r 109, farmer 70.
Shulenburg Alvin, r 113, farmer 30.
Shulenburg Fred J., (West Candor) r 105, dairy 18 cows, farmer 57, and leases of S. E. Gridley 250.
Shulenburg Horace, (West Candor) r 105, farmer.
Shulenburg James, r 56, farmer 100.
Silvernail Hiram, (Strait's Corners) r 139, resident.
Silvernail John, (Strait's Corners) r 139, farmer 79.
Simmons Edward, laborer, h Humiston.
Simpson Franklin, (Willseyville) r 4, farmer 50.
Slate Alfonzo, (West Candor) r 59, farmer.
Slate Francis, r 58, laborer.
Slate Nelson, (Jenksville) r 49, farmer, works estate of Arnold Blanchard 90.
Slater Bartholomew G., farmer on shares with Peter Carr 85, h Owego.
Slater Harry, clerk, h Owego.
Slawson James G., blacksmith, Foundry, h do.
Smith Alanson J., r 53, farmer 100.
Smith Angeline C., widow Jesse A., resident, bds. Owego.
Smith Charles S., saloon, Main, bds. Railroad.
Smith Clarissa Mrs., resident, h Mountain ave.
Smith Edgar M., farmer 50.
Smith Fred W., ass't cashier First Nat. Bank, h Main.
Smith H. Alanson, (Catatonk) r 133, postmaster, station agent, and general merchant.
Smith Hannah M., (Catatonk) r 127, widow Alanson Smith, farm 27.
Smith Henry, school director, lumberman, and farmer 160, h Owego.
Smith James, (Willseyville) r 1, farmer 15.
Smith James J., (Catatonk) r 115, farmer, works for Emma Smith 13.
SMITH J. LEWIS, deputy postmaster and town clerk, h Owego.
Smith John J., carpenter and farmer 17, and with Lucius H. 35.
Smith Judson, r 37, laborer.
Smith Lewis W., (Catatonk) r 127, laborer.
Smith L. Everett, r 95, brakeman.
Smith Lavelle, r 37, carpenter.
Smith Lucius H., r 95, carpenter and builder.
Smith Mantlebert H., farmer with his father Edgar M., 50.
Smith Nelson, (Willseyville) r 1, laborer.
Smith Wakeman B., farmer 218, h Main.
Smith William, farm laborer, h Owego.
Smith William B., druggist, bds. Main.
Smith William R., r 37, carpenter.
Smullen George B., (Weltonville) r 20, blacksmith.
Smullen Patrick, (Weltonville) r 120, blacksmith.

TOWN OF CANDOR.

Snover John F., r 64, farmer 90.
Snow Roswell, (Caroline Center, Tomp. Co.) r 10, farmer.
Snow Walstein, (Caroline Center, Tomp. Co.) r 10, farmer 161.
Snow William H., r 39, farmer 60.
Snyder Benjamin C., r 13, farmer 141.
Snyder Dewitt M., (Willseyville) r 1, saw and cider-mill and farmer 126.
Snyder Lewis H., laborer, h Mountain ave.
Snyder Samuel, r 56, resident.
Snyder William H., r 56, foreman E. C. & N. R. R.
Spaulding Alonzo, r 9, farmer 90.
SPAULDING URBON P., fire and life insurance, and loan and investment and real estate, Main, h Kinney.
Speers Joel W., (Willseyville) r 30, farmer 8 and leases of Amanda Willsey 175.
Spellman Michael, (Catatonk) r 115, farmer 36.
Southwick Aaron B., (Strait's Corners) r 140, farmer 104.
Stafford Horace G., (Owego) r 131, farmer 52.
Stafford Randolph, (Strait's Corners) r 137, farmer, leases of Arba Campbell, of Owego, 160.
Starks James O., off r 6, farmer with John 65.
Starks John, off r 6, farmer with J. O. 65.
Starkweather Charles, r 28, farmer 67.
Starkweather Joel, millwright and carpenter, h Pond.
Starkweather Lewis S., resident, bds. Pond.
Stevens Andrew T., (Willseyville) r 3, painter and farmer 26.
Stevens David, r 29, farmer 25.
Stevens Della, r 32, wife of John, farm with Mary J. Southwick, of Halsey Valley, 163.
Stevens George, (Willseyville) r 1, farmer, leases of David Stevens 30.
Stevens James M., (Willseyville) r 1, basket-maker and farmer 25.
Stevens John, r 32, farmer, works for Della Stevens 81½, and leases of Mary J. Southwick, of Halsey Valley, 81 1-2.
Stevens Lafayette, r 29, laborer.
Stevens Loren, (Willseyville) r 1, fireman.
Stevens Wilber, off r 36, farmer 25.
Stever Frank, (Jenksville) r 49, laborer.
Stewart Adelbert, r 70, farmer 20.
Stewart Augustus, barber, bds. Railroad.
Stewart Charles, barber, Main, h Railroad.
Stewart Henry B., tin-peddler, h Hulmboldt.
Stinard Abigail D., widow Oglesbary, resident, h Pond.
STINARD ALANSON K., (Jenksville) r 49, farmer 26.
Stinard Andrew, laborer, h off Owego.
Stinard Sylvester, (Jenksville) r 50, breeder and trainer of horses, proprietor of stock horse Prince, and farmer, leases of J. W. McCarty 244.
Stone Charles E., r 41, farmer.
Stone Eli, (Willseyville) laborer.
Stone Nelson, r 95, leases of the heirs of Geo. Andrews 143.
STOWELL ALMOND F., contractor and builder, Railroad, h do.
Strait Adelbert, (Willseyville) farmer, leases of Lewis Griffin 185.
Strait Henry, r 73, farmer 26.
Strait Sylvester, (Strait's Corners) off r 139, farmer, leases of Wm. Harlan 130
STRONG ANSON B., r 45, farmer 13, works for Hebron Strong 50 and for Orange Johnson 44.

TOWN OF CANDOR.

Strong Charles S., r 24, farmer 133.
Strong Eugene B., (Willseyville) r 3, assessor, manuftr. of tubs, firkins, etc., and farmer 75.
Strong Hebron, r 45, farmer 50.
Strong Joel H., r 98, dealer in wool, hides, pelts and produce.
Strong Josiah C., r 41, farmer 40.
Strong Manley, (Jenksville) r 50, laborer.
Strong Raymond, r 98, lumberman.
Sturdevant Judson, r 119, farmer 5.
Swartwood Edmund, (Strait's Corners) r 143, farmer, leases of Alfred Evelien, of Tioga, 82.
Sweetman Joanna, widow David, resident, h Owego.
Tacey Alexander, carpenter, h Church.
Tacey Melvin, laborer, h Church.
Taylor Abram, (West Newark) r 81, farmer 437.
Taylor Eugene C., (Weltonville) r 86, farmer 33.
Taylor Martin W., (West Candor) r 109, farmer 82.
Taylor Merton L., (Weltonville) r 86, farmer 50.
Taylor Samuel E., (Weltonville) r 86, farmer 84.
Taylor Walter, r 12, farmer, leases of J. S. Whitney 239.
Taylor William J., (West Newark) r 81, farmer.
Taylor William J., (Weltonville) r 86, teacher, apiarist 50 colonies, farmer, leases of Samuel Taylor 84.
Templeton Albert J., tinsmith, h Foundry.
Terwilliar Abigail J., (Owego) r 118, widow of Nathan, leases of Franklin W. Truman, of Owego, 200.
Terwilliger Andrew J., (Strait's Corners) r 111, prop. English coach stock horse, Tim Valons, farmer 136.
Terwilliger Levi G., (Catatonk) r 133, musician and sawyer.
Terwilligar Solomon E., (Catatonk) r 133, blacksmith.
Terwilliger Stephen E., (Strait's Corners) r 109, farmer.
Thayer John B., (South Danby, Tomp. Co.) r 34, farmer with William H.
Thayer William H., (South Danby, Tomp. Co.) r 34, farmer, leases of Marvin Reed, of Ithaca, 140, and of Eleanor Dewitt, of Danby, 62.
Thomas George H., (Weltonville) r 81, farmer 80.
Thompson Anthony H., r 38, farmer 41.
THOMPSON JEROME, (McCarty & Thompson) cashier, First Nat. Bank, also farmer in Spencer 420, h Main.
Thornton James J., r 93, basket-maker.
Throop William, r 35, farmer 33.
Tidd Francis T., farm laborer, h Foundry.
Tidd Mary E., laundress, h Foundry.
Toft George, (Catatonk) r 114, farmer 4, works for Elizabeth Orcutt 55.
Townley Mary J., widow James L., resident, h Owego.
Townley Reid W., farmer, h Owego.
Tracy Maria E., (Catatonk) r 133, widow James, resident.
Truman Lyman R., (Owego) r 132, farmer 130.
Tubbs Charles N., r 41, carpenter and with Ebenezer, farmer $25\frac{1}{2}$.
Tubbs Ebenezer, r 41, carpenter, and farmer with Charles N., $25\frac{1}{2}$.
Tubbs Isaac, r 41, tin-peddlar, and farmer 61.
Tubbs J. Thomas, tin-peddler, h Main.
Tubbs Orlando, r 69, farmer 20.
Tucker Charles E., r 29, farmer.

Tucker Frank, (Willseyville) r 30, laborer.
Tucker Matthew, (Willseyville) r 30, laborer.
Tucker William, r 29, farmer 108.
Turk John, retired, h Owego.
Turk Levi, carpenter, h R. R. ave.
TURNER GEORGE, (Strait's Corners) r 143, carpenter, and farmer 103.
Tuttle Warren H., 104, farmer 75.
Tyler Charles, off r 88, farmer 37.
Tyler Edward, r 119, laborer.
Tyler James, off r 88, farmer.
Ulrick Henry W., r 25, farmer, leases of John Ulrick, of Tioga, 161.
VanDebogart Francis, retired, h Church.
VanDebogart Frank L., general merchant, Main, h do.
Van Debogart Lawrence, (Willseyville) r 30, carpenter, and farmer 100.
Van Debogart Peter, dealer in agl. implements, Main, h do.
Van Deerveer Warren C., (Strait's Corners) r 142, farmer 110.
Van Dermark Joseph, r 65, farmer.
Van Dermark Peter, laborer, h Main.
Van Dermark Wayland L., r 65, farmer 37.
Van Dermark Wilson, r 23, farmer, leases of Morgan White 156.
VAN DEUSER H. & M., (Catatonk) r 133, proprietors saw-mill, also dealers in lumber and potatoes, and farmer 47.
VAN DEUSER HENRY, (Catatonk) (H. & M. Van D.) r 133.
VAN DEUSER JERRY, (Catatonk) (H. & M. Van D.) farmer 5.
VAN DEUSER MARTIN, (Catatonk) (H. & M. Van D.) r 133.
VanEtten George, r 5, refused to give information.
VanEtten George F., r 29, farmer 60.
Vanglone Schuyler, (Jenksville) r 13, farmer.
VanGorder Charles E., peddler, h R. R. ave.
VanGorder Elias, (Weltonville) r 82, laborer.
VanKleeck James, retired, h Owego.
VanKleeck Jane, r 36, wife of Charles H., farm 106.
VanKleeck John M., r 36, farmer.
VanLuven Simon, justice of the peace, Main, h Owego.
VanLuven Robert, (Strait's Corners) r 137. farmer 48.
VanPelt Sarah, widow Garrett, resident, h Owego.
VanScoy Augusta, r 40, widow Knowlton, farm 130.
VAN SCOY BURT R., r 70, fruit grower, and farmer 108.
VAN SCOY ISAAC D., (Jenksville) r 50, farmer 108.
VanScoy Simeon, r 40, farmer, works for Augusta VanScoy 130.
VanVleet Theodore, lumber dealer, Main, h do.
VanWoert Lebbeus, r 56, laborer.
VanWoert Levi, (West Candor) r 59, farmer 90.
VanWoert R. Smith, farmer, h Main.
VanZyle Stephen, r 69, farmer 10.
Vergason George, (Strait's Corners) r 140, wool buyer, and farmer 93.
VERGASON IDDO. prop. Allen House, Main.
VERGASON SOLOMON, r 112 cor. 114, manuf. and dealer in lumber, dairy 18 cows, and farmer 620.
Vergason Stephen, (Strait's Corners) r 142, farmer 125.
VOSE ENOCH, (West Candor) r 108, contractor and builder, also farmer.
Vorce Volney, (Weltonville) farmer 72.
Wake James, r 67, farmer.

Walker John, laborer, h Owego.
Walts Conrad, (Strait's Corners) r 109, farmer 80.
Ward and VanVleet Misses, (Elmira A Ward and Eva D. VanVleet) dealers in millinery and fancy goods.
WARD HARVEY H., farmer 75, h Owego.
Ward Hiram, farmer 75.
Ward Oscar, farmer.
Ward Oswald J., live stock dealer, h Owego.
Wardwell & Cooper, (West Candor) (William C. and J. H.) r 62, groceries.
Wardwell William R., drug clerk, bds. Main.
Warner John C., r 93, farmer, works for Minda Warner 45.
Warner Richard E., r 44, farmer with Shelden P., leases of R. P. Warner 254.
Warner Richard P., r 44, farmer 254.
Warner Shelden P., r 44, farmer with Richard E., leases of R. P. Warner 254.
Watkins Ephraim C., (Flemigville) laborer.
Watrous Sherman, farm laborer, h Foundry.
Watson James, resident, h Owego.
Webster Edwin, (Owego) r 132, dealer in live stock, and farmer 275.
Wentnorth John W., farm laborer, h Church.
Wentworth Noyes D., painter, h Church.
Wheeler Abram T., cider-mill and farmer 33.
Wheeler Charles T., (Owego) r 124, farmer 86.
Wheeler Frank G., (Owego) r 124, farmer.
Wheeler Ira E., r 63, farmer.
Wheeler John H., farmer, h Railroad ave.
Wheeler Mary, r 41, widow Lewis, farm 59.
Wheeler Myron F., r 41, farmer.
Whipple Marietta R., widow Solomon, resident, h Owego.
White Abram, (Strait's Corners), r 141, farmer 70.
WHITE A. FRANK, (Willseyville) (White Bros.)
WHITE BROS., (Willseyville) (A. Frank, Charles O. and Edward M.) r 30, manufacturers of White's patent bent chairs and patent folding tables.
White Charles B., (Willseyville) r 1, farmer 300.
WHITE CHARLES O., (Willseyville) (White Bros.) r 30, commercial traveler.
WHITE EDWARD M., (Willseyville) (White Bros.) r 1.
White Jacob N., (Strait's Corners), r 141, farmer 50.
White John B., (Strait's Corners) r 110, farmer 83.
WHITE MARY A., widow Leonard, resident, h Owego.
White Morgan A., (Willseyville) groceries and manuftr. and dealer in lumber, and farmer 1,065.
Whitley Andrew J., r 7, farmer 90.
Whitley Demoma, (Willseyville) r 30, laborer.
WHITLEY FLORILLA S., r 65, widow John, Jr.
Whitley George M., r 29, farmer 28.
Whitley Ira, r 29, farmer.
Whitley Newton D., r 7, farmer.
Whitley Sarah, r 28, wife of Joseph, h and lot.
Whitley Philip A., r 29, farmer 27.
Whitley Warren, r 29, farmer 133.
Whitmarsh Ambrose, (Catatonk) r 115, farmer 60.
Whitmarsh Andrew J., r 95, laborer.
Whitmarsh Charles, laborer.

TOWN OF CANDOR.

Whitmarsh Eben, r 116, dairy 11 cows, and farmer 96.
Whitmarsh Edward, (Catatonk) r 129, farmer 200.
Whitmarsh Edwin, (Catatonk) r 129, farmer 59.
Whitmarsh James, r 116, resident, age 87.
Whitmarsh John, (Catatonk) r 115, farmer.
Whitmarsh Luther, (Catatonk) r 129, farmer.
Whitmarsh Robert L., (Catatonk) r 134, farmer 100.
Whitmarsh Simon, (Catatonk) r 129, farmer.
Whitney George, r 71, laborer.
Whitney Joseph S., live stock dealer and farmer 230, h Railroad.
Whitney Martin D., r 88, agt. for Auburn Art Union Co.
Whitney Perry B., r 56, farmer 50.
Wiest George A., (West Newark) r 77, farmer, leases of Abram Taylor 270.
Wilber William H., (Speedsville, Tomp. Co.) r 18, farmer 100.
Willard Lewis D., speculator, and farmer 40.
Williston Horace, Rev., pastor M. E. church, h Owego.
Williams Enoch S., (Booth & Williams) h Main.
Williams Ezra O., teamster, h Owego.
Williams George F. (Catatonk) r 126, farmer 50.
Williams George R., r 40, farmer, leases of Henry Merikle 97.
Williams LaFayette, (Catatonk) r 126, farmer 90.
Williams William I., (Catatonk) r 116, farmer 93.
Willsey Gaylord, retired, h Spencer.
Willsey Harriet A., (Willseyville) r 30, widow of William W., farm 175.
Willsey Margerite M., widow Warren, resident, h Spencer.
Willsey Martin E., farmer, h Bank.
Wilson Ephraim J., farmer 5.
Wilson William H., laborer.
Winfield Simon, (Strait's Corners) r 139, farmer.
Woodard Elias H., (Weltonville) r 82, blacksmith.
Woodard Mary G , (Weltonville) r 82, wife of E. H., dealer in groceries and provisions.
WOODFORD ALBERT H., r 63, farmer 160.
Woodford Asel H., (West Candor) r 62, farmer 10, and with Charles Woodford 58.
Woodford Chauncey C., farmer 97, h Owego.
Woodford Edwin F., r 63, farmer.
Woodford Edward G., (West Candor) r 63, farmer.
Woodford E. Jerome, (West Candor) r 62, agricultural implements, and farmer with Elbert C. 150.
Woodford Elbert C., (West Candor) r 62, carpenter, farmer, E. Jerome, 150.
Woodford Frank S., r 56, farmer with Sylvester 100.
WOODFORD GEORGE, (West Candor) r 62, farmer 220.
Woodford Myron L., (West Candor) r 63, farmer 156.
Woodford Rhoda. r 56, widow Luther, farm 125.
WOODFORD SYLVSTER, r 56, farmer with F. S. Woodford 100.
Wool Joseph D., (Willseyville) r 3, justice of the peace, and farmer 12.
Wolverton Charles A., (Owego) r 131, cooper.
Wright Calvin, (West Candor) r 109, farmer 57.
Wright Charles H., r 111, farmer 135.
Wright Edwin J., r 111, farmer.
Wright John, retired, h Kinney.

STARKEY & WINTERS, Wholesale and Retail Druggists, Owego.

TOWN OF NEWARK VALLEY.

Wright Leroy, (Strait's Corners) r 109, farmer 10.
Wright William A., r 37, farmer 60, and works for the heirs of Sterling J. Barber 97.
Young David, (Jenksville) farmer 85.
Zimmer Alvah, (West Candor) r 61, laborer.
Zimmer Ira, (Jenksville) r 47, farmer 125.

NEWARK VALLEY.

(*For explanations, etc., see page 3, part second.*)

(Postoffice address is Newark Valley, unless otherwise designated in parenthesis.)

Abbey Reuben, r 16, carpenter.
Abbott George, (Howlan & Abbott) h Mill.
Ackerman Cornelius R., (Jenksville) contractor and builder, and farmer 40.
ACKERMAN JOSEPH, r 21, district collector and farmer 125.
Allen Charles W., (Jenksville) off r 1, retired.
Allen James, r 16, retired.
ALLEN JAMES H., Jenksville) r 2, farmer on shares with F. W. Richardson, 200.
Ames Henry W., r 16, farm laborer.
Ames Stephen W., r 18, farmer 100.
Ames William, r 6, carpenter.
Andrews Charles F., r 9, farmer 100.
Andrews Deborah, r 55, widow Chester, resident.
Andrews Ezra J., r 42, farmer 52.
Andrews Frank, r 42, teacher.
Andrews Heman N., r 42, farmer 48.
Andrews Jane, r 9, widow Luther, farm 200.
Andrews Jesse, r 42, farmer, on shares with W. Elwell, 40.
Andrews Judson, r 42, farmer 43.
Andrews Lucinda, r 42, widow Daniel, resident.
Andrews Sarah, r 9, resident.
Angell Elworth J., contractor and builder, also small fruit grower, h Whig.
Angell Thomas, (Ketchumville) r 9, retired Methodist preacher and farmer 40.
Arnold Frederick C., harness-maker, bds. Elm.
Arnold Harley, r 25, farm laborer.
Arnold James, r 25, farmer 89.
Ashley Frank D., clerk, h Whig.
Avery Samuel M., (Jenksville) r 1, postmaster.
Ayres Charles H., laborer, bds. Maple ave.
Ayers James, cooper, h Maple ave.
Ayers John S., tinsmith, h Maple.
Bailey Charles, (Maine, Broome Co.) r 26, farmer for his mother Mrs. M. Bailey.

STARKEY & WINTERS, promptly fill Mail and Telephone Orders.

Bailey Henry, (Maine, Broome Co.) r 26, farmer for his mother Mrs. M. Bailey.
Bailey Hiram C., (Maine, Broome Co.) r 26, farmer 125.
Bailey Margaret, (Maine, Broome Co.) r 26, widow Amos, farmer 70.
Baldwin Charles, r 38, farmer.
Baldwin Royal C., r 38, farmer 10.
Baldwin William, farmer, leases of E. Barber 22.
Ball A. Rodney, r 5, farmer, with his son William H., 60.
Ball Fred, emp. N. K. Waring, h Elm.
BALL HENRY W., (Jayne & Ball) h Maple.
Ball Margaret, widow Frank, resident, h Elm.
Ball William H., r 5, farmer 60 on shares with his father A. Rodney.
Ballard Addison L., laborer, h East ave.
Ballard Andrew M., emp. tannery, h Whig.
Ballard Ann, (Ketchumville) r 10, resident.
Ballard George W., deputy sheriff, h Maple.
Ballard George W. Mrs., laundress and general work, h Maple.
Ballard Horatio, r 25½, farmer 62.
Ballard John, r 26⅓, farmer 50.
Ballard Lewis, r 26⅓, farmer 50.
Barber Frederick W., emp. Donley Marble Works, h Whig.
Barber George, r 38½, farmer 100.
Barber Virgil C., carpenter, h Rewey ave.
Barclay Mitchell, emp. tannery, h off East ave.
Barnes Charles H., r 16, farmer 52.
Barnes Lewis W., r 16, farmer.
Barrett Holmes, retired, bds. Main.
Barrett Monroe, (West Newark) r 22, farmer 200.
BARROTT JOSEPHAS, (Weltonville) r 40, farmer 175.
Barton James H., r 6, farmer 85.
Barber William C., painter, h Maple.
Bean Fred C., (Maine, Broome Co.) r 47, farmer 100.
Becker Charles, retired, h Elm.
Beecher Lambert, harness-maker, h Maple.
Belcher J. Waldo, painter and paper-hanger, h Brook.
BELCHER SIDNEY, r 40¼, lumberman, and farmer 150.
Belden Uriah L., blacksmith, off Water, h Whig.
Belden William H., (West Newark) r 22, blacksmith.
Bement Celia, resident, bds. Whig.
Bement Egbert, milk dealer, and farmer 75, h Whig.
BENHAM CHARLES M., r 35, farmer for his father Martinus L.
Benham Martinus L., r 35, book-keeper in Utica, also farm 75.
Benton Lyman C., (Jenksville) r 1, shoemaker.
BENTON WILLIS S., (Jenksville) r 1, groceries, also reporter for Owego *Gazette* and Newark Valley *Herald*.
Benton Wilson, (Jenksville) r 1, farmer.
BERKLEY CHARLES E., r 53, carpenter, and farmer 43.
Berkley Egbert D., r 53, farmer 60.
Berkley Elizabeth, r 53, widow Charles, resident.
Berlin David, laborer, h Dam lane.
Bevier Daniel, farmer, bds. Whig.
Bevier Elizabeth, widow Ralph, resident, h Whig.
Bieber Allie V., r 42, dressmaker.

Bieber Catherine, widow Henry, resident, bds. Whig.
Bieber Philip, r 42, live stock dealer, and farmer 73.
BIEBER ROMAINE F., lawyer, Water, h Whig.
Billings William, farmer, bds. Main.
BISHOP FRANCIS M., physician and surgeon, Water, h Elm.
Bishop Lamont, carpenter, h Water.
Bishop Lewis D., carpenter, h Water.
Blewer Adelaide, r 40, widow Henry, resident.
Blewer J. Frank, r 40, farmer 200.
Blewer Jesse, r 40, farmer, with his mother Mary.
Blewer Mary E., r 40, widow Charles, farm 95.
Blewer Sarah J., r 60, widow Charles, resident.
Borthwick Delphine, (Jenksville) r 1, resident.
BORTHWICK D JAMES, (Jenksville), r 1, farmer.
Borthwick George H., (Jenksville) r 22, assessor and farmer 50, and leases of
 D. J. Borthwick 112.
Bowen Eugene, r 15½, farmer 50.
Boyce J. Edgar, painter, h Maple ave.
Boyce Henry W., retired, h Main.
Bradley Elmina, widow Lambert, resident, bds. Main.
Bradley Mary A., widow Lambert, h Main.
Brick Thomas, laborer, h Moore.
Briggs Sally, r 16, widow Salem, resident.
Brink John J., (West Newark) r 22, farmer 90.
Brink Peter G., (West Newark) r 22, justice of the peace, and farmer 110.
Brockway Joseph B., r 6, farmer 74½.
Brockway Lewellyn, r 6, farmer with his father Joseph B.
Brougham (Helen and Sarah), milliners, Water, h do.
Brougham William, r 53, farmer 50.
Brown Elmina, widow Amos P., resident, h Main.
Brown Mary A., dressmaker, Main, bds. do.
Brown Orpha Mrs., laundress, bds. Bridge.
Buckley Patrick, night watchman, h Maple.
Buffington Chauncey L., (Ketchumville) r 11, blacksmith, and farmer 25.
BURCH & WELLS (L. S. B. and L. E. W.) saw, planing and grain thresh-
 ing mills, Main.
BURCH LEVI S., (Burch & Wells) h Maple.
Burch Mary A., resident, h Main.
Burchard Harvey J., (Ketchumville) r 9, justice of the peace and apiasist.
Burr William H., veterinary surgeon, bds. Whig.
BURR WILLIAM J., physician and surgeon, office Whig, h do.
Burroughs Cornelius S., (Clinton & Burroughs) r 9, h do.
Bushnell Calvin, r 15, farmer 64.
Bushnell Edwin G., (Ketchumville) r 9, farmer 101.
Bushnell Frank G., r 15, commissioner of highways, dairy 9 cows, farmer 93.
Bushnell Philo C., farmer for his father Calvin 64.
Bushnell Theron H., telegraph line repairer, h Whig.
Bushnell Zina H., retired, h John.
Butler John, farmer 200, h Main.
Buttles William R., retired, bds. Bridge.
Byington Alphonso, general merchant, Main, bds. do.
Byington Clayton, speculator, h Main.
Byington Savilla, widow Lawyer, resident, h Main.

6

BYINGTON SHERMAN W., postmaster and meat-market, Main, h do.
Cady Gershom, (Ketchumville) r 9, farmer 16.
Cady Luther, (Ketchumville) r 14, farmer 125.
Caldwell William J., deputy postmaster, h Main.
Cameron Eugene, (Ketchumville) r 9, farmer 202.
Cameron Harry A., farmer on shares with E. Saddlemire, h Main.
Cameron John, r 41, farmer on shares with G. B. Sutton 100.
Campbell Harrison, (West Newark) r 22, farm laborer.
Cargill Heman, retired, bds. Main.
Cargill Julius C., resident, bds. Bridge.
CARGILL WILLIAM, furniture and undertaking, Main, h do.
Carpenter Anna C., widow Joshua L., resident, h Main.
Carty Henry J., laborer, h Main.
Cary Thomas A., farmer 82, h Main.
Castline Moses J., (Weltonville) r 40, farmer 35.
Chamberlain Daniel, r 16, retired.
CHAMBERLAIN THEODORE F., r 16, assessor and farmer 84.
Chambers Charles, wagon-maker, Water, h do.
Chapman Canfield, contractor and builder.
CHAPMAN EDGAR E., hardware, Water, h Main.
Chapman George M., contractor and builder, h Main.
Chapman Lyman F., groceries and provisions, Water, h Main.
Chapman Noyce P., retired, h Silk.
Chittenden Lester, r 40½, school collector and farmer 175.
Christensen Peter, laborer, h Whig.
Clark Edgar, (Ketchumville) r 14, farmer 100.
Clark Elizabeth, r 15, invalid, resides with G. M. Dickinson.
CLARK ENOS M., r 25, bridge builder and farmer 50, and leases of L. B. West 180.
Cleveland John, r 56, farm laborer.
Clifford John M., r 29, farmer 120.
CLINTON & BURROUGHS, (R. W. C. & C. S. B.) r 9, steam saw-mill.
Clinton Alice E., clerk, bds. Elm.
Clinton Edwin V., farmer 22, h Main.
Clinton Emma, widow Stephen P., h Elm.
Clinton George L., laborer, h Elm.
CLINTON JULIAN S., r 35, farm 120.
Clinton Henry W., retired, h Main.
Clinton Lydia B., r 42, widow George, resident.
Clinton Morris D., r 42 farmer 111.
CLINTON ROYAL W., lumber dealer and farmer, h Main.
Clizbe Jay, clergyman, (Cong.) retired.
Cole Edward, (Ketchumville) r 12, farmer.
Coney Alfred T., emp. tannery, h Main.
Coney Lewis J., laborer, h Main.
Cook Eugene D., farm laborer, bds. Bridge.
Cook Henry H., r 24, farmer.
Cook Lovisa F., laundress, h Bridge.
Cook Orson L., farm laborer, bds Bridge.
COOLEY BENJAMIN F., boarding-house and farmer 25.
Cooley Charles H., bridge builder, h Silk.
Cooley John, (Ketchumville) r 10, farmer 155.
Cortright Angeline A., (Weltonville) r 40, resident.

Cortright Josephus M., (Weltonville) r 40, farmer 65.
Cortright L. Elton, (West Newark) r 22, farmer 147.
Cortright Willie N., (West Newark) r 22, farmer with his father Elton.
Councilman Edwin W., r 35, apiarist, 60 swarms, poultry raiser and farmer 40.
COUNCILMAN JIRA F., r 19, farmer with his father Timothy S.
Councilman Timothy S., farmer, h Whig.
CRONCE JOHN H., r 15, farmer 70.
Crounse Charles G., r 24, farmer 50.
Culver Frank, resident, h East ave.
Curtis Isaac, farmer 6, h Main.
Custard William, r 40, farmer 50.
DAGGETT BARNEY, (West Newark) r 22, farmer 86.
Dalton William, r 15½, farmer 30.
Davern William. r 25, farmer 55.
DAVIDGE EUNICE, (Davidge, Landfield & Co.) widow John, h Whig.
Davidge John, resident, bds. Whig.
DAVIDGE, LANDFIELD & CO., (S. B. D., J. B. L. and Eunice D.) sole-leather mnfrs.; also, lumber in Pa. and W. Va., Main.
DAVIDGE SHERWOOD B., (Davidge, Lanfield & Co.) h Whig.
DAVIS FRANKLIN, prop. saw-mill and farm 100 on r 25, h Whig.
Davis John T., engineer and farmer with his father, Franklin, bds. Whig.
Davison D. Henry, (West Newark) r 22, carpenter.
Dean Charles E., (Ketchumville) r 10, farmer.
Dean Charles H., (Ketchumville) r 9, farmer 32.
Dean Franklin G., r 39, farmer 175.
Decker Abram D. W., cartman, h Whig.
Decker Abram L., laborer, h East ave.
Decker Ira, emp. William's saw-mill, h Elm.
Decker Joseph, stage express to Owego, h East ave.
DeGARAMO JAMES, r 15, farmer 51.
DeGaramo Peter, r 15, farmer 120.
De Garamo William, r 35, farmer 58.
DeGROAT JAMES F., r 40½, lumberman.
Delaney James, off r 25, farm laborer.
Delaney John, off r 25, farmer 96.
De Laney Michael, emp. tannery, h off East ave.
Delaney William, off r 25, farm laborer.
Dennison Joseph H., r 5, farmer 24.
Dickerson Austin, farmer 25, h John.
Dickinson Lyman, r 42, farmer 60.
Dickinson Orville, r 42, resident.
Dickson George M., (Connecticut) r 15, farmer 52.
DIMMICK & YOUNG, (O. D. & H.Y.) props. Dimmick House, also dealers in coal, lime, brick and cement, and produce shippers, opp. Depot.
DIMMICK HOUSE, Dimmick & Young, props., opp. Depot.
DIMMICK OSSIAN, (Dimmick & Young) bds. Dimmick House.
Dimmick Simeon L., (Ketchumville) r 11, retired Methodist minister, and farmer 60.
Dingman Andrew, r 53, farm laborer.
Dingman Ostrom, r 53, farm laborer.
Doan Daniel, r 25, school trustee, and farmer 65.
Dohs Daniel, retired builder, h Main.
Dohs George, furnace builder, and farmer 11.

Doney Catherine M., r 58, teacher.
Doney John A., r 58, farmer with his mother Saloma.
Doney Randall, (Connecticut) r 9, emp. lumber mill.
Doney Saloma C. Mrs. r 58, farmer 114.
DONLEY BROS., (James G. & Robert) all kinds of granite and marble work, Maple, also branch at Greene, N. Y.
DONLEY ROBERT, (Donley Bros.) h Watson.
Dooley Catherine, widow John, resident, h East ave.
Downey Robert, emp. tannery, h East ave.
Duran Mrs., resident, h Ward.
Durfee Samantha, widow Amasa, resident, h Rewey ave.
Duygan James, (Connecticut) r 15, farmer 50.
Duygan John, r 15, farmer for his father James.
Edwards Albert, stage express, Newark Valley to Whitney's Point, h East ave.
Elwell Catharine, widow Rev. King, h Main.
Elwell Morris, resident, h Main.
ELWELL WILLIAM, general merchant, Main, h do.
Fairchild Salley A., r 24, widow Hiram Z., resident.
Fellows Russell S. dentist, Main, h do.
Fellows William A., carpenter, h Whig.
Finch Charles, (Ketchumville) postmaster, and general merchant.
Fisk James, r 51, farm laborer.
Fivaz Jules B., farmer 40, h Whig.
Flanagan John H., retired, h Elm.
Flanagan Susie, dressmaker, Elm, bds. do.
FLANAGAN WILLIAM J., foreman Donley Bros. marble works, also prop. orange grove in Hernando, Fla., h Elm.
Fogle Elias E., 52, farmer.
Fogle George F., r 51, farmer.
Fogle Jacob, r 51, farmer 80.
FORD ALBERT N., general merchant, Water, h Elm.
Ford Herbert, clerk, bds. Elm.
Ford Ichabod A., farmer 83, h Main.
FRANK CHARLES, jeweler, Water, h Whig.
Freeland Lyman, r 21, farmer 110.
French Charles, r 25, farmer 31.
French Jerry, r 25, farmer for his father Charles.
Gage Rilla, r 60 farmer 44.
GAGER ULYSSES S., r 45, farmer for Peter Settle, also dealer in Champion drills.
Gale Hiram, (Ketchumville) r 9, reformed Methodist minister, and farmer 12.
Gaskill Levi C., r 41, carpenter, and farmer 60.
Gates Norton S., farm laborer, h Bridge.
Gleason George, r 39, farmer.
Gleazen Julia, resident, h Rewey ave.
Gleazen Sabrina, resident, h Rewey ave.
Golden Augustus H., (West Newark) r 22, cooper.
Golden Prentis E., (West Newark) r 22, school trustee, and cooper.
GOODFELLOW HEZEKIAH, r $40\frac{1}{2}$, mason, and farmer 50.
Gould Arthur J., r $15\frac{1}{2}$, farmer 50.
GOULD MELVIN J., r 4, farmer, leases of D. Sturtevant.
Gould Thaddeus, stationary engineer, h Silk.
Gould Warren Mrs., resident, bds. Brook.

TOWN OF NEWARK VALLEY.

Grenell Sherman, r 25, farmer 100.
Griffin Hiram, r 39, farmer 105.
Griffin Irving D., r 39, farmer with his father Hiram.
Griner George Mrs., resident, h Elm.
Griswold Eben, r 41, farmer 25, and 275 in Pennsylvania.
Grummons Truman, sawyer, h Moore.
GUYON CHARLES S., r 23, farmer 70.
Hale Adelbert, (Maine, Broome Co.) 127, farm laborer.
Hale Jerome H., (Connecticut) r 15, farmer, leases of Frank Ashley 100.
Hale Simeon, r 15, farmer with his son Jerome H.
Hall Abner G., r 19, farmer 90.
Hall Polley B., resident, bds. Whig.
Hall Sheridan G., (Jenksville) r 22, constable, also shoemaker, and farmer 35.
HAMMOND ADELBERT C., r 16, carpenter and joiner, also farmer 37.
Hammond Levi B., r 16, farmer 56.
Hammond Melville F., r 6, carpenter and joiner, and farmer 90.
Hancy William B., r 23, farmer on shares with M. Mead 160.
Hand Delmer C., laborer, h Maple ave.
Hardendorf George M., (Ketchumville) r 13, farmer 100.
Hardendorf Henry D., (Ketchumville) r 13, farmer 30.
Harris Emma, r 16, widow John, resident.
Harris Isaac, tailor, h Bridge.
Harris Luther C., r 5, farmer 46.
Harris William H., (Connecticut) r 15, farmer 50.
Harvey Catharine, widow Abel, resident, h East ave.
Harvey Jed, laborer, h East ave.
Harvey Mark, laborer, h Maple.
HAVENS GEORGE, shoemaker, Water, h do.
Henderson Alexander, r 24, farmer 170.
Henderson Irving, r 24, farmer with his father Alexander.
Henry George, emp. tannery, h Main.
Herrick Perlee, r 40, farmer 175.
Hess David, resident, h Maple.
Higbe Charles, retired farmer, h Main.
Hill Chauncey, (Ketchumville) r 11, resident.
Hilligas Charles, (Maine, Broome Co.) r 26, farmer 57.
HILLIGAS LORENZO D., mason and builder, h Maple.
Hinsdale Frank, r 23, farmer 160.
HINSDALE FRANK W., r 23, farmer 130.
Hinsdale James E., r 21, farm laborer.
HOFF ERASTUS, r 19, farmer 165.
Hoff George, retired, h Whig.
Holden Ermina, r 41, teacher.
Holden Harlan P., farm laborer, h Main.
Holden Hiram, r 41, farmer 110.
Holden Laura E., r 5, widow Walter, resident.
Holdrege Ira J., (Ketchumville) r 11, shoemaker.
Holes John, farm laborer, h Moore.
Holladay Anna M., milliner, Water, h do.
Holladay Eli J., egg buyer, h Water.
Holladay Herbert, farmer, h Water.
Holland Vienna, widow Abram, resident, h Main.
Hollenbeck Chester, (Maine, Broome Co.) r 48, farmer 200.

Hollenbeck Harrison, (Maine, Broome Co.) r 48, farmer 60.
Hollenbeck Whitfield, (Maine, Broome Co.) r 29, farmer 100.
Hollister Herbert, r 15½, farmer 56.
Holmes Jerome D., dealer in horses, h Main.
Holmes Rufus, dealer in horses, h Main.
Hooker Charles B., painter and paper-hanger, Whig, h do.
Hooker Frederick, r 15, farmer for Frank G. Bushnell.
Hooker John J., bridge builder, h Maple.
Hooker Mary E., teacher, bds. Whig.
Hopkins George, emp. N. K. Waring, h Whig.
Hooper Peter Q., farm laborer, h Silk.
Hotchkin Mary E., widow Marshal, resident, h Main.
Hover Albert, (West Newark) r 22, farmer 85.
Hover Albertus C., (West Newark) r 22, farmer 25, and leases of W. Watkins 125.
Hover Cornelius, (West Newark) retired.
Hover Hannah, r 20, widow Gilbert, resident.
Hover James, r 20, farm laborer.
Hover Lucinda A., r 38, widow Charles, carpet-weaver.
Hover Marvin L., (West Newark) r 22, carpenter.
Hover Willis E., (West Newark) r 22, postmaster, and farmer 66.
Howard Anderson, marble and granite polisher, h Maple.
Howard Barzillia S., laborer, h Maple ave.
Howard Uriel A., painter, John, h do.
Howard William R., r 21, farmer.
Howland Henry H., (Howland & Hill, Auburn) creamery, h Elm.
Howland Jane E., resident, h Main.
Hulslander John H., r 24, small beer manuf.
Humphrey Cyrus, r 24, farmer, leases of W. Tappan.
Humphrey Edward G., (Jenksville) off r 1, farm laborer.
Humphrey Jacob V., r 24, milk dealer.
HUNT LEWIS, fire and life insurance, Water, h Bridge.
HUTCHINSON HORACE W., hardware, Water, h Whig.
Hyden Charles, (Ketchumville) r 9, farmer 72.
Hyden John, laborer, h Main.
Hyden Henry, retired, h East ave.
Jackson Nelson E., r 16, farmer 50.
Jackson O. Lester, carpenter, h Whig.
Jackson Robert, r 25, farmer, leases of Alfred Roulet 140.
Jackson William H., (Byington & Jackson) h Whig.
Japhet Levi, r 15½, farmer 55.
Japhet Mrs., resident, h Ward.
JAYNE & BALL, (G. F, J. and H. W. B.) meat market and produce dealers, Water.
JAYNE ANNA M., teacher, bds. Whig.
JAYNE GEORGE F., (Jayne & Ball) h Whig.
Jayne Henry F., produce dealer and farmer, h Whig.
Jennings Mary, widow David, resident, bds. Whig.
Johnson Clark H., r 41, farmer 350.
Johnson Jefferson, r 16, farmer 80.
Joslin Almond, (Flemingville) r 61½, lumberman and farmer.
Joslin Daniel, (Flemingville) r 61½, lumberman and farmer 97.

STARKEY & WINTERS, Wholesale and Retail Druggists, Owego.

Joslin Edward A., r 41, farmer.
Joslin Joseph D., r 41, telegraph operator.
Kaley Ira, laborer, h John.
Kattell Erskine, r 35, farm laborer.
Keith Frank R., (Jenksville) r 1, farm laborer.
Keith Lucius A., (Jenksville) r 1, carpenter.
Kelleher Timothy, laborer, h Dam lane.
Kelleher Thomas, hostler, bds. Dam lane.
Kellogg Alva D., r 41, farmer 40.
Kellum Bradford, (Maine, Broome Co.) r 47, farmer 20.
Kellum Frederick, (Main, Broome Co.) r 47, farmer, leases of Freeman Madison 100.
Kennedy Charles, r 25, farmer 90.
Kennedy J. Arthur, laborer, h Watson.
KENNEDY JOSEPH L., r 25, farmer with his father Charles.
Kennedy LaMont, r 25, farmer with his father Charles.
KENYON CHARLES E., r 53, dealer in Wiard plows, farmer 50 and in Owego 100.
Kenyon Edwin, r 23, farmer 18.
Kenyon Frank, r 53, farmer.
Kenyon Lorenzo, r 23, farmer 42.
Kenyon Lydia, r 23, widow Howland, resident.
Kenyon Raymond, r 53, farmer.
Kershaw C. Benjamin, r 41, farmer 73.
Ketchum Seneca, (Ketchumville) r 12, prop. hotel and farmer 80.
Kinney Edward G., school trustee, h Whig.
Knapp Frank J., r 40½, farmer.
Knapp George, off r 41, farmer with his father Gaylord.
Knapp M. Gaylord, off r 41, farmer.
Knapp William T., r 58, farmer 95.
Kniskern E. Ann, widow George, resident, h Moore.
Lainhart Abram, r 46, farmer 96.
Lainhart Arthur, (Maine, Broome Co.) r 50, farmer for his father Aaron 140.
LAINHART ELIAS, r 51, farmer 135.
Lainhart Ephraim, farmer 30, and leases of W. Elwell 150, h Whig.
Lainhart John, (Ketchumville) r 14, farmer 300.
Lamb J. Bruce, (Maine, Broome Co.) r 14, farmer 90.
Lane Jacob, r 15½, farmer 50.
LANDFIELD JEROME B., (Davidge, Landfield & Co.) h Main.
LAWRENCE HORACE F., r 61, farmer 30.
Lawrence Melton, r 15, farmer for W. H. Harris.
LAWRENCE MILES A., r 16, school trustee, also farmer 20.
Lawrence Sarah A., r 61, widow Joel, carpet-weaver.
Lawrence William J., r 15, farmer 100.
Leach Daniel F. Rev., pastor Baptist church, h Whig.
Leach R. Jennette, widow John, resident, h Main.
Legg Melville M., carpenter, h Spring.
Leonard Arthur, farm laborer, bds. Franklin.
Leonard Augustus N., retired, bds. Franklin.
Leonard Grace A., dressmaker, bds. Franklin.
Leonard Herbert, marble-cutter, h Franklin.
Lipe Albert, r 55, farmer, leases of Romaine Bieber 50.

STARKEY & WINTERS, Druggists. Owego. Close Prices to Dealers.

Lipe Austin, r 57, farmer with his father Jacob.
Lipe David, r 58, farmer 45.
Lipe George F., r 57, farmer with his father John W.
LIPE GILBERT, r 57, farmer with his father Jacob.
Lipe Jacob, r 57, farmer 125.
Lipe John W., r 57, farmer 165.
Lipe Lyman, r 42, farm laborer.
Livermore Bert J., clerk, h Main.
Livermore James M., retired farmer, h Main.
Livingston Eugene, r 45, farmer 55.
LOCKWOOD DANIEL, (Ketchumville) r 9, farmer 117.
Loomis Anson, (Maine, Broome Co.) r 50, farmer 79.
LOOMIS GEORGE W., resident, h Bridge.
Loomis Myron L., (Maine, Broome Co.) r 49, farmer, works on shares for his father 50.
Lord John, farm laborer, h East ave.
Loveland Elizabeth H., teacher, bds. Whig.
Loveland Henry B., sugar orchard 500 trees, farmer 115, h Whig.
Loveland William, farmer with his father Henry B., bds. Whig.
Luck Ozias F., r 35, carpenter.
Lull Charlotte Mrs., resident, h Maple.
Lull George T., farm laborer, h Maple ave.
Lynch J. Henry, r 25, farm laborer.
Madan R. Jennie, (Jenksville) r 1, widow Benjamin C., seamstress.
Mahar John, r 25, farmer 150.
Marean Alson J., r 61, farmer 25.
Marean Lucien B., off r 60, resident.
Marinus David, r 21, farmer 82 1-2.
Marshall John, r 26, farm laborer.
Matile Mary L., widow G. August, h Elm.
McCabe William, laborer, h East ave.
McCrady William H., r 25, farmer 78.
McCullough Catharine, r 45, widow William, farm 38.
McCullough Lorenzo D., r 53, farmer 150.
McMahan Patrick, laborer, h Whig.
McPherson George B., r 5, farmer with his father John.
McPherson John, r 5, farmer 225.
McPherson Robert, r 5, retired farmer.
McVean Charles U., (Ketchumville) r 13, farmer 120.
Mead Clyde V., (Jenksville) r 1, farmer with his father Rogers D.
Mead Levi, (Weltonville) r 40, farmer 45.
Mead Lewis J., r 40 1-2, farmer.
Mead Martin, farmer 15, h Moore.
Mead Marvin, r 25, farm laborer.
Mead Nelson C., r 24, farmer 116.
MEAD ROGERS D., (Jenksville) r 1, orchard 400 trees and farmer 400.
Mead William R., r 40, farmer 85.
Meara Margarite, resident, h Elm.
MERRILL LUCINDA B., widow Abel, resident.
Millen Arthur L., (Jenksville) r 1, farmer with his father Elisha.
Millen Elisha, (Jenksville) r 1, farmer 114.
Millen Myron L., (Jenksville) r 1, farmer with his father Elisha.
Miller Daniel H., r 5, carpenter, also farmer 24.

Miller Sarah, widow Robert B., resident, h Main.
Minard Theodore, farmer on shares with Thomas Cary 70, h Main.
Minturn A. Mary, dressmaker, bds Main.
Minturn Amelia F. Mrs., teacher, h Main.
Mix Eugene P., blacksmith, Main, h Franklin.
Monell Wilford, (Ketchumville) r 9, farm laborer.
Monell William F., r 41, farmer 187.
Monigan Barney, emp. tannery, h East ave.
Monigan Patrick C., emp. tannery, bds. East ave.
Moon Levi B., cooper, Spring, h do.
Moon W. Adelbert, stationary engineer, h Elm.
Mooney Kernen, emp. tannery, h East ave.
Moore Frank, r 25½, farmer 100.
Moore Lucy M., r 41, widow David R., resident.
Moore Mary, r 41, resident.
Moore Winnie, (Ketchumville) r 9, farmer 300.
More Cornelia, r 35, resident.
Moseman Naomi J., widow William, h Silk.
Moses Frederick E., miller, bds. Main.
Moses Philander P., prop. Newark Valley custom mill, Main, h do.
Mott William H., r 60, farmer 25.
Munson Nathan J., r 15½, farmer 81.
Murray Thomas D., section foreman S. C. R. R., h Elm.
Muzzy Charles, r 24, farmer 50.
Muzzy Emily, resident, bds. Main.
Muzzy Frank H., r 6, farmer 100.
MUZZY GEORGE B., r 6, surveyor, and farmer 100.
Mynard Benajah, r 18, farmer.
Neal Amy, teacher, bds. Brook.
Neal Harvey, stone mason, h Brook.
Neal Mary, teacher, bds. Brook.
Neal Nettie, teacher, bds. Brook.
Neal Orlie Mrs., dressmaker, h Brook.
Nearing Ira, (Maine, Broome Co.) r 49, farmer 250.
Neff Asel, basket-maker, h East ave.
Neff Stephen, laborer, h Main.
Nicholson Colonel H., (Connecticut) r 15, farmer 40.
Nicholson Grant, r 15, farmer for his father C. H.
Niefer George P., r 46, farmer with his brother John 160.
Niefer John, r 46, farmer with his brother George P. 160.
NIXON CHARLES D., prop. Jenksville steam mills, residence in Owego.
Nixon Ephraim, r 40½, retired.
NIXON GEORGE H., (Jenksville) r 1, sup't Jenksville steam mills.
Nixon Isabella, (Jenksville) r 1, widow William, resident.
Nixon Jane F., (Jenksville) r 1, widow George G., resident.
Nixon John G., (Jenksville) r 1, general store.
*NOBLE & PURPLE, (C. L. N. and G. E. P.) props. Tioga County *Herald*, Water.
NOBLE CHARLES L., (Noble & Purple) h Main.
Noble C. S. Miss, farm, h Main.
Noble David W., farmer 75, h Main.
Noble E. George, farmer 30, h Main.
Noble James T., farmer, h Main.

NOBLE LYMAN B., dealer in eggs and poultry, bds. Main.
Noble Mary L., resident, bds. Main.
Noble Washington A., farmer, h Main.
Nolan Mary, widow John, general housework, h Main.
Nolan Patrick, emp. tannery, h East ave.
Nolton Byron, r 55, farmer 51.
Nolton William, carpenter, h Maple.
North Sarah A., r 24, widow Samuel D., resident.
Nowlan & Abbott, (E. G. N. & G. A.) blacksmiths, Main.
Nowlan Edward G., (Nowlan & Abbott) h Main.
Owen James K., (Ketchumville) r 11, farmer 30.
Owen Wesley, (Ketchumville) r 11, watch and clock repairer.
Pangburn Stephen, r 15 1-2, farmer 56.
Partridge John B., (West Newark) r 22, farmer.
Patrick Leroy, (Maine, Broome Co.) r 49, farmer, leases of Turner estate 150.
Patterson Alfred, off r 39, farmer 100.
PATTERSON D. WILLIAMS, genealogist, h Main.
Payne Ellis, (Maine, Broome Co.) r 47, farmer 50.
Pearl Albertine Mrs., housekeeper, h Main.
Pease George W., (Ketchumville) r 9, farmer, leases of Fred North 20.
Pease Henry F., (Ketchumville) r 12, carpenter.
Pease Morris, (Ketchumville) r 12, farmer.
Pellett George, r 21, farmer 30.
Pellett William M., r 21, farmer 132.
Perry Cephas, (Ketchumville) r 13, farmer 30.
Perry George, stone mason, h Ward.
Phelps Diana, widow Jason, resident, h Main.
Phillips Harriet, widow William, resident, h Moore.
Phillips John M., painter, h Moore.
Phipps George, (Ketchumville) r 12, peddler.
Pier Bradford S., r 46, farm laborer.
Pierce Hiram C., r 16, farmer 25.
PIERSON CHARLES O., harness-maker, Water, h Elm.
Pierson William, r 6, retired farmer.
Pinney Egbert B., traveling salesman, h Silk.
Pitcher Adelbert, (Maine, Broome Co.) r 28, farm laborer.
Pitcher Alfred, r 30, farmer 50.
Pitcher Allie De F., r 35, farmer for his father, Harrison.
Pitcher Eli (Maine, Broome Co.) r 28, farmer 80.
Pitcher Harrison, r 35, farmer 111.
Pitcher James, (Maine, Broome Co.) r 29, farmer, leases of Frank Lewis 50.
Pitcher Nathan, (Maine, Broome Co.) r 29, farm laborer.
Pitcher Silas, (Maine, Broome Co.) r 29, farmer 90.
Pitcher Wesley, off r 35, farmer, leases of David J. Shear 50.
Pollard Ira J., (Ketchumville) r 9, teamster.
PRENTICE ELMER E., r 20, farmer.
PRENTICE ULYSSES G. Jr., r 4, farmer with his father William F.
Prentice William F., r 4, farmer 110.
Prentice William G., emp., William's saw-mill, h Franklin.
PURPLE GILBERT E., (Noble & Purple) h Main.
Quail William, r 8, farm laborer.
Quick Frederick, r 52, farmer.
Race Lucy A., resident, bds. Whig.

Raleigh Orrin, emp. N. K. Waring, h Maple.
RANDALL OSCAR S., general merchant, Water, h do.
Recordon Theodore, r 60, farmer 50.
Reeves William J., r 20, excise commissioner, and farmer 145.
Rewey Emeline, widow Oliver, resident, h Main.
Rice James, laborer, h Main.
Rice John, retired, h Silk.
Rich Marion F., (Connecticut) r 15, farmer, works on shores for William Bushnell 50.
RICHARDSON FRED W., traveling salesman, and farmer 200, h Whig.
Riley Andrew, clerk, h Maple.
Riley Andrew B., carpenter, also dealer in wagons, h Maple.
Riley Kate, widow Michael, laundress, h off East ave.
Riley Maggie, clerk, h Water.
Riley William, (Ketchumville) r 13, blacksmith and farmer 25.
Robbins Clark M., (West Newark) r 22, farm laborer.
Robbins George, traveling hair-dresser, h Maple.
Robbins George E. Mrs., dressmaker, h Maple.
ROBERTS JOHN O., groceries and provisions, and wholesale dealer in butter and eggs, Water, h Elm.
Rockwood Lorenzo F., station agt. S. C. R. R., also agt. U. S. express, and telegraph operator, h East ave.
ROGERS CORNELIUS R., physician and surgeon, Main, h do.
Rogers Edward, (Maine, Broom Co.) r 47, farmer 16.
Ross John, (Maine, Broome Co.) r 27, farmer 50.
Roulet Alfred, farmer 140.
Roulet Felix, traveling salesman, h Elm.
ROYS ALPHEUS D., (Roys & Todd) h Main.
ROYS & TODD, (A. D. R. & Mrs. P. E. T.) general merchants, Main.
Russell Henry, (Main, Broome Co.) r 14, farmer 93.
Ryan Mary, widow Michael, bds. Brook.
Ryan William, principal school, h Main.
Saddlemire Alexander, r 26, farmer 80.
Saddlemire Anna E., r 30, widow David, resident.
Saddlemire Daniel J., r 31, carpenter, and farmer 25.
Saddlemire Elias, r 41, farmer.
Saddlemire Emily Mrs., r 26, farm 40.
Saddlemire Ephraim, (Main, Broome Co.) r 29, farmer 61,
Saddlemire Fenton R., r 31, farmer with his father, Noyes P.
Saddlemire Frank, r 57, farmer 60.
Saddlemire Jacob H., r 25, egg buyer, and farmer 78.
Saddlemire Jerome, r 43, farmer 111.
Saddlemire Manfred, r 26, farmer for his mother, Mrs. Emily Saddlemire.
Saddlemire Noyes P., r 31, farmer 188.
Salisbury William H., (Weltonville) r 40, farmer on shares with J. W. Barrett.
SANDWICK JOHN K., barber, water, h Whig.
Schnapp Jacob, Jr., r 53, farmer 25.
Schoolcraft Hattie E., r 42, widow Lucius, resident.
Schoolcraft John, laborer, h East ave.
Schoolcraft John D., r 35, farmer 19.
Schoolcraft Minor, r 42, farm laborer.
Schoolcraft Paul, r 35, resident.
Schoolcroft Abagail, r 45, widow David, resident.

TOWN OF NEWARK VALLEY.

Schoolcroft Adam, (Maine, Broome Co.) r 29, farmer 102.
Schoolcroft Earnest, r 26, farmer, leases of D. Pitcher estate 200.
Schoolcroft Henry, r 34, farmer 40.
Searles Ezra, r 61, mason and farmer 50.
Searles Jack E., r 41, painter.
Sears Lizzie M., dressmaker, Elm, bds. do.
Sears Sophronia M. Mrs., resident, h Elm.
Sebastian Christina, r 53, widow G. O., resident.
Settel Deidamia, r 46, widow John, resident.
Settel Oscar, r 46, farmer 300.
Settell David, retired, h White.
Settell Elmer E., r 32, farmer with his father, Ira D.
Settell George, r 51, farmer 90.
Settell Ira D., r 32, farmer 177.
SETTLE PETER, r 45, farmer 105.
Shafer Egbert, r 41, farm laborer.
Shaffer Charles E., r 25, farmer 50.
Sharp Osmer, (Ketchumville) r 9, farm laborer.
Sharp Robert B., (Ketchumville), r 11, blacksmith and farmer 152.
Shaw Laura M., widow Joel, h Main.
Shaw Philander M., farmer 62, h Main.
Shay James, laborer, h Maple ave.
Shear David J., resident, h Elm.
Shear John I., r 35, farmer 64.
Sheldon Harley G., retired farmer, h Main.
Sherman Hiram L., carpenter, h Maple.
Sherman Peter, (Ketchumville) r 13, farmer.
SHERWOOD GEORGE F., supt. Davidge & Landfield's tannery, h Maple.
Sherwood Warren D., sewing machines, h Main.
Shoultes Chauncey, r 53, farm laborer.
Shoultes Edward W., r 32, farmer with his father, William H.
Shoultes Frederick, r 53, farmer 95.
Shoultes George, r 53, farmer 50.
Shoultes Ira., off r 53, farmer 100.
Shoultes Ira A., r 35, farm laborer.
Shoultes William H., r 32, farmer 75.
Shulenburg Wallace H., r 41, farm laborer.
Simmons Joseph, retired, h Elm.
SLOSSON GEORGE W., justice of the peace, h Maple.
SMITH ALFRED, (Jenksville) r 51, horse-breeder and farmer 120; farm for sale.
Smith Benjamin F., resident, h Main.
SMITH EDWIN P., farmer, h Main.
Smith Elijah, (Maine, Broome Co.) r 27, farmer, works on shares for Frank Lewis 315.
Smith Harvey B., resident, h Brook.
Smith Jabez C., farmer, leases of E. P. Smith 70.
SMITH JOEL E., r 41, farmer 25.
SMITH JOHN E., r 40½, excise com. and farmer 100.
Smith John S., resident, h Bridge.
SMITH L. M. & SON, (Lewis H.) drugs and wall-paper, 5 Water.
SMITH LEWIS H., (L. M. Smith & Son) h Water.
SMITH LUCIUS M., (L. M. Smith & Son) h Water.

Smith Randolph L., r 40 1-2, farmer 58.
Smith William H., r 5, farmer 45.
Smullen Charles M., (Jenksville) r 1, blacksmith.
Snapp Edward E., r 53, farmer 106.
Snapp Emeline, r 53, widow George, resident.
SNAPP FRANK, r 53, farmer 90.
Snapp Henry O., r 15, farmer 75.
Spaulding Lucius W., r 41, farmer 160.
Spaulding Luther J., retired, h Main.
Spaulding Marcus M., retired, h Main.
Sprague Almander, retired, h Main.
Sprague Henry A., resident, h Main.
Sprague Lewis H., resident, h Main.
Stannard Aretus R., emp. Donley Brothers, h Brook.
Stannard Henry, r 26 1-2, farmer 100.
Stannard Hiram R., bakery, Water, h do.
Stannard John M., r 25, farmer 104.
Stevens Aaron C., r 41, millwright and turner.
Stevens Elvira Mrs., r 42, resident.
STEVENS HENRY W., r 42, apiarist, small fruit grower and poultry.
Stevens William W., r 41, farmer 23.
Stever Fred A., painter, h Whig.
Stinard Jane H., r 4, widow James D., resident.
Stowell Alexander D., r 16, farmer 18.
Strait Edward, r 19, farmer, leases of J. R. Johnson 63.
Strait Joseph, (Connecticut) r 8, lumberman and shingleman.
Strong Fanny C., (Jenksville) r 1, widow Isaac B., resident.
Strong Fred W., (Jenksville) r 1, farmer, leases of J. Evans 10.
Strong Orin, (Jenksville) r 1, farmer 200.
Sturtevant David M., carriage painter, Brook, h Whig.
Sutphen Horace, (Jenksville) r 1, supt. Nixon farm.
SUTTON GEORGE B., r 41, artist and farmer 100.
Sweet Charles E., (Ketchumville) r 13, blacksmith.
Sweigler Robert, r 58, farmer 45.
TAPPAN CHARLES, small fruit grower and farmer, bds. Whig.
Tappan John C., farm laborer, h Whig cor. Moore.
Tappan Rebecca A., widow Asher C., resident, Whig cor. Moore.
Tappan Revere C., physician and surgeon, Main, h do.
Tappan Riley A., farmer 150.
THORNTON C. FRANK, stone mason and prop. of quarry, East ave.
Thornton Chauncey G., resident, h Franklin.
Thornton George, r 16, farm laborer.
Thornton Mary E., laundress, h Franklin.
TIBBITTS ELI D., retired farmer, Main.
TIDD JOHN, r 41, retired.
*TIOGA COUNTY HERALD, (Noble & Purple) weekly, issued Saturday, Water.
TODD FRANK H., clerk, h Main.
TODD PHEBE E., (Roys & Todd) h Main.
Tompkins George, (Ketchumville) r 10, farmer.
Towner Lucy M., r 4, widow Milo B., resident.
Treible Wilson Rev., pastor M. E. church, h Main.
Tripp Emma, (Maine, Broome Co.) r 47, widow Frank, resident.

TOWN OF NEWARK VALLEY.

Turner Charles, (Maine, Broome Co.) r 49, farmer 113.
Turner Leroy, (Maine, Broome Co.) r 49, farmer 400.
VanDemark John, (Weltonville) r 40, farmer 62.
VanDemark Lucius, r 16, farm laborer.
VanGlowe Abram, (Jenksville) off r 1, farm laborer.
VanPatten Richard H., farmer 40, h East ave.
Wade Edgar O., r 41, farmer with his father William H.
Wade William H., r 41, farmer 86.
Waldo Betsey C., resident, h Main.
Waldo William D., r 6, farmer 46.
Walter Charles, off r 41, farmer 63.
Walter Clarence S., r 41, carpenter and joiner.
Walter Eugene C., r 39, farmer 30.
Walworth Clark, r 23, farmer 140.
Walworth LaVern, r 4, farmer 96.
Walworth William, r 23, farmer with his father Clark.
Waring Norman K., manuf. fly-rods, Spring, h do.
Warner Frank, (Connecticut) r 9, emp. lumber-mill.
Warner William, (Connecticut) r 9, emp. lumber-mill.
Washburn Stoddard, farm laborer, h Maple ave.
Waterman Charles H., r 5, farmer, leases of A. C. Matthews 128.
Watkins William, (West Newark) r 22, farmer.
Watrous Frank, r 15, farmer 185.
Watson Abbie J., widow Seth, bds. Whig.
Wells Henry L., book-keeper for Davidge, Landfield & Co., h Main.
Wells Jane B., widow Frederick, farm 130, h Main.
WELLS LUCIUS E., (Burch & Wells) h Main.
Wells William F., farmer with his mother Jane B., bds. Main.
Westfall E. Frank, r 55, farm laborer.
Westfall Frank, r 56, farmer 15.
Westfall Frederick W., r 16, farmer with his father Joseph F.
Westfall Joseph F., r 16, farmer 100.
White George W., (Jenksville) custom grist and saw-mill.
WHITING BROS., (J. E. and W. V. B.) wagon and carriage makers, repairing done with neatness and dispatch, Brook.
WHITING WARREN V. B., (Whiting Bros.) h Main.
WHITING JERRY E., (Whiting Bros.) h Main.
Whitmore Horace L., leather finisher, h Whig.
Whitmore Martha, widow Hezekiah, resident, h Whig.
Williams Edson, r 41, farmer, leases, of James Reed 100.
Williams Lucius E., saw, planing and feed-mill, and dealer in coal and lumber, off Main, h Rewey ave.
Williams Margaret, widow Almeran, bds. off Bridge.
Williams Oliver G., laborer, h Maple.
Williams Royal R., farmer 85, h off Bridge.
Williams Theodore, carpenter, h Elm.
Willis Henry, (Maine, Broome Co.) r 47, farm laborer.
Willis Horace B., (Maine, Broome Co.) r 47, farmer 43.
Wilson Elnora, widow Charles F., resident, h Main.
Winship Charles B., boarding-house, Maple.
Winship Henry, retired, h Main.
WOOD HENRY A., billiard room and shoemaker, Water, h do.

STARKEY & WINTERS, Wholesale and Retail Druggists, Owego.

Wood Joseph, retired, h Rewey ave.
Woodard Andrew J., laborer, bds. Maple.
Wright Malborn W., resident, h Main.
Wright Sarah, widow Giles, resident, h Main.
YOUNG HIRAM, (Dimmick & Young) bds. Dimmick House.
Young John, r 51, farmer 96.
Young Wilson, r 51, farmer with his father John.
Zimmer Addie Mrs., nurse, h Whig.
Zimmer Asa W., r 45, farmer with his father Elias.
Zimmer Charles, r 31, farmer.
Zimmer Charles W., r 45, farmer with his father Elias.
Zimmer Daniel, r 53, farmer 70.
Zimmer Delmar, r 43, farmer with his father Seymour E.
Zimmer Edgar, (West Newark) r 22, farm laborer.
Zimmer Edward, r 45, farmer with his father Seymour E.
Zimmer Edward, r 46, farmer 85.
Zimmer Elias, r 45, farmer 180.
Zimmer Eva M., teacher, bds. Whig.
Zimmer Henry S., r 35, farmer 65.
Zimmer Jacob, r 26, farmer 20.
Zimmer Lyman, r 26, farmer 125,
Zimmer Manier, (Maine, Broome Co.) r 29, farmer 93.
Zimmer Miner S., r 34, farmer 54.
Zimmer Nathaniel, (Maine, Broome Co.) r 47, farmer 96.
Zimmer Peter A., r 40 1-2, farmer 115.
Zimmer Peter B., r 30, farmer 200.
Zimmer Ransom J., r 30, farmer 128.
Zimmer Seymour E., r 45, farmer 112.
Zimmer Sherman, r 45, farmer with his father Seymour E.
Zimmer Wesley, r 45, farmer with his father Elias.

NICHOLS.

(*For explanations, etc., see page 3, part second.*)

(Postoffice address is Nichols, unless otherwise designated in parenthesis.)

Adams Eliza S., (Hooper's Valley) r 5, resident.
Adams Maria, widow Absalom, resident.
ADAMS STEPHEN B.(Hooper's Valley) r 5, McCormick Harvesting Machine Company's agt. for Tioga County, and farmer 140.
Alen Clarence B., (Owego) r 20, farm laborer.
Allen John, (Owego) r 10, farm laborer.
Allen Robert A., laborer, h Main.
Allington Emily J., (Hooper's Valley) r 1, resident.
Allington Sarah A., (Hooper's Valley) r 3, widow Rev. Jacob, farm 34.
Ames Lloyd H., (Owego) r 21, stationary engineer.

STARKEY & WINTERS, promptly fill Mail and Telephone Orders.

TOWN OF NICHOLS.

Ames Orley L. Mrs., laundress, h River.
Anderson H. Beecher, hostler, bds. Main.
Angell Benjamin P., retired, h Main.
Angell Charles D., (Hooper's Valley) r 1, farmer, leases of Pearsall & Gray 250.
Annable Lovisa, r 40, widow, resident.
ANTHONY FLOYD H., groceries and provisions and livery, Main, h do.
Atwood Harrison, r 10, farm laborer.
BABCOCK WILLARD, farmer, h Railroad.
Babcock William, laborer, h Main.
Baird Frances C., resident, bds. River.
BAKER BROTHERS, (W. W. and R. B.) props. Nichols creamery.
Baker Frank B., emp. creamery, bds. Cady ave.
BAKER ROBERT B., (Baker Bros.) h Cady ave.
BAKER WILLIAM W., (Baker Bros.) h Cady ave.
Barnes George W., (Hooper's Valley) off r 5, farm laborer.
Barr George, r 30, farm laborer.
Barr John, r, 30, farmer 150.
Barr John, Jr., r 2, farmer.
Barr Lawrence, r 30, farm laborer.
BARSTOW MARY L., resident, bds. River.
Barstow Oliver A., (Hooper's Valley) r 5, retired.
BAXTER FREDERICK H., r 26, farmer.
Baxter George T., off r 26, farmer, leases 200.
Beach Ernest C., miller, bds. Main.
Bennett Abraham, (Hooper's Valley) r 5, resident.
Bennett Elizabeth, r 26, widow Elijah, farm 25.
Bensley Fred, (Hooper's Valley) r 1, farmer.
BENSLEY JOHN, (Hooper's Valley) r 1, school trustee and farmer 200.
Bensley John C., (Hooper's Valley) r 1, farmer.
Bixby Charles R., carpenter and builder, h Cady ave.
Bixby Chester, carpenter, h Main.
Bixby George W., r 37, farmer.
Bixby Schuyler, r 37, farmer on shares with Jos. Reynolds 130.
BIXBY SMITH R., contractor and builder, h River.
Blair Linus, r 23, farm laborer.
Bliven Cranston, member of school board; also, dealer in produce and general merchandise, Main, h River.
Bliven Cranston V. S., retired, bds. River.
Boardman Elizabeth P., r 10, widow Edward, resident.
Bonham Jonas, retired, h Cady ave.
Booth Franklin, (Hooper's Valley) off r 5, farmer.
Boyce David M., laborer, h River.
Bradley Hiram, (Tioga Centre) r 10, farmer on shares with C. Lounsberry.
Bradley Marcus, farmer on shares with Warren A. Smith 60, h River.
Briggs Ebenezer, (E. Nichols) r 39, farmer 56.
Briggs Edward W., (E. Nichols) r 22, farmer 91½.
Briggs Elihu, (E. Nichols) r 22, farmer 94.
Brigg Herman I., off r 9, stock dealer and farmer 87½.
Briggs Ira, r 39, farmer 75.
Briggs Julius, (E. Nichols), r 46, farmer.
Briggs Melvin, (E. Nichols) r 40, apiarist and farmer.
Brott David, (Owego) r 21, farmer.
Brougham John W., emp. Harris, DeGroat & Co., h Main.

Brown Elizabeth, off r 2, widow Peter, resident.
Brown Fanny, widow, h Main.
Brown George, retired, h Oxford.
Brown James M., r 8, carpenter.
Brown John W., r 1, farmer 6.
BROWN S. OTIS, off r 2, farmer 114.
Burrell Isaac, farm laborer, h River.
Burrell Lott S., laborer, bds. River.
Butolph Frank E., r 9, farmer 76.
Butolph Leroy, r 37, farmer 115.
Butolph Sybil, r 48, farm 35.
Cady George M., (Latham & Cady) also physician and surgeon, bds. River.
CADY GEORGE P., physician and surgeon, River, h do.
Cady William, retired, bds. Cady ave. (Died July 2, 1887.)
Campbell Amos B., (Owego) r 42, cooper and farmer on shares with Charles Dunham 80.
Campbell George W., (Hooper's Valley) r 5, laborer.
Campbell Smith, r 9, farmer 31.
Campion Frank, r 12, teacher and farmer.
Carpenter Allen O., farm laborer, h Cady ave.
Carter Alexander, (East Nichols) r 47, farm laborer.
Childs Marcus W., principal of the Union School.
Chubbuck Francis Rev., (Hooper's Valley) r 1, retired M. E. clergyman and small fruit grower.
CLAIR HIRAM, (Hooper's Valley) r 3, farmer 253.
Clair William H., (Hooper's Valley) r 3, farmer with his father Hiram.
CLAPP SAMUEL, lumber dealer and farmer 60, bds. River.
Clarke Howard W., traveling salesman, h Cady ave.
Cogswell Henry S., (East Nichols) r 47, farmer, leases of G. Newman 50.
COLE HORACE, r 3, farmer.
Cole Truman, 27, farmer 114.
Coleman & Horton, (E. C. & G. H. H.) hardware, stoves and tinware, Main.
Coleman Emmet, (Coleman & Horton) also postmaster, bds. Nichols House.
Conant Edward H., painter, h River.
Conant Luther, boots and shoes, Main, h River.
Cortright Charles F., r 37, laborer.
Cortright Elijah, r 24, cooper.
Cortright John, (Tioga Center) r 10, laborer.
Coryell Arthur, (Hooper's Valley) r 4, farm laborer.
Coryell Augusta, widow Henry P., resident, h Cady Block.
Coryell Emanuel, (Hooper's Valley) r 4, farmer 65.
Coryell Emanuel, Jr., (Hooper's Valley) r 4, farm laborer.
Coryell Mary, teacher, bds. Cady Block.
CORYELL ROBERT P., r 1, school trustee and farmer 250.
Crandall Charles, r 10, farmer on shares with I. Dunham.
CRANDALL GEORGE E., (Tioga Center) r 10, farmer.
Crandall William, r 10, basket-maker.
Cure Andrew J., r 10, farmer.
Curkendoll William, r 10, carpenter and small fruit grower.
Davenport Abraham, r 30, farm laborer.
Davenport Amelia Mrs., (Hooper's Valley) r 2, farm 30.
Davenport Charlotte D., r 30, farm 25.
Davenport Ellen, (Hooper's Valley) farm 30.

Davenport Ira, (Hooper's Valley) r 2, farmer.
Davenport Joseph, r 2, farmer.
DEAN JULIA A., (Hooper's Valley) r 3, farm 34.
DEAN NATHAN S., r 1, apiarist 30 swarms, fruit grower, and farmer 60.
De Bolder Lawrence, r 24, farmer 42.
De Bolder William E., stationary engineer, h Walnut.
De Groat J. Fields, (Harris, De Groat & Co.) h Main.
De Groat William, (Owego) r 16, blacksmith.
Derring Herman, r 9, laborer.
Doty Charles H., laborer, bds. Cady ave.
Doty George W., retired, h Cady ave.
Drake C. Sidney, clerk, bds. Nichols Hotel.
Duncan James (E. Nicholas), r 40, farm laborer.
Dunham Benjamin, (Owego) r 36, carpener, and farmer 74.
Dunham Charles, (Owego) r 32, farmer 100.
Dunham Charles, r 49½, farmer with his father Samuel.
Dunham Charles L., r 10, farmer.
DUNHAM EBENEZER, produce dealer, Main, h do.
Dunham Elemer E., (Owego), r 35, farm laborer.
Dunham Frances J., (Owego), r 36, teacher.
Dunham Harriet P., (Owego) r 33, widow Anson, resident.
Dunham Harvey W., r 10, farmer 135.
Dunham Isaac, r 10, farmer 300, and in Penn. 100.
Dunham James, (Owego) r 17, farmer, leases of John Smith 100.
Dunham Joseph M. r 10, farmer.
Dunham Mary E., resident, h Main.
Dunham Melissa S. Miss, (Owego) r 16, resident.
Dunham Nehemiah, (Owego) r 35, farmer 50.
Dunham Platt, (Owego) r 32, farmer 50.
Dunham Platt Jr., (Owego), r 42, farmer 114.
Dunham Samuel, (Owego) r 32, farmer.
Dunham Samuel, r 49 1-2, farmer 71.
Dunham Sands, r 23, farmer.
Dunham Stephen H., r 10, farmer 135.
Edsall Benjamin F., carpenter, h Howell.
Edsall Brice P., retired, h Walnut.
Edsall Ida O., widow David, resident, bds. River.
EDSALL JOHN R., town clerk, also general merchant and dealer in agricultural implements, Main, bds. Walnut.
Edwards Ann E., (Hooper's Valley) r 5, widow Albertus, resident.
Edwards Cyrus, (Hooper's Valley) r 5, farm laborer.
Ellis George, r 29, farmer.
Ellis George, Jr., (Hooper's Valley) r 5, carpenter and ferryman.
Ellis Hiram, (Hooper's Valley) r 28, farmer on shares with S. Kirby estate 67.
Ellis John, (Waverly) r 30, farmer 15.
Ellsworth Aurelia, widow Francis H., resident, h River.
Ellsworth Elwin F., painter and paper-hanger, bds. River.
Ellsworth Henry N., carpenter, also farmer 31, h Cole.
Elsbree Emily C., widow Manning, resident, h head of Main.
Evans Amanda C., (Tioga Centre) r 22, widow Cyrus G., farm 52.
Evans Cyrus, (Tiga Center) r 13, farmer 50.
Evans Edward E., well driver, also agt. for wind-mils, h Walnut.
Evans Elijah K., r 8, contractor and builder, and farmer 20.

Everitt Elmore, r 8, supervisor, and farmer 38.
Everitt Frederick M., tinsmith, h Main.
Everitt George E., farmer, h Main.
Everitt Harvey C., farmer 50, h Main.
Everitt Hovey E., drug clerk, bds. r 8.
Everson George T., (Owego) r 17, farm laborer.
Everson Oliver C., (Owego) r 17, farm laborer.
FARNHAM OSCAR E., r 49½, patentee egg preserving rack, also prop. wood turning shop, and cidar-mill, and farmer 4½.
FENDERSON JOHN, prop. Nichols steam flour, saw and planing-mills, h River.
Ferris Horace, (Owego) r 17, farmer 50.
Field Lucas T., (Hooper's Valley) r 5, postmaster.
Ford George, r 9, farmer.
FORMAN JOHN, r 10, member of school board, excise commissioner, small fruit grower, and farmer 200.
Forman Miles, resident, h Main.
Forman Smith, r 10, farmer with his father John.
Fox Alfred J., farmer.
Fox Harry, r 26, retired.
Fox Isaac D., farmer 25, on shares with F. C. Lowman.
Goetchins Maurice L., r 1, farmer.
Goodenough Delos, boots and shoes, Main, h do.
Goodsell William S., (Athens, Pa.) r 1, farmer 50, and leases of H. Kiff 70.
Goodsell Zina, r 26, farmer 50.
Granger Daniel, (Owego) r 20, farmer 36.
Granger George M., (Owego) r 17, farmer 25.
Greene Joseph G., (Owego) r 19, farmer on shares with S. Evans.
Griswold Martha, (Waverly) r 1, widow Henry, farmer 25.
Griswold Thoms, (Waverly) r 1, farmer 50.
Hamel Charles E., (Owego) r 18, watch repairer.
Hamel Clark, (Owego) r 18, gardener.
Harden Ida Mrs., dressmaker, off Main.
Harden Samuel W., farmer 26, h off Main.
Harris, DeGroat & Co., (O. P. H., J. F. DeG. and R. C. H.) wholesale dealers and shippers of hay, grain, potatoes and general farm products, Main.
Harris Elizabeth D., widow Nathaniel B., resident, h Main.
Harris Oliver P., (Harris, DeGroat & Co.) Main.
Harris R. Corsa, (Harris, DeGroat & Co.) h Main.
HAUVER GEORGE L., (Owego) r 16, farmer, leases of J. Hunt estate 90.
Hazard Lois, r 10, widow Dwight, resident.
Hazard Willis W., r 8, farm laborer.
Herrick Henry B., (Waverly) r 30, farmer 6¼.
HERRICK WILLIAM, r 1, apiariast 11 swarms, assessor, and farmer on shares with Julia A. Dean 31.
Hill Abner, r 10, farm laborer.
Hill Morris M., (Hooper's Valley) r 3, farmer.
Hilligass David, (Hooper's Valley) r 4, district collector, and farmer 27.
Hilligass Jacob, r 49, farmer.
Hoover William, (Hooper's Valley) r 5, retired.
Horton Betsey, widow Stephen S., h River.
Horton G. Henry, (Coleman & Horton) also farmer 300, h River.
Howell Arthur M., r 49½, farmer.

TOWN OF NICHOLS.

Howell John J., r 8, resident.
Howell John L., retired, h Main.
HOWELL ROBERT, r 49½, geologist, mineralogist, and farmer 127, and in Pennsylvania 20.
HUNT ADONIJAH, (Owego) r 37, prop. saw and grist-mill, and farmer 140.
Hunt Brothers, (Enos and Seth) r 10, farmers 60.
Hunt Charles E., clerk, bds. Main.
Hunt Ebenezer, r 10, farmer 53.
HUNT ELIZABETH, (Owego) r 36, farm 194.
HUNT EZRA C., (Owego) r 21, farmer 110.
Hunt George B., (Owego) r 17, farmer with his father Thomas J.
Hunt John W., (Waverly) r 1, farmer 160.
Hunt Julia S., (Owego) r 17, widow Jonathan, 2d, farm 40.
HUNT MARCELLA, (Owego) r 36, farm 194.
HUNT SAMUEL, (Waverly) r 1, farmer 155.
HUNT SISTERS, (Owego) (E. and M. Hunt) r 36, farmer 194.
Hunt Thomas J., (Owego) r 17, farmer 188.
Hunt Timothy, (Owego) r 13, farmer.
HUNT WILLISTON, r 10, farmer 115.
Hyres Frances, widow Jerry W., resident, h Main.
INGERSOLL GEORGE A., r 10, member of school board, also stock breeder, and farmer 103.
Jansen Abram, (Owego) r 33, retired.
Johnson Charles H., r 23, farmer 47.
Johnson Eliza J., r 10, widow Parley, resident.
Johnson John A., r 23, farmer.
Johnson John E., r 10, farmer 40.
Jones Charles M., laborer, h Railroad.
Jones Eveline, r 49, resident.
Jones Lewis, r 39, road commissioner and farmer 100.
JOSLIN EDWARD, dry and fancy goods, millinery and wall-paper, Main, h do.
Joslyn Louisa, (Owego) r 21, widow Peter, resident.
Kane Michael, laborer, h Cady ave.
Keech Miles W., r 46, mason, carpenter and farmer.
KEECH T. WILBER, r 39, farmer, leases of his mother Laura 50.
Kelso Harry, r 38, cigar-maker.
Kennedy John M., telegraph operator, bds. Main.
Kent Pulaski P., (Owego) r 17, farm laborer.
KETCHAM ELI G., (Owego) r 35, justice of the peace, school trustee and farmer 226.
Ketcham William, butcher, Main, h Walnut.
KIRBY ALLEN B., agent D. L. & W. R. R., also, U. S. express agent, Main cor. Life.
Lane David J., (Owego) r 17, apairist and farmer.
Lane Fred H., (Owego) r 17, teacher.
Lane George S., (Tioga Centre) r 13, farmer 127.
Lane Harvey P., (Tioga Centre) r 13, farmer.
Lane Lucinda, (Owego) r 16, widow Amos, farm 46.
Lane Warren A., (Owego) r 17, school trustee and farmer 47.
Laning Charles P., carpenter, h Howell.
LaRue Isaac L., prop. hotel, Main.

STARKEY & WINTERS, Wholesale and Retail Druggists, Owego.

TOWN OF NICHOLS. 101

Latham & Cady (S. H. L. and G. M. C.) druggists, toilet articles and confectionary, Main cor. River.
Latham Sidney H., (Latham & Cady) h Main.
Lisenby Charles F., r 8, farmer on shares with E. Dunham 240.
Lisenby John, r 1, farm laborer.
Lollis William, r 16, nurse.
Losaw Daniel, r 25, farmer.
Lounsberry Benjamin, (Owego) r 17, farmer 138.
Lounsberry Frederick, (Owego) r 21, farmer.
Lounsberry George, (Tioga Centre) r 11, farmer 100.
Lounsberry George F., (Tioga Centre) r 11, farmer 62.
LOUNSBERRY HARRIET E., (Tioga Centre) r 10, farm 50.
Lounsberry Harriet E., (Tioga Centre) r 10, widow James, farm 60.
Lounsberry Horace, (Tioga Centre) r 13, farmer 241.
Lounsberry Horace, Second, (Owego) r 21, farmer 70, and with Horace Lounsberry, First 241.
Lounsberry James, (Tioga Centre) r 22, farmer 113.
Lounsberry John, (Owego) r 21, saw-mill and farmer 159.
Lounsberry Platt, (Tioga Centre) r 10, retired farmer 28.
LOUNSBURY WILLIAM R., r 12, excise commissioner and farmer 64.
Loveland Mary A., widow Lewis, laundress, h Main.
Loveland Seth H., (Waverly) r 1, saw-mill and carpenter.
LOWMAN FREDERIC C., r 3, breeder of thoroughbred short-horn cattle and farmer 525; stock for sale at all times.
Lunn William H., r 8, farm laborer.
Lurcock Adelbert, r 3, farm laborer.
Lurcock Frederick, (Tioga Centre) r 12, farmer.
Lurcock William, emp. De Groat, Harris & Co., h Main.
Lynch William, r 9, laborer.
Mallory Frederick O., (Owego) r 32, farmer, leases of J. Smith, Jr., 50.
Mallory John L., (Owego), r 23, local preacher, carpenter, and farmer 35.
Mallory Susan, widow Harrison, resident, bds. Cady ave.
Mallory William W., barber, Main, h Cady ave.
MARSHALL TIMOTHY B., r 49, town collector, and farmer 50.
Mason Fritz, gardener, h Main.
Matthews Hiram P., r 38, apiarist 25 swarms, small fruit grower, and farmer 113.
MATTHEWS ISAIAH, r 38, cigar manufacturer, and prop. cider-mill.
MATTHEWS STEPHEN P., (Owego) off r 32, retired physician, and farmer 40.
Matthews Susie, widow Ephraim, art teacher, h Cady Block.
McNeil George K., constable and collector, h Main.
Measer Ernest H., r 30, farmer 70.
Merrill Albert S., carpenter and builder, h Howell.
Mettler James L., (Waterman & Mettler) h Cady ave.
Mikels George H., laborer, h Howell.
Mikels J. Henry, r 12, farm laborer.
Miller Edmund S., blacksmith, Main, h Oxford.
Miller James, off r 23, farmer.
Miller William, off r 23, farmer.
Mills Delavan, r 39, farmer 90.
Mills Francis, r 37, school trustee, and farmer 140.

STARKEY & WINTERS, Druggists, Owego. Close Prices to Dealers.

MITCHELL IDA A., art teacher, h Cady ave.
MITCHELL MARY J., art teacher, h Cady ave.
Mitchell Sally C., widow Nathan, resident, h Cady ave.
Mollet Betsey, (Owego) r 19, widow Peter, farm 70.
Moody George, r 26, farm laborer.
Moody George H., r 26, farmer 45.
Moore Edwin T., (Owego) r 22, building mover, and farmer 114.
Moore Frank H., (Owego) r 36, farmer.
Moore George, r 37, farmer 260.
Moore Ruth A., (Owego) r 36, widow Hezelton N., resident.
Morey Robert, off r 9, farmer.
Morse Frank J., R. R. section hand, bds. Main.
Mosher Edwin, carpenter, h Main.
Moulton Morris B., farmer 12, and 160 in Penn., h Main.
Neal Henry C., off r 2, farmer 52.
Neal Linus, r 23, farmer.
Neal Nehemiah E., furniture dealer and carriage painter, Cady ave., h do.
Newland Samuel, (Owego) r 18, carpenter.
Newman George, (East Nichols) r 47, farmer 200.
NICHOLS HOTEL, J. Platt, prop., River.
Nichols James, (East Nichols) r 44, farmer.
Nichols John E., (East Nichols) prop. threshing machine and farm laborer.
Northrop Charles T., (East Nichols) r 44, farmer 25.
Olmstead Joseph, ferryman, h Ferry.
Orsburn Charles, (Hooper's Valley) r 1, farmer.
Orsburn Miers, (Hooper's Valley) r 1, farmer 240.
Orsburn Miles, (Hooper's Valley) r 1, farmer.
Osburn William, retired, h Cady ave.
Paris Peter, r 10, farmer on shares with Ebenezer Hunt 53.
PARK JOSEPH, (Waverly) r 1, farmer 162.
Pearl Eunice, (East Nichols) r 35, widow Daniel, farm 103.
Pearl Fred G., (Owego) r 35, farmer 50.
Pearl Walter H., (Owego) r 17, farmer 25.
PEARSALL L. BURR, (Hooper's Valley) r 5, prop. steam saw-mill and farmer 386, and in Penn. 300.
Peck William C. Rev., (Hooper's Valley) r 3, Free Baptist, retired.
Peet Henry, (Owego) r 19, farm laborer.
Pendleton Caleb F., foreman Nichols creamery, bds. Cady ave.
PETTY FOSTER, (Hooper's Valley) r 1, farmer.
Pitcher Eliza, widow John, resident, h River.
Pitcher Elvira, (Owego) r 18, widow Heman, farm 125.
Pitcher John, (Hooper's Valley) r 5, farm laborer.
Pitcher William A., emp. creamery, bds. River.
Platt Frank, clerk Nichols Hotel, River.
PLATT JOHN, prop. Nichols Hotel, Main.
Presher Benjamin, (Tioga Center) r 21, farm laborer.
Quilty Michael, r 8, farmer 50.
Ratchford John, miller, bds. Main.
Reed Adeline, (Owego) r 17, widow Ezra, farm 70.
Reeves Ella, widow George, dressmaker, h River.
Reynolds Albert S., r 39, farmer 50.
Reynolds Amanda, r 9, widow Vincent, resident.
Reynolds Enoch J., r 8, farmer on shares with A. Waterman 80.

REYNOLDS ISUM I., r 48, farmer 80, and leases of Miss S. Butolph 35.
Reynolds John E., r 9, farmer 170.
REYNOLDS JOHN S., r 8, member of school board, and farmer 160.
Reynolds Joseph, r 37, retired farmer.
Reynolds Lester, farm laborer, h Main.
Richardson Ester A. Mrs., (Owego) r 32, resident.
Robertson Albert, (Owego) r 13, farmer 72.
Robertson Charles T., (Owego) r 13, farmer.
Robinson William O., traveling salesman, h Main.
Rogers John H., (Hooper's Valley) r 2, farmer.
Rogers Lorenzo, drayman, h River.
Roper Frank H., (Owego) r 18, milk dealer, and farmer 54, and 25 in Owego.
Ross Leonard B., cabinet-maker, and undertaker, Main, h River.
Russell Frederick W., (E. Nichols) r 44, farmer.
Russell Horace G., r 8, farmer with Ulysses G., leases of J. H. Morey 304.
Russell Justin A., (E. Nichols) r 44, farmer 75.
Russell Ulysses G., r 8, farmer with his brother Horace, leases of J. H, Morey 304.
Ryan Johanna, widow William, resident, bds. River.
Sanford Jay, (Owego) r 17, farmer 100.
Scott Alonzo J., laborer, bds. Cady ave.
Scott David C., farm laborer, h Cady ave.
Scott Ella F., dressmaker, Cady ave., bds. do.
Scott George B., emp. DeGroat, Harris & Co., h Main.
Scott Libbie M., dressmaker, bds. Cady ave.
Scott Perry L., laborer, bds. Cady ave.
Searles Aaron P., (E. Nichols) r 44, farmer.
Sears Charles, (Owego) r 21, farmer on shares with L. H. Pitcher 105.
Sears David, (Owego) r 21, farmer on shares with Ezra Hunt 110.
Sears Spencer, (Owego) r 36, farmer.
Seymour Herrick H., (Owego) r 16, farmer 170.
Sharp Charles, laborer, h Railroad.
Sharp Rufus G., r 8, miller.
Sherwood Casper I., general merchant, Main, h River.
Sherwood Silas, r 7, poor-master, and farmer 68½.
Sherwood Thomas B., (Tioga Center) r 22, farmer on shares with Mrs. Amanda Evans 52.
Sherwood Wesley W., (Tioga Center) r 10, apiarist, and blacksmith.
Shipman Edmund, r 24, farmer 6.
Shipman Selem, r 24, laborer.
SHOEMAKER EDGAR, r 1, farmer 97.
SHOEMAKER HORACE A., r 23, farmer.
Shoemaker Lyman H., harnessmaker, Main, h do.
Shoemaker William R., r 1, farmer 180.
Sibley Herbert L., (Owego) r 35, farmer, leases of S. Sibley 125.
Sibley John G., (E. Nichols) r 43, farmer 150.
Sibley Samuel, (Owego) r 35, retired farmer.
Sibley William H., (E. Nichols) r 43, farmer with his father John.
Sisk Harriet, r 49½, widow John, resident.
Sisson Wheeler, (Hooper's Valley) r 4, farm laborer.
Smith Charles H., (Owego) r 16, farmer 80.
Smith Charles O., (Owego) r 23, farmer 90.
SMITH HARVEY R., (Owego) r 10, farmer 100.

Smith Jane B., (Hooper's Valley) r 1, widow Washington, farm 120.
Smith Jay L., (Owego) r 32, farmer.
Smith John, (Owego) r 16, retired.
SMITH JOHN., Jr., (Owego) r 18, milk dealer, and farmer 230.
Smith Oliver P., (Hooper's Valley) r 5, blacksmith.
Smith Samuel B., r 16, retired.
SMITH SISTERS, (Catherine E. and Phebe A.) farm 120.
SMITH WARREN A., justice of the peace, deputy postmaster, and farmer.
Stanton Eben, r 27, farmer on shares with Z. Goodsell 100.
Stanton Frank E., r 27, farmer with his father Eben.
Stauff Elizabeth, (Hooper's Valley) r 28, farm 50.
Stauff Frederick, (Hooper's Valley) r 28, farm laborer.
Stauff George C., (Hooper's Valley) r 29, farmer.
Stauff Henry, (Hooper's Valley) r 28, farm laborer.
Steen Benjamin, (Owego) r 43, farm laborer.
Steward Charles B., (Hooper's Valley) off r 1, farmer with his father Jacob.
Steward Franklin P., (Hooper's Valley) off r 1, farmer.
Steward Jacob, (Hooper's Valley) off r 1, farmer 145.
Steward Thaddeus, (Hooper's Valley) r 3, small fruit grower, and farmer 97.
Steward Thaddeus J., (Hooper's Valley) off r 1, farmer.
Strong Sadie, clerk, bds. Main.
Sullivan Dennis O., mason, h Cady ave.
Sullivan Fred J., farm laborer, bds. River.
Sullivan John, farm laborer, h River.
Sullivan J. Whitmore, emp. E. Dunham, bds. River.
Taylor Lucretia, widow Stephen R., resident, h Howell.
Thorn Warren, (Owego) r 21, farmer on shares with James Nelson, Jr. 75.
Townsend James, (Owego) r 16, farm laborer.
Tripp Seymour C., watch repairer and jeweler, Main, h at Smithboro.
Turner G. M. Dallas, carpenter and joiner, h Cole.
Turner Harvey, wagon-maker, off Main, h Walnut.
Turner Jacob, mail carrier, bds. Walnut.
Van Demark Charles, farmer, h River.
Van Demark Emma Mrs., milliner, bds. Main.
Van Dermark Beniah, r 9, farm laborer.
Van Dermark Josiah, (Hooper's Valley) r 4, farmer 9.
Van Deusen Ella G., teacher, bds. Main.
Van Deusen H. Newton Rev., pastor M. E. church, h. Main.
Van Gorder Aaron, (Hooper's Valley) r 2, farmer 30.
Van Gorder Allen, (Hooper's Valley) r 28, farmer 126.
Van Gorder Edward S., r 16, sawyer.
Van Gorder Esther, r 16, widow Enos, resident.
Van Gorder George, r 1, farmer.
Van Gorder John, (Waverly) r 1, farm laborer.
Vannatta William, (Owego) r 18, farm laborer.
Van Ness Belle H. Mrs., groceries and provisions, Main, h Cady ave.
Van Ness Elias, manager of store for Mrs. B. H. Van Ness, h Cady ave.
Van Ness John H., r 48, farmer, leases of Jos. Olmstead 150.
Van Ness Myron, (Hooper's Valley) r 3, farmer 150.
Van Ness William W., shoemaker, Main, h River.
Van Norstran Andrew L., traveling salesman, h River.
Van Norstran Dora, teacher, bds. River.
Verguson Israel, (Owego) r 17, farmer.

Verguson Phoebe M., (Owego) r 17, widow L. Nelson, resident.
Vincent Oliver L., r 16, laborer.
Wait Austin D., (Owego) r 33, farmer 86.
WAIT GEORGE A., (Owego) r 50, farmer 75, and leases in Penn. 50.
Wait Jefferson, (E. Nichols) r 44, farmer.
Wait Joseph, (E. Nichols) r 44, farmer 25.
Walker Aaron, (Owego) r 12, farm laborer.
Walker Eliot, (Owego) r 32, farm laborer.
Ward Mahala, (E. Nichols) r 41, widow Abraham B., farmer 42.
Warner Jane, (Hooper's Valley) r 4, widow Frederick, resident.
Warner Sarah, widow Oscar T., h Walnut.
Warwick Laura D., widow William, h Cady ave.
Washburn Henry H., r 30, retired farmer.
WASHBURN JOHN H., (Hooper's Valley) off r 29, farmer 50.
Washburn Joshua, r 28, farmer 40.
WATERMAN & METLER, blacksmiths, Main.
Waterman Abraham, (Hooper's Valley) r 5, farm laborer.
WATERMAN ALONZO C., r 8, apiarist 20 swarms, and farmer 80.
WATERMAN BENJAMIN M., (Waterman & Mettler) h Main.
Waterman Charles, (Hooper's Valley) off r 5, farm laborer.
Waterman Charles H., r 8, blacksmith.
Waterman James H., r 8, carpenter.
WATERMAN JOHN G., r 8, blacksmith.
Waterman Thomas, (Hooper's Valley) farmer on shares with M. Van Ness 160.
Waterman Walter S., meat-market, Main, h do.
Webb Vestus R. (Waverly) r 1, laborer.
Webber Andrewson A., (Hooper's Valley) r 3, farm laborer.
Welch John F., R. R. section foreman, h River.
Wells Charles S., painter, bds. River.
Westbrook Levi, cigars and fruit, Main, h River.
Wheeler Charles J., r 10, laborer.
WHIPPLE ANDREW G., (Owego) r 33, school trustee and farmer 179.
White Anson, (East Nichols) r 51, farmer 50.
White Carrie H., (East Nichols) r 40, teacher.
White Charles L., (East Nichols) r 40, farmer with his father Henry.
WHITE DANIEL, (East Nichols) r 46, farmer 100.
White Elizabeth A., (East Nichols) widow Enoch, postmistress, and farm 30.
White Frank P., r 7, farmer with his father Platt White.
White George, (East Nichols) r 40, school trustee and farmer 60.
White Harriet, r 23, widow Lyman, resident.
White Hattie C., (East Nichols) r 43, teacher.
White Henry, (East Nichols) r 40, farmer 185.
White J. Lawrence, (Owego) r 22, overseer of the poor and farmer 128.
WHITE JOSEPH W., (East Nichols) r 45, assessor and farmer 168.
White Leonard, r 46, farmer 71.
White Myron P., (East Nichols) farmer 50.
White Perry F., (Owego) r 21, farmer on shares with Rachel Newland 40.
White Perry H., (East Nichols) r 43, farmer 100.
WHITE PLATT, r 7, farmer 80.
White Samuel H., (East Nichols) r 45, school trustee and farmer.
White Wellington, r 46, farmer 125.
White William, (East Nichols) r 43, farmer 140.

WHITE WILLIAM W., (Owego) r 21, assessor, apiarist 32 swarms and farmer 175.
Whiting Edward I., (Owego) r 17, farmer 26.
WICKHAM ALBERT, (Owego) r 16, farmer on shares with H. H. Seymour 170.
Wiggins Absalom J., emp. DeGroat & Harris, h Cady ave.
WIGGINS CLOID B., r 8, contractor and builder.
Wiggins George, r 8, carpenter and millwright.
Wiggins Silas, gardener, h Cole.
Wilber David, (Owego) r 32, farmer 25.
Wilber Horace, (Owego) r 32, farmer.
Wilbur Spencer, (Owego) r 18, farmer on shares with Mrs. E. Pitcher 125.
Williams George, laborer, bds. Main.
Williams George F., barber, Main, h do.
Williams Harry G., barber, bds. Main.
Williams Squire L., r 8, laborer.
Williams Stephen, r 8, stone-mason.
Wilson James M., M.D., Rev., pastor Presbyterian church, h Cady ave.
Wilson James P., medical student, bds. Cady ave.
Wilson John, r 49, farm laborer.
Wilson Louisa, widow George, laundress, h Main.
Wiswell Leon O., teacher, h Cady ave.
Witty Kate, (Owego) r 19, widow Thomas, resident.
Wood Allen, (Owego) r 42, farmer 50.
Wood Charles O., r 7, farmer 16.
Woodard Thaddeus, (Waverly) r 1, farm laborer.
Woodruff Joseph J., (East Nichols) r 43, farmer, leases of W. White 93.
Wright Caleb, r 8, prop. Dunham's mill.
Wright James, (Owego) r 17, farm laborer.
Wright Nancy W., r 8, carpet-weaver.
Yarrington James, (Owego) r 20, farm laborer.
Young O. Warren, (Owego) r 16, school trustee and farmer 90.

OWEGO.

INSIDE CORPORATION.

(*For explanations, etc., see page 3, part second.*)

(Postoffice address is Owego, unless otherwise designated in parenthesis.)

Abel Alonzo, carpenter, h 84, McMaster.
Abel Frank W., clerk, bds., McMaster, cor. Temple.
Aberhart Peter, baker, h over 56 North ave.
ADAMS HORACE B., tinwork, stoves and plumbing, 40 Lake, h 18 Ross.
Adams Joseph, retired, bds. Forsyth Block, North ave.

STARKEY & WINTERS, Wholesale and Retail Druggists, Owego.

OWEGO—INSIDE CORPORATION.

Adams Newton W., printer, h Forsyth Block, North ave.
Adams Ray, baker, h 100 Talcott.
AH-WA-GA HALL, G. W. Fay, agent, 203 Front.
AH-WA-GA HOUSE, B. J. Davis prop., Front, cor. Church.
Allen Alexander P., traveling salesman, h 26 George.
Allen Charles, farmer, h n Dean's Tannery.
Allen Edward, tanner, h n Dean's Tannery.
Allen Eugene, emp. Dean's Tannery, h n tannery, North ave.
Allen Guerdon L., collector for U. S. Express Co., h George.
Allen James, laborer, bds. 93 Erie.
Allen John, laborer, h 45 Erie.
Allen Lucius H., physician and surgeon, 140 Main, h do.
ALLEN LUCIUS H., 2nd, meat cutter, h 56 George.
Allen Matthew, laborer, h 47 Erie.
Allen Matthew J., laborer, bds. 93 Erie.
Allen Patrick, laborer, h 93 Erie.
Anderson Johnson M., (J. W. Jansen & Co.,) and with W. H. Bailey produce, h over 60 Main.
ANDREWS GEORGE F., attorney and counselor at law, 214 Front, h 117 Liberty.
Andrews Philetus, farmer, h 566 Fifth ave.
Andross & Groo, (W. W. A. and L. G.) wholesale commission fruit dealers, 136 North ave.
Andross Keziah, widow Stebbins, 46 Temple.
Andross William W., (Andross & Groo) 136 North ave, h 46 Temple.
Anthofer Anna, teacher German, bds. 54 Liberty.
Archibald Almon W., resident, h 35 Front.
Archibald Charles, farmer with his father, South Side.
Archibald Samuel, farmer 50, leases of A. N. Potter, South Side.
Arnold Charles E., painter, bds. 240 Temple.
Arnold George M., brakeman, bds. 240 Temple.
Atchison William J., clerk, bds. over 54 North ave.
Atkins Galen H., shoemaker, h 40 Lake.
Auffhammer Eugene, teacher of languages, h 215 Prospect.
Augusta Lucinda, tailoress, bds. 524 Main.
AYER WARREN L., physician and surgeon, 207 E. Main, h 203 do.
Ayers Elmer, porter Park hotel, bds. do.
Ayers Julia, widow Capt. Henry, bds. 51 Front.
BABCOCK JOHN B., machinest, h 240 E. Temple.
Babcock Zachary T., clerk, h over 69 North ave.
Bailey Deborah, widow Alexander, h 620 Fifth ave.
Bailey Mary Mrs., tailoress, h 194 East Temple.
BAILEY W. H. & CO. (W. J. Mawhiney) hay, grain and potatoes, 164 North ave.
BAILEY WILLIAM H., (W. H. Bailey & Co. and J. W. Jansen & Co.) overseer of the poor, h 80 East ave.
BAIRD LEWIS J., fireman, h 10 Adaline.
Baird Sabrina, widow John, h 10 Adaline.
Baker Charles, brakeman, h 222 North ave.
Baker Edwin T., clerk, h South Side.
Baker Frank M., supt. Addison & Northern Pennsylvania R. R., h Main.
Baker James R., farmer, h 173 North ave.

STARKEY & WINTERS, promptly fill Mail and Telephone Orders.

BAKER JULIA A., widow John D., h Spencer block, Lake.
BALL JOHN P., general variety and auction, 170 Front, h 27 Front.
Ball Mariette, widow George, bds. 5 Spruce.
Ball William W., clerk, bds. Front.
BANDLER ROBERT, clothing, hats, caps and gent's furnishing goods, 19 and 21 Lake, h 13 Park.
Banta Alonzo H., harness-maker, h 204 Bell.
Barber Edbert, farmer, bds. 405 Front.
Barden Ezra D., traveling salesman, h 234 North ave.
Barnes Clarissa Mrs., resident, bds. 313 Main.
Barnes Eliza, widow William, resident, h 123 Liberty.
Barnes Katie, telegraph operator, bds. 73 Liberty.
Barnes Theodore, farmer, h 103 Liberty.
Barnett John W., plumber, h 157 Erie.
BARRETT JAMES M., physician and coroner, Main cor. North ave., h 63 Liberty.
Barstow Oliver A., retired, bds. McMaster.
Bartholomew Phoebe A., resident, bds. rear 18 Adaline.
Bartlett Oscar J., blacksmith, h 94 Talcott.
Barton Eugene F., (G. W. Barton & Son) h over 59 North ave.
Barton George W., cigar manuf., 191 Main, h 166 Temple.
BARTON ISAAC, (Isaac W. Barton & Co.) produce, h 71 Liberty.
BARTON ISAAC W. & CO., (Frank H. Catlin) produce.
Barton Maggie E., widow Festus L., bds. 473 Front.
Barton Walton A., town clerk and book-keeper, h 202 East Temple.
Basford Albert, laborer, h 76 South Depot.
Basford Henry, harness-maker, h near tannery, North ave.
Basford Hiram, laborer, bds. 24 Temple.
Basford James, shoemaker, 150 River, South Side, h do.
Bassett James A., teller Owego Nat. Bank, h 41 Paige cor. Main.
Battersby Joseph, retired, h 359 Main.
Batterson Helen, clerk, bds. 38 Spencer ave.
Bauer Caroline Mrs., dressmaker, h 26 Adaline.
Bauer Elizabeth, dressmaker, 26 Adaline, h do.
Baxter Daniel M., laborer, h 489 Front.
BEACH & PARMELEE, (O. S. B. and A. W. P.) druggists, Main cor. North ave.
Beach D. & Co., (G. W. Derrickson) manufs. cordage, and dealers in sporting goods, 197 Main.
Beach Darius, (D. Beach & Co.) h over 197 Main.
BEACH OTIS S., (Beach & Parmelee) h McMaster.
Beach William, emp. planing-mill, h 60 McMaster.
Beard David O., barber, bds. Lake.
Beard James C., retired farmer, bds. 380 Main.
Beard James C., Jr., sup't Beard Manuf. Company, h 380 Main.
Beard Manuf. Co., (W. A. and G. A. King) manufs. of saddlery, 24, 26 and 28 Lake.
Beardsley Nathaniel A., harness-maker, 291 Prospect.
Beaumont John H., botanic drug store, 135 North ave., h do.
Beck Charles, laborer, h 208 North ave.
Beck Edward, medical student, bds. 115 West ave.
Beck Edward S., teacher, h 115 West ave.
Beck Frank, law clerk, bds. 115 West ave.

Beck George P., resident, bds. 115 West ave.
Beck Louie A.. clerk, bds. 115 West ave.
Becker Delevan, conductor Erie R. R., h Spencer Block, Lake.
Becker Fayette A., carpenter, h Fifth ave.
Beebe Hiram A., retired, h 345 E. Main.
Beecher Frederick, baggageman, h 115 North ave.
Beecher Lambert, emp. King & Co., bds. 118 Temple, h at Newark Valley.
Beeman Harman S., cartman, h 117 North ave.
Beers Charles, farmer 150, h 221 Main.
Beers Edwin W., carpenter, h South Side.
Beers Frank J., baker, confectioner, and oyster dealer, 55 North ave., h do.
Belden Martha M., widow Henry A., h Temple.
Bell James, laborer, bds. 225 Erie.
Bell Mary A., widow Charles T., h 394 Main.
Bell William, laborer, h 225 Erie.
Bennett Caroline, widow William, h 80 Temple.
Bennett Dana, engineer, h 264 North ave.
Bennett Harry A., clerk, bds. Temple cor. Church.
Bennett Hattie A., dressmaker, bds. 80 Temple.
Bennett Nathaniel, shoemaker, Fox, h do.
Bennett Nelson R., engineer, h 102 Temple.
Bennett William, hostler, h Main.
Benson Hattie A., artist, bds. 112 Fox.
Benson Mary A., cook and laundress, h 112 Fox.
Benson Robert F., laborer, bds. 112 Fox.
Benson W. Henry, gardener and sexton, h 112 Fox.
Bergen Bridget, widow James, saloon and confectionary, 80 So. Depot, h do.
Bergen Timothy, laborer, h 94 Spencer ave.
Berger Andrew F. F., clothing and gents.' furnishing goods, Lake, h 72 Talcott.
BERRY JOSEPH, (Sporer, Carlson & Berry) h 373 Front.
Besler C. William, prop. Excelsior Soap Factory, cor. Temple and Liberty, h 95 Main.
Bicknell Hiram D., locomotive engineer, h Spencer, cor. George.
Bignall Juliet C., widow Burnett B., resident, h 90 Spencer.
Bikely Frederick, employee Gas Company, h 440 Main.
Billings Georgie Miss, clerk, h 61 Forsyth.
BILLINGS HENRY, pres. Owego village, h 109 Main.
Billings John A., magr. W. U. Tel. office, 30 Lake, h 73 Liberty.
Billings Mary E. Mrs., boarding-house, 73 Liberty.
Billings Mary E., widow William, h 61 Forsyth.
Billings Nancy, widow Henry, h 198 E. Temple.
Billings Richard, resident, bds. 198 E. Temple.
Billings Will, printer, bds. 73 Liberty.
Bing Wah, Chinese laundry, 71 North ave., h do.
Bird Henry, laborer, h 109 Paige.
Bird Lawrence, laborer, h 113 Paige.
Birdsall Benjamin, bartender, bds. 154 North ave.
Blair Parmelia, widow Stephen O., resident, bds. 92 Adaline.
Bliss Francis A., (Bliss, Thompson & Co.) h 30 William.
Bliss, Thompson & Co., (F. A. B., A. C. T. and George Truman, Jr.) wool dealers, 174 Front.
BLOODGOOD DARWIN H., clerk U. S. Ex. Co., h 33 Park.

BLOODGOOD FRANK S., manager Telephone Exchange, h 33 Park.
Bly Benjamin F., laborer, h Constine's lane.
Boardman Edward W., fireman, h over 130 North ave.
Bodle Sarah A., widow James, bds. 66 Church.
Bonham Emma, widow John S., bakery 3 Park, h do.
Booth Fred E., telegraph operator, bds. Delphine.
Booth Celestia, widow of Ransom, h 92 Liberty.
Bostwick Lewis W., farmer 100, h 61 Talcott.
Boughton William H., painter, h 45 Adeline.
Bourke John, laborer, 289 Front.
Bouquet Albert, saloon and restaurant, 13 Lake, h do.
Bouquet Frank, emp. Drill Works, h n Dean's Tannery.
Bouquet George, tanner, h n Dean's Tannery.
Bowen Abbey A., dressmaker, over Owego Nat. Bank, h do.
Bowen Franklin L., resident, h 236 North ave.
Bowen Timothy, laborer, h West ave.
Boyd Mary, widow Andrew, bds. 134 Talcott.
Boylen Frank F., clerk, h over 72 North ave.
Bradbury Amanda L., widow Charles, h 89 William.
BRADLEY CHAUNCEY A., market gardener, h South Side.
Brady John, laborer, h 36 John.
Brady Thomas F., recording clerk county clerk's office, h 162 West ave.
Brainard Burnette E., clerk, bds. 249 Prospect.
Brainard Henry C., printer, h 249 Prospect.
Brant F. Lester, clerk, bds. 195 Main.
Brant Hiram H., liquor dealer, 169 Main, h 70 Liberty.
Brant Julia, dressmaker, 122 River, South Side, h do.
Brant Nelson, saloon, 195 Main, h do.
Bravo Eugene J., clerk, bds. over 23 Lake.
Bridgman Alfred T., traveling auditor D. L. & W. R. R., h Main.
Briggs Belle M., widow George N., h 359 Front.
Briggs Diana G., M. D., widow Isaac S., resident, h 5 Park.
Briggs Mary L., M. D., physician, 5 Park, h do.
Briggs N. Smith, farmer, bds. 5 Park.
Briggs William F., brakeman, h 204 East Temple.
Brink Edward T., well-driver, h 448 Front.
Brink Eliza D., widow Nelson, market garden, fruit nursery, etc., h 577 Main.
Brink John, laborer, h Canal.
Britenbaker Jennie, widow George, saloon and restaurant, Delphine, h do.
Brobasco Westbrook G., farm laborer, h South Side.
Brockway Francis E., deputy county treas., teller First Nat. Bank, h 24 Paige.
BROCKWAY LEON L., prop. parlor job printing house, 34 Lake, bds. 24 Paige.
Brooke James W., tailor, h 29 Temple.
Brooks Chester P., traveling salesman, bds. 153 Temple.
Brooks Chloe M., deputy county clerk, Court House, h 153 Temple.
Brooks David, locomotive engineer, h over 72 North ave.
Brooks Edward P., clerk, bds. North ave.
BROOKS HORACE A., justice of the peace and conveyancer, over 191 Main, h 153 Temple.
Brooks James L., mason, h Gere.

Brooks Lucy G., widow Benjamin, h 153 Temple.
Brooks Martha, resident, bds. 153 Temple.
Brooks M. Mandane, resident, bds. 153 Temple.
Brott Anna, widow John W., nurse, 162 West ave.
Brott Anthony P., farmer 15 and leases of Peter Brott 36, h 82 Temple.
Brott Joseph, porter Ahwaga House, h 121 Franklin.
Broughman R. Frank, book-keeper, h 67 West ave.
Brown Abram, laborer, h 73 Fox.
Brown Charlotte M., widow Frederick, h 18 Front.
Brown Della, widow James, millinery, 67 North ave., h do.
Brown Ebenezer S., traveling salesman, h 122 West ave.
Brown Edward, farmer, h 273 North ave.
BROWN GEORGE, (L. & G. Brown) h off North ave. near S. C. R. R. round house.
BROWN H. CORYDON, book-keeper Owego Mutual Benefit Association, Lake, h 78 Chestnut.
Brown John, hotel and restaurant, and liquor dealer, 171 Main, h do.
Brown John J., butcher, h over 82 North ave.
BROWN L. & G., (Lyman & George) farmers 50, apiarists 135 swarms, and manufs. of apiarist's supplies, off North ave. n S. C. R. R. round house.
BROWN LYMAN, (L & G. Brown) h off North ave. n S. C. R. R. round house.
Brown Lyman, farmer, bds. 273 North ave.
Brown Mary E. Mrs., h 111 Paige.
Brown M. J., clerk Central House, bds. do.
BROWN PATRICK, tel. operator D. L. & W. depot, h 182 River, S. Side.
Brundage Daniel, blacksmith, h John R.
Bruneman August, laborer, h 268 North ave.
Bryan Esther C., widow George H., dressmaking, Spencer block, Lake, h do.
Buckbee Frances, widow Ezra, h 364, Front.
BUCKBEE, PETERSON, WOOD & CO., (P. C. Peterson, C. L. Wood, C. E. Schoonmaker, and F. J. Burgess) dry goods, carpets and millinery, 190 and 192 Front.
Buffum Charles, drug clerk, h Paige.
Buffum Edward, bar-tender, h over 167 Main.
Buffum Ellen E., widow George W., h 20 Paige.
Bulloch Lewis, barber, bds. 63 Spencer ave.
Bunzey Adelbert T., clerk, bds. 36 William.
BUNZEY JOHN H., salesman, h 36 William.
Bunzey Nelson P., farmer, h Pumpelly, So. Side.
Burbank Horace J., apprentice, bds. 70 Spencer.
Burbank Joseph T., baker, h 70 Spencer ave.
Burdick Edgar L., harnessmaker, h r 38 Temple.
Burdick Lewis C., cleaning and dying, 67 Fox, h do.
BURGESS FRANK J., (Buckbee, Peterson, Wood & Co.) h Fox cor. Liberty.
BURNETTE CHARLES R., printer, *Gazette* office, h 62 Liberty.
Burns Nellie T., saleslady, bds. 530 Main.
Burrows James, restaurant and saloon, 218 Front, h do.
Burt Martha, widow James M., h 359 Front.
Burton Nathaniel T., bakery, 61 North ave. h do.
Burton Reuben E. Rev., pastor First Bapt. church, h 19 Ross.
Bush James L., peddler, h Constine's Lane.

Butler James, barber, 65 North ave., h 89 Fox.
Cable Edmund, baggagemaster, bds. 289 Main.
CABLE FREDERIC O., postmaster, h 289 Main.
Cafferty Edward, gardener, h Water.
Cafferty Margarett, widow William J., bds. Water.
Cain Patrick, laborer, h John R.
Caley Charles, farm laborer, h 18 Adaline.
Calkins Benjamin S., emp. D. L. & W. R. R, bds. Dugan House.
Cameron Charles, painter, h 98 Spencer ave.
Cameron Charles A., resident, bds. 208 E. Temple.
Cameron Delray A., clerk, h 61 Liberty.
Cameron Frederick H., law clerk, bds. 208 E. Temple.
Cameron John, clerk, 208 E. Temple.
Cameron Larne J., resident, h over 170 Front.
Cameron Robert, retired, h over 170 Front.
CAMP GEORGE SIDNEY, atty. at law and farm 132, h Front near Park.
Camp Hermon H., (H. H. Camp & Co.) h 24 Front.
Camp H. H. & Co. (Lucy A. Camp) foundry, 136 Front.
CAMP JOHN, baggageman, h 447 Main.
Camp John, shoemaker, bds. 52 Fox.
Camp Lucy A., (H. H. Camp & Co.) widow Henry W., h 24 Front.
CAMP MARY L. MRS., art teacher, h 259 Erie.
Camp William, brakeman N. Y. & Erie R. R., h 368 Main.
CAMP W. HARRISON, postal clerk, h 259 Erie.
CAMPBELL ARBA, tanner, dealer in phosphates and other fertilizers; farm in Tiogo 300, Candor 250, in Rome, Pa., 200, h 289 Front.
CAMPBELL'S TANNERY, A. Campbell prop., Talcott.
Campion Edward, tinsmith, h Fulton.
Campion Michael, tinsmith, h 68 McMaster.
Campion William, emp. gas company, h 495 Main.
CARD ALBERT A., foreman contract work, h over 7 Adaline.
Card George, farmer in Candor 40, h 7 Adaline.
Card Irving, farm laborer, bds. 7 Adaline.
Carleton Edward D., gardener, h 161 Talcott.
Carleton Fanny A., dressmaker, bds. 161 Talcott.
Carlson John M., piano tuner, h 63 Paige.
CARLSON OTTO M., (Sporer, Carlson & Berry) h Paige cor. Bell.
Carmichael Charles S., manuf., h 194 East Temple.
Carpenter Charles B., book-keeper 200 Front, bds. at Ah-wa-ga House.
Carpenter Collins A., salesman, h 38 George.
Carrigan Henry K., tanner, h near Dean's tannery.
Carrigg Michael, machinist, bds. 118 Paige.
Carrigg Patrick, yardmaster Erie R. R., h 118 Paige.
Carter Charles, stationary engineer, h 120 River, South Side.
Carter Frances F., hair-worker, h 89 Fox.
Carter Sarah Mrs., resident, h over 109 North ave.
Cartledge Elizabeth, widow John, bds. 499 Front.
Cartwright Estes, clerk, bds. Front.
Case Ellis L., carpenter and painter, h 216 East Temple.
Case Nancy, widow Chauncy F., bds. 216 East Temple.
Casey Margarett, widow John, h 64 Paige.
Casey Thomas F., laundry 210 Front, h do.
Casterline Evi E., carpenter Erie R. R., h 108 Chestnut.

Catlin Calvin H., clerk Ah-wa-ga House, bds. do.
Catlin Charles A., wind-mills, bds. 75 Talcott.
Catlin Charles M., supt. saw-mill, h 75 Talcott.
CATLIN FRANK H., (I. W. Barton & Co.) bds. 337 Front.
Catlin John, clerk, bds. North ave.
Catlin Mary E., dressmaker 75 Talcott, bds. do.
Catlin Sarah E., dressmaker 75 Talcott, bds. do.
Catlin Thomas, laborer, h 228 North ave.
Caughlin Catherine, widow Patrick, h 31, Erie.
*CAULDWELL & GRAY, (J. A. C. and J. C. G.,) engines, boilers, castings, mill-work, and boiler-iron jails, McMaster cor. Delphine.
CAULDWELL JAMES A., (Cauldwell & Gray) h 56 Spencer ave.
Cauldwell James A., Jr., clerk, bds. 56 Spencer ave.
CENTRAL HOUSE, W. G. Gardener, manager, cor. Main and Lake, Free buss to all trains.
Chaffee Caleb J., resident, h 122 Main.
Chaffee Catherine, widow Barney, h off Water.
Chaffee Martha, dressmaker, bds. off Water.
Chamberlain Lee N. & Son, (Stephen) boots and shoes, Chamberlain block, Lake.
Chamberlain Lee N., (L. N. Chamberlain & Son) wholesale boots and shoes, Lake, h 317 Front.
Chamberlain Stephen, (L. N. Chamberlain & Son) wholesale boots and shoes, Lake, h 37 Paige.
Chambers George, bartender, bds. 161 North ave.
Chappel Frederick, emp. King & Co., bds. 14 West ave.
Chappel Hattie, tailoress, bds. 14 West ave.
Chappel Lyman, retired, h 14 West ave.
Chappell Matilda, widow William, laundress, 100 Talcott.
Chatfield George S., (Storrs, Chatfield & Co.) h 149 Front.
Chatfield John R., (Storrs, Chatfield & Co.) h 44 Front.
Chatfield Lucy B., widow of Thomas I., h 337 Front.
Cheeks Abraham, tinsmith, h 240 Prospect.
Cheeks Ellen, resident, h 238 Prospect.
Cheeks Enoch J., laborer, h 263 Prospect.
Cheeks Moulton, carpenter, h 508 Main.
Cheeks Samuel L., laborer, h 240 Prospect.
Chillson Hope Miss, resident, h 15 Temple.
Chitry Charles E., postal clerk, h 318 Front.
Chitry Francis, silversmith, h 374 Main.
Chitry William F., traveling salesman, bds. 374 Main.
Chittenden Josie M., widow W. Gus, bds. 147 Main.
Church Lewis W., clerk, h Fifth ave.
CITY STEAM LAUNDRY, (J. B. Keeler and J. A. Mabee) 83 North ave.
CLARK C. A. & H. A., attys. and counselors at law, Academy Bldg., Court.
CLARK CHARLES A., (C. A. & H. A. Clark) h Main.
Clark Fred, painter, h 16 Paige.
CLARK H. AUSTIN, (C. A. & H. A. Clark) h Main.
CLARK HERMAN C., confectionary and tobacco, 68 North ave., h do.
Clarke Eliza B., widow Timothy, h 53 Liberty.
Clarke Lizzie A., teacher, bds., 53 Liberty.
Clem Anton, tailor, h over 76 North ave..
CLEVELAND ALBERT P., supt. Cruciform Casket Co., h 26 W. Fox.

Coakley James, telegraph repairer, h 92 Paige.
Cobb Alanson L., emp. Casket Co., h 37 Delphine.
Cobleigh Harrison, blacksmith, h 249 Erie.
Cobleigh Ida J., dressmaker, bds. 249 Erie.
Coburn Andrew, resident, h 135 Main.
COBURN & STRAIT, (E. D. C. & E. E. S.) books, stationery and wall-paper, 17 Lake.
Coburn Ebenezer, resident, h 135 Main.
COBURN EDWARD D., (Coburn & Strait) h 67 Liberty.
COBWEB BOTTLING WORKS, Pat. Maloney prop., cor. Paige and Fox.
Coe Jesse W., lumber, h River, South Side.
Coe Jesse W., Jr., lumberman with his father, bds. River, South Side.
Cole Ida M., dressmaker, 261 Erie, bds. dc.
Cole Ira J., blacksmith, h 261 Erie.
Cole Russell S., painter, h 84 Temple.
Cole Smith B., carpenter, h 40 Adaline.
COLEMAN JULIET, clothing, 9 and 11 Lake, h 212 Main.
Coleman Louisa, widow James, laundress, h 121 Green.
Coleman Morris, mgr. for J. Coleman, h 212 Main.
Coleman William, bookkeeper, 9 and 11 Lake, bds. Main, cor. Church.
Colgan Christopher, cigarmaker, bds. 92 South Depot.
Colgan Edward, drug clerk, h 7 Fox.
Colgan Mary, widow Thomas, h 92 South Depot.
Collins Daniel, mechanic, h 98 Paige.
Collins Dennis, harness-maker, h 18 Paige.
Collins Ellen, dressmaker, bds. Delphine.
Collins John, laborer, h Delphine.
Collins Joseph J., emp. Cobweb Bottling Works, bds. Green.
Collins Timothy, brakeman, h 109 Green.
Collins Timothy, Jr., emp. Cobweb Bottling Works, bds. Green.
Collins William, shoemaker, Lake, h 108 Spencer ave.
COMFORT MELVILLE L., jeweler and optician, 25 Lake, bds. Ah-wa-ga House.
Conant Frank L., carpenter, h 122 Franklin.
Conant James C., (Corchran & Conant) h Prospect.
Cone Cynthia C., widow Charles, h 82 Temple.
Congdon Daniel O., (Congdon & Robinson) h 188 Temple.
Congdon Nettie A., widow George E., seamstress, h 102 Fox.
Conklin Ira, teamster, h River, South Side.
Conklin Larne H., under sheriff, Main cor. Court, h do.
Conklyn Michael, retired, h 223 E. Temple.
Conley Emma M., widow John, laundress, h 448 Front.
Conlon Bridget, widow Timothy, laundress, h 112 Green.
Conlon John T., engineer, h 116 Green.
Connell John, laborer, h 109 Spencer ave.
Connell Patrick, track-walker Erie R. R., h 23 Fox.
Connell Thomas, laborer, h 250 East Temple.
Connell Timothy, tanner, h Canal.
Connelly Bridget, widow David, h 68 Paige.
Constine Michael, resident, h 123 Green.
Cook Allen E., switchman, h Constine's Lane.
Cook John, emp. casket shop, h 31 Fox.
Cook John, emp. livery, h 35 Talcott.

Cook Nelson C., locomotive engineer, h 41 Fox.
Cook William, brakeman, h 195 East Temple.
Conley La Forest B., tanner, h 30 West Main.
Cooper Byron, farmer, h 147 Talcott.
Cooper Frank E., clerk, h 195 East Temple.
Coppins Amelia E., milliner, bds. 152 Central ave.
Coppins James H., engineer, h 152 Central ave.
Corchran & Conant, (J. T. C. & J. C.) contractors and builders, 62 Temple.
Corchran John T., (Corchran & Conant) h 51 George.
Corchran Nathan F., cabinet-maker, h 61 Adaline.
Corey William H., station agent D. L. & W. R. R., h 268 Main.
Cornell Charles, emp. foundry, h Adaline.
Cornell Edward, laborer, h off Water.
Cornell Edwin W., (H. W. Cornell & Son) h 18 John.
Cornell Elizabeth, widow David, bds. 29 Talcott.
Cornell Harmon W., (H. W. Cornell & Son) h 112 Chestnut.
Cornell H. W. & Son, groceries and provisions, 405 Main.
Corrigan John, Jr., traveling salesman, bds. 117 Chestnut.
Corrigan John, clerk, h Chestnut.
Corseni F., fruit dealer, 10 Lake.
Cortright Albert, grocery, North ave., h 22 Fox.
Cortright Charles E., brakeman, bds 237 Erie.
Cortright Dorcas, widow Nicholas, h 44 West Main.
CORTRIGHT HOUSE, J. A. Cortright & Son, props. 157 North ave.
CORTRIGHT J. A. & SON, (Mahlon A.) props. Cortright House.
CORTRIGHT JAMES A., (J. A. Cortright & Son) h 157 North ave.
Cortright John, clerk, h 201 East Temple.
Cortright John Mrs., dressmaker, 201 East Temple, h do.
CORTRIGHT MAHLON A., (J. A. Cortright & Son) h 157 North ave.
CORTRIGHT REUBEN W., brakeman, h 237 Erie.
Cortright Richard W., emp. foundry, bds. 44 W. Main.
Cortright Theodore, groceries and provisions, 64 North ave, h 62 Liberty.
Corwin Estelle H., clerk, h Church.
Corwin Harriet E., saleswoman, bds. East Main.
Courtright Charles, emp. foundry, h 100 Franklin.
Couton Adolph R., resident, bds. 265 Main.
Couton Charles E., retired, h 265 Main.
Covert Mary A., widow William H., h 232 North ave.
COYLE WILLIAM, livery, 73 North ave., h do.
Crabb Alice, widow Robert, h 150 Central ave.
Crabb Daniel, emp. foundry, h 50 W. Main.
Crabb George, hostler, bds. 150 Central ave.
CRABB ISAAC, market gardener, and wholesale dealer in vegetables, h Water.
Crabb Robert, h 212 North ave.
Crandall Ellis, jeweler, bds. 63 Paige.
Crandall Morris, painter, h 265 Erie.
Cramer Jennie W., widow Wallace E., bds. 99 Franklin.
CRANS ABRAM F., physician and surgeon, 126 North ave., h do.
Crans Egbert, carpenter, h 67 Central ave.
Crater Marinda, resident, h 91 Franklin.
Croak Thomas, liveryman, 73 North ave., bds. do.
Croff Isaac, cartman, h 146 River, South Side.

Croft Charles, hostler, bds. 56 Front.
Crowel Margaret, widow John, resident, h 50 W. Main.
Crowley Charles, laborer, h 90, S. Depot.
Crumley Thomas F., laborer, h 124 Paige.
Cuddeback William A., retired, h 38 William.
Cummings William, currier, h near Dean's tannery.
Cuneo Pietro, confectionery, 181 Front, h 8 Main.
Curtis Alson, conductor, h 29 Talcott.
Curtis A. Maria, widow Oliver D., h 101 Franklin.
Curtis Mary, widow, h 567 Front.
Cushman Eliza, resident, h 67 Forsyth.
Cusick John, laborer, h 129 Chestnut.
Cutler Thomas, gardner, h Canal.
Daggett Charles W., manager Postal Telegraph & Cable Co., bds. 34 Fox.
DANA CHARLES, custom boot and shoe maker, 65 North ave., h 322 Front.
Dana Lena J., saleswoman, bds. 322 Front.
Danforth Fred, emp. King & Co., bds. 118 Temple.
Danforth Joseph A., drayman, h Commerce.
Daniels Emily M., widow Dr. Ezekiel, h 217 Main.
Darrow Asa A., retired, h South Side.
DARROW FRANK A., (Mead & Darrow) h South Side.
Darrow Hill, mechanic, h 105 North ave.
DAVIS BURR J., prop. Ah-wa-ga House, Main cor. Church.
Davis William, steward Ah-wa-ga House, bds. do.
Dawes Etta, tailoress, bds. 229 Prospect.
Dawes Joseph M., locksmith, 69 North ave., h 229 Prospect.
Day Marvin, resident, bds. 313 Main.
Day Warren, farm laborer, bds. 596 Fifth ave.
Day William, farm laborer, h 596 Fifth ave.
Dean Alanson P., retired, h 63 Paige.
DEAN CALVIN B., livery, hack and sale stable, Church, h 30 do.
DEAN CAMERON B., ticket agent N. Y. L. E. & W. R. R., rooms Main.
Dean Charles R., (Shaw & Dean) h 274 Main.
DEAN H. N. & SON, (Ransom B.) props. tannery, North ave.
Dean James A., contractor and builder, Spencer ave., h do.
Dean John E., produce, h 122 River, South Side.
Dean Mary, widow H. Nelson, 255 Front.
Dean Mortimer C., yard-master S. C. R. R., h 248 North ave.
DEAN RANSOM B., (H. N. Dean & Son) vice-prest. Owego Nat. Bank, h in Adams, Mass.
Dean Sumner R., bar-keeper Ah-wa-ga House, bds. do.
Dearstine Charles, brakeman, bds. 124 Chestnut.
Dearstine Elias, brakeman, bds. 124 Chestnut.
Dearstine Jane A., widow John, h 124 Chestnut.
Decker Abram C., laborer, h South Side.
Decker Alexander, market gardener, h Fifth ave.
Decker Andrew J., laborer, h Canal Front.
Decker Frederick, emp. King & Co., bds. Canal Front.
Decker John, soda and mineral waters, Fifth ave., h do.
Decker John, laborer, h 220 North ave.
Decker Morgan, night-watchman, h 553 Front.
Decker Phoebe, widow Anson, books, stationery and wall-paper, 186 Main, h 472 do.

Decker Samuel H., laborer, h 24 Temple.
Decker Silas, emp. foundry, h North ave. cor. Temple.
Decker William, brakeman, h 36 W. Main.
Decker Victor, resident, h Main.
Decker Ward, manager of store for Mrs. A. Decker, bds. 472 Main.
Dee James, telegraph operator, bds. 313 Main.
Degarmo Alonzo, billiards, South Depot, h 178 River, South Side.
Delevan Irving J., produce and live stock, Front, h 233 do.
DeLong John Mrs., h 105 Talcott.
DeLong Pertilla, widow George, h 125 Talcott.
DEMUN CLINTON L., Singer sewing machines, 155 North ave, bds. European House.
Denison Alonzo H., laborer, h 146 River, South Side.
Dennis Catharine, widow Charles, h 111 Paige.
Dennis Mary, resident, h 223 North ave.
Densmore Anson, farmer, h South Side.
Densmore Eliza, widow John, bds. Delphine.
Densmore Franklin J., laborer, h 215 Prospect.
Densmore John J., emp. casket company, h Delphine.
Densmore William H., laborer, h over 168 Front.
DEPOT D. L. & W. R. R., River, South Side.
DEPOT N. Y., L. E. & W. R. R., North ave.
Derrickson George W., (D. Beach & Co.) h over 197 Main.
Deremer Theresa A. Mrs., resident, h over 177 Main.
DE VALLIERE ERNEST, baggageman, h 55 Spencer ave.
De Valliere Nina A., sales-lady, bds. 55 Spencer ave.
Devine Mary, tailoress, bds. South Depot.
DeWitt Catharine, widow Joseph, resident, h 58 Liberty.
DeWitt Elizabeth, widow Thomas, resident, h 25 George.
DEWITT HENRY B., saloon, 76 North ave, bds. Central House.
Dewitt Margaret, resident, bds. 25 George.
Deyo Jay, cartman, bds. West ave., n Creek.
Diamond Irvin, carpenter, h 126 McMaster.
Dibble Clement, laborer, h Division.
Dickerson Fountain F., bartender, h Liberty.
Dildine Albert, fireman, h 73 East ave.
Dildine William J., cigarmaker, bds. 73 East ave.
Dingman Henry B., painter, h Decker Block, Main.
Dodd Thomas, railroad conductor, bds. 113 North ave.
Dodge Alfred, retired farmer, h 387 Front.
Dodge Edmund, upholster and furniture repairer, h 479 Front.
Dodge Emily Mrs., h 88 Paige.
Dodge Joseph A., clerk, h over 69 North ave.
Dollaway Frank L. Miss, resident, h 65 Central ave.
Donovan James H., R. R. section foreman, h 18 W. Main.
Donovan Mary A., dressmaker, 102 Paige, bds. do.
Donovan Michael, laborer, h 102 Paige.
Doody John, laborer, h 112 Spencer ave.
Doody Patrick, laborer, h 112 Spencer ave.
Dooley Alice, widow James, h 117 Erie.
Dooley James F., cigarmaker, bds. 117 Erie.
Dorcas Hannah, widow Moses, h 110 Paige.
Dorsey Alma J., dressmaker, 207 E. Temple, bds. do.

OWEGO—INSIDE CORPORATION.

Dorsey James, painter, h 123 Chestnut.
Dorsey Sarah E., widow Allen R., h 207 E. Temple.
Dorsey William, tinsmith, bds. 123 Chestnut.
DORWIN, RICH & STONE (W. E. D., G. E. R. and J. F. S.) millers office 177 Front, mills foot of Main.
DORWIN WILLIAM E., (Dorwin, Rich & Stone) h Glen Mary.
Dotson Matthew, chimney sweep, h John R.
Doty Elijah, tailoring, cleaning and repairing, rear 63 North ave., h 69 Adaline.
Douglas Charles, traveling salesman, h over 80 North ave.
Dowd Anna E., dressmaker, 5 Park, h do.
Dowd Charles H., blacksmith, h 574 Main.
Dowd Mary A., bds. 574 Main.
DOWNS EDWIN D., D. D. S., dentist, 192 Front, h 239 do.
Doyle Bridget, widow Patrick, h 93 Spencer ave.
Doyle Mary, housekeeper, Pumpelly, South Side.
Doyle Mary, widow Dennis, saloon 121 Franklin, h do.
Doyle Peter, J., (Richards & Doyle) bds. Ah-wa-ga House.
Drake Dolly, emp. King & Co., bds. 118 Temple.
Drake Eli B., farmer and cooper, 74 Temple, h 95 Liberty.
Driscoll Cornelius, blacksmith, h 279 E. Temple.
Druckenmiller Charles, prof. music, bds. 73 Liberty.
Duel Betsey, widow Samuel L., h 193 North ave.
DUGAN CHARLES B., prop. Dugan House, 139-145 Front.
DUGAN HOUSE, Charles B. Dugan, prop., 139–145 Front.
Dugan Jeanette, widow Hugh, h Dugan House.
DUGAN JOHN, grocer 173 Front, h 64 North ave.
Duncan Agnes, clerk, bds. Paige.
Duncan Stephen, carpenter, h 85 Paige.
Dundon John, laborer, h 141 Erie.
Dundon John, Jr., laborer, bds. 141 Erie.
Dunham Frederick, clerk, h 191 E. Temple.
Dunham Hannah, boarding-house, 118 Temple.
Dunham Mahlon G., bartender, h 88 Page.
Dunn Dennis, book-keeper, Dean's tannery, bds. Decker blk., Main.
Dunn Jeremiah, tanner, h n Dean's tannery.
Dunn Michael J., laborer, h 530 Main.
Dunn Paul, currier, bds. n Dean's tannery.
Dunn Thomas W., express messenger, bds. 530 Main.
Dunning Catharine, widow Horace, h 322 Front.
Duren Loren D., foreman casket company, h 3 Adaline.
Duren W. Warren, laundryman, bds. 109 Fox.
Durfee Edgar S., carpenter, h 137 North ave.
DURFEE FRANK G., cutter, also correspondent Elmira *Advertiser*, h 99 Liberty.
Durkee Charles R., carpenter, h 32 Main.
Durphy Lyman D., retired lumber dealer, h Durphy block, Lake.
DURUSSEL & SON, (L. F. & G. A.) jewelers, 35 Lake.
DURUSSEL GEORGE A., (Duressel & Son) h 275 Main.
DURUSSEL LEWIS F., (Durussel & Son) h 191 E. Temple.
DUTCHER MERRITT T., physician and surgeon, over 15 Lake, h do.
Dwelle & Link, (J. C. Dwelle and C. A. Link) Clothing, Front.
Dwelle Clinton W., clerk, bds. 249 Front.

Dwelle Jefferson C., (Dwelle & Link) h 249 Front.
Earsley Belle Mrs., dressmaker, Commerce, h do.
Earsley Harriet, resident, h 259 McMaster.
EARSLEY JOHN F., drayman, h Commerce.
Easton John M., resident, bds., Main.
EASTON DAVID T., lawyer, over 168 Front, h 571 E. Main.
Eastwood Charles K., clerk, bds. Ah-wa-ga House.
Eberhart George D., Lockwood Mail and express, 43 Talcott, h do.
Eckert A. F., conductor, h over 58 North ave.
Eckter Frank, drayman, bds. 188 West ave.
Eckter Fred, resident, 188 West ave.
Eckter Louis, stone mason, h 188 West ave.
Eckter Marvin, well driver, bds. 188 West ave.
Eddie Ester A., widow David S., cook, h 102 Fox.
Eddy Wilber H., laborer, h 206, North ave.
Edson George, carpenter, h over 107 North ave.
Eldridge Mrs., widow James, h Front.
Ellis Alexander D., manuf. shirts, and agent for John Wanemaker, h Church.
Ellis A. H. Mrs., milliner, h Front.
Ellis Lydia J., widow Virgil, 34 Paige.
Ellis Stella A., clerk, h 34 Paige.
ELLIS WILLIAM H., (Goodrich & Co.) bds. 271 Front.
Elston George, laborer, h over 86 North ave.
Ely Alfred G., (Ely Brothers) h Front.
Ely Brothers, (Alfred G., Charles C. and Frederick) Ely's cream balm, 235 Greenwich street, New York.
Ely Charles C., (Ely Brothers) h Front.
Ely Frederick, (Ely Brothers) h Front.
Embody Abram, resident, bds. 7 Adaline.
EMERY DAVID H., (Raymond & Emery) h 56 West ave.
Emery Paul, h 52 Fox.
EMPIRE SOAP WORKS, (James B. Keeler, prop.) 191 McMaster, office 83 North ave.
Engelbreckt Peter, pianos, h rear 182 River, South Side.
Erie Express Co., Foster N. Mabee, agent, 18 Lake.
EUROPEAN HOUSE, John Hayes, prop., 151 North ave.
Evans Andrew, butcher, h 160 McMaster.
Evans Charles W., baggage-master, h 53 Paige.
Evans Josiah R., carpenter, h 4 William.
Everhart Peter, baker, h over 56 North ave.
Every William B., 62 North ave., wholesale liquors, h over do.
Ewalt —, tailor, bds. 73 Liberty.
Excelsior Soap Factory, C. W. Beseler prop., 37 Temple.
Fahey Michael, laborer, h 133 Erie.
Fairchild Samuel F., Agent, hats, caps and gents.' furnishings, 27 Lake, h 55 Central ave.
Fancher Herman P., wood-turner, h 55 Talcott.
Farnham Albert S., teamster, bds. 235 E. Temple.
Farnham Melissa, widow Edwin, h 235 E. Temple.
FAY GEORGE W., excise commissioner and insurance, 203 Front, h 334 Main.
Ferguson Frederick, emp. foundry, bds. 151 Talcott.
Ferguson Irving, emp. foundry, bds. Talcott.

OWEGO—INSIDE CORPORATION.

Ferguson Laura, widow John, resident, h 113 Liberty.
Ferguson Royal B., foreman Gere, Truman, Platt & Co., h 7 George.
FERGUSON T. JEFFERSON, carpenter, h 151 Talcott.
Ferris Samuel W., pattern maker, h 110 McMaster.
Fiddis Emeline Mrs., bds. 104 West ave.
Fiddis Lucy A., teacher, bds. 93 Franklin.
Fiddis Lucy G., widow Robert, resident, h 93 Franklin.
Field John H., conductor, h 13 George.
Finch Smith, carpenter, h 170 West ave.
FIRST NATIONAL BANK OF OWEGO, (George Truman, Sr., prest., W. S. Truman, cash., F. E. Brockway, teller) 179 Front.
Fisher George, sewing machine repairer, North ave., h South Erie.
Fisher James, molder, h 113 Liberty.
Fitzgerald Catherine, widow, Morris, resident, 120 Fox.
Fitzgerald Deborah, cleaning and dying, 105 Fox, h do.
Fitzgerald Edward, emp. Drill Works, h 43 Temple.
Fitzgerald Thomas, painter, bds. 120 Fox.
Fitzgibbons John, watchman, h Bell.
Flamer Isaiah, barber, 154 Front, h 184 River, South Side.
Flamer Julia, widow Jeremiah, h 184 River, South Side.
Flanigan James P., laborer, h 21 Adaline.
Flanigan Mary, dressmaker, bds. 21 Adaline.
Flanigan Patrick, laborer, h 106 South Depot.
Flanigan Thomas F., machinist, bds. 21 Adaline.
Foley James, laborer, h 113 Spencer ave.
Foot Frederick, bridge builder, bds. Lackawanna House, South Side.
Foot Sarah M. Mrs., dressmaker, bds. River, South Side.
Ford George, resident. bds. over 17 Lake.
Ford Lewis, livery, 132 North ave., h do.
Ford Lucius, carpenter, h 607 Main.
Forgason Charles, carpenter, bds. over 19 Lake.
FORGASON THADDEUS C., V. S., veterinary surgeon, stable Central ave. rear Park Hotel, h over 19 Lake.
Forsyth Charles E., clerk, bds. 245 Erie.
FORSYTH ELDRIDGE, retired, h 67 Forsyth.
Forsyth Eleazur V., emp. Erie R. R., h 11 Adaline.
Forsyth Eva B., dressmaker, bds. 11 Adaline.
Forsyth George F., painter, bds. 245 Erie.
FORSYTH GILBERT T., decorative painter, h 435 Main.
FORSYTH HUBBARD T., house and decorative painter and paper-hanger, h 245 Erie.
FORSYTH JAMES, resident, h 113 Front.
Forsyth Rachel, widow George, bds. 60 Forsyth.
FORSYTH WILLIAM S., landscape, frescoe and decorative painter, h 60 Forsyth.
Foster & Hampton, (J. F. & J. W. H.) barbers, 129 North ave.
Foster Joseph, (Foster & Hampton) h 129 North ave.
FOSTER LEONARD, r 27, prop. saw and feed-mill. all kinds of pine and oak lumber on sale at lowest market prices, farmer 135, h McMaster.
Foster William C., clerk, h Fulton.
Fowley Michael, laborer, h 216 North ave.
Fox Lydia N., widow Edward, carpet-weaver, h 142 Central ave.
Fox Stuart E., emp. foundry, h 115 Chestnut.

Fralley Robert, baggageman, h 144 Central ave.
France Francis, emp. casket shop, bds. 142 Central ave.
FRANK JOHN, physician, 115 Main, h do.
Franz Conrad, tailor, h Gere.
Fraser Daniel, traveling salesman, bds. 143 Temple.
Fraser Reuben, farmer 140, h 143 Temple.
Fredenburg Catharine, widow Virgil, h 265 North ave.
Fredenburg Edward E., law student, bds. 215 North ave.
Fredenburg Fred J., laborer, h 215 North ave.
Freehill Maria, widow Patrick, boarding-house and lodging, 64 South Depot.
Freight-house and Office Erie R. R., South Depot, head Spencer ave.
French Charles O., farm laborer, h Constine's Lane.
French Orrin, laborer, h 460 Main.
Frisbie Sarah Mrs., laundress, h 5 Adaline.
Fritcher George, retired, bds. 128 Temple.
Frutchey Erastus, teamster, h Temple.
Fulton Market., (P. Hyde and G. Saltsman) general store, 32 Fulton.
Gaher Henry, tailor, bds. 73 Liberty.
Gale William E., station agent S. C. R. R., h 47 George.
Gallagher Dryden, widow William, bds. 41 Paige.
GARDNER WILLIAM G., manager Central House, Main cor. Lake.
Garey Henry J., brakeman, h 236 E. Temple.
Garvey Michael, laborer, h 111 Erie.
Garvey Patrick, emp. Erie R. R., h Delphine.
Gates Anna, widow Simon, bds. 229 Main.
Gavell Edward, cigar manuf., over 169 Main, h do.
Gavin Catherine, resident, bds. 125 Chestnnt.
Gavin Mary, widow Patrick, h 125 Chestnut.
Geary Patrick, laborer, h 22 Temple.
Genung Abram C., carpenter, h 118 Franklin.
Gere Adaline, widow Bradford, 192 North ave.
GERE EUGENE B., attorney at law, 112 Front.
GERE THEODORE D., (Gere, Truman, Platt & Co.) h 118 Main.
GERE, TRUMAN, PLATT & CO., (T. D. G., F. W. T., T. C. P. and C. F. Johnson) manufs., "Champion" wagons, grain and fertilizer drills, harrows, etc., Central ave.
Gibbons John H., laborer, bds. Constine's lane.
Gibson Charlotte, widow Stephen D., h 205 North ave.
Gibson Donald, bridge builder, h 205 North ave.
Gibson Frank, laborer, h 205 North ave.
Gibson Sarah, widow Edward G., resident, h 127 North ave.
Gilbert Charity, widow John H., h 115 Temple.
Gilday Edward, clerk, bds. 54 Delphine.
Gilday John, emp. foundry, bds. 54 Delphine.
Gilday Michael, laborer, h 54 Delphine.
Gilday William, emp. foundry, bds. 54, Delphine.
Giles Chester, emp. foundry, bds. Canal.
Gill Ellen, widow Christopher, h 16 Paige.
Gillett Luther W., (Riley & Gillett) Front, h 114 McMaster.
Gillett J. Fred, clerk, bds. 114 McMaster.
GILLSON WILLIAM H., bridge carpenter, h 116 West ave.
Gilman Herbert, stage driver, bds. Lackawanna House, South Side.
Gilman Milton H., prop. mill-yard, lumberland in Sullivan Co., Pa., h Front

Gilman N. M. Mrs., millinery, 204 Front, h do.
Ginnane Joseph, emp. foundry, h 161 West ave.
Ginnane Mary, widow Edward, h 135 West ave.
Ginnane Mary A., teacher, bds. 161 West ave.
Ginnane Thomas, laborer, h 448 Front.
Glaseo Thomas, gardner, h 112 Paige.
GLEZEN OSCAR B., att'y at law, and justice of the peace, Academy Bldg., Court, h 9 Front.
Goodnough William, expressman, h 268 North ave.
GOODRICH & CO., (J. W. Goodrich and W. H. Ellis) drygoods, 196 Front.
Goodrich David L., surveyor, h 388 Front.
Goodrich Frank, sewing-machine agent, h over 80 North ave.
GOODRICH JAMES W., (Goodrich & Co.) h 27 Front.
Goodrich Lyman T., traveling agent, h 425 Front.
Goodrich Samuel, yard-master Erie R. R., h 123 Liberty.
Goodspeed Eliza A., widow Joel J., h 57 Paige.
Goodspeed Elizabeth, teacher, bds. 57 Paige.
Goodwill Burdett D., laborer, h 22 Temple.
Goodwill Martha M., widow James G., h 22 Temple.
Gordon Martha N., widow William C., resident, h 229 Main.
Gordon Samuel, laborer, h off North ave. near S. C. R. R. round-house.
Gorman Dorinda M., widow Capt. John, h 383 Front.
Gorman James, switchman, bds. 64 South Depot.
Gorman Orrin T., shipping-clerk, Gere, Truman, Platt & Co., h 339 Main.
Goss Seward, retired, h 25 Ross.
Gotleiber Victor, policeman, bds. 88 Chestnut.
Gould Adam C., blacksmith, Temple, h 16 do.
Gould Appleton H., leather-cutter, h 290 Prospect.
Gould Ephraim, retired, h Talcott.
Gould Ephraim C., drayman, bds. 112 West ave.
Gould Frederick, emp. Drill Works, h 87 Liberty.
Gould Jane, widow Wilber D., h 234 Main.
Gould Joel S., retired, h 146 Talcott.
Gould Joseph, laborer, h Canal Front.
Gould Marion D., emp. foundry, bds. 16 Temple.
Gould Morris P., emp. foundry, h 8 Temple.
GOULD WILLIAM L., blacksmith, h 112 West ave.
GRAND ARMY HALL, over 76 North ave.
GRAND UNION TEA COMPANY, Milton T. Knight, agt., 42 Lake.
Granger Cora A., teacher, bds. 135 Main.
Grant Simon, produce, bds. 264 Main.
Graves Henry A., news, cigars and confectionary, 49 Lake, h 62 Church.
Gray George, painter, h Delphine.
GRAY JOHN C., (Cauldwell & Gray) h McMaster opp. Academy.
Gray John H., clerk, h North ave.
Green James W., miller, h 119 Liberty.
Greenleaf Emeline, widow John M., bds. 105 Main.
GREENLEAF JOHN T., physician and surgeon, 101 Main, h 105 do.
Greenwood Frank A., printer, bds. 80 William.
Greenwood James, custom boot and shoemaker, 188 Front, h 80 William.
Greenwood James W., emp. foundry, bds. 80 William.
Greenwood John E., emp. U. S. Express Co., bds. 80 William.
Greenwood Lizzie M., dressmaker, 80 William, bds. do.

Griffin Emma, laundress, 138 Talcott.
Griffin Margaret Mrs., h 148 Fox.
GRIFFING SAMUEL B., village alderman and salesman, h 226 E. Temple.
Grimes James, brakeman, h 27 Adaline.
Grimes Sarah, widow James, Jr., bds. 36 William.
Groat Abram W., confectionery and cigars, 115 North, h do.
Groo Lines, (Andross & Groo) residence in New Jersey.
GROSS JERRY S., lawyer, 178 Main, h do.
Hall George H., dry goods, h 122 Main.
Hall Granville W., carpenter, bds. Cortright House.
Hall James D., apprentice, bds. 105 Franklin.
Hall Mary, widow Edward, h 105 Franklin.
Hall Michael, confectionery, h 59 Church.
Hall William, laborer, h Water.
Hallock Andrew J., brakeman, h 61 Forsyth.
Hamilton Joel A., contractor and builder, h 3 Front.
Hammond ——, laborer, h 136 Main.
HAMMOND EDGAR, baker, h over 69 North ave.
Hammond Edwin, printer, h Buckbee Block.
Hampton James W., (Foster & Hampton) h 129 North ave.
Handlon Jerry, saloon-keeper, bds. 133 North ave.
Haner John, tanner, h 274 North ave.
Hannon John, laborer, h 107 Fox.
Hannon Patrick, laborer, 88 South Depot.
Hannon Thomas, local mail agent, h South Depot.
Hansell George I., book-keeper, Storrs, Chatfield & Co., h River, So. Side.
Hanvey Eliza, resident, h 2 W. Main.
Hanvey Hugh, retired, h 2 W. Main.
Hanvey John, retired, bds, 2 W. Main.
Hanvey Rosanna, resident, 2 W. Main.
Hard Horace, miller, h W. Main.
HARDER EMMOTT, boots and shoes, 23 Lake, h 279 Main.
Harding George A., farm laborer, h Pumpelly, South Side.
Harding Grant, laborer, h 222 North ave.
Harding Hannah T., widow Robert, h 143 Temple.
Harding Osee, widow John, h 222 North ave.
Harding Ward, baggageman, bds. 222 North ave.
*HARGRAVE WILLIAM G., artist and photographer, 38 and 40 Record block, Lake, h do.

Awarded First Premium at the Tioga County Fairs of 1885-1886. Satisfaction Guaranteed to all.

W. G. HARGRAVE,
Artistic * Photographer
38 AND 40 LAKE ST., OWEGO.

Copying and Enlarging of Old Pictures is one of our Special Features. Twenty-five Years New York City Experience.

OWEGO—INSIDE CORPORATION.

Harold Edward, R. R. section foreman, h 149 Fox.
Harold James J., foreman Owego *Blade*, h 149 Fox.
Harrington Thomas, track foreman D. L. & W. R. R., h 122 Fox.
Harris Scott, cashier Erie express office, h 68 Liberty.
Harris William M., book-keeper, 180 Front, bds. 12 Liberty.
Harris William S., resident, h 377 Main.
Harrison James, laborer, h 24 Temple.
Harrison John B., R. R. signal tender, h 11 East ave.
Harrison Lewis, clerk, bds. 115 North ave.
Harrison Samuel, teamster, h 36 W. Main.
Harrison S. M. Mrs., resident, h 115 North.
Harrison William L., harness-maker, 127 North, h do.
Harros Daniel, cartman, h 153 Erie.
Hart Alfred, laborer, bds. 256 Prospect.
Hart Daniel, machinist, h 483 Front.
Hart Horace, miller, h 12 Temple.
Hart Lewis, laborer, h 104 South Depot.
Hartnett Maria, resident, h John R.
Hartnett Michael, emp. Haywood's Marble Works, h 100 South Depot.
Haskins Edward T., engineer, h 34 George.
HASTINGS & STRATTON, (J. M. H. & E. S.) dry and fancy goods, 186 Front.
HASTINGS JAMES M., (Hastings & Stratton) school commissioner, h 351 Main.
Hastings Rebecca, widow William, bds. 351 Main.
Haughy Robert, laborer, h 108 Green.
Haupt Frank, emp. King & Co., bds. 118 Temple.
Havland Harriet, widow George, h 254 North ave.
Havland Ruth, widow Frederick, housekeeper, Spruce.
Hawes Judson, harness-maker, bds. 133 North ave.
Hawkins Philander, tanner, h n Dean's Tannery.
Hayden James J., emp. King & Co., bds. 31 Delphine.
Hayden Maggie, tailoress, bds. 87 Paige.
Hayden Mary Mrs., resident, h 87 Paige.
Hayden William P., retired, h 31 Delphine.
Hayden William P., Jr., foreman King & Co., bds. 31 Delphine.
HAYES JOHN, prop. European House, 151 North ave.
Hayes Michael J., peddler, h 185 E. Temple.
Hayes Richard J., bartender, bds. European House.
Haynes George L., painter, h 42 William.
Hays Richard L., laborer, bds. Water.
HAYWOOD CHARLES M., marble and granite work, 80 North ave., h 42 Temple cor. Liberty.
Haywood Harry C., marble-cutter, bds. 42 Temple.
Hazzard Ella, clerk, bds. 118 Temple.
HEAD KATE Mrs., nurse, 104 West ave.
HEAD MELINDA, widow John M., resident, h 152 Talcott.
HEATON CARLTON R., physician and surgeon, treas. Cruciform Casket Company, and medical director O. M. B. Association, Park cor. Main, h do.
Hemstrought Abram V., carpenter, h 198 E. Temple.
Herrick John J., market gardner, 577 Main, bds. do.
Herrick Laura A., teacher, bds. 577 Main.

Hevland George W., emp. Grain Drill Works, h 242 North ave.
HEWITT FREDERICK C., retired, h 223 Front.
HEWITT GURDON, retired, h 223 Front.
HIBBARD GEORGE R., crockery, 84 Front, h Spencer ave.
Hibbard Jemima, widow Ralph, bds. 101 Franklin.
Hibbard Ralph W., cabinet-maker, h 112 Franklin.
Hickey James, cigarmaker, bds. 301 Prospect.
Hickey John, laborer, h 301 Prospect.
Hickey John, clerk, bds. 68 South Depot.
Hickey Lizzie C., dressmaker, 399 Main, bds. do.
Hickey Mame, tailoress, bds. 68 South Depot.
Hickey Mary, widow Patrick h 68 South Depot.
Hickey Thomas, shoemaker, h 399 Main.
Hicks Horace H., blacksmith, h 52 Fox.
Hierstiner Moses, resident, h 88 Chestnut.
Hill Alfred, janitor, h William.
HILL BROTHERS, (H. H. and C. C.) dentists, Front.
HILL CHARLES C., Dr., (Hill Brothers) h Binghamton, N. Y.
Hill Charles F., special claim agt. for pensions, h 354 Front.
Hill Charles O., manuf. and dealer in lumber and shingles (estate of James Hill,) 89 Central ave., 99 do.
Hill Edward, coachman, bds. William.
Hill Fred C., atty. at law and clerk Surrogate's court, Court House, h Main.
HILL HARRIET, widow James, h 84 North ave.
HILL HOMER H., (Hill Brothers) bds. Dugan House.
Hill James, (Estate) manuf. and dealer in lumber and shingles, 89 Central ave.
HILL LUCY, widow Chauncey, bds. 254 E. Temple.
Hinckley Alphonso J., restaurant and saloon, 189 Main, h do.
Hines Belle, widow Rufus W., h 447 Main.
Hines Louise, clerk, h 447 Main.
Hitchcock Eugene, cartman, h Canal.
Hoagland Alexander D., commercial traveler, h Buckbee block, Lake.
Hoagland Emma D., dressmaking, Buckbee block, h do.
Hoagland James R., laborer, h John R.
Hobler George, telephone operator, McMaster.
Hobler Philip, engineer, h 255 McMaster.
Hodge Caroline A., widow Henry J., resident, h 86 Temple.
Hodge Ella A., dressmaker, 86 Temple, bds. do.
Hodge Frederick S., painter, h 41 Temple.
Hodge Henry J., painter, h Water.
Hodge Joseph, laborer, h Constine's Lane.
Hogan Catharine, widow Philip, h 38 W. Main.
Hogan Catharine M., dressmaker, 60 Delphine, bds. do.
Hogan James, laborer, h 60 Delphine.
Hogan James J., fireman, bds. 60 Delphine.
Hogan John F., second hand store, 57 North ave., h do.
Hogan Roger P., reporter, h 38 W. Main.
Hoghey Sarah, widow James, h 118 Fox.
Holes George, carpenter and saw filing, 7 Park, h do.
Hollenback David J., farmer, h 117 North ave.
Hollenback Sisters, (Mary and Alice) farm 200, h 412 Front.
Hollensworth Jeremiah M., barber 22 Lake, h 158 Temple.

Hooper Warren, tanner, h 62 George.
Hopkins John, cigar-maker, bds. Park Hotel.
Horgan Jerry, retired, h 56 Delphine.
Horgan Katie, dressmaker, 56 Delphine, bds. do.
Horgan Mary, widow John, h 56 Delphine.
Horigan Daniel J., prop. Erie House, 70 South Depot.
Horn Eva, widow Matthias, bds. Gere.
Hornbeck Cornelius F., machinest, h 273 Erie.
Horrigan Margaret, widow Michael, tailoress, h 152 Green.
Horrigan William, barber, 152 North ave., h Green.
Hortnet Andrew, emp. foundry, bds. 109 Spencer ave.
Hortnet Mary, laundress, h 109 Spencer ave.
Horton John J., resident, h 105 North ave.
Hoskins Franklin F., machinest, h 8 Temple.
Hoskins James B., delivery clerk freight depot, h 65 Spencer ave.
Hoskins Mary M., widow Fayette F., bds. 223 East Temple.
HOSKINS WATSON L., insurance and jeweler, 185 Front, h 311 Main.
Houk Cora B., book-keeper, 184 Main, bds. 122 Temple.
Houk Frederick G., clerk, bds. 122 Temple.
Houk Harry, clerk, bds. 131 Talcott.
Houk Jennie M., book-keeper, 184 Main, bds. 122 Temple.
HOUK JONATHAN S., hardware, 184 Main, h 122 Temple.
Houk Lewis C., tinsmith and plumber, h 131 Talcott.
*HOUSE EPHRAIM H., coal, wood and lumber dealer, and farmer 75, office 229 McMaster, h 220 Main.
House Oakley, clerk, h 57 Church.
House Oakley A., horse farrier, h 76 South Depot.
Hover Robert, produce buyer, h 274 North ave.
Howard Orville, carpenter, h 7 Spruce.
Howe Olin R., pastor Park Cong. church, bds. 290 Main.
Howe Rufus, farmer, h 45 West Main.
Howe Ransom, cartman, h 115 Temple.
HUBBARD & KING, (I. M. H. & O. G. K.) furniture and undertaking, 29 Lake.
Hubbard Charles, emp. foundry, h rear 59 Church.
Hubbard Emeline M., widow Henry N., resident, h 275 Main.
Hubbard Henry D., clerk, 210 Front, h 160 Temple.
Hubbard Thomas, barber, Lake, h 60 Spencer ave.
HUBBARD TRUMAN M., (Hubbard & King) h Lake.
Hubbard Willis, emp. foundry, bds. rear 59 Church.
Huber Albert D., (Nichols & Huber) h 161 Main.
Hugaboone Matthias, laborer, h 460 Main.
Hughs Almira Mrs., laundress, h 32 Adaline.
Hughs George, stationary engineer, h John R.
HULL ALFRED H., resident, h 120 Chestnut.
Hull Byron O., resident, bds. 120 Chestnut.
Hull Frederick K., retired, h over 17 Lake.
Hull Hattie R., teacher, bds. 340 Main.
Hull Margaret S., teacher, bds. 340 Main.
Hull Mary A., h 340 Main.
Hulslander Levi T., dry and fancy goods, 59 North ave., bds. Central House.
HUMISTON FRANK M., (White & Humiston) h over 194 Front.
Hunt Arthur E., wind-mills and pumps, 134 Front, bds. Dugan House.

Hollister Charles J., silversmith and sewing machine agent, Fox cor. Central ave., h do.
Hollister George W., clerk, bds. 283, Prospect.
Hollister Joseph D., painter, Canal, h do.
Hollister Julius, silversmith, and sewing machine agt., Fox cor. Central ave., h do.
Hollister Mercy, widow Horace J., h Canal.
Hollister Myron E., printer, h 283 Prospect.
Hollister William S., painter, h Canal.
Holmes Oscar H., coachman, h 104 Paige.
Holmes Thomas H., clerk, bds. 358 Front.
Holt Mary, widow Edwin H., resident, h 94 Fox.
Home Rufus C., mason, Main, h do.
Hooker Archie S., carpenter, h 113 Franklin.
Hooker Warren, bridge carpenter, h George.
Hunt Emily J., widow William, h 14 Lake.
Hurlburt E. Burritt, flour, h 211 Main.
Hutchins Frank F., United States express agent, h 314 Main.
Hutchinson Alice M., teacher, bds. 232 E. Temple.
Hutchinson James, carpenter, 232 E. Temple, h do.
Hutchinson William, watch-maker, bds. 243 Main.
Hyde & Winters, (C. H. H. and J. B. W.) groceries and provisions, Front cor. Court.
Hyde Charles H., (Hyde & Winters) h 358 Front.
Hyde Earl, telephone operator, h Main.
Hyde Earl Mrs., dry goods and notions, Main.
Hyde Francis Mrs., bds. 67 Erie.
Hyde Merritt, emp. U. S. Express Co., h 91 Talcott.
Hyde Nelson H., wood-worker, 135 Talcott, h do.
Hyde Otis B., sup't cemetery, h 243 Main.
Hyde Perry, book-keeper, Hyde & Winters, also prop. Fulton Market, h Main cor. Fulton.
Hymes Edgar W., miller, h W. Main near Mill.
Ingersoll Charles A., teamster, h 18 Lake.
Isenburg William, cartman, h 190 River, South Side.
Jackson John, dentist, 12 Lake, h do.
Jackson John T., photographer, 12 Lake, bds. do.
Jackson Lois M., widow George W., dressmaker, 63 Liberty, h do.
Jackson Sarah, widow James, h Commerce.
Jackson W. Mianda, widow Harvey, h West ave., near creek.
Jansen Jesse W., (J. W. Jasen & Co.) also physician and surgeon, 60 North ave., h do.
JANSEN J. W. & CO., (W. H. Bailey and J. M. Anderson) drugs, medicines, and paints, 60 North ave.
JENKS ELIZA J., widow Sabin M., resident, h 15 Front.
JEWETT HARRY, retired, h 108 Liberty.
JOHNSON ABIGAIL M., caterer, widow Joshua C., h 459 Main.
Johnson Calvin, laborer, h 225 Prospect.
Johnson Caroline, widow David, resident, h 45 Front.
Johnson Charles W., retired, bds. 32 William.
Johnson Cyrene Mrs., resident, h 81 Liberty.
Johnson Edward J., groceries and provisions, 100 North ave., h North ave., cor. Chestnut.

OWEGO—INSIDE CORPORATION.

Johnson Edward S., emp. agricultural works, h over 100 North ave.
JOHNSON FRANCES M., music teacher, also caterer for weddings, parties and private teas, Saratoga potatoes furnished to dealers, h 459 Main.
Johnson Frank H. Mrs., resident, h 85 North ave.
Johnson Harlen F., resident, h 275 E. Temple.
Johnson Henry, horse-trainer, h 98 Spencer ave.
Johnson Hiram R., resident, h 12 Talcott.
JOHNSON HORACE A., painter and paper-hanger, and decorative work, 52 George, h do.
Johnson James H., postal clerk, h 358 Main.
Johnson Lottie G., teacher, bds. 358 Main.
Johnson Thomas D. Rev., pastor St. Patrick's church, h Main.
Johnson Winfield, drug clerk, h 358 Main cor. Ross.
Jones Albert, laborer, h 493 Front.
Jones George W., mason, h 517 Front.
JONES JAMES E., carpenter, pattern and general job shop, 191 McMaster, h 116 Franklin.
Jones John, lumber at Nanticoke, Pa., h 41 Front.
Jones John B., moulder, h 254 E. Temple.
Jones Moses C., laborer, bds. 69 Fox.
Jones Peter, coachman, h 96 Spencer ave.
Jones Pierson, laborer, h 69 Fox.
Joslyn H. B., cabinet-maker, h 118 Temple.
Joslyn Hulda Mrs., resident, h over 57 North ave.
JOSLYN JUDSON, bridge carpenter, h 7 Hill.
Kaley Charles, laborer, h 11 Fox.
Kaley John W., emp. King & Co., h 90 Talcott.
Kaley William H., carpenter and stone mason, h over 177 Main.
Kanane Frank, gardener, bds. 43 Delphine.
Kanane Mary, tailoress, bds. 43 Delphine.
Kanane Patrick, laborer, h 43 Delphine.
Keefe Owen, blacksmith, h 283 E. Temple.
KEELER ALBERT H., contractor and builder, and dealer in lime, cement and fertilizers, h Temple cor. Central ave.
Keeler Charles P., mason and contractor, h rear 68 Paige.
KEELER JAMES B., (City Steam Laundry) prop. Empire Soap Works, Temple cor. Central ave.
KEITH GEORGE W., brakeman, h 15 East ave.
KEITH MARY B., widow Luther T., bds. 15 East ave.
Kellogg Charles T., contractor and builder, h 262 Prospect.
Kellogg Julia, widow Charles, h 73 Forsyth.
Kellogg Ulysses P., carpenter, h 22 Fulton.
Kelly Julia F., widow Frederick P., dressmaker, 246 E. Temple, bds. do.
Kelly Matthew, laborer, h 112 Green.
Kempson Emily P., widow Peter T., h 80 McMaster.
Kendall Frank B., traveling salesman, h 96 Franklin.
Kennedy Lee, insurance, h 73 West ave.
Kennedy Peter G., barber, h 106 Paige.
KENYON ALBERT J., chief engineer, U. S. Navy, h 163 Temple.
KENYON JAMES, retired, h 163 Temple.
Kenyon Joel C., druggist, 5 Lake, h do.
Kershner Eugene K., clerk Dugan House, bds. do.
Ketchum John, hack driver, h Main.

Ketchum La Fayette F. Rev., Reformed Methodist, h 92 Franklin.
Kettle John, porter Dugan House, bds. do.
Kidder James H. Rev., rector St. Paul's Church, h 100 Main.
Kidder Phœbe Mrs., resident, h 195 North ave.
Kiernan Margaret, dressmaker, bds. Canal.
Kiernan Patrick, laborer, h Canal.
Kile Lowell E., laborer, h over 67 North ave.
Kimball Ebenezer, bridge builder, h 126 McMaster.
Kimball Helen, widow Calvin S., artist, bds 425 Main.
King & Co., (W. A. and G. A. K.) manufs. of and wholesale dealers in harnesses, 24, 26 and 28 Lake.
King Charles H., barber, Ah-wa-ga House, bds. 112 Fox.
King George A., (King & Co.) h 58 Paige.
KING ORLANDO, (Hubbard & King) county supervisor, bds. Ah-wa-ga House.
King Seth L., machinist, h 234 Main.
King William A., (King & Co.) h 250 Front.
King William H. Rev., retired Bapt., h 369 Front.
Kingcade Charles, shoemaker, h 90 Paige.
Kingcade Charles Mrs., dressmaker, 90 Paige, h do.
Kingfield Ellen Mrs., mailing clerk, postoffice, h 184 E. Temple.
Kingfield Fanny B., book-keeper, 196 Front, h 184 E. Temple.
KINGMAN LEROY W., editor and pub. Owego *Gazette*, h 2 Academy.
Kingman Lyman R., bartender, h North ave.
Kingman Maria L., widow Leroy W., h 260 Main.
Kinney Susan J., widow J. Alphonso, h 18 Fulton.
Kinney Willis D., printer, bds. 18 Fulton.
Kipp George, butcher, h 111 North ave.
Kline Orion, carriage-maker, h 144 Temple.
Knapp Maria R., widow Dr. Jerome, bds. Front.
Knight Catharine, widow Cornelius, h 56 Forsyth.
KNIGHT ELIZABETH, dressmaker, bds. 59 Church.
Knight Mary J., widow Moses, h 59 Church.
KNIGHT MILTON T., agt. G. U. Tea Co., bds. Dugan House.
Knight Milton W., carpenter, bds. 56 Forsyth.
Korbmann Rosa, widow Christian, h over 13 Lake.
Labarron Sarah A., widow Edson, h 234 North ave.
Lackawanna House, Ira J. VanDemark, prop., 176 River, South Side.
LaGrange Abram, carpenter, bds. 52 West ave.
LaGrange Charles, carriage-painter, h 52 West ave.
Lainhart George, variety store, 212 Front, h 132 Main.
Lake Martha D. Mrs., resident, h 58 Spencer ave.
Lake Thomas B., meat-market and grocery, 119 North ave., h 65 Talcott.
Lake William A., butcher, h over 119 Lake.
Lamb Charles B., brakeman, h 174 North ave.
LAMEREAUX NATHAN, saloon, 76 North ave., bds. 57 Church.
LaMonte Fred S., (LaMonte & Rodman) produce, h 442 Front.
LaMonte Samuel M., retired, h 105 Liberty.
Lane Bert J., clerk, bds. 12 Adaline.
Lane Leonard, clerk, bds. near Dean's tannery.
Laning John, retired, h. 143 Main.
Larkin Thomas, laborer, h 62 Talcott.
Lawheed Joseph W., boarding-house, 118 Temple.

Lawrence Laura, widow William, bds. 69 Church.
Lawrence Oscar S., emp. Erie Express Co., h 69 Church.
Lawrence William A., jeweler, h McMaster.
Lawrence William D., express messenger, h 58 Church.
Layton Daniel, laborer, h 238 E. Temple.
Layton James F., laborer, bds. 238 E. Temple.
Layton John J., printer, bds. 239 E. Temple.
Leach Benjamin C., grocery and music, North ave., h do.
Leach John J., locomotive engineer, h 158 McMaster.
Leach Tillie C.. music teacher, bds. North ave.
Leahy James J., (P. Leahy & Son) bds. 310 Main.
Leahy Patrick & Son, (James J.) groceries, provisions, and meats, Main cor. North ave.
Leahy Patrick, (P. Leahy & Son) h 310 Main.
Lee Albert S., barber, 109 North ave., h do.
Lee William, farm laborer, h 534 Main.
Legg Dolphus, emp. D., L. & W. R. R. freight depot, h 198 North ave.
Legg Louis H., law clerk, bds. 69 Church.
Lenon John, clerk, bds. European House.
Leonard Allen, carpenter, h Water.
Leonard Emily C., resident, h 313 Main.
Leonard Frank, laborer, h W. Main, near Mill.
LEONARD GEORGE S., loan, investment and insurance, 209 Front, h Main.
Leonard John, saloon, 135 North ave., h do.
Leonard Laura A., resident, h 313 East Main.
Leonard Lewis S., clerk. h over 195 Main.
LEONARD NATHANIEL, laborer, h Canal.
LEONARD WILLIAM B., retired, h Front.
Leonard Willis B., tobacco grower, h Pumpelly, South Side.
Leroy Peter H., laborer, h Prospect, cor. Green.
Letts Armena, widow John D., resident, h rear 18 Adaline.
Levene Abram, tailor, h 42 Temple.
Lewis Fred W., machinist, h 109 Fox.
LEWIS GEORGE B., M. D., physician and surgeon, Lake, cor. Main, rooms do.
Lewis Milo, contractor, Owego Casket Company, h 95 West ave.
Lewis Robert, laborer, h 93 Paige.
Lillie George W., retired, h 103 River, South Side.
Lillie Jared. saloon, 104 North ave., h do.
Lincoln & Co., (C. K. Lincoln) coal and wood, 59 Central ave.
Lincoln Charles K., (Lincoln & Co.) h 294 Main.
Link Charles A., (Dwelle & Link) h 348 Front.
Livermore Cyrus E., clerk, h 20 Ross.
Livermore Otis W., general repair shop, rear 117 North ave., h 84 Chestnut.
Livingston Amos, groceries and provisions, 56 North ave, h do.
Loader Richard, painter, h 64 Forsyth.
Locke Mary E., carpet weaver, h 91 Fox.
LOCKE REUBEN B., carpenter, h 241 Erie.
Long Jeremiah, resident, h 25 Temple.
Loring Benjamin W., retired lieut. U. S. revenue marine service, h 351 Front.

STARKEY & WINTERS, Wholesale and Retail Druggists, Owego.

Loring Benjamin W., Jr., law student, bds. Front.
Lounsbury William H., boot and shoemaker, 63 North ave., h 37 Main.
Lovejoy Charles L., photographer, Front cor. Court, h 313 Main.
Lynch Daniel, bartender, bds. 7 Fulton.
Lynch Martin S., atty. at law, Lake, cor. Main h 495 Main.
Lynch Michael, mason, h 7 Fulton.
Lynch Michael, (Wall & Lynch) h Chestnut.
Lynde Marion, widow James G., resident, bds. 51 Front.
Lynn Luzern, laborer, h 65 Adaline.
LYON & RIPLEY, (F. D. L. & H. C. R.) boots and shoes, 188 Front.
Lyon & Robinson, (J. R. L. & G. R.) liquor dealers, 187 Main.
LYON FRANCIS D., (Lyon & Ripley) h 7 Park.
Lyon John R., (Lyon & Robinson) h 60 Paige.
Mabee Foster N., agent Erie Express Co., h 333 Main.
MABEE JOHN A., (City Steam Laundry) h Temple cor. Central ave.
Mabee William, emp. Owego Casket Company, bds. 73 Liberty.
Macbeth Margaret, resident, h 22 William.
MADAN ANDREW J., emp. James Hill estate, h 111 Talcott.
Male William, carpenter, h 22 William.
Maloney Ann, resident, h 121 Erie.
Maloney Bridget, resident, h 121 Erie.
Maloney Catherine, widow Michael C., h 98 Temple.
Maloney Catherine A., clerk, bds. 98 Temple.
Maloney Julia, resident, h 121 Erie.
Maloney Minnie, dressmaker, bds. 73 Liberty.
Maloney Owen T., bookbinder, h 98 Temple.
MALONEY PATRICK, prop. Cobweb Bottling Works, Paige cor. Fox, also general grocery and liquors, 122 Paige, h do.
Maloney William P., clerk, bds. 122 Paige.
Manas Julia, dressmaker, bds. 7 East ave.
Manas Patrick, R. R. signal tender, h 7 East ave.
Manning Caroline M. Mrs., millinery, 206 Front, h do.
Manning Ellen, dressmaker, bds. Division.
Manning James, foreman Owego *Times*, h over 193 Main.
Manning Josephine, tailoress, bds. Division.
Manning Lewis, printer, bds. 133 North ave.
Manning Margaret, widow John, h Division.
MANNING MARION L., shoemaker, h 206 Front.
Manning Mary, widow James, bds. 57 Church.
Manning Michael J., laborer, bds. Division.
Manning William H., carpenter, 113 Main, h do.
Mareane James, engineer, bds. 150 Central ave.
Maroney Daniel, laborer, h 245 E. Temple.
Maroney John F., groceries, 56 North ave, h over do.
Marquart Gideon, farmer, bds. 139 North ave.
Marquart Levi, retired, h 17 West ave.
Marquart Levier, bds. Commerce.
Marquart Simeon, farmer, h 139 North ave.
Marquett John M., shoemaker, h 473 Front.
Marquett Larenzo, clerk, bds. 473 E. Front.
Marquette Alanson A., resident, h 230 Prospect.
Marquette Jerome N., clerk, 14 W. Main.

STARKEY & WINTERS, Druggists, Owego. Close Prices to Dealers.

Marshall Mrs., resident, h 167 North ave.
Martin Benjamin B., carriage-trimmer, bds. 73 Liberty.
Marvin Harrison, orderly at State Capitol, h 94 Liberty.
Mason Allen J., painter, bds. 113 Chestnut.
Mason Harriet Mrs., widow Roswell A., laundress, h 113 Chestnut.
Matson Cynthia E. Miss, resident, h 14 Front.
Matson John L., furniture and undertaking, 183 Front, h 27 Park.
Mawhiney Edward, bookkeeper, 164 North ave., bds. 5 Spruce.
MAWHINEY WILLIAM J., (W. H. Bailey & Co.) h 5 Spruce.
May William, laborer, h 209 Prospect.
Maynard William, shoemaker, h 64 Spencer ave.
MAYOR EDWARD A., D. D. S., dentist, over 173 Front, h Academy.
Mayor William E., D. D. S., dentist, over 173 Front, bds. Academy.
McArthur John, confectionery, 107 North ave., h do.
McCofferty Anthony C., horse-dealer, bds. European House.
McColly Thomas, resident, bds. United States Hotel.
McCARTHY FLORENCE, laborer, h 604 Fifth ave.
McCarthy John, laborer, h 119 Fox.
McCarthy John P., clerk, bds. 604 Fifth ave.
McCaslin John H., (Smith & McCaslin) blacksmith, h 190 River, So. Side.
McCullock ———, h 107, Chestnut.
McCormick Daniel, brakeman, h 99 Fox.
McDonald John, mason, bds. 18 West Main.
McDowell Fayette, cabinet-maker, h Canal.
McDowell Betty, widow Augustus, bds. Ah-wa-ga House.
McGiffin John L., emp. grist-mill, h 102 Chestnut.
McGratch Patrick, laborer, h 115 Paige.
McKee Robert, retired, h 387 Main.
McKenzie Alexander C. Rev., pastor First Pres. church, h 321 Front.
McLean Ezra, carpenter and builder, h 172 Talcott.
McManus Rose, widow Patrick, laundress, h 91 Fox.
McMaster Frank, liquor store, 70 North ave., h do.
McNulty Barney, tanner, bds. 133 North ave.
McNulty James, baggageman, h 107 River, South Side.
McNulty Thomas, emp. Dean's tannery, bds. near tannery, North ave.
MEACHAM CHARLES D., carpenter, h 99 Talcott.
Meacham Erastus, blacksmith, 221 North ave., h do.
MEAD & DARROW, (H. J. M. & F. A. D.) attorneys at law, Main cor. North ave.
MEAD HOWARD J., (Mead & Darrow) h Main, cor. Spencer ave.
Mericle Alfred, baggageman, h 200 North ave.
Mericle Charles D., clerk, h 439 Main.
Merritt Ephraim J., brakeman, h 167 North ave.
Merrick John, salesman, h 57 Main.
Metcalf Charles, miller, h 114 Central ave.
Metcalf Hannah M., widow Dr. A. E., h 207 East Main.
Middaugh Augustus B., carpenter, h 32 Adaline.
Middaugh Elijah, retired, h off Water.
Middaugh James E., laborer, h Canal Front.
Miller Edith L., tailoress, bds. 88 Adaline.
Miller Lorenzo, clerk, h Central ave.
Miller Mrs., widow Abram, h 405 Front.

MILLREA BROTHERS, (W. A., J. F. & T.) meat-market and grocery, 178 Front.
MILLREA J. FRED, (Millrea Bros.) h 377 Main.
MILLREA THOMAS, (Millrea Bros.) bds. Dugan House.
MILLREA WILLIAM A., (Millrea Bros.) h 55 Paige.
Mills Robert, cooper, h 102 McMaster.
Minehan John, tanner, h 64 Temple.
Minehan William, miller, bds. 14 W. Main.
Miner William D., book-keeper 174 Front, bds. Dugan House.
Mitchell Bartlett, tanner, h 107 River, South Side.
Mitchell Eliza A. B., widow Henry A., bds. 153 Temple.
Mitchell William J., emp. King & Co., bds. 107 River, South Side.
Moak Robert T., retired carpenter, h 130 North ave.
Moffitt James R., laborer, h 117 Green.
Moffitt Robert J., laborer, h 117 Green.
Moloney Agnes K., clerk, bds. 98 Temple.
Moneypenny Elizabeth, widow Robert L., resident, h 388 Main.
Monyhan George, hostler, bds. United States Hotel.
Moody Winfield S., harness-maker, h 59 Main.
Moon Reuben, cooper, h John R.
Moore & Ross, (T. F. M. & J. S. R.) carriage and wagon manufs., 146 North ave.
Moore Charles, wagon-maker, h 134 North ave.
Moore Helen E. B., widow Dr. Robert, resident, h 227 Front.
Moore Theodore F., (Moore & Ross) h 82 Chestnut.
Moran James, well driver, bds. 89 William.
Morann Thomas, blacksmith, h 105 Fox.
MOREHOUSE ALLIE, art teacher, h Spencer ave.
Morehouse Charles H., printer, h Spencer ave.
Morehouse John, carpenter, h off Water.
Morgan Delos, carpenter, h 18 Paige.
Morgan William B., horse-trainer, h 607 Main.
Morris Anna, widow John, bds. 104 Paige.
Morris Frank, clerk, bds. 110 Spencer ave.
Morris Patrick, laborer, h 110 Spencer ave.
Morris Thomas, resident, bds. 110 Spencer ave.
Morse Charles, printer, h 31 Temple.
Morse Henry H., butcher and farmer, h Pumpelly, South Side, h do.
Morse Mrs., resident, h 100 East ave.
Morse Newell, coal, wood and shingles, 133 Temple, h do.
Morton Durwent, laborer, h 169 North ave.
Morton Edward, laborer, h 215 North ave.
Morton Ida E., widow G. A., h 84 North ave.
Morton John, constable and tanner, h South Side.
Moulton Michael A., sewing machine repairer 10 Lake, bds. do.
Mulks Frank H., emp. foundry, h 130 Chestnut.
Munger Cynthia L., widow Alanson, h 285 Main.
Munn Sarah E. Mrs., resident, bds. 7 George.
Murray Ida Mrs., laundress, h 26 Talcott.
Muzzy Cornelius, clerk, bds. 279 Main.
Myers Andrew, butcher, h 6 West ave.
Myers Jessie, teacher, bds. 6 West ave.
Myers Philip, emp. casket works, bds. 6 West ave.

Neally Sarah F., teacher, bds. 560 Fifth ave.
Neaves Edmund J., clerk, bds. Front.
Nelson Bert E., drug clerk, bds. North ave. extension.
Nelson James, retired, bds. 48 West Main.
Nelson James, Jr., notions, 48 West Main, h do.
Nelson Willa M., dressmaker, bds 21 George.
Nelson William, engineer, h 21 George.
Newell Frank, carpenter, h 117 Central ave.
Newell Friend G., cabinet-maker, rear 17 Lake, h 57 Liberty.
Newell Gilbert, resident, h 34 Fox.
Newell Gilbert C., emp. foundry, bds. 77 West ave.
Newell Orvin L., emp. foundry, h 77 West ave.
*NEWGEON MARY F., physician, 295 Main, h do.
Newiand James D., laborer, h 248 North ave.
Newman Adolphus, (Newman Bros.) h 47 Temple.
Newman Brothers, (A. & G.) dry goods and millinery, 31 and 33 Lake.
Newman George, (Newman Bros.) h 47 Temple.
NEWMAN SIMON, optician, h 54 Temple.
Newton Charles D., printer, h 43 Talcott.
Newton Frank, laborer, h 152 River, South Side.
Newton George, emp. Chamberlain's boot and shoe factory, h 125 Main.
Nichols George A., (Nichols & Huber) h 161 Main.
Nichols Susan B., widow Thomas M., h 55 Front.
Nichols Susan B. Miss, resident, bds. 55 Front.
Nichols Washington, resident, h 55 Front.
NIXON CHARLES D., loan and investment, real estate and lawyer; also prop. Jenksville steam mills, Front cor. Court, bds. Ah-wa-ga House.
Nixon Walter, harness-maker, h over 168 Front.
N. Y., L. E. & W. R. R. Depot, Cameron B. Dean, agent, North ave., cor. Depot.
Noble Asa S., carpenter, h 12 Adaline.
Noonan David E., carpenter, h 96 Franklin.
Noonnan Daniel, mason, h Paige.
Norris Charles P., carriage-smith, h 266 Prospect.
Norris George E., lamp-lighter, h 521 Front.
Norris Hampton M., barber, bds. 266 Prospect.
Norris Theodore, teamster, bds., Decker Block, Main.
Northrop Tilly, book-canvasser, bds. 113 Chestnut.
Northrop William T., painter, h 113 Chestnut.
Norton Harriet A., widow Colden O., h 164 Temple.
Norwood Erastus, retired, bds. 7 Hill.
Nugent Mary, pastry-cook Ah-wa-ga House, bds. do.
Nutt Hamer, emp. King & Co., bds. 118 Temple.
N. Y. & PA. TELEPHONE AND TELEGRAPH CO., Frank S. Bloodgood, manager, 178 Main.
NYE ARTHUR E., (Nye Brothers) h Fox.
NYE BROTHERS, (M. G. & A. E.) bakers and confectioners, 44 Lake.
NYE MELVIN G., (Nye Brothers) bds. Fox.
Oakley Timothy B., counselor at law, 214 Front, h River Road.
ODD FELLOWS' HALL, W. Stewart, janitor, over 80 North ave.
Odell Hiram A., engineer, h 36 George.
Ogden Aaron, tobacconist, 7 Lake, h Front.
Ogden Frederic L., traveling salesman, bds. Front.

Ogden Harriet A., widow Walter, h 229 Main.
Ogden Priscella C., widow Isaac, h 194 River, South Side.
Ogden S. Jane, widow Jehiel, resident, h 125 Main.
OHART S. JAY, att'y and counselor at law, Academy Bld'g, Court, h at Tioga Center.
Ohern Bartholomew, track foreman S. C. R. R., h near tannery, North ave.
Ohmar Patrick, gardener, bds. Front.
Olmstead Franklin H., machinist, bds. 227 Erie.
Olmstead Freeborn W., machinist, h 227 Erie.
O'Neil Maggie, clerk, 61 East ave.
O'Neil Michael, laborer, h 61 East ave.
Orcutt J. Allan, carpenter, h 126 Chestnut.
Orcutt Isaac D., bridge carpenter, h 45 Fox.
O'ROURKE MICHAEL F., keeper Auburn prison, h Lake.
Ostrander Edward, emp. King & Co., bds. 14 West ave.
*OWEGO CRUCIFORM CASKET CO., (John Jones, pres't; J. J. VanKleeck, sec'y; and C. R. Heaton, treas.) burial caskets and undertakers' supplies, lumber, sash, doors, and blinds, 42, 44 and 46 Delphine.
*OWEGO DAILY AND WEEKLY RECORD, (Scott & Watros) 172 Front.
Owego Gas Light Co., A. P. Storrs, Jr., pres't, office Front cor. Lake.
*OWEGO GAZETTE, (weekly) Leroy W. Kingman, editor and publisher, 28 Lake.
*OWEGO IRON WORKS, Cauldwell & Gray, props., McMaster cor. Dalton.

OWEGO IRON WORKS

CAULDWELL & GRAY, Proprietors.

FOUNDRY AND MACHINE SHOPS.

WE MANUFACTURE NEARLY ALL KINDS OF CASTINGS.

Engines and Boilers Repaired

ALSO MACHINE WORK DONE ON SHORT NOTICE.

We Manufacture Patent Cast Iron Standards and Lasts for Shoemakers' use.

OWEGO NATIONAL BANK, (Charles E. Parker, pres't; R. B. Dean, vice-pres't; C. A. Thompson, cashier; J. A. Bassett, teller) 6 Lake.
OWEGO POSTOFFICE, F. O. Cable, postmaster, Lake.
*OWEGO TIMES, (Weekly) W. Smyth & Son, props., 193 Main.
OWEGO TIMES BINDERY AND BLANK-BOOK MANUF., W. Smyth & Son, props., 193 Main.
OWEGO WATER WORKS, George Y. Robertson, sup't, 69 North ave.
Owen Elias H. Mrs., h 314 Front.
Padgett Gurdon E., emp. Canawanna mills, bds. Canal.
Padgett William S., laborer, h off Water.
Paine Thomas, saloon and restaurant, 229 North ave., h do.

OWEGO—INSIDE CORPORATION.

Park George W., carpenter, h 74 Fox.
Park Hotel, (Nichols & Huber, props.) 161 Main.
PARKER CHARLES E., county judge, surrogate, and att'y at law, pres't Owego National Bank, Court House, h 108 Main.
PARKER STELLA, widow John M., h 113 Front.
Parmelee Alburn S., manager Western Union and Erie telegraph offices, Erie Depot, h 77 Liberty.
PARMELEE ALBURN W., (Beach & Parmelee) h Main.
Parmeter Edward, lumber, h 3 Spruce.
Parris Stephen, billiards, h 206 Front.
Partridge Frank J., soapmaker, h George.
Partridge John F., resident, h 48 George.
Partridge John F., Jr., soapmaker, bds. 48 George.
Partridge Walter B., clerk, bds. 48 George.
Partridge William J., baggageman S. C. R. R. depot, h 91 Talcott.
Patghard Gordon, laborer, h Canal.
Patrick George W., resident, bds. Park Hotel.
Payne Frank A., hack driver, bds. Central ave.
PAYNE FRANK F., printer, bds. Main.
Payne John, gardener, h 256 Prospect.
Payne William A., porter Ah-wa-ga House, bds. do.
Peabody Oliver A., harness-maker, h 19 John.
PEARSALL ANDREW T., physician and surgeon, Taylor Block, h Main cor. Spencer ave.
Pearsall Dwight, engineer, h 192, North ave.
Pearsall Gilbert, medical student, bds. Main cor. Spencer ave.
PEARSALL RANSOM S., justice of the peace, over 168 Front, h in Apalachin.
Pease George, shoemaker, 160 North ave., h do.
Pease Johanna, widow David, bds. 56 George.
Peck Ezra J., principal of academy and supt. of schools, h 104 Main.
Peck Nancy M., widow Rev. Philetus B., h 347 Main.
Peck Sarah N., resident, bds. 347 Main.
Peck William A., resident, h 105 Talcott.
Pelham John W., cooper, h 39 Temple.
Pelham William, cooper, bds. 133 North ave.
PELLUM MARGARET MRS., shampooer of ladies' hair, also hair worker, h 459 Main.
Penney Ella G., book-keeper, bds. 59 Spencer ave.
Penney Joseph H., cutter, h 59 Spencer ave.
PENNY CORNELIUS S., bridge carpenter, h 16 Adaline.
Penny Frederick C., clerk, h 31 Church.
Perkins Frederick, carpenter, h 21 Fulton.
Perrine Joanna, widow John K., h Buckbee Block.
Perry Harley, emp. foundry, bds. 118 Temple.
Perry John M., blacksmith, h 30 Temple.
Perry Lottie A., teacher, South Side, bds. do.
Perry William H., carpenter, h South Side.
Pert Thomas, express messenger, h 31 Front.
Pert William, tel. op., bds. 31 Front.
Peters William, resident, h 162 McMaster.
PETERSON PETER C., (Buckbee, Peterson, Wood & Co.) h 16 Ross.
Phelps E. B., retired physician and surgeon, Front cor. Paige.

Phillips Augustus H., retired, bds. 113 Franklin.
Phillips Betie, clerk, bds. 68 Adaline.
Phililps Carrie, clerk, bds. 228 Front.
Phillips James H., bridge carpenter, h 68 Adaline.
Phillips William H., gardener, bds. 68 Adaline.
Pike Augusta, widow Horace, h 8 W. Main.
Pinney Hammon D., books, stationery and wall-paper, 45 Lake, h 437 Front.
Pippett Mary, widow James, laundress, h 101 Fox.
PITCHER DANIEL M., wool, hides and pelts, 175 Front, h 325 Main.
Pitcher Lena, resident, h over Lake cor. Main.
Plakenpol John, farmer, h n Dean's Tannery.
PLATT FREDERICK E., cashier Tioga Nat. Bank, h 256 Main.
Platt George, resident, h 33 Church.
Platt George Mrs., cancer specialist, h 33 Church.
Platt Henry B., (Gere, Truman, Platt & Co.) rooms 33 Park.
Platt Harry P., supt. for Gere, Truman, Platt & Co., bds. Court.
Poltzen Peter, piano-maker, h n Dean's Tannery.
Porter Frances S., widow Rev. George P., bds. 322 Main.
Postal Telegraph and Cable Co., (C. W. Daggett, mgr.) 40 Lake.
Potter Asa N., retired, h 87 Main.
Potter Isaac L., carpenter, h 100 Chestnut.
Powell William, gardener, h Front.
Powell William H., jeweler, bds. Front.
Prendergast John, pattern-maker, h 78 Paige.
Prendergast John, Jr., resident, bds. 78 Paige.
Pride Eliza, widow William, h Water.
Prime Aaron P., gardener, h Constine's lane.
Pritchard Albert J., clerk, h Spencer Block, Lake.
Probert Daniel, laborer, bds. Canal.
Probert Emma, dressmaker, bds. Canal.
Pultz Frank, photographer, bds. 38 Lake.
Pultz Griffin, locomotive engineer, h 51 Fox.
Pultz Griffin, Jr., music teacher, bds. 51 Fox.
Pumpelly Caroline A., resident, bds. 113 Front.
Pumpelly Gurdon H., wholesale leaf tobacco dealer, and farmer 250, h Pumpelly, South Side.
Pumpelly James F., real estate dealer and farmer, h Pumpelly, South Side.
Purdy Emma D., music teacher, bds. 147 Main.
Purple George B., expressman, h 102 Liberty.
Purple Jasper L., contractor, h 99 Franklin.
Putnam Archibald, painter, h 425 Main.
Putnam Frederick, (Leverson & Putnam) h Main.
Putnam Frederick J., painter, h 427 Main.
Putnam Jennie C., milliner, bds. 425 Main.
Putnam Louis H., house-painter and music teacher, bds. 425 Main.
Putney Cyrus, shoemaker, h 97 Paige.
Quetschenbach Anna, widow Walter, h 269 Erie.
Quetschenbach Grace, dressmaker, 269 Erie, bds. do.
Quetschenbach Joseph, cigarmaker, bds. 269 Erie.
Quinn Ann, resident, h 88 South Depot.
Quinn Frank, laborer, bds. 18 West Main.
Quinn Julia, dressmaker, bds. 18 West Main.
Quinn Richard, brakeman, h 5 Fox.

Rader Lawrence W., plumber, h South Side.
Rady Kate E., widow Hugh, dressmaker, h 124 Paige.
Randall Frank, carpenter, h 607 Main.
Randall Samuel, carpenter, h 607 Main.
Ransom John, laborer, h 111 Paige.
Ransom Margaret, widow Robert, h 115 Fox.
Rapp Charles F., salesman, bds. Dugan House.
RAYMOND & EMERY (F. L. R. and D. H. E.) carriage and wagon manufrs., Central ave. cor. Temple.
Raymond Chauncey L., mgr. of store for Mary F. Raymond, h 199 Main.
RAYMOND FRANK L., (Raymond & Emery) h 29 Fox.
Raymond George C., carriage-maker, h 72 McMaster.
Raymond Mary F., groceries and meats, 199 Main, h do.
Raymond Mrs., resident, h 64 Spencer ave.
Raymond William B., clerk, bds. Ah-wa-ga House.
Raymond William B., farmer 75, h 228 Main.
Raymond William W., clerk, bds. over 199 Main.
Ready James, laborer, h 149 Erie.
Redding Hugh, dyeing and cleaning, 65 Central ave., h McMaster.
REED SARAH, widow Timothy C., resident, h 26 Ross.
Regan Edward, bartender, bds. 16 Lake.
Regan Jane, widow Thomas, resident, h 109 Paige.
Regan Jerry, cigarmaker, h 99 Erie.
Regan John, saloon and restaurant 16 Lake, h do.
Relyea Andrew, carpenter, h 26 Fulton.
RENWICK WILLIAM C., (Battelle & Renwick of New York city) h 79 Front.
Reynolds Peter, carpenter, h 270 North ave.
Reynolds Smith, peddler, bds. 133 North ave.
Rhinevault Myron, blacksmith rear 81 North ave., h 53 Talcott.
Rice Catherine, resident, h 65 Adaline.
Rich George E., (Dorwin, Stone & Rich) h 40 Front.
Richards & Doyle (W. N. R. & P. J. D.) wholesale and retail liquors, 168 Front.
Richards William N., (Richards & Doyle) bds. Ah-wa-ga House.
Richardson Wesley L., carpenter, 557 Front.
Rightmire Charles H., carpenter, h 17 George.
Rigney Thomas, harness-maker, bds. 64 South depot.
Riley & Gillett, (M. R. & L. W. G.) blacksmiths, 140 Front.
Riley George, blacksmith, h 140 Central ave.
Riley James, laborer, h Constine's lane.
Riley James, blacksmith 81 North, h 34 Main.
Riley Martin, (Riley & Gillett) h 27 Fox.
Ringrose Ellen, widow Patrick, h 117 Franklin.
Ringrose John, clerk, bds. 117 Franklin.
Ringrose Thomas J., printer, bds. 117 Franklin.
Ringrose William E., (Shaw & Ringrose) bds. 117 Franklin.
RIPLEY HENRY C., (Lyon & Ripley) h 359 Main.
Ripley Sarah P., resident, h 53 Paige.
Roach David, blacksmith, h 113 Spencer ave.
Roach Ellen, widow David, h 100 Spencer ave.
Roache David, laborer, h 231 Temple.
Roak Alvin P., salesman 198 Front, bds. Main.

OWEGO—INSIDE CORPORATION. 139

Roberts J., traveling salesman, bds. 67 Central ave.
Roberts Lincoln, emp. drill shop, bds. 67 Central ave.
Robertson Frank W., bds. 123 North ave.
ROBERTSON GEORGE Y., supt. water works, h 489 Main.
Robertson Jason J., street commissioner, h 79 Talcott.
Robertson A. Jerry, chief of police, h 123 North ave.
Robertson Peter, gardener, h 489 Main.
Robertson Peter J., emp. Erie freight-house, h 26 John.
Robertson Ralph H., clerk, h 9 Spruce.
Robertson Will P., emp. foundry, bds. 79 Talcott.
Robinson Alexander, laborer, h 98 Fox.
Robinson Alvin T., carpenter, h Adaline.
Robinson Bert E., emp. casket company, bds. Adaline.
Robinson Charles, harness-maker, bds. 177 Main.
Robinson Edwin, moulder, bds. 115 Temple.
Robinson Elvira, widow J. Owen, bds. Adaline.
Robinson George, laborer, h 121 Green.
Robinson George, carpenter, h 115 Temple.
Robinson George, (Lyon & Robinson) h over 187 Main.
Robinson Jacob H., blacksmith and farmer 61, h 552 Main.
Robinson James V., bar-tender, h North ave. cor. Fox.
Robinson Martin V., clerk, bds. Adaline.
Robinson Matthew, saloon, 20 Lake, bds. Dugan House.
Robinson William, constable, h 109 North ave.
Rockwell Marvin, emp. foundry, h 116 Chestnut.
RODMAN CHARLES, county sheriff and produce, Front, and Main cor. Court, h do.
Rodman Edward D., deputy sheriff and produce dealer, Main cor. Court, h do.
Rogers Arthur L., saloon, 152 Front, h do.
Rogers Elias H., emp. drill works, h Fox cor. Central ave.
Rogers James T., assistant postmaster, bds. Ah-wa-ga House.
Roland John, laborer, bds. near tannery, North ave.
Roll Joseph, cigar-maker, bds. 269 Erie.
ROMINE CHARLES F., house, sign, fresco and decorative painter and paper-hanger, 121 Erie, h do.
Romine Clarence W., painter and paper-hanger, 119 Chestnut, h do.
ROMINE DEMOSTHENES, piano-varnisher, h 279 Prospect.
ROMINE EDWIN B., house-painting and decorating, Opera House Block, h 95 Fox.
Romine Joseph, painter, bds. 119 Chestnut.
ROMINE PERCIVAL H., scenic, fresco, ornamental and house-painting, paper-hanging, etc., 81 Fox, h do.
Romine Samuel L., painter, h 104 Fox.
Rose Jane, widow Albin, h 164 Temple.
Ross Allie M., dressmaker, 42 William, bds. do.
Ross Delia, widow Horatio, h 42 William.
Ross Ed. L., machinest, bds. 93 West ave.
Ross John S., (Moore & Ross) bds. Ah-wa-ga House.
Ross Oliver L., salesman, h 492 Main.
Ross William E., laborer, h 15 Fox.
Rounsville Caroline E., widow Charles J., resident, bds. 15 Front.
Rowe Henry W., clerk, h over 19 Main.

Rowe Joseph, blacksmith, h 100 Liberty.
Rowe Louise, clerk, bds. Front.
Rowe M. & G., (Mary & Gussie) dressmakers, 192 Front, h do.
Rubert Charles B., jeweler, bds. Dugan House.
Rumph David, lather, h 217 North ave.
Russell Howard A., emp. Erie R. R., h 54 Fox.
Russell Van Ness, retired, h 91 Talcott.
Ryan Annis, widow Thomas, h Canal.
Ryan Charlotte, widow Joseph, resident, h near Dean's tannery.
Ryan Michael, laborer, h 17 Park.
Ryan Patrick, laborer, h 19 West ave.
Ryan Thomas E., moulder, h 65 George.
Ryan William, machinist, bds. Canal.
Sackett Hattie, teacher, bds. 100 Front.
Sackett Mary T., widow Charles, resident, h 100 Front.
Sackett Richard G., express messenger, bds. 45 Front.
Saltsman George, clerk, bds. 488 Main.
Sample Arche, laborer, h 493 Front.
Samuels Yetta, widow Jacob, h 60 Spencer ave.
Sanford Dayton M., clerk, h 108 Liberty.
Sanford William Rev., African M. E. Zion church, bds. 106 Paige.
Saxton Edward, carpenter, h 96 Liberty.
SCHNEPPER JACOB, supt. Canawanna mill, h Water.
SCHOONMAKER CHRISTOPHER E., (Buckbee, Peterson, Wood & Co.) bds. 313 Main.
Schoonmaker John, cooper, h Railroad.
Schoonmaker John, cooper, h 112 Liberty.
Schopp Francis A., mason, bds. Pumpelly, South Side.
Schopp John P., gardener, bds. Pumpelly, South Side.
Schopp Peter, mason and farmer, h Pumpelly, South Side.
Schopp Stephen M., farmer, bds. Pumpelly, South Side.
Schopp William T., farmer, bds. Pumpelly, South Side.
SCOTT & WATROS, (C. S. Scott and O. J. Watros) publishers *Owego Record*, 172 Front.
Scott Charles, farmer with his brother Edmund 250, h 6 Adaline.
SCOTT CLAYTON S., (Scott & Watros) h William.
Scott George, cartman, h 206 North ave.
Scott Lee, laborer, h 531 Front.
Scott Lizzie, teacher, bds. 6 Adeline.
Scott Harriet, resident, h Fox cor. Central ave.
Scrafford Robert, janitor, h 226 North ave.
Searles John T., (J. T. Searls & Son) h over 136 North ave.
Searles J. T. & Son, (Louie F.) groceries and provisions, 136 North ave.
Searles Lot, carpenter, h 97 Central ave.
Searles Louie F., (J. T. Searles & Son) h 119 West ave.
SEARS JOHN G., district attorney, Lake cor. Main, h 56 Front.
Seely Lewis, boarding, 133 North ave.
SETTEL LYMAN L., atty. at law, Postoffice Bldg., bds. Ah-wa-ga House.
Severn Franklin L., bridge builder, h 318 Front.
Severson & Putnam, (G. R. S. and F. P.) saloon and pool-room, 78 North ave.
Severson & Williamson, (G. S. & C. W.) saloon 53 North ave.
Severson Edward, steward Ah-wa-ga House, bds. do.
Severson George, (Severson & Williamson) h Main cor. Forsyth.

Severson George R., (Severson & Putnam) h 417 Main.
Severson Mary, dressmaker, bds. 417 Main.
SEYMOUR LOUISA L., widow Dr. Elias W., 113 North ave., h do.
Shanahan Patrick H., clerk, h 87 Liberty.
Shaughnessy Luke, marble-worker, h 100 McMaster.
Shaw & Dean, (C. E. S. and C. R. D.) merchant millers, 110 Central ave.
Shaw & Ringrose (E. J. S. and W. E. R.) wholesale and retail grocers, Lake cor. Main.
Shaw Charles E., (Shaw & Dean) h 276 Main.
Shaw Elmer J., (Shaw & Ringrose) h Church.
Shaw William, farmer, h South Side.
SHAW WILLIAM H., saloon, 156 Front, h do.
Shay Bridget, widow Henry, h 89 Paige.
Shay James, laborer, bds. 113 Erie.
Shay John, clerk, bds. 44 Fox.
Shay John, laborer, h 113 Erie.
Shay Maggie, tailoress, bds. 44 Fox.
Shay Mary A., dressmaker, bds. 113 Erie.
Shay Nellie, tailoress, bds. 44 Fox.
Shay Owen, railroad car inspector, h 44 Fox.
Shays George, meat market, 82 North ave., also fish market 84½ do., h 60 West ave.
Shays Jonas, groceries and provisions, 72 North ave, h 63 McMaster.
Shays Lucinda, widow Hiram, h 60 West ave.
Shays Rilla, bookkeeper, bds. 60 West ave.
Shea John, laborer, h 505 Front.
Shea William, emp. Cobweb Bottling Works, bds. Chestnut.
Shehan Timothy, mason, h 105 Paige.
Sheldon & Yates, (W. H. S. and A. Y.) groceries and provisions, 131 North ave.
Sheldon Erastus, sawfiler, h over 131 North ave.
Sheldon William H., (Sheldon & Yates) h 117 Central ave.
Shepard W. Henry, carpenter, h Main.
Sheridan Robert E., moulder, h 395 Main.
Sherlock Robert J., tailor, h 524 Main.
Sherman Frederick S., farmer, h South Side.
Sherman Harriet, widow Reuben, h South Side.
Shields James, section foreman Erie R. R., h 566 Fifth ave.
Shipman Ernest R., clerk, bds. Adaline.
Shipman Prosper, emp. Gere, Truman, Platt & Co., h Adaline.
Shipman Rufus, emp. Gere, Truman, Platt & Co., h 131 Talcott.
Shuler Andrew, clerk, bds. 147 Talcott.
Shupp Lawrence, shoemaker, 18 Lake, h do.
SIBLEY OLIVER P., (Stiles & Sibley) also produce dealer, and farmer 100, h 96 Chestnut.
SIGNOR ALBERT, pianos, organs and spring-beds, 207 Front, h Fifth ave.
Signor Loreta, saleswoman, bds. Fifth ave.
Simmons George, stationary engineer, bds. off North ave. n S. C. R. R. round-house.
Simmons John, emp. Casket Factory, bds. off North ave. n S. C. R. R. round-house.
Sinon Patrick, laborer, bds. 103 Erie.
Sinon Robert, laborer, h 103 Erie.

Sinon Susan, widow John, h 67 Erie.
Sisson Cornelia, widow, h over 102 North ave.
Sisson Sarah, teacher, h over 102 North ave.
Sisson William D., carpenter, h 18 Fulton.
Skeels Frederick, resident, h over 64 North ave.
Skeels Irving D., postal clerk, h over 17 Lake.
Skellenger Emma E., dressmaker, 51 Forsyth, h do.
Skellenger James C., moulder, bds. 73 George.
Skellinger Martin E., conductor, h 73 George.
Skellinger William H., brakeman, h 51 Forsyth.
Skillman David, mason, h 219 North ave.
Skinner Emily, widow Charles P., resident, h 80 Main.
SLATER FRANK B., variety store and job printing, 75 Paige cor. Temple, h do.
Slater Phœbe A., widow David, bds. 75 Paige.
Slocum Ethan A., emp. drill works, h W. Main near Mill.
Smead David J., harness-maker 150 Front, h 49 Temple.
Smith Catherine, widow Silas J., laundress, h Gere.
SMITH CHARLES F., groceries, bds. Central House.
Smith Charles W. H., book-keeper Lake, h 99 Green.
Smith Chauncey G., tailor, h 443 Main.
Smith Edward, moulder, bds 79 George.
Smith Enos, resident, bds. 229 Main.
SMITH FRED W., milk products and farm produce, 38 Lake, h Fifth ave.
Smith George W., laborer, h 79 George.
Smith George W., laborer, h 208 North ave.
Smith Hannah, widow Philip, resident, h 32 Temple.
SMITH HATTIE A., art teacher, bds. 443 Main.
Smith Herbert, clerk, bds. 73 Liberty.
Smith James L., hats, caps, robes, &c., 8 Lake, also book-keeper 190 Front, h 15 John.
Smith John, laborer, h 94 Fox.
Smith John, laborer, h 220 North ave.
Smith Jonathan M., clerk, h Main.
Smith Joseph W., (Smith & McCaslin) h River, South Side.
Smith Julius, baggageman, h 21 Fox.
SMITH LEWIS, blacksmith 168 North ave., h 96 Temple.
Smith Patty A., widow Milo, h 18 William.
Smith Philip, emp. foundry, bds. 32 Temple.
Smith Samuel H., freight agent Erie R. R., h 30 Paige.
Smith Samuel L., hatter, h 23 John.
Smith William, blacksmith, bds. 96 Temple.
Smith William E., ice peddler, bds. 117 North ave.
Smith William H., engineer, h 59 West ave.
Smith William L., blacksmith, bds. 96 Temple.
Smullen Edward, laborer, h 26 W. Main.
SMYTH WILLIAM & SON, (William A.) props. *Owego Times*, and bindery and blank-book mnfy., 193 Main.
SMYTH WILLIAM, (William Smyth & Son) h 110 Temple cor. Church.
SMYTH WILLIAM A., (William Smyth & Son) h 70 Church.
Snyder George, life insurance, h over 63 North ave.
Solomon Eleanor P., widow William C., h 32 William.
Solomon Cecil, emp. casket company, bds. 32 William.

OWEGO—INSIDE CORPORATION. 143

Somers Daniel T., carpenter, h 130 Talcott.
Soper Frances, wid. Frederick, h 123 Green.
Southerland Washington R., resident, h 134 Talcott.
SOUTHERN CENTRAL RAILROAD DEPOT, Delphine.
Spaulding Enoch R., barber, 47 Lake, h 63 Spencer ave.
Spaulding Francis, barber, bds. 63 Spencer ave.
Spaulding Harriet S., widow John, h 65 East ave.
Spaulding Harry B., apprentice, bds. 65 East ave.
SPEERS WILLIAM S., hay and general produce, 207 North ave., h 52 Church.
Spelecy Thomas, R. R. track foreman, h 96 South Depot.
Spelecy William, laborer, bds. 96 South Depot.
SPENCER WILLIAM H., pianos, organs and sewing machines, h 220 East Temple.
SPORER, CARLSON & BERRY, (F. S., O. M. C. & J. B.) piano manufs. and dealers in musical merchandise, 58 North ave.
SPORER FRANCIS M , (Sporer, Carlson & Berry) h 97 Main.
Sprague Rowland, 'bus-driver, bds. Ah-wa-ga House.
Spring Liba G., resident, h 65 East ave.
Sprong Eugene, resident, h 254 North ave.
Sprong Hannah J., widow John V., h 12 Talcott.
STANBROUGH JOHN B., hardware and stoves, 180 Front, h do.
Stanbrough Lyman T., lawyer, bds. Front.
*STARKEY & WINTERS, (J. C. S. & E. W.) drugs and medicines, cor. Front and Lake.

STARKEY & WINTERS,
Druggists and Chemists

The Prescription Department is in charge of a graduate of the College of Pharmacy, of the City of New York, and who was formerly with Caswell, Hazard & Co., of that city.
Since taking the Ely Drug Store, they have established a reputation for skillfulness and accuracy in selecting, manufacturing and dispensing Drugs and Medicines, which has gained for them the entire confidence of the public.

COR. FRONT AND LAKE STS., - OWEGO, N. Y.
Persons out of town can order by mail or telephone.

STARKEY EMMA A., (Starkey & Winters) widow Dr. John E., bds. 3 Park.
Starr A. Lorena, book-keeper, 15 Lake, bds. 290 Main.
STARR CHARLES P., jeweler, 15 Lake, h 290 Main.
STEARNS PHINEAS S., physician, bds. Park Hotel.
Stebbins Ann E., widow Charles, h 560 Fifth ave.
STEBBINS BARNEY M., insurance and real estate, 34 Lake, h 33 Paige.
Stebbins Charles L., traveling salesman, bds. 560 Fifth ave.
Stebbins Fanny, teacher, bds. 560 Fifth ave.
Stebbins George M., book-keeper, 34 Lake, bds. South Side.
Stebbins John E., resident, bds. South Side.
Stebbins William M., resident, h South Side.
Steele Don, book-keeper Owego Nat. Bk., h over Cole's clothing store, Lake.

Steele G. Odell, groceries and provisions, 177 Front, h 30 Ross.
Steele John F., harness-maker, h 164 Temple.
Steen Bert, coachman, bds. Canal.
Steen Stogdill S., farmer, h near Dean's tannery.
STEEVENS NORTON A., foreman Champion Wagon Works, h 90 Chestnut.
STEPHENS W. HENRY, mechanic, h 577 Front.
Stevens Alexander, laborer, h 63 North ave.
Stevens Charles J., emp. grain drill works, h near tannery, North ave.
Stevens Frank Mrs., resident, h 105 North ave.
Stevens John, piano-maker, h Canal.
Stevens Romeo, shoemaker, h 32 John.
Stever Alvin C., resident, h over 167 Main.
Stever Amanda E. Mrs., dressmaker, over 78 North ave., h do.
STEVER PETER, butcher, 74 North ave., h over do.
Stewart James W., minstrel performer, Constine's Lane.
Stewart Wilmot L., soap-maker, h 28 Temple.
STILES & SIBLEY, (F. H. S. & O. P. S.) agricultural implements, North ave.
Stiles Charles L., physician and surgeon, 228 Front, h do.
Stiles George, clerk, bds. 67 Central ave.
Stiles Mary, resident, bds. 206 Front.
Stillman Phineas, harness-maker, bds. Decker Block, Main.
Stockwell R., harness maker, bds. Decker Block, Main.
Stone Eli W., teller Tioga Nat. Bank, h Front.
Stone James T., (Dorwin, Rich & Stone) h Front.
Stone William P., retired merchant, h Front.
Storm Cora, teacher, bds. 36 Adaline.
Storm Elias P., farmer, leases of E. Brown 25, h 36 Adaline.
Storm Elizabeth, widow Jonn C., resident, h 42 George.
Storm John C., carpenter, bds. 42 George.
Storms George, cartman, h 25 Adaline.
STORRS AARON P., (Storrs, Chatfield & Co.) h River, South Side.
STORRS AARON P., Jr., (Storrs, Chatfield & Co.) h River, South Side.
STORRS, CHATFIELD & CO., (A. P. S., J. R. C., A. P. S., Jr., and G. S. C.) hardware, Front cor. Lake.
Stout Richard S., resident, h 212 E. Temple.
STRAIT EDWARD E., (Coburn & Strait) h King Block, Lake.
Strait Julia A., widow William, bds. 48 Talcott.
Strait Seeley P., resident, h 190 E. Temple.
Strang Anna L., widow Charles R., resident, h 83 Paige.
Strang Benjamin H., teamster, h 20 Talcott.
STRANG GEORGE H., teaming, h 47 Talcott.
STRATTON EDWIN, (Hastings & Stratton), h 383 Front.
Straus Alfred M., clerk, bds. 147 Main.
Straus Julius L., prop. "New York Bazaar," ladies' furnishing goods, 43 Lake, h 147 Main.
Strong Lewis, carpenter, h 258 North ave.
Sullivan Ellen, widow John, resident, h Temple.
Sullivan Frank, resident, bds. 1 Temple.
Sullivan Hannah, widow Nathaniel, cook, h 87 Fox.
Sullivan James, contractor and builder, 58 Liberty, h do.
Sullivan William, salesman, bds. 1 Temple.

Swartout Abram, emp. foundry, h 159 Temple.
Swartout Caroline, teacher, bds. 159 Temple.
Swartout Helen, teacher, bds. 159 Temple.
Swartwout George W., laborer, h 70 Fox.
Sweeney Dennis J., painter, bds. 137 Erie.
Sweeney Edward F., fireman, h 50 Delphine.
Sweeney James, book-keeper, h 126 Fox.
Sweeney John, brakeman, bds. 180 North ave.
Sweeney John E., saloon, 88 North ave., bds. 126 Fox.
Sweeney Kate, widow Edward, h 180 North ave.
Sweeney Maggie G., tailoress, bds. 137 Erie.
Sweeney Margaret, widow Thomas, h 101 Erie.
Sweeney Margaret L., widow Dennis, h 137 Erie.
Sweeney Matie L., book-keeper, Lake, bds. 137 Erie.
Sweeney Michael, laborer, bds. 101 Erie.
Sweeney Michael, engineer, h 180 North ave.
Sweeney Thomas, laborer, bds. 101 Erie.
SWEET BROS. (J. R. and est. of G. W.), boots and shoes, 54 North ave.
SWEET JOHN R., (Sweet Bros.) h over 54 North ave.
Sweet Rose E., widow George W., livery, rear 64 and 68 North ave., h over 64 do.
Sweig Saul, tailor, bds. 93 Liberty.
Sykes Maria B., widow Edward, boarding-house, 313 Main.
SYKES THEODORE P., carpenter, h 52 Liberty.
Talcott Francis B., harness-maker, h 67 Paige.
Talcott George, farmer 70, h North ave. cor. Talcott.
Talcott Harriet, widow William C., h 363 Front.
Tate Emma, teacher, bds. 51 Front.
Taylor Alonzo A., gardener, h John R.
Taylor Annie M., widow James E., h 194 River, South Side.
Taylor Daniel G., retired, h 317 Front.
Taylor Ellen, tailoress, bds. 73 Liberty.
Taylor James H., book-keeper Campbell's Tannery, bds. Front cor. Paige.
Taylor James R., blacksmith, bds. South Side.
TAYLOR JOHN J., lawyer, Front cor. Court, h Front.
TAYLOR JOHN L., resident, h 377 Front.
Taylor Julia, widow William C., h over 100 North ave.
Taylor Susan, widow James, resident, h 41 Fox.
Taylor Robert J., fancy goods and notions, bds. 377 Front.
Temple M. D. Mrs., widow Austin J., h 125 Main.
Tench Richard, emp. Dean's tannery, h near tannery, North ave.
Terrill L. Fontenell, contractor, h 100, Franklin.
TERWILLIGER BENJAMIN D., mason and bricklayer, h 120 North ave.
Terwilliger Jesse E., brick-mason, h 305 Prospect.
Thatcher Sumner, locomotive engineer, h 137 North ave.
Thayer Arthur P., emp. Gere, Truman, Platt & Co., h 44 Adaline.
Thayer William, harness-maker, h Main.
*THE OWEGO MUTUAL BENEFIT ASSOCIATION, J. J. Van Kleeck, sec'y, 30 Lake.
THOMAS ALEXANDER J., florist and green-house, Main h do.
THOMAS CHARLES C., retired, h 322 Main.
Thomas Ida C., teacher, bds. 44 Talcott.
Thomas Lewis, mail-carrier, h over 59 North ave.

OWEGO—INSIDE CORPORATION.

THOMAS MOSES H., dealer in the "Bradley" reapers, mowers and horse-rakes, full line of Syracuse chilled plows, cultivaters, and sulky plows, the "clipper" chilled, reversible and sulky plows, of Elmira, and a general line of agricultural implements, 64 Temple, h 112 Liberty.
Thomas Samuel H., hotel and restaurant 54 South Depot, h do.
Thomas William H., saloon and restaurant, 154 North ave., h do.
Thomas William W., farmer 60, h 44 Talcott.
Thomas Wilnettie, teacher, bds. 44 Talcott.
Thompson A. Chase, (G. T. Sons & Co.) h 101 Front.
Thompson Ambrose B., machine shop 62 Temple, h 93 West ave.
THOMPSON ANTHONY D., excise commissioner, and Erie R. R. conductor, h 382 Main.
THOMPSON CLARENCE A., cashier Owego Nat. Bank, h 18 Front.
Thompson George H., book-keeper Gere, Truman, Platt & Co., bds. 311 Main.
Thompson George W., laborer, h 105 Green.
Thompson Harry G., clerk Owego Nat. Bank, bds. E. Main.
Thompson John M., sewing machines and organs, 107 North ave., bds. do.
Thorington Levi, gardener, h 178 River, South Side.
Thorn Warren, teamster, bds. 8 W. Main.
Thornton Jeremiah, basket-maker, h 32 W. Main.
THURSTON CHESTER P., grocery, 176 Front, and village clerk, h 145 Temple.
Thurston George, farmer, h 105 North ave.
Thurston Frederick G., groceries and fish, 130 North ave., h over 111 do.
Thurston George S. clerk, bds. over 63 North ave.
Thurston William C., clerk, h over 63 North ave.
Tickner Byron J., harness-maker, bds. Dugan House.
Tierney Charles, harness-maker, h over 17 Lake.
Tilbury Edgar E., clerk, h Temple.
Tilbury Edward, emp. L. Matson, h North ave.
Tillotson James E., confectionery and cigars, 86 North ave., h Temple cor. Spencer ave.
TINKHAM HARRIET, widow David P., h 127 North ave.
Tinkham Lois, widow Standish S., h 120 North ave.
TIOGA NATIONAL BANK OF OWEGO, (T. C. Platt, prest., F. E. Platt, cashier) 199 Front.
Tomkins Eber L., postal clerk, bds. Ah-wa-ga House.
Towsand Alva, emp. Erie freight house, h 102 Spencer ave.
Towsand Jeremiah, brakeman, h 67 McMaster.
Tracy Ellen P., widow George W., resident, h 57 Central ave.
Treat Betsey, widow Sylvester, h Decker Block, Main.
Trimnell John, laborer, h 100 Spencer ave.
Tripp Daniel, watch repairer 10 Lake, h do.
Tripp Frank, painter, h 204 North ave.
Truax Anna E, widow Isaac R., h 91 Liberty.
Truesdell Lewis W., tinsmith, plumber, &c., h 64 McMaster.
Truman Benjamin L., groceries 182 Front, h 329 Main.
Truman Emily M., widow Lyman, h Front.
TRUMAN FRANCIS W., (Gere, Truman, Platt & Co) h Front.
TRUMAN G. SONS & CO., (G. & G. Truman, Jr., and A. Chase Thompson) produce, 174 Front.

TRUMAN GEORGE (Truman, Sons & Co.) also prest. First Nat. Bank, h 374 Front.
TRUMAN GEORGE, JR., (Truman, Sons & Co.) bds. 374 Front.
Truman Gilbert T., county supt. of the poor, h 391 Front.
Truman, Stephen S., clerk., bds. Main.
TRUMAN WILLIAM S., cashier First Nat. Bank, h 347 Front.
Trutchey Erastus, express driver, h 45 Temple.
Tuch Isaac, dry and fancy goods, 198 Front, h 54 Temple.
Tuch Louis, retired, bds. 60 Spencer ave.
Tuch Meyer H., variety store, 202 Front, h 317 E. Main.
Tuch Morris R., salesman, bds. 54 Temple.
Tuck George, manager Whiteson's clothing store, Front, h 264 Main.
Tucker Oren, drayman, h 57 Adaline.
Turner Edwin B., retired Congregational clergyman, h 371 Main,
Tuthill Demon C., retired, h 121 Temple.
Tuttle Joel A., produce, h 21 Fulton.
Tuttle Minnie, milliner, bds. 92 Adaline.
Tuttle Wilbert, emp. foundry, h 92 Adaline.
Tuttle William H., emp. foundry, h 92 Adaline.
Tyler Isaiah, laborer, h South Side.
United States Express Co., F. F. Hutchins, agent, 34 Lake.
Upham Macus K., carpenter, h 5 Temple.
UPTON ALBERT H., sup't Dean's tannery, bds. 279 Main.
VanAuken Alvin, hack-driver, h 22 John.
VanAuken Benjamin, hackman, h 72 Central ave.
VanAuken Russell, porter Central House, bds. do.
VanBrunt Henry, carpenter, h 20 Temple.
VanBrunt Margaret, widow William, h 20 Temple.
VanBuren Elmer L., stage-driver, h 23 Temple.
VanDemark Rebecca, widow James, bds. 27 Adaline.
VanDerlip Wesley W., brakeman, h 168 Temple.
VanFleet James, mason, h Blade building.
VanGorder Elizabeth, widow Charles E., h 118 Paige.
VanGorder Fred C., machinist, h 118 Paige.
*VAN KLEECK JOHN J., county clerk, fire and life insurance, sec'y Cruciform Casket Co., western loans and investments, Court House, h 228 Main.

J. J. VAN KLEECK,

Fire Insurance and Real Estate Agent,

AND NEGOTIATOR OF

FIRST-CLASS WESTERN FARM MORTGAGE SECURITIES.

Buildings and property insured in the best of companies, at current rates, and losses fairly and promptly adjusted.

Parties wishing to sell or buy Real Estate, can generally be accommodated by entrusting their wants to me.

No further need of having your money lie idle. All my Western Farm Mortgages are No. 1, and the land increases in value every year. Interest and principal payable at your own bank on the day it becomes due. No person who has allowed me to loan their money has ever lost a single dollar in the fifteen years of my experience.

My only charge to the investor is one dollar on each $100 invested at time of making the loan. Letters of inquiry solicited, and promptly answered.

J. J. VAN KLEECK,
Owego, Tioga Co., N. Y.

Vanover David, ice-peddler, h 138 Central ave.
Vanover Frank W., clerk, bds. River, South Side.
Vanover Jacob, carpenter, h River, South Side.
Vanover James H., carpenter, h River, South Side.
VANOVER WESLEY, emp. Chamberlain's boot and shoe factory, h 54 Liberty.
VanPatten Abram, resident, bds. 582 Main.
VanPatten Frederick, farm laborer, h 582 Main.
Vargason Welton W., emp. Gere, Truman, Platt & Co., h Gere.
Vermilyea Abram, carpenter, h 39 West ave.
Vetter John G., tanner, h near tannery, North ave.
Vickery Almira B., widow John, h 84 Paige.
VICKERY CHARLES S., piano tuner, h 84 Paige.
Vincelett John, mason, h 79 Forsyth.
Vose Charles E., resident, bds. 240 E. Temple.
Vose Nancy B., widow J. Parker, h 240 E. Temple.
Vroman Peter, farmer, bds. 32 Temple.
Wade Charles M., carpenter, h 119 West ave.
Wade George N., groceries and provisions, 1 West ave., h do.
Wade Lewis N., cartman, h 175 North ave.
Wade L. N. Mrs., dressmaking, 175 North ave., h do.
Waggoner John, laborer, h off Water.
Wagner Clarence L., upholster, h near Dean's tannery.
Walbridge Charles M., fireman, h 40 Talcott.
Walker Amos, carpenter, h Adaline.
Walker Henry L., conductor, h Erie near Main.
Walker Jesse, harnessmaker, bds. over 177 Main.
Walker Lydia C., widow William, h 136 Temple.
Walker Ransom, D. D. S., dentist, over 200 and 202 Front, h do.
Walker Rial H., carpenter, h Buckbee Block.
WALL & CO., (Mrs. Charles and C. T. Wall) boots, shoes and rubbers, 200 Front.
WALL ABIGAIL F., (Wall & Co.,) widow Charles, h Front.
WALL CLARENCE T., (Wall & Co.) h Front.
Wallace Harry, clerk, bds. 67 Central ave.
Wallace Lewis, laborer, h rear 123 North ave.
Wallis Stephen S., law student, h in Tioga.
Walsh Lewis A., clerk, bds. 122 Paige.
Walsh William M., tailor, h 502 Main.
Walts John, bridge carpenter, bds. 43 Talcott.
Walter Ralph H., farmer, leases of Mrs. Julia Kellogg 70, h 73 Forsyth.
Wand James, laborer, bds. 63 Spencer ave.
Ward Anna E., widow Willard W., h 499 Front.
Ward Daniel, laborer, h 109 Franklin.
Ward Edward, emp. foundry, bds. 109 Franklin.
Ward Ezra, mason, h South Side.
Ward Frances L., dressmaker, bds. South Side.
Ward Kate M., book-keeper, 229 McMaster, h 48 West ave.
Ward John F., clerk Ah-wa-ga House, bds. do.
Ward Laura F., teacher, bds. South Side.
Ward Michael, laborer, bds. 109 Franklin.
Ward Patrick, drayman, h 47 West ave.
Ward Polly R., widow William, h 51 West ave.

Ward Thomas J., drayman, h 48 West ave.
WARNER FRANK H., contractor and builder, Fox, h 122 Franklin.
Warner Montgomery, saloon and restaurant, 203 Front, h do.
Warner William M., baker, h Buckbee Block.
Warren Lamira, widow Charles W., h 102 Chestnut.
Warrick Lillie J., teacher, bds. 363 Front.
Watkins Annie, clerk, bds. Main.
Watkins Charles D., lawyer, over 168 Front, h 571 East Main.
Watkins Frederick, blacksmith, bds. 142 Central ave.
Wrtkins Hollis, stationary engineer, 212 North ave.
Watkins Miner D., clerk, bds. Ah-wa-ga House.
Watkins William, traveling salesman, h 391 Main.
WATROS ODELL J., (Scott & Watros) h 234 North ave.
Watson Harmon S., drover, h Canal Front.
Watson James, painter, h 89 Franklin.
Watson Wallace, emp. casket shop, h 61 George.
Way William E., carpenter and saw-filer, 174 North ave., h do.
Webb James, carriage-painter, 72 Temple, h 97 Forsyth.
WEBSTER GEORGE H., painter and paper-hanger; decorative work a specialty, 242 East Temple, h do.
WEBSTER GILBERT E., meat-market, 133 North ave., h over 131 do.
Webster James, resident, h 25 John.
Webster Mason, painter, h 4 Fox.
Webster Rachel E., widow Charles, h 350 Main.
Webster William H., painter, bds. 88 Adaline.
Wedon Herbert, harness-maker, bds. Decker Block, Main.
Weed & Co., (J. D. & G. W. Weed) custom saw, grist and planing-mill, River, South Side.
Weed George W., (J. D. & G. W. Weed) h River, South Side.
Weed John D., (J. D. & G. W. Weed) h River, South Side.
Weed Joseph H., emp. Weed & Co.'s mill, bds. River, South Side.
Welch Charles, carpenter, h Adaline.
WELCH DAVID A., contractor and builder, cane-chairs reseated and general repairing, 243 Prospect, h do.
WELCH GEORGE H., clerk, bds. 243 Prospect.
Welch Harriet, widow Hiram, bds. 243 Prospect.
Welch William H., contractor and builder, 267 Prospect, h do.
Wentz Sarah, widow Rev. William, h 101 Franklin.
Whipple Daniel A., farmer, h 139 Main.
Whipple Sisters, (Martha A., Addie and Emma) dressmakers, 139 Main, h do.
Whipple William, hostler. bds. Ah-wa-ga House.
Whitaker A. B. Mrs., widow, bds. 41 Front.
WHITE & HUMISTON, (P. H. W. and F. M. H.) drugs and medicines, 194 Front.
White Charles, meat market, 36 Lake, h 64 Liberty.
White Darius, mason, h over 154 Front.
White Delia, widow Perry, milliner, h 51 Fox.
White Frederick, bartender, bds. 187 McMaster.
White Henry O., emp. King & Co., bds. 64 Liberty.
White John, carpenter, h 26 William.
WHITE PAUL H., (White & Humiston) bds., Ah-wa-ga House.
White Roderick, laborer, h 187 McMaster.
White Tryphena P., dressmaker, bds. 58 Spencer ave.

OWEGO—INSIDE CORPORATION.

Whiteson Isidor, (George Tuck, manager) clothing, 201 Front, h at Cortland.
Whitfield Samuel, laborer, h 239 Prospect.
Whitfield Samuel Mrs., laundress, 239 Prospect.
Whitmarsh Polly, widow Daniel, bds. 18 Fulton.
Whitney Nathan R., engineer, h 128 Temple.
Whitton Fred, meat-cutter, h 103 Paige.
Wicks L. Emmet, bookkeeper, 19 and 21 Lake, bds. 239 Main.
Wiggins Maria, widow John, h John R.
Wilbur Lebbeus, traveling salesman, h 496 Main.
Wilbur William E., boots, shoes and restaurant. 182 Main, h do.
Wilcox Sarah A. Mrs., resident, h 67 Paige.
WILCOX JOHN A., repair foreman Erie R. R. car shop, h 239 Main.
Williams Abram, gunsmith, h 132 Main.
WILLIAMS ALBERT S., bridge inspector, h 106 Chestnut.
Williams Burton, emp. C. M. Haywood, h 147 Temple.
Williams Charles D., laborer, h 99 Paige.
Williams Chester D., bridge carpenter, h 59 West ave.
Williams Daniel, gardener, h John R.
Williams Edward W., carpenter, h 119 Main.
Williams Fred D., drug clerk, bds. Park Hotel.
Williams George, porter, bds. 115 Fox.
Williams Henry F., produce, h 32 William.
Williams Laura M., widow Thomas, h George.
Williams Maria A., widow Thomas, h 115 Fox.
Williams Marshall G., salesman, h 27 Ross.
Williams Morgan, teamster, h Water.
Williams Nathan L., emp. Campbell's tannery, bds. George.
Williams William B., farm laborer, h George.
Williamson Charles, (Leverson & Williamson) h Erie.
Williamson Loesa, resident, bds. 241 Erie.
Willis William, laborer, h 257 Prospect.
*WILSON JAMES, physician and surgeon, 295 Main, h do.
WILSON OPERA HOUSE, S. F. Fairchild, manager, Lake.
Winans Edwin W., clerk, h 58 Spencer ave
Winions William, laborer, h 149 Erie.
Winne Catharine, widow Peter, h 11 Fox.
Winnie Franklin, farmer h 11 Fox.
Winner James, cartman, h Division.
Winow Simon P., barber, bds. Fox.
Wilsey Kelsey, painter, h over 62 North ave.
Wilson Samuel, tanner, bds. 187 McMaster.
Wilts Portis L., emp. drill works, h 140 Central ave.
Wiltse Kelsey, painter, h 104 Spencer ave.
Wiltse William, saloon, 65 North ave.
WINTERS EDGAR, (Starkey & Winters) h John.
Winters Judson B., (Hyde & Winters) h Main cor. Spencer ave.
Witters Ralph C., retired, h 94 Chestnut.
Woeppel Alvis, gardener for A. J. Thomas, bds. Main.
WOOD CHARLES L., (Buckbee, Peterson, Wood & Co.) bds. 364 Front.
Wood George H., blacksmith, North ave., h 104 Franklin.
Wood Hester, widow William, h 76 Talcott.
Wood Lydia, dressmaker, 76 Talcott, bds. do.

STARKEY & WINTERS, Wholesale and Retail Druggists, Owego.

Woodard Lucretia, widow Joseph, h 4 West ave.
Woodburn David M., laborer, h 43 Talcott.
Woodford Bissell, farmer 200, h 417 Front.
Woodford Charles G., teller First Nat. Bank, bds 374 Main.
Woodford George R., clerk, bds. 417 Front.
Works Frederick, emp. casket factory, h over 161 Main.
Works Russell S., shoe-cutter, h Park cor. Main.
Worthington Jennie, widow Robert, resident, h 51 Front.
Woughter Adelaide, widow Lysander G., bds. 15 Adaline.
Woughter Charles, emp. Lincoln coal yard, h 104 Spencer ave.
Woughter Eugene F., emp. foundry, h 15 Adaline.
Wright Albert G., retired, h 222 E. Temple.
Wright Frank N., moulder, h 89 Paige.
Wright Frederick, painter. h 222 E Temple.
Wright Joseph A., tinsmith, bds. 467 Front.
Wright Patrick, laborer, h 121 Paige.
Writer Gabriel M., conductor N. Y. L. E. & W. R. R., h 381 Main.
Writer Lena M., teacher, bds. 381 Main.
Wyckoff Abram, type-writer and stenographer, bds. Dugan House.
Wyman William, harness-maker, 112 North ave., bds. Central ave.
Wyman William, tailor, h 78 Paige.
Yates Alanson, (Sheldon & Yates) h 114 Liberty.
Yates Mary L. Mrs., teacher, h 194 River, South Side.
Yerks Catherine, resident, bds. 31 Adaline.
Yerks Clarissa, carpet-weaver, h 31 Adaline.
Yerks Emmet, farm laborer, h 40 Adaline.
Yerks William A., carpenter, h 246 E. Temple.
Yost Mary E. Mrs., hair-worker, h over Owego Nat. Bank.
Yothers Charles D., book-keeper First Nat. Bank, h 433 Front.
Yothers Horace, telegraph operator, D. L. & W. depot, bds. 433 Front.
Young H. Earl, clerk, bds. 455 Main.
Zimmer Al, carpenter, h 66 Adaline.
Zweig Samuel, clerk, bds. Central House.

OWEGO

OUTSIDE CORPORATION.

(For explanations, etc., see page 3, part second.)

(Postoffice address is Owego, unless otherwise designated in parenthesis.)

Ahern Daniel, (Apalachin) r 69, book-keeper.
Akerly Charles, (Campville) r 54, laborer.
Akerly Jerry, (Campville) r 54, laborer.
Aldrich Aaron, (Apalachin) r 81, farmer.
Aldrich Charles, (Apalachin) off r 81, farm laborer.
Aldrich Charles E., r 95, farmer with his mother Minerva H.
Aldrich Frederick, (Apalachin) retired, h Main.
Aldrich Heman B., (Apalachin) resident, bds. Main.

STARKEY & WINTERS, promptly fill Mail and Telephone Orders.

OWEGO—OUTSIDE CORPORATION.

Aldrich Melvin O., r 95, farmer 20.
Aldrich Minerva H., r 96, widow Olney, farm 50.
Alger Phineas, r 56½, cooper.
Allen John, (Gaskill's Corners) r 35, farm laborer.
Allen Reuben, (Flemingville) r 4, retired farmer.
Ames Lydia, (Apalachin) r 80, resident.
AMES PHINEAS N., r 65, farmer 6.
Anaville Charles, r 117, farmer, leases of Mr. Thomas 130.
Andrews Romeo, r 40, butcher and cattle dealer.
Annable Jarvis B., r 95, farmer 50.
Anson Mary, (Apalachin) widow Amos, resident, h Main.
Appleby Francis, (Union Broome Co.) r 30, farm laborer.
Arnold George, (Apalachin) r 70, farmer.
Ayer Mary A., (Apalachin) widow Isaac, resident, h Main.
Ayer Warren, (Apalachin) r 83, farmer 125.
Ayers Charles, r 94, physician.
Ayers Loren F., r 94, farmer.
Bailey James, r 42, farmer 82.
Bailey Thomas, r 42, farmer.
Bakeman David, (Gaskill's Corners) r 25, farmer 3.
Bakeman Philip, (Gaskill's Corners) r 12, farmer 95.
Baker Albert E., r 54, farmer for C. LaMonte.
Baker Charles, (Apalachin) carpenter, h Ferry.
Baker E. Vandaber, (Flemingville) r 6, farmer 54, and in Newark Valley 25.
Baker William, (Flemingville) r 6, farm laborer.
Ballard James, (Campville) r 54, peddler.
Ballou Hartwell M., r 12, wagon-maker, carpenter and farmer 25.
Ballou Wendell D., r 56½, music teacher.
Banney John F., (Apalachin) r 103, farmer with his father Ransom.
Barker Chauncey, (Apalachin) r 113, farmer 30.
Barker Chauncey, Jr., r 113, farmer 36.
Barker Simeon, (Apalachin) r 113, farmer.
Barnes Newton W. Rev., (Apalachin) pastor M. E. Church, h Church.
Barnes Reed A., r 67, farmer 75.
Barney E. Allen, (Apalachin) resident, h Church.
Barney Ransom (Apalachin) r 103, farmer 55.
Barnhart Alanson D., r 69, farm laborer.
BARRETT EUGENE, (Gaskill's Corners) r 25, farmer 117.
Barrett Simeon L., (Flemingville) r 40, farmer 80.
Barton Albert, (Apalachin) r 87, farmer.
Barton Andrew J., (Flemingville) r 5, farmer 100.
Barton Charles, (Apalachin) r 108, farmer with his mother Jane.
Barton Charles L., (Apalachin) r 87, butcher.
Barton Effy A. Mrs., off r 54, prop. LaMonte ferry.
Barton George H., (Apalachin) off r 108, farmer 40.
Barton Jane, (Apalachin) r 108, widow Isaac, farmer 107.
Barton Lester, (Union, Broome Co.) r 28, farmer 40.
Barton Louis A., r 94, carpenter and farmer 47.
Barton Rebecca W., r 101½, widow Morris W., resident.
Barton Renselaer, off r 54, blacksmith and farmer.
Barton Smith, Jr., (Apalachin) r 108, farmer 80.
Barton Thomas, (Apalachin) r 86, farmer.
Barton Thomas, r 87, carpenter and farmer.

Barton Virgil P., (Flemingville) r 5, farmer 80.
Barton William, (Apalachin) r 89½, farmer 45.
Barton William, (Apalachin) produce, h William.
Barto Charles, (Apalachin) laborer, h Church.
Bateman Isaac, (Campville) r 48, farmer 40.
Bates German A., (Apalachin) r 113, farmer with his father Gilford.
Bates Gilford, (Apalachin) r 113, farmer 40.
Beach George W., (Apalachin) physician and surgeon, Main, h Ferry.
Beach Olive, r 56, widow Nathan, farmer 33.
Beardslee William L., (South Owego) r 128, farmer 114.
Becker Fayette, r 54, retired farmer.
Beebe Orin, (South Apalachin) r 110, postal clerk and farmer.
Beebe Reuben (South Apalachin) r 110, farmer 119.
Beecher Edgar R., r 39, farmer with his father, Isaac S.
Beecher Isaac S., r 39, farmer 71.
BEEMAN HORACE W., r 116, wood-sawing and feed-mill, and farmer 40.
Beers Charles M., r 32, farmer 47.
Beers Julia M., r 40, widow James, farmer 65.
Belknap John J., (Campville) r 71, farmer 120.
Belknap Parmelia Miss, (Campville) r 71, resident.
Bell John, (Apalachin) trackman, bds. Exchange Hotel.
Benjamin Albert, r 95, farmer 55.
Benjamin J. Allan, r 95, farmer with his father Albert.
Benjamin James, r 95, retired.
Benjamin James U., r 117, farmer 165.
Benner Louise E., (Apalachin) music teacher, bds. Main.
Benner Ordelia, (Apalachin) widow Philip R., resident, h Main.
Bennett William (Campville) r 49, farmer.
Berdine Laramie, (South Apalachin) r 10, widow William, resident.
Berdine William P., (South Apalachin) r 110, farmer 186.
Billings Charles, (Little Meadows, Pa.) r 110, farmer 28.
Billings Norman, (Apalachin) r 110, farmer 55.
Billings Ransom, (Apalachin) r 102, farmer on shares with Almon Hotchkiss.
Bills Alonzo, (South Apalachin) r 111, deputy postmaster.
Bills Amari, (Apalachin) off r 107, farmer 30.
Bills James H., r 98, school trustee and farmer 100.
Bills Maria, (Apalachin) r 110, widow Warren, farm 125.
Bills Nehemiah, (Apalachin) laborer.
Bills Paul, (Apalachin) r 101½, farmer 6.
Bills Ulysses, r 99, farmer 25.
Bishop Gilbert, (Apalachin) carpenter, h Main.
Blair Asa, (Flemingville)) r 40, farmer.
Blair Ezra, r 39, farm laborer.
BLOW AMANDA, r 120, widow Francis, farm 50.
Blow Arthur, r 116½, farmer on shares with H. Codner 90.
BLOW FRANK L., r 59, prop. threshing-machine and farmer 25.
Blow George, r 96, farmer with his father Henry.
Blow Henry, r 96, farmer 80.
Blow William, r 120, farmer 18, and on shares with his mother Amanda 50.
Bodle Arthur, r 59, farmer.
Bornt Anna Mrs., r 54, farm 35.
Bornt Frederick, (Campville) r 48, farmer 80.
Bornt Levi, (Union, Broome Co.) r 73, farmer 91.

Bornt Peter, (Campville) r 50, farmer 10.
Bornt Samuel, (Campville) r 48, farmer 40.
Bornt William H., (Union, Broome Co.) r 73, farmer with his father Levi.
Bostwick Curtis, r 95, farmer 52.
Bostwick Fred, r 116½, farmer 138.
Bostwick Melvin F., r 40, farmer 105.
Bostwick Oliver, r 120½, farmer 50.
Bostwick Spencer, r 117, farmer 70.
Bostwick Thomas, r 117, farmer 85.
Bostwick Willis, r 117, farmer 40.
Bourst Menzo, r 61, farm laborer.
Bowen Isaac A., r 96, law student.
Bowen Jonathan P., r 96, farmer 50.
Bowen William J., r 94, farmer, leases of J. F. Holmes 55.
Boyce John R., (Apalachin) clerk for Sleeper & Whitaker, bds. Main.
Bradley Otis, r 56½, farmer 33.
Bradt Anthony, r 37, farmer 15.
Bradt Frank, r 43, farmer, works on shares for his father John 108.
Bradt John, r 38, farmer 108.
Bradt Peter, r 43, farmer 40.
Brainard Polly, (South Owego) r 99, widow Albert, resident.
Branch Andrew, (Campville) r 54, shoemaker.
Branch Charles, (Campville) r 54, brakeman.
Brewster John, (Apalachin) off r 102, farmer 50.
Briggs Anson, r 14, farmer 60.
Briggs Charles, r 54, farmer, leases of Mrs. George Smith 83.
Brink Jefferson H., r 58, farm laborer.
Brink Mulford, (Union, Broome Co.) r 71, farmer for his father John 60.
Brink William, (Apalachin) r 69, farm laborer.
Brooks Henry G., (Campville) r 53, farmer 69.
Brooks John, (Campville) r 53, retired farmer.
Brooks John G., r 95, farmer 19.
Brougham Henry A., r 94, farmer 10.
Brougham Joseph, (Union Center, Broome Co.) r 28, farmer, leases of William Conell 200.
Brougham Peter, (Union Center, Broome Co.) r 11, farmer 50.
Brown Asel, (Little Meadows, Pa.) r 110, farmer 50.
Brown Edgar, (Apalachin) r 81, farmer.
Brown Frank, (Litte Meadows, Pa.) r 110, farmer, 98.
Brown Frank L., (Apalachin) painter, h Cross.
Brown George, (Union, Broome Co.) r 80, school trustee, and farmer 125.
Brown Royal S., (Apalachin) butcher, h Main.
Brown Simeon, (Apalachin) r 83, farmer 27.
Brown William H., (Apalachin) farm laborer.
Brownell Benjamin W., r 40, farmer 50 and wood lot 36.
Brownell George, r 40, farmer with his father Benjamin W.
Brownell John C., (Flemingville) r 22, farmer 84 and wood lot 86.
Brumage Ann, (Flemingville) r 5, widow William, resident.
Brumage David, (Flemingville) r 5, farmer 20.
Buck Alonzo D., r 54, farmer 46¼.
Buck Charles W., r 54, carpenter and farmer.
Buck George H., r 54, carpenter.
BUNZEY CHARLES H., r 63, farmer, works on shares 150.

OWEGO—OUTSIDE CORPORATION.

Bunzey Sophia, r 63, widow Jacob, resident.
Burgett Robert, r 20, farmer 80.
Burton Amelia, (South Owego) r 128, widow Obadiah, farm 100.
Burton Ann, (Apalachin) r 83, widow Benjamin.
Burton Oliver, (South Owego) r 128, farmer 50.
Cafferty Asa, (Campville) r 71, farmer 120.
Cafferty Fayette, (Campville) r 48, farmer 55.
Cafferty Frank B., r 54, farmer 50.
Cafferty James, (Union, Broome Co.) r 74, farmer 200.
Cafferty James, Jr., (Union, Broome Co.) r 74, farmer 50.
Cafferty Myron, r 93, farmer, leases of James Armstrong 105.
CAMP GURDON H., (Apalachin) horse dealer, h Main.
Camp Nathan, (Campville) r 71, farmer 129.
Camp Orin, r 54, threshing machine and farm laborer.
CAMPBELL & LAMPHERE, (Apalachin) (I. W. C. & G. U. L.) saw and planning-mill, depot.
Campbell David S., r 94, farmer 85.
CAMPBELL ISAAC W., (Apalachin) (Campbell & Lamphere) h depot.
Campbell John A., r 94, farmer with his father.
Campbell Joseph, r 93, farmer, leases of Elin Gould 160.
Campbell Joseph, Jr., r 93, emp. Coe's saw-mill.
Campbell Ralph, r 94, fireman Coe's mill.
Cane Ezra, r 65, farmer on shares with Mrs. Steele 105.
Cane Peter, r 65, farmer with his father Ezra.
Card Abel, (Apalachin) r 108, farmer 27.
Card Albert, (Apalachin) r 108, farmer with his mother Eliza 24.
Card Charles, (Apalachin) r 108, farmer 24.
Card David, (Apalachin) r 108, farmer 32.
Card Eliza, (Apalachin) r 108, widow Harrison, farm 24.
Card Henry, (Apalachin) r 108, farmer with his mother Eliza 24.
Card Isaac, (Flemingville) r 4, engineer.
Card John, (Apalachin) r 108, farmer with his father David 32.
Carleton M. Dwight, r 69, farm laborer.
Carman Charles, (Apalachin) r 80, farm laborer.
Carpenter Albert J., r 97, farmer 54.
Carpenter Ann M., r 40, widow Joseph S., resident.
Carrier A. B., (Apalachin) laborer, h River.
Carrier Hartley, (Apalachin) r 113, farmer, leases of Simeon Barker 50.
Carte Louise, r 54, widow Eli, farmer 50.
Case Daniel, (Campville) r 71, farmer 50.
Case Hiram, (Campville) r 48, farmer 50.
Case Marilla D., (Campville) widow Zenos, resident.
Case Peter, (Union, Broome Co.) r 71, farmer 50.
Castle Albert, r 4, laborer.
Catlin George L., (Apalachin) r 96, supt. Marshland stock farm.
Catlin Jacob, (Apalachin) farmer 40, h Main.
Central House, (Apalachin) Alanson Goodenow, prop., h do.
Chaffee Elizabeth, r 96, widow Oliver P., resident.
Chandler Harrison, r 120½, farmer.
Chapman Horace, r 96, resident.
Chidester John, (Little Meadows, Pa.) r 133, farmer.
Childs Mark W., (Campville) r 54, school teacher.

Clapham Harry J., (Flemingville) r 2, manager and prop. Globe Theatre Co., and farmer 160.
Clark David L., (Apalachin) r 68, farmer 75.
Clark James, r 93, farmer 100.
Clanson Albert, (Apalachin) r 70, farmer on shares with W. Hilton 50.
Codner Charles N., r 116, farmer with his father Nelson.
Codner Hiram, r 116, farmer 90.
Codner John, (East Nichols) off r 118, farmer 100.
Codner Nelson, r 116, farmer 100.
Coffin Frank, (South Apalachin) r 128, farmer with his father.
Coffin Harvey, farm laborer.
Coffin Lucy, (South Owego) r 128, widow Henry, resident.
Coffin William H., (South Apalachin) r 128, farmer 75, and on shares with F. D. Coffin 130.
Cole Abram, r 40, farmer 75.
Cole Helen, r 40, matron County Alms House.
Cole William T., off r 65, farmer 25.
Coleman Peter, (Campville) r 54, trackman.
Conant Emery, (Little Meadows, Pa.) r 110, farmer.
Congdon Amos, (East Nichols) r 119, farmer 100.
Conklin Alfred, r 39, farmer 100.
Conklin Charles H., r 54, farmer, leases of Mrs. Anson Decker 60.
Conklin David, (Apalachin) farm laborer, h River.
Conklin Lewis D., r 60, mason.
Conklin Marcus A., (Apalachin) bds. River.
Conklin Matthew H., (Apalachin) laborer, bds. River.
Conklin William, r 40, carriage-maker.
Connant Simeon, r 117, blacksmith.
Connell Edward, r 60, farmer 20.
Connell Joseph, r 60, resident.
Connor Martin, (Campville) r 54, trackman.
Cooper Charles, (Union, Broome Co.) r 30, farmer 70.
Cooper George P., (Apalachin) r 80, farmer on shares with F. Aldrich 40.
Cooper Hiram, (Apalachin) r 84, farmer.
Coots Henry D., r 42, milk dealer and farmer, works on shares for Reuben Fraser 140.
Corbin Arthur L., (South Owego) r 122, farmer 30, and on shares with Myron Prince 100.
Corbin George, r 69, farm laborer.
Corbin Neweil, (South Apalachin) r 110, farmer 50.
Cornell Daniel, (Union Center, Broome Co.) r 28, farmer 150.
Cornell Eli, (Union Center, Broome Co.) r 28, farmer 150.
Cornell Eugene, (Union, Broome Co.) r 29, farmer 64.
Cornell Henry, r 56, blacksmith.
Cornell Thomas, (Union, Broome Co.) r 47½, farmer 70.
Courtright Herbert N., (Apalachin) r 106, shoemaker.
Cragan John, (Apalachin) mason, h William.
Crandall Amos J., r 98, farmer on shares with Asa Stanton 135.
Crater Samuel, r 97, farmer 50.
Crawford Arthur, r 27, farmer 100.
Crawford Merrills J., (South Owego) r 122, farmer 100.
Creemon Aaron, (Apalachin) off r 80, farmer.
Crounse Henry E., (Gaskill's Corners) r 45, farmer 175.

Crum James, r 99, farmer 20.
Curtis Bertie D., (Gaskill's Corners), r 35 invalid.
CURTIS HARMON, (Gaskill's Corners) r 35, postmaster and prop. saw and feed-mill and grocery.
Curtis Harvey, r 56½, nurseryman 2.
Daniels Darwin H., (Union Center, Broome Co.) r 11, farmer 50.
Daniels Douglas, (Union Center, Broome Co.) r 11, farmer 60.
Daniels George F., r 56, farmer 20.
Daniels Gustavas, (Union Center, Broome Co.) r 11, farmer 70.
Darling Albert, (Little Meadows, Pa.) r 110, farmer 70.
Davidson John, (South Apalachin) r 111, farmer 107.
Davis Leslie R., r 95, farmer with his mother Mary A.
Davis Mary A., r 95, widow James, farm 19.
Davis Walter J., r 95, farm laborer.
Davis William, r 40, farm laborer.
Davison Lucius, (Apalachin) r 107, farmer 70.
Decker Albert L., r 59, farm laborer.
Decker Emanuel, (Union, Broome Co.) r 47, farmer.
Decker Gideon, r 42, farm laborer.
Decker John S., (Apalachin) carpenter.
Decker John W., r 41, farmer 85.
Decker Jonathan, r 46, laborer.
Decker Marvin W., r 65, farm laborer.
Decker Narcis Mrs., r 27, resident.
Decker Wayne, r 31, farmer.
GeGroat J. DeWitt, r 67, musical instruments, and milk dealer.
DeGroat Lorenzo, r 67, farmer 99.
Delaney Richard, (Apalachin) trackman, bds. Exchange Hotel.
Dennison Cerene, r 99, widow Henry, farm 25.
Dennison George, r 99, farmer with his mother Cerene.
Dennison Joseph, r 116, farm laborer.
Deuel Augustus S., r 93, farmer 59.
Dexter Adelia, r 54, widow Frank B., farmer 40.
Dexter Edwin J., (Campville) r 54, carpenter and farmer.
Deyo William, r 37, farmer, works for Michael Lynch 100.
Dickinson Ira W., (Campville) r 73, Methodist clergyman, and farmer 44.
Dickinson McKenzie, (Campville) r 54, postmaster and grocery.
Dingman Abraham, (Apalachin), retired, h William.
Dingman John, (South Owego) r 128, farmer 160.
Dodge Asa J., r 93, farmer 70.
Dodge Benjamin F., r 93, farmer.
Dodge Daniel S., r 93, farmer 120.
Dodge John G., r 56, expressman.
Donnelly Joanna, 93, widow John, resident.
Donnelly Matthew, r 93, farmer 141.
Donnovan John, off r 54, track-hand.
Doty James, r 20, farm laborer.
Dougherty James R., r 20, farmer.
Dowd James, (Little Meadows, Pa.) r 135, farmer.
Downs William, (Apalachin) blacksmith, h Main.
Doyle Bernard, (Apalachin) laborer, h Main.
Drake Charles, (Apalachin) off r 102, farmer 40.
Drake Tamar, (Apalachin) r 87, widow Jerome.

Duane Burr, r 99, farmer 100.
Duane John, r 99, farmer 100.
Dunham Asa, r 99, farmer 131.
Dunham Burdett N., (South Apalachin) r 108, farmer.
Dunham Chauncey R., r 43, dairy 35 cows and farmer for G. S. Camp 130.
Dunham Dudley J., (South Apalachin) r 108, farmer.
Dunham Jennie, (South Apalachin) r 108, teacher.
Dunham Nathan Y., r 99, farmer.
Dunham Sylman, (South Apalachin) r 108, farmer 95.
Dunham Willard F., r 99, farmer.
Dutton Mortimer E., (Apalachin) r 69, boarding-house.
Easton Mary, (Apalachin) r 83, widow Julien G., resident.
Edward Edward, (Campville) r 54, blacksmith.
Edwards Edson, (Apalachin) r 110, resident.
Edwards Fred, (Apalachin) r 83, farmer with his father Ira.
Edwards Ira, 1st, (Apalachin) r 83, farmer 65.
Edwards Ira, (Apalachin) butcher and farmer, h Main.
Edwards Nelson, (Apalachin) r 107, resident.
Edwards Susie, (Apalachin) r 83, dressmaker.
Eldred Nelson, r 27, farmer 60.
Eldridge Chester, off r 27, farm laborer.
Eldridge Simeon, (Union, Broome Co.) r 29, laborer.
Elliott Francis H., (Apalachin) painter, h Main.
Ellis Airy Mrs., r 39, resident.
Ellis Nathan H., r 40, prop. grist and flouring-mill.
Evans Truman (Campville) r 54, carpenter.
EXCHANGE HOTEL, (Apalachin) John S. Ryan, prop., Main.
Fairbanks Benjamin R., (Apalachin) hostler Exchange Hotel, bds. do.
Fairbanks Benjamin R., (Apalachin) r 110, laborer.
Fairbanks Harriet E., (Apalachin) r 110, farm 47½.
Terbush Lancelott B , (Flemingville) r 16, blacksmith, wagon-maker and feed-mill, h r 4.
Ferguson David, (South Owego) r 123, farmer with Mrs. Slawson 160.
Ferguson Eugene B., (Flemingville) r 15, farmer 100.
Fessenden Adelbert N., (Apalachin) resident, h Cross.
Fessenden Nelson Rev., (Apalachin) Wesleyan Methodist, h Cross.
Finch Jehial S., r 22, farmer 79.
Finch Russell, r 22, farmer 25.
Fish Frank E., (Apalachin) r 113, farm laborer.
Fisk Darwin, (Gaskill's Corners) r 35, farm laborer.
Fleming John, (Flemingville) r 40, farmer 120.
Fleming Luke, (Flemingville) r 4, farmer 54.
Folker Frank, (Apalachin) r 69, farm laborer.
Ford Charles H., (Gaskill's Corners) r 35, carpenter.
Ford George L., (Gaskill's Corners) r 25, farmer 350.
Foster David, (Apalachin) farm laborer.
Foster Electa, r 27, widow Daniel R., resident.
Foster Phileman A., (Apalachin) r 101½, farmer 6.
Fox Alanson, off r 95, farmer 75.
Fox Albert, (Apalachin) off r 113, retired.
Fox Allen, r 95, farmer 50.
Fox Charles, off r 91, apiarist, and farmer 32.
Fox Fred, r 67, farmer 51.

Fox Fred E., (Apalachin) r 84, farmer with E. Jones 31.
Fox George, (Apalachin) off r 108, farmer.
Fox Ira, (East Nichols) r 118, farmer 50.
Fox James, (Apalachin) r 113, farm laborer.
FOX JEROME, (Gaskill's Corners) r 25, farmer, works on shares for Charles Becker 120
Fox John, (Gaskill's Corners) r 35, laborer.
Fox Julia A., (Apalachin) widow Charles T., resident, bds. Cross.
Fox Lewis L., (Apalachin) telegraph operator, h William.
Fox Oliza, r 60, resident.
Fox Russell, (Apalachin) r 113, farmer 53.
Fox Thomas, (Campville) r 53, farm laborer.
Fox William, r 120½, farmer 100.
Fox William S., (Apalachin) contractor and builder, h William.
Frear Elias, (Apalachin) r 113, farmer.
Frear Hannah, r 54, widow John, farmer 40.
French William, r 91, farmer 75.
Fuller Benjamin F., (Apalachin) carriage-maker, Main, h William.
Fulmer Charles, r 27, farmer 112.
Fulmer Peter, (Gaskill's Corners) r 34, farmer 80.
Fulmer Philip, r 22, farmer 45.
Gage Ellen, r 54, widow Jeremiah, resident.
Gage Ezra M., r 14, farmer 50.
Gage Mary A. Mrs., (Apalachin) teacher, bds. Cross.
Gage Miner, r 37, apiarist 50 swarms, and farmer 75.
Gage Walter, r 37, apiarist 38 swarms, and farmer 37.
Garrison Chester, (Apalachin) r 108, farmer 35.
Garrison James, (Apalachin) r 70, farm laborer.
Gaskill David W., r 32, farmer 40.
Gaskill Frank, r 54, milk peddler.
Gaskill Paul, (Gaskill's Corners) r 45, farmer 110.
Gaskill Stephen H., (Gaskill's Corners) r 45, farmer for his father Paul.
Gaskill Wilder J., (Apalachin) retired merchant, h Main.
Gaskill William C., (Apalachin) farmer 13, h Main.
Gibson David W., (South Apalachin) r 111, farmer on shares with Orin Bebee 100.
Gibson Frank, (Little Meadows, Pa.) r 135, farmer.
Gibson George, (Apalachin) off r 108, farmer.
Gibson William, (Apalachin) laborer, h Ferry.
Gifford Albert R., (South Owego) r 122, farmer with his mother Sophia H.
Gifford David S., (South Owego) r 122, farmer 100.
Gifford Sophia H., (South Owego) r 122, widow Russell D., farm 85.
Gile Orton, r 60, gardener.
Giles Alexander, (South Owego) r 126, farmer.
Giles Ebenezer, (South Owego) r 126, farmer 50.
GILES JOHN S., (Apalachin) r 87, pres't School Board, small fruit and hop grower, apiarist 200 swarms, and farmer 115.
Glann George W., (Apalachin) r 80, farmer.
Glann James H., (Apalachin) r 83, farmer 160.
Glann Martin, (Apalachin) r 85, farmer 50.
Glann William (Apalachin) r 83, farmer 140.
Glover Anson, (Apalachin) r 110, farmer.
Glover George (Apalachin) r 110 farmer.

Glover Stephen B., (Apalachin) r 119 farmer.
Goodenow Abram (Apalachin) r 102, farmer 42.
Goodenow Alanson, (Apalachin) prop. Central House, and farmer 26.
Goodenow Chauncey B., (Apalachin) clerk Central House, bds. do.
Goodenow Henry, (Apalachin) r 87, farmer 38.
Goodenow Isaac, (Apalachin) farmer 5.
Goodenow John W., (Apalachin) hostler Central House, bds. do.
Goodenow Peter, (Apalachin) r 87, resident.
Goodenow Ransom B., (Apalachin) r 114, farmer on shares with his father Abram, 140.
Goodrich Edwin, r 69 farmer.
Goodrich Matthew, r 95, farmer 87.
Goodsel A. Ford, r 56, farmer 61.
Goodspeed Alden, r 118½, farmer 100, and leases of Abner Goodspeed 50.
Goodspeed James, (East Nichols) off r 118, farmer 100.
Gould Andrew C., r 94, farm laborer.
Gould Charles P., r 94, farm laborer.
Gould Elin, (Apalachin) r 87, resident.
Gould George W., r 114, farmer with George Sandford.
Gould Smith, (South Owego) r 123, farmer 160.
Gould Stanley H., r 101½, farmer, leases of Joel Tuttle, 60.
Gower Charles, (Union Center, Broome Co.) r 9, farmer.
Gower Thomas, (Union Center, Broome Co.) r 9, farmer.
Graves Chester W., (South Owego) r 115, farmer 260.
Graves E. Talmage, (South Owego) r 115, teacher.
Graves Horace, (Little Meadows, Pa.) r 131, farmer 100.
Gray John H., (Apalachin) (Kinney & Gray) h Main.
GREEN A. L. & R. D., (Gaskill's Corners) r 25, groceries and provisions.
GREEN ALLEN L., (A. L. & R. D. Green) (Gaskill's Corners) r 25, h r 35.
Green Mary A., (Apalachin) r 87, widow Nathan, resident.
GREEN R. DEVERE (A. L. & R. D. Green) (Gaskill's Corners) r 25.
Green Will M., (Apalachin) r 102, farmer.
Griffin Alfred, r 56½, retired carpenter.
Griffin Alvah, (Campville) r 48, farm laborer.
Griffin Edward E., r 56, farmer, leases of Mrs. B. W. Spencer 65.
Griffin Emily, r 56½, widow Seth.
Griffin Fanny, (Gaskill's Corners) r 25, widow Alvah, resident.
Griswold George M., r 93, school trustee and farmer 92.
Griswold Jacob, (Apalachin) laborer, h Ferry.
Groesbeck Betsey, r 68, widow Cornelius, farm 70.
Groesbeck Charles H., r 67, farmer, leases of his father Isaac 50.
Groesbeck Frank P., r 68, farmer on shares with Mrs. Betsey Groesbeck.
Groesbeck George B., (South Owego) r 99, farmer on shares with Elin Gould.
Groesbeck George S., r 61, contractor and builder.
Groesbeck Isaac W., r 68,'farmer 170.
Groesbeck Theodore P., r 68, farmer with his father Isaac W.
Groesbeck William, (Apalachin) r 88, farmer, leases of I. W. Groesbeck 50.
HAGADORN FRANK E., r 95, farmer with his father William A.
Hagadorn William A., r 95, farmer 108.
HALL EUNICE E. Mrs., (Flemingville) r 40, prop. Flemingville Hotel, special attractions for summer boarders.
HALL GEORGE W., (Flemingville) r 40 hotel.

Hall Peter, (Apalachin) r 87, laborer.
Hall Temperance (Apalachin) r 87, widow John, resident.
Hall William, (Little Meadows, Pa.) r 131, farmer 50.
Halsted Thomas D., (Gaskill's Corners) r 25½, farmer 52.
Hammond Frederick, r 17, farmer 50.
Haner Addison L., r 96, carpenter and farmer 64.
Haner Irving J., r 96, farmer with his father Levi J.
Haner Levi J., r 96, farmer 45.
Haradon Julius S., r 54, gardener.
Harden Ford, (Flemingville) r 4, laborer.
Harrington George W., (South Owego) r 123, farmer 34.
Harrington Lyman D., r 96, farmer 41.
Harrington Russell, r 96, farmer 41.
Harris David, (South Owego) r 123, farmer 168.
Harris Levi (Apalachin) r 107, resident.
Harris Linus, (South Apalachin) r 111, farmer 100.
Hart Daniel, off r 46, farmer 37.
Harvey Charles, (Apalachin) off r 80, farmer, works for Charles Gland 50.
Hatfield Harry, (Apalachin) laborer, h Main.
HAUVER FRANK M., r 64, farmer 35, and leases of James Archibald 160.
Hayes Henry (Apalachin) r 68, lumberman.
Hayes Ira P., (Apalachin) r 89½, farmer 36.
Hayner David H., (Campville) r 52, farmer 340.
Hemstrought Charles, (Campville) r 50, farmer 20.
Hemstrought Harvey, (Campville) r 54, farmer 24.
Hemstrought Jacob, (Campville) r 54, brakeman and farmer 45.
Hemstrought James, (Campville) r 54, wagon-maker and farmer 30.
Hemstrought Jesse, (Campville) r 54, laborer.
Hemstrought Joseph, (Campville) r 51, farmer 50.
Hemstrought Lovejoy, (Campville) r 54, laborer.
Hendershott Adelbert, r 40, emp. grist-mill.
Herrick Bert, r 40, farm-hand county alms-house.
Herrick Edward P., (Flemingville) r 40, retired farmer.
Herzig Julius, r 37, farmer, works for Mrs. Shannon 37.
Hiawatha House, on Hiawatha Island, estate of E. G. Brown, of N. Y. city, Eugene F. Baton, lesee.
Hickein John, r 69, farm laborer.
Hickey John, (Apalachin) r 106, farmer 112.
Hickey Patrick J., (Apalachin) r 106, farmer with his father John.
Hickok Gideon F., (South Owego) r 122, farmer 25.
Hicks Eber, (Apalachin) off r 108, farmer 40.
Higbee George, r 46, farmer 135.
Higbee Orson, r 46, farmer with his father George.
Higbee Sidney C., r 46, farmer with his father George.
Hills George H., (Apalachin) r 113, farmer 130.
Hills John F., (Apalachin) r 113, resident.
Hills Marvin L., (Apalachin) r 113, farmer with his father George H.
Hills Phoebe, (Apalachin) widow Abner.
Hiller Levi G., (Apalachin) r 110, lawyer.
Hilton George, (Apalachin) r 89½, farmsr 50.
Hilton William, (Apalachin) farmer 45, h Main.
Hoagland Fred, r 56, farmer with his father William.
Hoagland William, r 56, farmer 60.

Hoary Edward, (Campville) r 54, trackman.
Hodge William, r 39, laborer.
Holbrook Albert, r 94, lumberman.
Holbrook Frank r 94, lumberman.
Holbrook George, r 94, lumberman.
Holbrook Herman, r 94, lumberman.
Holden Edward P., r 22, farmer 100.
Holden Fred, (Flemingville) r 3, farm laborer.
Holden John F., r 22, farmer with his father Edward P.
Holden Jonathan P., (Apalachin) r 102, farmer with I. W. Barton, 200.
Holden Melvin, (Flemingville) r 3, farm laborer.
Holden Oliver, (Flemingville) r 3, farmer 120.
Hollenbeck William, r 43, farmer 110.
Hollister Edwin S., (Gaskill's Corners) r 24, farmer 75.
Hollister Eliakim H., (Gaskill's Corners) r 24, farmer 73.
Hollister Watson P., (Gaskill's Corners) r 24, farmer 143
Holmes Anson C., r 91, farmer with his father Elston.
Holmes Asher, (Apalachin) retired, h Main.
HOLMES BROS., (Apalachin) (James & Gilbert) dealers in horses, Depot.
Holmes Elston, r 91, farmer 200.
HOLMES GILBERT, (Apaiachin) (Holmes Bros.) also potato dealer and farmer 200, h Main.
HOLMES JAMES, (Apalachin) (Holmes Bros.) also commissioner highways, insurance agent and farmer 16.
Holmes John, (Apalachin) r 70, notary public, lumberman, and farmer 200.
Holmes John, Jr., clerk for Kinney & Gray, h William.
Holmes Ransom S., (Apalachin) farmer, leases of John Thurber 40, h Main.
Holmes Susan W., (Apalachin) widow Stephen, resident, bds. Main.
Hopkins Clark, (Union, Broome Co.) r 47, farmer.
HOPKINS LANCY N., (Apalachin) drugs and medicines, Main, h do.
Hopler Peter Q., (Flemingville) r 4, laborer.
Hotchkiss Almond, (Apalachin) farmer 40, h Main.
Hotchkiss Edward, off r 27, farmer 90.
Howe Peter R., (Apalachin) r 102, farmer 40.
Howe Ralph, r 40, farmer 36.
Howell & Tracy, (Apalachin) (G. W. H. & P. T.) blacksmiths and horseshoers, Main.
Howell Charles W., (Apalachin) blacksmith.
Howell George W., (Apalachin) (Howell & Tracy) h Main.
Howes Joshua F., r 94, farmer.
Hoxie Raymond J., (Apalachin) r 101, farmer 50.
Hullett Oney, r 27, teamster.
Hull Catharine, r 25, widow Clark, resident.
Hull Dwight, (Gaskill's Corners) r 25½, farmer 23.
Hull George W., (Gaskill's Corners) r 25, farmer 60.
Hull Wellington G., r 25, farmer 78.
Hunt Bros & Co. (John, Charles, Samuel and Susan) r 43, farmer 224.
Hunt Charles, (Hunt Bros. & Co.) r 43, farmer.
Hunt Charles H., (Apalachin) r 70, farmer for Mrs. Mersereau.
Hunt Ellen, r 43, widow John, resident.
Hunt John, (Hunt Bros. & Co.) r 43, farmer.
Hunt Harriet L., (Apalachin) r 70, widow Thomas H., resident.
Hunt Samuel, (Hunt Bros. Co.) r 43, farmer.

Hunt Susan, (Hunt Bros. & Co.) r 43, farm.
Hyde William, r 20, cooper.
Ingersoll Eugene F., r 46, cooper.
Ingersoll Guy, r 27, farmer for his father James H.
Ingersoll Irving, r 46, farmer 97.
Ingersoll James E., (Union, Broome Co.) r 72, farmer, works on shares for John Wenn 112.
Ingersoll James H., r 27, farmer 100.
Jakway Fred D., r 66 farmer, leases of Rev. Mr. King 68.
Jaycox Alvin, (Gaskill's Corners) r 25, farm laborer.
Jenks Byron J., r 93, farmer 211.
Jennings Ransom, (Little Meadows, Pa.) farmer, leases of A. Jennings 70.
Jewett Charles, (Apalachin) r 104, produce.
Jewett George, (Apalachin) r 88, farmer 43.
Jewett Maurice W., (Apalachin) r 69, retired.
Jewett John, (Union, Broome Co.) r 71, farmer 40.
Jewett John W., (Union, Broome Co.) r 71, farmer 112.
Johnson Albert, r 40, attendant County Insane Asylum.
Johnson Andrew J., (Apalachin) r 104, contractor and builder.
JOHNSON DANIEL, r 40, sup't County Alms House and Asylum, and in Candor farm 208.
Johnson Horace, r 43, farm laborer.
Johnson John, r 22, farm laborer.
Johnson Nathan A., r 28, farmer, leases of Mrs. Hauver 20.
Johnson Stillman, r 40, blacksmith.
Johnson Taylor, r 21, farmer 50.
Jones Edward, (Apalachin) r 84, carpenter, and farmer 31.
Jones George, (Apalachin) r 87, farm laborer.
Jones Pardon, (Apalachin) carpenter.
Joslin Daniel F., (Flemingville) r 3, farmer 18.
Judge Thomas L., r 120½, farmer 8.
Judge Thomas, Jr., r 120, farmer 72.
Judge William, (Little Meadows, Pa) r 132, farmer.
Judge William H., r 120, farmer 36.
Kaley Adam I., (Flemingville) r 4, carpenter, and works farm 53.
Kaley John, (Gaskill's Corners) r 25½, farmer 25.
Kattell Willard, (Flemingville) r 3, farm laborer.
Keeler James, (Union, Broome Co.) r 30, farmer 8.
Kellum Ambrose, (Apalachin) wagon-maker, Main, h do.
Keltz Henry, (Union Center, Broome Co.) r 28, farmer.
Kent Fred, r 91, farm laborer.
Kent Gibson, (Apalachin) r 113, farmer 10.
Kent Mary A., r 91, widow Amos. resident.
Kenyon Egbert, (Union Center, Broome Co.) r 11, farmer 40.
Ketchum Charles H., r 97, butcher, and farmer 42.
Ketchum Dell, r 97, farmer 15.
Ketchum Frederick, r 97, farmer with his father Charles H.
Keth Jackson, (Campville) r 48, farmer 75.
Kettell George, (Gaskill's Corners) r 35, farmer, works for John Scrofford 75.
Kile George O., r 95, prop. feed and shingle-mill, and farmer 130.
King Andrew, (South Owego) r 126, farmer 70.
Kinney & Gray, (Apalachin) (J. D. K. and J. H. G.) general merchants, Main cor. Depot.

OWEGO—OUTSIDE CORPORATION.

Kinney John D., (Warren Center, Pa.) (Kinney & Gray) also store at Warren Center, and at Burchardville, Pa., h at Warren Center, Pa.
Kinney Thomas, (Apalachin) r 69, farm laborer.
Kipp Clinton, r 46, farmer 51.
Kipp Wallace, r 46, butcher, and farmer 20.
Knapp Amos, (Apalachin) r 87 farmer.
Knapp Charles R., (Apalachin) hardware, flour and feed, boots and shoes, Main, h do.
KNAPP FRANK J., (Apalachin) postmaster and tinsmith, h Main.
Knapp Henry, (Apalachin) r 110, farmer.
Knapp Ira, (Apalachin) 108, farmer 80.
Knapp James, (Apalachin) r 110, farmer.
Knapp Joel. (Apalachin) r 110, farmer 7.
KNAPP WILBUR F., (Apalachin) groceries and provisions, Main, h do.
Knapp William (Apalachin) r 110, farmer.
Knickerbocker Harvey, r 56½, laborer.
Knight Ambrose, (Apalachin) off r 80, farmer.
Knight Irvin, (Apalachin) off r 80, farmer.
Kyle Thomas, r 56½, farmer 130.
Ladd Isabella, r 91, widow Cyrus, resident.
Lainhart Addison, r 35, farmer 135.
Lainhart Simeon, (Gaskill's Corners) r 34, farmer 60.
Lainhart Thomas, (Union, Broome Co.) r 30, carpenter.
Laird George H., (Apalachin) insurance, h Church.
Laird George H. Mrs., (Apalachin), dressmaker, h Church.
LA MONTE CYRENE M., r 54, farmer 115, and prop. Hiawatha Island and picnic grounds.
La Monte David M., r 68, breeder fine horses, and farmer 75.
La Monte Hannah, r 54, widow Marcus, resident.
LAMPHERE GRANT U., (Apalachin) (Campbell & Lamphere) h Depot.
Lampman Jared, (Little Meadows, Pa.) r 130, resident.
LANE A. LINDSLEY (Apalachin) r 69, farmer 80.
Lane Don C., (Apalachin) r 83 farmer.
Lane Edgar S., (Apalachin) r 69, farmer with his father A. Lindsley.
Lataurette Androette, (Campville), r 49, farmer 88.
Leasure George, (South Owego) r 123, carpenter, and farmer 10.
Leonard Leonard, (Apalachin) r 108, farmer 80.
Letts Matthew, (Gaskill's Corners) r 45, farmer.
Lewis Edgar, (Apalachin) r 69, farmer 50.
Lewis Hiram, (Apalachin) r 69 farmer.
LEWIS ISAAC W., (Apalachin) physician and surgeon, and farmer 314, and in Kansas 160, and in Iowa 80, h Main.
Lewis Maria, r 56. widow of James, carpet-weaver.
Like George W., (Apalachin) r 106, agricultural implements, and farmer 56.
Like William, (Apalachin) r 106, farm laborer.
Lillie Charles T., (Apalachin) r 108, farmer on shares with John Decker.
Lillie George M., (Apalachin) r 108, farmer 35.
Lillie Lucina, (Apalachin) r 108, widow Jared, resident.
Lillie Merritt F. (Apalachin) r 108, farmer 66.
Lillie William, (Apalachin) r 108, mason, and farmer 63.
Lindsly Hiram, r 40, carpenter.
Livingston Amos, r 54, gardener 7½.

STARKEY & WINTERS, Wholesale and Retail Druggists, Owego.

Livingston Christiana, widow Peter, r 67 resident.
Livingston John, (Campville) r 71, lawyer in New York city and farmer 83.
Livingston Marcus, (Campville) r 51, farmer 66.
Livingston Peter, (Campville) r 48, farmer 160.
Lory Joseph (Apalachin) r 83, bartender.
Lory Kaziah, (Apalachin) r 83, widow David, resident.
Lown Catherine, (South Owego) r 122, widow Jacob, resident.
Lown William P., (South Owego) r 122, horse-dealer and farmer 47.
Lucas Daniel T., r 99, farmer, works on shares with Mr. Drake 80.
Lyke Peter (Campville) r 54 farmer 120.
Lyke Rufus F., r 91, farmer 30.
Mabee Robert, (Apalachin) r 87, farmer.
Mack Thomas, off r 54, track-hand.
McGee Griffin, r 43, farm laborer.
Mahar Michael, r 41, farmer 72.
Maloney Jeremiah, (Apalachin) r 103, farmer 92.
Marean Duane, (Flemingville) r 6, farmer 42.
Marean George, (Union, Broome Co.) r 31, farmer 113.
Mason Albert G., r. 27, farmer 60.
Mason Albert G., Jr., r 27, farmer 12.
Mason Samuel, r 22, locomotive engineer.
Mason Samuel, r 22, farmer 42.
Mason Thomas, r 22, farmer with his father Samuel 77.
Mason William (Apalachin) off r 108, farmer.
Maston Charles, r 120½, farmer 10.
Maston John, r 120½, farmer 40.
Mayhew Charles, (Little Meadows, Pa.) r 110, painter.
Mayhew George W., (Apalachin) resident, h Main.
McCann George E., (Campville) r 54, upholsterer.
McCann J. William, (Campville) r 54, farmer 44.
McCaslin Alexander (Apalachin) blacksmith Main, h do.
McClain Charles, (Gaskill's Corners) r 35, farm laborer.
McClain Polly, r 20, widow Charles, farm 20.
McClary Rexford, (Union, Broome Co.) r 71, farmer 46.
McCoy Stiles, r 56½, retired farmer.
McDonald Cameron, r 40, painter.
McHenry Francis B., (Apalachin) farmer, h Church.
McHenry James (Apalachin) r 103, farmer with his mother Sally J.
McHenry Sally J., (Apalachin) r 103, farmer 92.
McMahon Thomas, off r 54, track-hand.
McNeil Roswell C., (Campville) r 54, farmer.
McNeil Sarah, (Campville) r 54, widow Roswell C., resident.
Mead George, off r 22, farmer 175.
Mead Holloway, (Flemingville) r 2, farmer 90.
Mead John, (East Nichols) r 119, farmer 50.
Mead Ransom H., (Gaskill's Corners) r 12, farm laborer.
Mead William E., (Gaskill's Corners) r 35, farmer 150.
Meade Fayette E., r 20, farmer 83.
Meade Maria, r 20, widow Isaac, resident.
Meads Peter, (Little Meadows, Pa.) r 135, farmer.
Mericle Jacob, r 118½ farmer 112.
Mericle James H., r 116, farmer 52.

STARKEY & WINTERS, Druggists, Owego. Close Prices to Dealers.

Meircle John, r 116½, farmer 110.
Mericle William H., r 116½ farmer 110.
Merrick Austin B., off r 65, farm laborer.
Merrick John B., r 65, farmer for L. H. Pitcher.
Mersereau Adeline, r 69, widow George, farm 100.
Mersereau Frank, r 68, farmer 150.
Mersereau Grant, r 68, farmer 150.
Millage Brinton, (Campville) r 52, farmer 64.
Miller Augustus, (Apalachin) farm laborer, h Church.
Miller Cornelia, (Gaskill's Corners) r 11, widow Alexander, farm 40.
Miller Emanuel, (Apalachin) cooper.
Miller John, (South Apalachin) r 128, farmer 50.
Miller John, Mrs., r 56, residen.
Miller Jonas, (Gaskill's Corners) r 11, farmer for his mother Cornelia.
Millrea Edward, r 39, farmer for his father, Thomas.
Millrea Thomas, r 39, farmer 110.
Mills Gurdon T., (Union, Broome Co.) r 31, farmer 5.
Moe Ezra, (South Apalachin) r 112 farmer 56.
Moe Sherman, (Little Meadows, Pa.) r 110, farmer 40.
Montanyea Buffum D., (Campville) r 54 farmer 65.
Moot Peter, r 20, farmer 60.
Morgan Alexander, (Union. Broome Co.) r 29, farmer 50.
Morgan William, off r 27, farmer 100.
Morton David, (South Apalachin) off r 108, farmer 70.
MORTON LEVI, (Apalachin) boot and shoe dealer, also custom work, Main, h do.
Moss Samuel, r 99, farmer, leases of James Clark 50.
Mott Frank C., (Apalachin) r 80, farm laborer.
Mott Israel D., r 54, stone-mason.
Mott Lorenzo, r 90, resident.
Murphy Edward, (Apalachin) retired, h Church.
Myers John, off r 54, emp. Mrs. E. A. Barton.
Myers Joseph H., r 91, farmer 23.
Narsh Frederick, r 32, farmer, leases of Leonard Foster.
Narsh Marvin A., r 56½, farmer 6.
Nash Allen, (Gaskill's Corners) r 25, painter.
Newman Maria, (Apalachin) r 84, widow Nelson S., resident.
Newman Warren A., (Apalachin) r 84, farmer 34.
Newman William, (Flemingville) r 16½, farmer 24.
Nichols Betsey, (Apalachin) widow William, h Main.
Nichols Charles, r 68, farmer 112.
Nichols Charles H., r 67, farmer with his father Justus.
Nichols George, r 60. farmer 160.
Nichols George S., r 60 farm laborer.
Nichols Justus, r 67, farmer 145.
Nichols Robert, r 60, farmer with his father George.
Nichols Washington, (Apalachin) r 102½, apiarist, and farmer 35.
Nichols Will F., (Apalachin) hostler.
Noteware Frederick H., (South Apalachin) r 110, farmer 90.
Noteware Wallace R., (South Apalachin) r 110, apiarist, and farmer 170.
Noteware Walter R., (Apalachin) r 89½, farmer 35.
Northrop Arthur T., r 23, farmer, leases of Lainhart estate 300.
Ogden Catherine E., (Apalachin) widow Isaac, resident, h Main.

Ogden Frank C., (Apalachin) teacher, bds. Main.
Olmstead Augustus, r 80, farmer 120.
Olmstead Daniel B., (Apalachin) r 80, farmer 71.
Olmstead Maria S., (Apalachin) r 80, widow Avery, farm 200.
Olmstead Luman, r 40, farmer.
Olmstead Robert, r 80, farmer with his father Augustus, 120.
Olmstead Seth, r 40, grocery, and farmer 28.
Olmstead Whiting W., r 40, farm laborer.
O'Neill James M., r 22, farmer 89.
Orford Charles F., (Apalachin) carpenter, h Church.
Orford David (Apalachin) shoemaker, h Church.
Padgett Allen W., r 40, farm laborer.
Pangburn Jacob, (Union, Broome Co.) r 28, farmer 50.
Pearl Charles E., r 95, farmer, leases of his father Loring C.
Pearl Frederick J., r 95, farmer, leases of his father Loring C.
Pearl Diana B., r 95, widow Austin, resident.
PEARL LORING C., r 95, farmer 240.
PEARL MYRAM W., off r 65, farmer, leases of J. F. DeGroat 123.
Pearsall Grace L., (Apalachin) teacher, bds. William.
PEARSALL RANSOM S., (Apalachin) justice of the peace and farmer, h William.
Pease Joseph N., r 39, farmer 130.
Pendleton Jenks, (Little Meadows, Pa.) r 132, farmer.
Pendleton Loren, (Little Meadows, Pa.) r 132, farmer.
Pendleton Monroe, (Little Meadows, Pa.) r 133, farmer.
Perkins Barney, (Apalachin) r 89 1-2, peddler, and farmer 5.
Perkins Maggie, r 40, matron County Insane Asylum.
Perry Charles F., (South Owego) r 122, farmer on shares with L. B. Truman, 250.
Perry George H., (South Owego) r 122, farmer with his father Charles F.
Pettigrove Laura J., r 40, farm 47.
Pettigrove Sewell, r 40, miller, and farmer 6.
Phalen Patrick, r 14, farmer, works on shares for William P. Stone, 110.
Phelps George, (Gaskill's Corners) r 25, farm laborer.
Phelps Jesse, (Flemingville) r 40, farmer 11, and in Candor 100.
Phelps Philip, (Gaskill's Corners) r 25, farmer 50.
Phelps William, r 56, farmer 16.
Phillips James, (Apalachin) r 90, farmer 101.
Phinleyson Richard, (Apalachin) off r 108, farmer.
Pitcher Harvey, r 65 resident.
Pitcher Leroy H., r 65, agricultural implements, and farmer 100.
Potter John, (Flemingville) r 16, farmer for Frank Scott.
Potter Wendall, farmer 78.
Powell John H., (Union, Broome Co.) r 47, farmer.
Powers Angeline, (Apalachin) r 110, widow John J., resident.
Powers Francis J., (Apalachin) r 110, farm laborer.
Powers Frederick A., (Apalachin) r 110, farm laborer.
Post Gardner, (Apalachin) r 85, farmer 75.
Pray Ephraim, (Apalachin) r 83, resident.
PRITCHARD ASA, (Flemingville) r 3, farmer 37, and wood lot 14.
Pritchard James, (Flemingville) r 4, farmer with his brother Truman 30.
Pritchard Herbert E., (Flemingville) r 3, farmer with his father Sylvester.
Pritchard Sylvester H., (Flemingville) r 3, farmer 126.

Pritchard Truman, (Flemingville) r 4, farmer with his brother James 30.
Pritchard William H., (Flemingville) r 2, farm laborer.
Probasco Elmer, r 68, farm laborer.
Probasco Frank M., r 67, farmer 75.
Probasco Gurdon, r 68, farm laborer.
Pultz Henry, r 17, farmer.
Pultz Henry, Jr., r 17, farmer.
Pultz Putnam, r 17, farmer 40.
Pultz Ransom, r 17, farmer 50.
Queeman West, (Apalachin) r 83, resident.
Quimby Adelbert H., (Apalachin) laborer, h William.
Quimby John W., (Apalachin) r 87, farmer.
Randall Henry, r 26, farmer 80.
Rauch George F., (Flemingville) r 3, farmer, leases of the Allen estate 38.
Recorden Charles, (Flemingville) r 5, farmer 87.
Reed James L., (Flemingville) r 4, blacksmith, and farmer in Newark 100.
Redding John, r 120, farmer 50.
Reynolds Albert L., r 94, farm laborer.
Richardson Austin, r 31, farmer for his father Cephas.
Richardson Cephas, r 31, farmer 90.
Richardson Harry, r 31, farmer for his father Cephas.
Richardson Jerome B., r 99, farmer 35.
Rinevault Amanda, r 40, widow Alfred.
Rising James H., (Gaskill's Corners) r 25, farmer 108.
Rising Jeanette, (Gaskill's Corners) r 25, widow John, farm 100.
Rising William H., (Gaskill's Corners) r 25, farmer 57.
Robbins Ephraim, (Union, Broome Co.) r 47, farmer.
Robinson Benjamin, r 56, farmer 25.
Robinson Bridget, r 22, widow Matthew, farm 118.
Robinson Henry, (Union, Broome Co.) r 74, farmer 64.
Robinson Howard, r 46, farmer 123.
Robinson Jacob, r 27, farmer 61.
Robinson John, r 22, farmer 118.
Robinson John L., r 94, farmer, leases of Frank Bliss 47.
Rockwood Charles, r 40, farm laborer.
Rodman Benjamin, (Union, Broome Co.) r 47, farmer 60.
Rodman Calvin, (Union, Broome Co.) r 47, farmer.
Rodman Nicholas, (Apalachin) r 68, farmer.
Romain Benjamin, r 27, farm laborer.
Romain Charles, (Campville) r 54, farmer 15.
Romain George, (Campville) r 54, laborer.
Romain Jesse, (South Owego) r 123, farmer on shares with D. Gifford.
Rounds Simeon, (Apalachin) r 83, cider and shingle-mill, and farmer 25.
Rowe Edward, r 54, gardener 17.
Rowley James, (Apalachin) r 87, resident.
Rulison George P., (Apalachin) mason, h Main.
Rundle James A., r 95, farmer on shares with Mrs. G. Van Bunschoten 76.
Russell Daniel, r 20, farmer.
Russell Elbridge, r 20, farmer 75.
Russell Minor, (South Apalachin) r 108, carpenter and wagon-maker.
Ryan Michael, (Apalachin) r 89½, farmer 56.
Ryan James, (Apalachin) r 70, farmer 35.
RYAN JOHN S., (Apalachin) prop. Exchange Hotel, h do.

Ryan Thomas, (Apalachin) laborer.
Ryan Walter, (Union Center, Broome Co.) r 11, farmer 100.
Sandford George, (South Owego) r 114, farmer 160.
Sandford Lewis C., r 98, farmer with his father Oliver B.
Sandford Oliver B., r 98, farmer 80.
Savey Edmund G., (Apalachin) carpenter, h Main.
Savey Seth, (Apalachin) r 87, carpenter.
Savey William, (Apalachin) carpenter and builder, h Main.
Sawyer George, r 56½, farmer with his father Nathan.
Sawyer Nancy M., r 54, widow William, farm 60.
Sawyer Nathan, r 54, farmer 50.
Sawyer Oscar W., r 54, farmer for his mother, Mrs. Nancy M.
Schoolcroft Peter, r 14, farmer 200.
Schoolcroft Philip, r 14, farmer 60.
Scott Abram, (Campville) r 69, cartman and mail-carrier.
Scott Clinton, r 40, farmer 50.
Scott Elizabeth, (Flemingville) r 16, widow Frederick, resident.
Scott Emery, (Flemingville) r 16, farmer with his father Frank.
Scott Frank, (Flemingville) r 16, farmer 92.
Scott Phoebe, r 40, widow Alonzo, farm 10.
Scrafford James, (Gaskill's Corners) r 25½, farmer 75.
Scrafford John, (Gaskill's Corners) r 35, farmer 75.
Scutt Dell, r 54, farm laborer.
Scutt George, r 54, farm laborer.
Scutt Isaac, r 54, farmer 4.
Searl Edward, r 37, farmer 86.
Searl Edward F., r 56, farmer 75.
Searles Amos, (Flemingville) farmer 14.
Searles Asahel, (Flemingville) r 4, farmer 50.
Searles Esther, (Flemigville) widow Chester, farmer 15.
Searles George, (Flemingville) r 4, Mason.
Searles Homer, (Flemingville) r 16½, prop. steam saw-mill and farmer 10.
Searles Lot, (Flemingville) r 16½, farmer 13.
Searles Luke E., (Flemingville) r 15, farmer, leases of G. Pultz 100.
Searles Nathan P., (Flemingville) r 16½, mason and farmer 90.
Severson George, (Campville) r 51, blacksmith.
Shaffer Abram, r 17, farmer 50.
Shaffer Abram, Jr., r 17, farmer.
Shannon Elizabeth, r 37, widow Cornelius, farm 37.
Shaw Hiram D., (South Owego) r 123, farmer 130.
Shay John, (Apalachin) section foreman D. L. & W. R. R., bds. Exchange Hotel.
Shay Wesley W., r 58, milk dealer and farmer, leases of B. Woodford 160.
Shellman Chauncey, (Campville) r 51, cobbler and ferryman.
Shepard Charles D. Rev., (Flemingville) r 40, pastor M. E. Church.
Sherwood Charles, r 56½, farmer, works on shares for George Young 128.
Sherwood Elsworth, (South Apalachin) r 128, farmer 150.
Sherwood George J., (Apalachin) r 106, stock-breeder and farmer 55.
Sherwood John, (Apalachin) r 70, farmer 25.
Sherwood Nathaniel, (Apalachin) r 88, farmer 50.
SHERWOOD VAN NESS (Apalachin) r 88, farmer with his father Nathaniel.
SHERWOOD WILLIAM H., (Apalachin) r 162, farmer 145.

Shirley Jonathan, r 38, farmer 13.
Shirley John, r 36, farmer 20.
Shirley Nathaniel, r 38, farm laborer.
Shirley Rial, r 36, farmer 30.
Shirley Samuel, r 37, farmer 40.
Shopp John, (Union, Broome Co.) r 28, farmer.
Short Frank (Apalachin) r 88, farmer with his father Uriah.
Short Fred, (Apalachin) r 88, farmer, leases of Uriah Short, Sr., 35.
Short G. Ransom, (Apalachin) r 89½, farmer 15.
Short Lorenzo, (Apalachin) r 88, farmer, leases of Uriah Short, Sr., 35.
Short Uriah, Sr., (Apalachin) r 88, farmer 152.
Short Uriah, (Apalachin) r 87, laborer.
Shultz John, (South Apalachin) off r 110, farmer.
Sibley Charles V., off r 97, farmer 65.
Sibley Elvira S., r 98, resident.
Sibley George D., (Flemingville) r 15, farmer, works on shares for S. Marquit 70.
Slawson George, (South Owego) r 126, farmer 75.
Slawson Schuyler M., r 99, farmer 35.
Slawson Milton, (South Owego) r 123, farmer 160.
SLEEPER THOMAS J., (Apalachin) (Sleeper & Whittaker) h Main.
SLEEPER & WHITTAKER, (Apalachin) (T. J. S. & W. W.) produce and general merchants, Main.
Slocum Humphrey C., r 54, farmer 25.
Smith Albert, (Apalachin) r 86, farmer.
Smith Aurelia, (Gaskill's Corners) r 25, widow James, resident.
Smith Charles F., r 14, farmer 200.
Smith Elizabeth, r 54, widow George, farm 83.
Smith Franklin E., (Apalachin) laborer, bds. Cross.
SMITH FRED W., r 54, milk dealer and farmer 323.
Smith George W., r 41, bridge builder.
Smith Henry W., r 65, deputy sheriff and farmer 32.
Smith Ira A., r 22, farmer 108.
Smith Jerome, (Campville) r 54, farmer, leases of Dr. Allen 100.
Smith Orville, (Campville) r 54, prop. cider-mill and farmer 100.
Smith Phoebe, r 54, widow Stephen W., resident.
Smith Robert C., (Gaskill's Corners) r 25, farmer 140.
Smith Robert E., (Gaskill's Corners) r 35, farm laborer.
Smith Royal Y., (Apalachin) r 86, farmer.
Snell Robert, r 98, farmer 10.
Snell Samuel B., r 98, emp. Coe's saw-mill.
Snooks Halsey, (Apalachin) r 113, chair-seating.
Snooks William D., (Apalachin) r 114, farm laborer.
Snyder Nett, r 61, widow Edward D., resident.
Southwick William, (Flemingville) r 5, sugar orchard 76 trees, and farmer 100.
Spencer A. Judson, farmer 180.
Spencer Arminda, r 59, widow Brinton W., farm 65.
Spencer George, (Campville) r 54, trackman.
Spencer Hiram, r 96, farm laborer.
Sprong Christopher C., r 20, farmer 75.
Sprong George, r 20, farmer.
Stage Clarence, (Flemingville) r 2, farmer, leases of Harry I. Clapham 125.
Stalker Charles, farm laborer.
Stalker George, r 31, emp. Leonard Foster.

STANTON ASA, r 96, surveyor and farmer 195.
Stanton Mary, (Union, Broome Co.) r 47, widow Edward, resident.
Stedman Lyman, (Flemingville) r 3, farmer 58.
STEDMAN WHEELER, (Flemingville) r 40, hay, coal, lumber, produce, and farmer 170.
STEELE AARON, (Apalachin) express and station agt. D. L. & W. R. R., and farmer 400, h Main.
Steele Aurelia, r 93, widow William, farm 105.
Steele E. Jennie, r 93, teacher.
Steele George, r 56, farmer 26.
Steele James, (Apalachin) farmer 42, h Main.
Steele Maria, (Apalachin) widow Lucius, h Main.
Steele Marinda, r 66, widow Aaron W., resident.
Steele Philetus, r 66, farmer, leases of Aaron W. Steele 160.
Steenburg Fred, (Apalachin) r 102½, farmer 70.
Steenburg Isaac, (Apalachin) r 107, farmer 30.
Steenburg Nicholas, (Apalachin) off r 108, farmer.
Stein Jacob, r 39, laborer.
Stephens Bert, (South Apalachin) r 110, farmer 100.
Stephens Henry, (South Apalachin) r 110, farmer 125.
Stephens Samuel J., r 116, farmer 52.
Stevens Charles, r 56, farm laborer.
Stockwell Frank, (Gaskill's Corners) r 45, farm laborer.
Stone Charles M., r 116, farmer 28.
Stratton James H., r 20, farmer, leases of Hiram Johnson 40.
Stratton John, (Union, Broome Co.) farmer.
Stratton Richard, r 20, wagon maker, and farmer 35.
Strong Beri, (Flemingville) r 4, farm laborer.
Strong Charles, r 39, farmer, leases of Mrs. Caroline Allen 90.
Strong Clayton B., r 66, farmer.
Strong Susan A., r 66, widow Levi, leases of Dr. Phelps 100.
Sturtevant Harrison C., r 20, farm laborer.
Stilson Eugene, (Apalachin) r 69, farm laborer.
Stilson Sarah E., (Apalachin) r 69, widow Hiram, farm 6.
Stinard Joseph, r 63, miller.
Stinard R. Charles, r 63 farmer.
Surdam P. Smith, (Union, Broome Co.) r 31, farmer 127.
Swartwood Joseph A., (Apalachin) gardener, h Cross.
Swart J. Walter, (Campville) r 51, farmer 42.
TALCOTT CHARLES, r 40, apiarist 35 swarms, and farmer 75.
Talcott Frederick, r 40, farmer.
Talcott Eunice B., r 40, widow Joel, resident.
Talcott George B., r 40, apiarist 70 swarms, 90 head sheep, and farmer 207.
Talcott William H., r 20, farmer 75.
TALLMADGE EZRA W., r 99, fruit grower, 600 apple trees, and farmer 116.
Taylor Frank, r 95, resident.
Teater Philip, (Union, Broome Co.) r 28, farmer 80.
Terbush Clark, (South Owego) off r 90, farmer 188.
Terbush Hiram, (Apalachin) r 106, farmer 46.
Thomas Jane E. Mrs., r 95, resident.
Thomas William, off r 56 1-2,, farmer 44.
Thompson John A., (Apalachin) r 69, farm laborer.
Thompson William, (Apalachin) shoemaker, Main, h William.

Thornton Abram, r 31, emp. Foster's saw-mill.
Thornton Thomas, r 27, basket and shoemaker.
Throop John G., (Apalachin) r 106, farmer 25.
Tilbury Charles F., (Campville) r 71, farmer 50.
Tilbury Frederick, (Union, Broome Co.) r 71, farmer 100.
Tilbury Herman M., (Campville) r 71, potato dealer, and farmer 40.
Tilbury Isaac, r 53, farmer 96.
Tilbury James, (Campville) r 71, farmer 100.
Tobey James D., (Apalachin) r 83, saw-mill, and farmer 30.
Tobey Ruel L., (Apalachin) r 83, farm laborer.
Toburn Richard, (Campville) r 54, trackman.
Tousley Silas G., r 54, farmer 50.
Towsand Frederick, off r 120, farmer 91.
Towsand Joel, r 120, farmer 100.
Towsand John, r 120 1-2, farmer 110.
Towser John, r 41, farm laborer.
TRACY BENJAMIN F., (Apalachin) (B. F. Tracy & Son) r 69.
TRACY B. F. & SON, (Apalachin) (Frank B.) r 69, props. Marshland stock farms.
TRACY FRANK B., (Apalachin) (B. F. Tracy & Son) r 69.
Tracy Frank Y., (Apalachin) (Howell & Tracy) h Cross.
Tracy Harrison (Apalachin) off r 110, farmer 110.
Tracy Harvey J., (Apalachin) r 83, stock raising and farmer 105.
Tracy Pardon, (Apalachin) (Howell & Tracy) h Church.
Travis Charles J., r 68, farmer with his father James.
Travis James, r 68, farmer 50.
Travis Samuel, (Apalachin) off r 102, farmer 50.
Travis William, (Apalachin) r 69, hostler.
Truman Aaron B., (Gaskill's Corners) r 35, farmer 203.
Truman Charles E., (Flemingville) r 40, postmaster, justice of the peace and farmer 70.
Truman Charles F., (Flemingville) r 40, farmer 150.
Truman Elias, r 120 1-2, farmer 160.
Truman Elias W., (Apalachin) r 87, farmer.
Truman Lyman B., (South Owego) r 123, postmaster and farmer 250.
Trusdell Morris, (Campville) r 71, farmer, leases of Michael Livingston 80.
Tucker Nelson, (Apalachin) off r 113, resident.
Tullock James A., (Flemingville) r 4, farmer 40.
Tuttle Jason, (Campville) r 51, laborer.
Tyrrell Henry I., r 116, farmer 33.
Tyrrell Walter D., farmer, leases of W. Fox estate 100.
Van Brunschoten George W., (Apalachin) r 110, farmer 6.
Van Dermark, r 69, farm laborer.
Van Gorder Ezra, (Apalachin) r 85, farmer.
Van Gorder James, (Apalachin) off r 110, farmer.
Van Gorder Jonathan, r 93, retired.
Vanorder Frederick, (Gaskill's Corners) r 45, farm laborer.
Van Riper Fred, (Apalachin) r 102, farmer.
Van Riper Morris, (Apalachin) r 90, farmer 27.
Verguson Edward, (Gaskill's Corners) r 25, farmer for F. W. Smith 240.
Verry Russell, (Little Meadows, Pa.) r 132, farmer.
Viele John N., off r 96, farmer 25.
Vincent Dexter C., r 46, cooper.

Vosburgh Stephen H., r 40, saw-filer.
Wade John, (Flemingville) r 5, farm laborer.
Wade Ozias D., (Flemingville) r 5, farmer 41, and in Newark 65.
Wait Charles B., (East Nichols) off r 119, farmer 90.
Wait Frederick C., (East Nichols) r 120, farmer 200.
Wait Henry, (East Nichols) r 119, farmer 112.
Wait Horace, (East Nichols) off r 119, farmer with his father Charles.
Wait John, r 54, farmer 50.
Wait John H., (East Nichols) r 119, farmer with his father William 225.
Wait William, (East Nichols) r 119, farmer 225.
Wait William H., r 54, farmer with his father John 50.
Walker Abram, (Campville) r 54, laborer.
Walker Frank, r 27, carpenter.
Walker George D., (Union, Broome Co.) r 30, farmer 128.
Walker Judson R., r 59, farmer, with his father Rial.
Walker Rial, r 59, farmer 36.
WALTER ARTEMAS, (Gaskill's Corners) r 35, farmer 250.
Walter Franklin A., (Gaskill's Corners) r 25, carpenter.
Walter Lester, (Gaskill's Corners) r 35, farmer for his father Artemas.
Walter Lyman, (Gaskill's Corners) r 35, farm laborer.
Walters Herman, (Gaskill's Corners) r 45, student.
Walters Margaret, (Gaskill's Corners) r 45, widow William, farm 300.
Walters Orin, (Gaskill's Corners) r 45, farmer, leases of Mrs. M. Walters 300.
Ward Charles, off r 113, farmer, leases of Ira Edwards.
Ward Daniel, off r 46, farmer with his father Richard 55.
Ward Richard, off r 46, farmer with his son Daniel 55.
Warrick Peter, r 32, retired farmer.
Warrick Samuel, (Union, Broome Co.) off r 47, farmer.
Welch Charles, r 43, farmer, works on shares for the Misses. Hollenback 275.
Welch James, (Gaskill's Corners) r 11, farmer 80.
Welch Herbert, r 37, farmer 40.
Wells Maria K., r 32, resident.
Wemple Isaac S., (Union, Broome Co.) r 30, farmer 84.
Wenn John, (Union, Broome Co.) r 71, farmer 100.
Wheeler Charles, (Apalachin) r 86, farmer.
Wheeler Fred S., (Campville) r 54, clerk.
Wheeler John, (Campville) r 54, groceries and provisions.
White Andrew, (Apalachin) r 101 1-2, farmer 110.
Whitmarsh Andrew, on Hiawatha Island, works on shares for C. M. LaMonte 100.
Whitney David H., (Campville) r 54, farmer 23.
Whitney Nathan S., (Campville) r 54, farmer.
WHITTAKER WELLINGTON, (Apalachin) (Sleeper & Whittaker) h Main
WHITTEMORE ALVIN, (Union, Broome Co.) r 28, farmer 85.
Whittemore Charles, r 27, farmer 80.
Whittemore Egbert, (Union, Broome Co.) r 29, farmer 17.
Whittemore Fred, (Union, Broome Co.) r 46, farmer, works on shares for Charles J. Stanton 162.
Whittemore George, (Union, Broome Co.) r 30, farmer 120.
Whittemore John, r 27, carpenter and farmer 40.
Whittemore Marcus, (Campville) r 48, laborer.
Whittemore Virgil, r 26, farmer 200.
Whittemore William, (Gaskill's Corners) r 43, farmer 140.

Wicks Lucius M., r 54, ice-dealer.
Wilcox Elizabeth Mrs., (Apalachin) resident, h Main.
Williams Emeline, r 117, widow James H., resident.
Williams George E., r 99, farmer 110
Williams Isaac F., r 95, farmer 41.
Williams Jacob, r 99, retired.
Williams John E., (Apalachin) harness-maker, Main, h Church.
Williams Lucy, r 95, widow Reuben, resident.
Williams Stephen L., r 95, farmer, and leases of Mrs. Lucy Williams 100,
WILLIAMS WRIGHT B., r 115, fruit-grower and farmer 100.
Williamson Ezra M., r 22, farmer 80.
Williamson George D., agt. for the "Sprague" farm wagon, and farmer, leases of Mrs. M. McLean 30.
Williamson Isaac, r 17, farmer.
Wilsey Otis, (South Owego) r 113, farmer 150.
Winans Ernest, r 117, farmer with his father Orlando.
Winans Orlando, r 117, farmer 110.
Winchell John J., (Flemingville) r 4, farmer 71.
Winne Ajelica, (Gaskill's Corners) r 35, widow Walter V., resident.
Winne Eugene, (Gaskill's Corners) r 35, farmer with his brother James 183.
Winne Jacob, r 14, farmer 30.
Winne James, (Gaskill's Corners) r 35, farmer with his brother Eugene 183.
Winship Frank, (Flemingville) r 4, farm laborer.
Witter Lyman, r 94, farmer 70.
Witter William, off r 96, shingle-maker and farmer.
Wolcott Aaron, (South Owego) r 128, farmer 50.
Wood Alva, (Apalachin) off r 108, farmer 37.
Wood Andrew J., off r 96, farmer 41.
Wood Catherine E., (Apalachin) r 114, widow Luman B., farmer 75.
Wood Charles E., (Flemingville) r 30, dealer in agricultural implements and well-driver.
Wood Charles H., r 60, cabinet-maker.
Wood Clarence, r 40, farmer.
Wood C. Leonard, r 60, emp. King & Co.
WOOD EDWARD B., (Apalachin) r 114, farmer with his mother Catherine.
Wood Frank T., (Gaskill's Corners) r 25, farmer 75.
Wood J. Henry, off r 96, farm laborer.
Wood Nelson, (Flemingville) r 5, farm laberer.
Wood Royal, (Apalachin) r 104, farm laborer.
Wood Royal P., r 40, farmer 85.
Wood Samuel H., off r 96. farmer with his father Andrew J.
Worrick Charles T., r 101½, farmer 70, and leases of Anna M. Boyce 110.
Worrick Freeman, (Apalachin) r 101½, farmer.
Worrick Nathaniel S., r 32, farmer 130.
Woughter Andrew C., (Union, Broom Co.) r 73, farmer 113.
Woughter Avery, (Union, Broome Co.) r 71, farmer 70.
Woughter Chester, (Union, Broome Co.) r 73, farmer 50.
Woughter Cornelius, (Union, Broome Co.) r 72, farmer 85.
Woughter Vol, r 54, farmer 57½.
Wright Adam, r 16, farmer, works on shares for Joseph Young 100.
Wright Elson, r 20, farm laborer.
Yarrington Sylvia, (Apalachin) widow Washington, bds. Main.

STARKEY & WINTERS, Wholesale and Retail Druggists, Owego.

TOWN OF RICHFORD. 175

Yates Daniel, (Campville) r 54, farmer 36.
Yates Frank, (Apalachin) r 85, farmer.
Yates George L., r 91, farmer with his father John.
Yates John, r 91, farmer 70.
Yates John S., (Apalachin) r 70, farmer 85.
Yates Mary A., r 91, resident.
Yearsley Aaron, (Apalachin) r 69, horseman.
Yearsley William, (Apalachin) emp. Marshland stock farm, h Main.
York Abram, (Apalachin) r 104, farm laborer.
Young Charles, r 20, farmer 50.
Young George, r 54, farmer 265.
Young Joseph, r 21, farmer 200.

RICHFORD.

(*For explanations, etc., see page 3, part second.*)

(Postoffice address is Richford, unless otherwise designated in parenthesis.)

Abbey Edward B., r 25, carpenter. and farmer 52.
Allen Carlton E., (Caroline, Tomp. Co.) r 26, farmer with H. C. Allen 134.
Allen Elmer, r 42, carpenter.
Allen George W., farmer 35, h Main.
Allen Henry C., (Caroline, Tomp. Co.) r 26, farmer 77, and with C. E. A. 134.
Allen James, physician and surgeon, h Main.
ALLEN J. W., (Finch & Allen) r 18, prop. saw-mill, lumber dealer, and farmer 330.
Allen Sidney B., (Caroline, Tomp. Co.) r 23, farmer 102.
Allen William B., commercial traveler, h Main.
Avery Ebeneazer, (Caroline, Tomp. Co.) r 26, farmer 12.
Ayers Elias, r 49, farmer 110.
AYERS FREDERICK A., r 37, farmer 110.
AYERS JAMES W., shoemaker, h Mill.
Ayers Jeptha L., r 46, laborer.
Ayers Job, r 28, farmer 230.
Ayers John L., r 46, farmer, leases of W. F. Wright, of Berkshire, 92.
Ayers Marietta, r 41, widow of Albert, farm 11½.
Ayers Rudolph, r 27, farmer 219.
AYERS WAYLAND B., r 28, farmer.
Barden Charles F., off r 26, farmer, leases of W. S. Goodrich 167.
Barden Edmund, r 18, carpenter.
Barden Ezra S., farmer 30, h Main.
Barden Frank, r 18, farmer 117.
Barnes Arba P., harness-maker, h Front.
Barnes George S., (Caroline, Tomp. Co.) r 22, farmer, leases of C. A. Fellows 100.

STARKEY & WINTERS, promptly fill Mail and Telephone Orders.

TOWN OF RICHFORD.

BARNES GRANT W., manuf. and dealer in harnesses, saddles, whips, nets, robes, and dusters, also county superintendent of poor, h Aurora.
Barney George E., r 18, farmer 30.
Beam Charles, (Caroline, Tomp. Co.) r 23, farmer 34.
Belden Edgar F., clerk for W. C. Smith & Co., and farmer with William F. Belden 156.
Belden Frederick C., r 39, farmer 160.
Belden George R., r 39, farmer.
BELDEN WILLIAM F., r 39, farmer 144.
Bell Augustus E., shoemaker, Main.
Benjamin Frank E., (Caroline, Tomp. Co.) r 23, farmer, leases of Sarah A. Benjamin, of McGrawville, 60.
Benjamin Luther U., (Harford, Cort. Co.) r 8, laborer, h and lot.
Berry Benjamin, (Harford Mills, Cort. Co.) r 12.
Blakeman Allen, (Harford Mills, Cort. Co.) r 14, farmer 161.
Blakeman Asahel, r 11, farmer 155.
Blakeman William, (Harford Mills, Cort. Co.) r 14.
Bliss Bert, laborer.
Bliss Franklin, prop. grist-mill, and farmer 30, opp. depot.
Boice William J., (Harford Mills, Cort. Co.) farmer 30.
Boyce Charles, (Harford Mills, Cort. Co.) r 10, laborer, h and lot.
Brace Francis, resident, h Aurora, served in Co. D, 76th N. Y. Vols.
BRIGHAM BOSTWICK, r 27, farmer 130.
Brink Theodore, r 45 1-2, farmer.
Brookins George W., r 33, farmer 25.
Brumage John, (Speedsville, Tomp. Co.) r 44, farmer 4.
Brusie Granville, (Harford Mills, Cort. Co.) off r 14, farmer, leases of Allen Blakeman.
BUNCE HARVEY A., r 49, farmer with William A., 65.
Bunce William A., r 49, farmer with Harvey A., 65.
Chaffee Varnum, r 37 cor. 50, farmer 72.
Chambers Samuel, (Slaterville, Tomp. Co.) r 3, farmer 90.
Chapman Amos E., r 35, farmer.
Clark Birdswell, (Berkshire) r 47, farmer, leases of Abram Clark, of Owego, 180
Clark Charles A., postmaster, and farmer 188 1-2.
Clark Erastus W., r 19, farmer 8.
Clark George, off r 18, laborer.
Clark John D., laborer, h Aurora.
Cleveland Ezekiel, off r 10, farmer 140.
Cleveland Justus, r 42, farmer 110.
Colby Lewis I., r 41, farmer 144.
Cole John, (Berkshire) r 48, farmer 28.
Coney William, (Harford Mills, Cort. Co.) r 14, laborer.
Congdon Peter, r 39, farmer 122.
CONRAD CHARLES H., r 37, farmer 28.
Cooper Ephraim A., (Slaterville, Tomp. Co.) r 3, prop. saw-mill and farm 12.
Cortright Charles, r 42, laborer.
Cortright James, sawyer, h Main.
Cox Sarah, r 31 1-2.
Crain Marvin, (Harford Mills) r 9, laborer.
Crandall Ira, (Caroline, Tomp. Co.) r 23, farmer 15.
Culver John L., (Harford Mills, Cort. Co.) r 11, farmer, leases of A. Boyce of Harford 47.

FINCH CHARLES R., farmer, and breeder of Clydesdale horses.
FINCH CLARENCE W., (H. S. & C. W.) (W. C. Smith & Co.) h Main.
Finch Elam, emp. H. S. & C. W. Finch.
FINCH H. S. & C. W., (Hotchkiss S. and Clarence W.) props. steam sawmill, and manufs. of lath, flooring, ceiling, etc., also woven wire mattress frames, corn knife, grass hook, and hay-knife handles, sythe boxes, extension table slides, bed slats, etc.
FINCH HOTCHKISS S., manuf. and dealer in soft and hard wood lumber, lath, posts and shingles, farmer 1,200, 12 houses and 20 vacant lots in Auburn. Fish property, West ave. cor. King st., and with J. W. Allen, block cor. State, Perry and Mill sts., Rochester.
Finch Philander W., justice of the peace, and dealer in live stock and produce, h Aurora.
Foote George M., farmer 50 in Candor, h Main.
Foster Brewster, r 35, farmer 60.
Foster Miles, r 42, farmer, leases of R. Holmes, of Newark, 74.

TOWN OF RICHFORD. 177

CURTIS CHARLES F., r 39, justice of the peace, breeder and dealer in horses, dairy 16 cows and farmer 200.
Curtis Loren H., r 39, resident.
Dalrymple Lydo H., (Harford Mills, Cort. Co.) farmer.
Dalrymple Samuel A. (Harford Mills, Cort. Co.) r 8, farmer 100.
Daniels H. & S. H., r 10 cor. 19, dairy 15 cows and farmers 180.
Daniels Heman, (H. & S. H.) r 10 cor. 19.
Daniels Samuel H., (H. & S. H.,) r 10 cor. 19, also civil engineer and surveyor.
Darlin Preston, (Slaterville, Tomp. Co.) r 3, farmer 4.
Davis Charles P., (Harford Mills) r 10, farmer, leases of Alfred Davis of Harford, 80.
Davis John M., r 33, teacher and farmer 188.
Decker Peter N., (Harford Mills, Cort. Co.) r 14, farmer 102.
Decker Rensselaer, (Harford Mills, Cort. Co.) r 13, farmer 40.
Decker Stephen, (Harford Mills, Cort. Co.) r 11, farmer 60.
Dennis Frank, r 16, farmer 50.
Dennis Franklin J., r 16, farmer 50.
Deuel Oliver, (Harford Mills) r 10, farmer 100.
Dimon John, (Harford, Cort. Co.) r 6, farmer 136.
Dodge Charles, r 35, farmer 73.
Donley David, cigar-maker, bds. Main.
Dow Dewitt C., (Slaterville, Tomp. Co.) r 3, farmer, leases of Mrs. Sumner, of Ithaca 230.
Dye Ansel M., r 17 cor. 11, blacksmith.
Dye Milton R., r 17 cor. 11, farmer 81.
Earsley Frederick L., r 26, farmer.
Earsley Richard, r 26, farmer 148.
Ellis Anson, r 17, laborer.
Ellis John, r 33, laborer.
Ellis Pison, r 31, farmer 34.
Ellis William, (Speedsville, Tomp. Co.) r 48, laborer.
Fellows Catherine A., (Caroline, Tomp.Co.) r 22, widow of Edward, farm 100.
Fellows Egbert M., (Harford Mills, Cort. Co.) r 8, farmer 131.
Fellows Gardner, (Harford Mills, Cort. Co.) r 21, farmer 116.
Fellows Lucius, (Harford Mills, Cort. Co.) r 9, farmer 120.
Fenner Alfred, r 18, laborer.
Fenner Arthur, (Harford Mills, Cort. Co.) r 15, laborer.
Freeland Eugene L., (Speedsville, Tomp. Co.) r 43, farmer, leases of S. Freeland 150.
Fries James M., (Harford Mills, Cort. Co.) r 14, farmer 25.
Friss Philip, r 35, farmer 50.
Fundis John, off r 30, dairy farmer 335.
Fundis John, Jr., off r 18, farmer, leases of John Fundis 54.
Gee Charles, farmer 25, h Main.
Gee Moses L., farmer 107, h Aurora.
Gee Noah, r 17, farmer 25.
Geer Calphernia, widow Henry, resident, h Main.
Geer George M., r 31 1-2, supervisor, and farmer 200.
Geer Ichabod H., r 31 1-2, resident.
Genung Edward, r 34, farmer, leases 80.
Genung Orrin L., r 45 1-2, wagon-maker and carpenter, also farmer 6.
Gilbert Milo, (Center Lisle, Broome Co.) r 51, farmer 58.

12

TOWN OF RICHFORD.

Gilbert William, (Center Lisle, Broome Co.) r 36, laborer.
Glezen Charles A., (Center Lisle, Broome Co.) r 35, farmer 246.
GOODRICH WILLIAM S., dealer in cattle, sheep, calves and swine, and farmer 167, h Main.
Gostley Peter, off r 17, farmer 30.
GRANGER EDMUND R., (Harford Mills, Cort. Co.) (Francis & Son) r 10.
GRANGER FRANCIS & SON (Harford Mills, Cort. Co.) (Edmund R.) r 10, prop. of saw and grist mill, and manuf. of yard-sticks, bee-hives, honey sections, shipping crates, potato crates, mouldings, brackets and novelty goods.
Gray Dennis, live stock and farm produce, also farmer 44, h Main.
Greaves Susan D., widow George, resident.
Griswold Lavina, (Harford Mills, Cort. Co.) r 14, widow William, farm 180.
Griswold William, (Harford Mills, Cort. Co.) r 14, laborer.
HALE SAMUEL B., r 37, farmer 60., served in Co. B 104th N. Y. Vols.
Hall Leonard, (Harford Mills, Cort. Co.) r 10, laborer.
Hamilton Alexander, r 33, farmer 20.
Hamilton Luther B., (Harford Mills, Cort. Co.) r 11, farmer 138.
Haynes Charles A., r 17, farmer.
Haynes Sylvester C., r 17, farmer 100.
Heath Ambrose B., r 40, farmer 37 1-2, leases of Nathaniel 28 1-2.
HEATH NATHANIEL, r 40, carpenter, and farmer, 28 1-2, served in Co. H 146th N. Y. Vols.
Heath Seymour, r 40, resident.
Hefron Leroy, (Slaterville, Tomp. Co.) r 3, portable saw-mill.
Herrick Amos, r 37, farmer 80.
Hill Charles H., r 26, laborer.
Hill Ignatius, r 30, resident.
Hill Wilson I., r 30, farmer 93.
Hoaglin Edward, r 43, farmer.
HOAGLIN MARVIN A., r 43, dealer in organs and sewing machines, and farmer 42.
Holcomb Adelbert, r 35, farmer 50.
Holcomb Timothy M., r 35, farmer.
Hopkins Daniel H., house, sign and carriage painting and paper-hanging, kalsomining, etc., h Main.
Horton Bros., (Orlando and Stephen L) r 46, farmers 140.
Horton Horace, section hand.
HOUK GEORGE, r 21, farmer 40, and leases of Lydia Houk 130.
Houk Lydia, r 21, widow Benjamin, farm 100.
HOWLAND HARRISON, (Center Lisle, Broome Co.) r 36, carpenter, and farmer 174.
Howland Wilber, (Center Lisle, Broome Co.)r 48, farmer 68.
HUBBARD LINDERMAN M., r 51, farmer 11 1-2.
Hulsander George, emp. H. S. & C. W. Finch, h Mill.
Hulslander Jacob, r 17, farmer, leases of M. L. Gee 107.
Hunt Daniel E., r 43, miller, and farmer 37.
Hutchinson Alzina, widow John, resident, h Railroad.
Hutchinson Edward, r 31 1-2, farmer, leases of George M. Geer 200.
Hutchinson Frank, resident, h Aurora.
Hutchinson Wesley J., carpenter, h Railroad.
Japhet George, r 35, laborer.

STARKEY & WINTERS, Wholesale and Retail Druggists, Owego.

TOWN OF RICHFORD. 179

Jayne Amzi L., r 30, farmer 115.
Jayne Charles F., r 30, farmer.
Jayne Samuel A., r 30, farmer 150.
Jennings George, r 40, laborer.
Jennings Henry A., r 35, breeder and dealer in horses, and farmer 170.
Jennings William H., off r 41, farmer 175.
Jewett Caroline, r 45, widow Richard, farm 96.
Jewett Charles F., (Berkshire) r 95, dairy 14 cows, farmer 125.
Jewett Lyman, r 45, farmer, leases of James Smith estate of Caroline 147.
Jewett Oliver, r 43, retired farmer.
Jewett Orrin, r 45, farmer, works for Caroline Jewett 96.
Johnson James B., r 40, farmer 100.
Johnson William, (Center Lisle, Broome Co.) r 36, farmer, leases of Gamaliel H. Tubbs 115.
Johnson William R., r 40, strawberry culturist, and farmer 50.
Jones Lucius A., farmer 16, h Main.
Jordan Franklin, (Berkshire) r 36, farmer.
Kent Isman, off r 18, farmer 10.
Keyes Thomas S., r 46, farmer 58.
King William W., (Harford Mills, Cort. Co.) r 10, carpenter, and farmer 30.
Krum Charles G., r 41 cor. 42, dairy 15 cows, farmer 240.
Lacey Charles, laborer, h Main.
Lacey George, r 42, laborer.
Lacey Louis V., telegraph operator.
Lacey Philip, laborer, h Main.
Lacey Rufus, laborer, h Railroad.
Lacy James, r 28 cor. 29, farmer 160.
Leach Daniel, r 44, farmer 45.
Leebody Henry, laborer, h Aurora.
Leebody Robert, r 40, laborer.
Leonard John B., 35, millwright, and farmer 25.
Lewis William, r 18, laborer.
Livermore Walton, sawyer, h Aurora.
Locke Benjamin, (Slaterville, Tomp. Co.) r 3, laborer.
Locke Henry D., (Slaterville, Tomp. Co.) farmer, leases of Mrs. S. A. White 250.
Marsh Aaron, r 46, dairy 12 cows, farmer 120.
Marsh Burr, (Center Lisle, Broome Co.) r 36, farmer 134.
Marsh Washington, r 35, farmer 70, served in Co. E., 76th N. Y. Vols., and Co. F., 1st Ver. Cavalry.
Marshall Charles, laborer.
Marshall Charles, r 31, blacksmith.
Marshall William, laborer, h Main.
Marshall Wilson, off r 18, farmer 13.
Matson Frank, (Harford, Cort. Co.) r 7, farmer, works for Orrin Matson 90.
Matson Lucy A., (Caroline, Tomp. Co.) r 24, widow Isaac, farm 17, and with Seth Matson 200.
Matson Ormal, (Harford, Cort. Co.) r 7, laborer.
Matson Orrin, (Harford, Cort. Co.) r 7, farmer 90.
Matson Seth, (Caroline, Tomp. Co.) r 24, farmer with Lucy A. 200.
Mayo William W., r 46, farmer.
McIntyre John, (Harford Mills, Cort. Co.) r 19, farmer.

STARKEY & WINTERS, Druggists, Owego. Close Prices to Dealers.

Meacham George W., r 37, farmer.
MEACHAM JAMES W., r 37, brick and plaster mason.
MEACHAM ORRIN N., r 37, carpenter, also mason, and farmer 32.
Meloy Charles T., r 33, farmer 50.
Meloy Frank P., r 33, lumberman, breeder and dealer in horses, and farmer 96½.
MILLER WILLIAM F., dealer in groceries and provision, and farm produce, Read & Co.'s fertilizers and champion mowers and reapers, and Perry spring tooth harrow, Main.
Mills George F., r 33, laborer.
Moore Charles H., justice of the peace and produce dealer, h Main, served in Co. G., 137, N. Y. Vols.
Moore Dana A., r 46, farmer 28.
Moore Emily A., r 46, widow Elijah, farm 112.
Moore Enoch N., r 33, laborer.
Moore Helen A., r 46, farm with Diadama Walker 71.
Moreland George D., general blacksmith, served in Co. G, 109th N. Y. Vols., h Main.
Morenus Chancey, r 33, farmer 100.
Morenus William H., r 33, farmer.
Morton Agnes, r 18, widow Spencer, resident.
Morton Edward, r 18, laborer.
Morton John, off r 10, farmer.
Morton Lewis, r 10, sawyer and farmer 20.
Morton William, r 10, mason, carpenter and farmer 18.
Myers Fred, (Harford Mills, Cort. Co.) r 11, lumberman and farmer.
Myres John S., (Harford Mills, Cort. Co.) r 11, farmer 53, served in Co. E, 157th N. Y. Vols.
Nash David, laborer, h Mill.
Neff Alexander, r 34, laborer, served in 109th Artillery, N. Y. Vols.
Neff Harrison, r 15, farmer 67.
Neff Jerome, r 34, farmer 60.
Newton Delay, r 31½, farmer 38.
Nigus Judson, (Harford, Cort. Co.) r 7, stone-mason.
Nixon Albert, r 31, laborer.
Norton Cyrus, (Caroline, Tomp. Co.) r 24, laborer.
O'Brien Dennis, farmer 50, h Main.
O'Brien James, r 26, farmer 130.
Ostrander Lorenzo, r 35, farmer 127.
Owens Levi, r 31 cor. 18, blacksmith, and farmer 20.
Owens Phineas, laborer.
Owens William, r 31, well-drilling.
Packard George, r 18, farmer 26.
Packard John, r 18, farmer 30.
Palmerton Fred H., r 49, laborer.
Palmerton George, r 37, farmer 40.
Parker William W., (Harford Mills) r 9, dairy 28 cows, farm 260.
Patch Edward H., (Berkshire) r 45½, farmer, works for Mrs. E. L. Patch, of Berkshire 222.
Perry Ebenezer, (Caroline, Tomp. Co.) r 5, farmer 20.
PERRY EDWIN A., r 43, steam-threshing and grist-mill, wagon maker, and farmer 110.
Perry Frank, r 44, music teacher, and farmer 25.

Perry Lewis, (Caroline, Tomp. Co.) r 5, laborer.
Perry Richard H., (Caroline, Tomp. Co.) r 51, resident.
Personius John J., (Slaterville, Tomp. Co.) r 3, farmer 8.
Phelan Patrick, section boss.
Phillips C. Martin, (Center Lisle, Broome Co.) r 48, farmer.
Phillips Franklin, (Center Lisle, Broome Co.) r 48, farmer 66.
Phillips W. Ardell, (Berkshire) r 47, leases of C. Arnold of Geneva 90.
Pierce Benjamin, (Harford, Cort Co.) r 6, dealer in charcoal, and farmer 60.
Pierce George H., (Harford, Cort. Co.) r 6, resident.
Pierce John, (Harford, Cort. Co.) r 21, laborer.
PIERCE WALLACE C., dealer in furniture and household goods, also undertaker and dealer in breech-loading shotguns and rifles, agent for the Ithaca breech-loading shotguns.
Polley Amos, r 31, farmer 275.
Polley Lemuel, r 31, farmer 68.
Polley Solomon, r 32, farmer 62.
Quail Fred, (Caroline, Tomp. Co.) r 4, laborer.
Rawley Daniel T., retired farmer.
Rawley George W., dentist and jeweler, Main.
Rawley Hiram B., general store.
Rice William, laborer, h Railroad.
RICH CHAUNCEY L., retired treasurer Southern Central R. R.
Rich Henry L., book-keeper, bds Main.
Rich Lucian D. station and express agent.
RICHFORD HOTEL, H. W. Theleman, prop.
Root Reuben, (Berkshire) r 46, farmer 43.
Robinson Asher, (Caroline, Tomp. Co.) farmer, leases of M. Robinson 90.
ROBINSON CALVIN J., att'y and counselor at law, notary public, and pension agent, h Main.
Robinson Fred J., telegraph operator, bds. Main.
Robinson Hiland, mechanic, h Main.
Robinson Isaac N., r 21, carpenter, and wagon repairer, also farmer 60.
Robinson James, telegraph operator, h Main.
Robinson Martin, r 42, farmer 290.
Rockefeller Egbert, (Harford Mills, Cort. Co.) r 11, farmer 135.
Rockefeller Henry, (Harford Mills, Cort. Co.) off r 14, farmer 30.
Rockefeller Jacob, (Caroline, Tomp. Co.) r 22.
Rockefeller John, (Caroline, Tomp. Co.) r 22, farmer 82.
Rockefeller Simeon W., (Harford Mills, Cort. Co.) r 12, farmer 100.
Rogers Mary Powell, resident, h Aurora.
Royce Dewitt, (Harford, Cort. Co.) r 5, farmer with Herman 63.
Royce Herman, (Harford, Cort. Co.) farmer with Dewitt 63.
Rusher William, (Harford, Cort. Co.) r 8, farmer, leases of Jane Sheldon, of Newark, 144.
Satterly Charles, r 17, farmer 5.
Satterly Ira, r 33, farmer 15.
Satterly Lyman J., r 17, farmer 18.
Satterly Willard, r 17, lumberman, and farmer 62.
Satterly William B., (Center Lisle, Broome Co.) r 36, farmer 41.
Sears Dioclesian, r 16, retired farmer.
Sears James M., r 16, stock breeder and dealer, and farmer 237.
Sexton Ransom, (Harford Mills, Cort. Co.) r 18, dairy 17 cows, farmer 160.
Sherwood Isaac, (Berkshire) r 47, dairy 15 cows, farmer 150.

TOWN OF RICHFORD.

Slater George, emp. H. S. & C. W. Finch, h Aurora.
Slater Joseph, r 16, farmer 22.
Slater Timothy, off r 18, farmer 15.
Smith Eliza, r 45, widow James, farm 147.
Smith Jerome, r 11, laborer.
Smith Julius C., millwright, and wagon-maker, h Aurora.
Smith Nicholas, (Harford Mills, Cort. Co.) r 14, farmer 80.
SMITH RALPH P., r 35, breeder and dealer in Clay and Hambletonian horses, dairy 30 cows, farmer 200.
Smith W. C. & Co., (H. S. and C. W. Finch) general store.
Smith William R., r 18, laborer.
STANLEY ANSON, (Center Lisle, Broome Co.) r 51, farmer 56.
Steele Andrew, (Caroline, Tomp. Co.) r 4, farmer 160.
Stephens Hector, teamster.
Stewart Lewis, r 31, laborer.
SWIFT CHARLES H., dealer in hardware, tinware, stoves and ranges, hanging lamps, Rogers Bros.' plated-ware, cutlery, alarm clocks. agate ware, churns and churn-powers, bird cages, horse-blankets, syrup cans, sap-buckets, tin-roofing, eave-troughs, tobacco and cigars, etc., Main, h Main.
Talbot Selah, r 11, farmer 32.
Talcott Horace B., r 17, farmer 25.
Talcott Jessie F., r 17, farmer 25.
Talcott Willard, r 17, farmer 27.
Tarbox Benjamin, r 10, farmer 40.
Theleman Frank, porter Richford Hotel.
THELEMAN HIRAM W., prop. Richford Hotel, and livery, also dealer in wagons, mowing-machines, horse-rakes, etc., and farmer 50.
Thomas Theodore F., r 42, farmer 6.
THOMPSON ALEXANDER, (Harford Mills, Cort. Co.) r 11, farmer $85\frac{1}{2}$.
Thompson Benjamin, r 44, cooper, and farmer $2\frac{1}{4}$.
Thompson Charles, r 16, farmer 40.
Thompson Charles H., r 44, farmer.
Thompson William H., (Harford Mills, Cort. Co.) r 11, farmer 22, leases of Mrs. E. N. VanDyke 80.
Tobey Josiah G., (Caroline, Tomp. Co.) r 26, prop. saw-mill, and farmer 118.
Tryon Daniel, (Harford Mills, Cort. Co.) r 11, farmer 64.
Tubbs Elbert, r 49, laborer.
Tubbs Freedom U., r. 34, widow Robert, farmer 35.
TUBBS GAMALIEL C., (Center Lisle, Broome Co.) r 36, prop. steam saw-mill, dealer in lumber and farmer 300.
TUBBS GAMALIEL H., (Whitney's Point, Broome Co.) farmer 100 and at Whitney's Point steam saw-mill, and mnfr. and dealer in lumber, doors, blinds, sash, mouldings and butter packages.
Turk George H., r 32, farmer, leases of Amos Polley.
Tyler Edward, (Harford Mills, Cort. Co.) r 10, clergyman (Chris.) and farmer 10.
Tyler Laura, widow Ezra, resident, h Main.
Vandemark Samuel, r 17, farmer 72 1-2.
Van Gorder Charles H., r 49, farmer 25.
Vincent Delia, (Harford Mills, Cort. Co.) r 10, widow Peter, farmer 142.
Vincent Henry, (Harford Mills, Cort. Co.) farmer, leases of James Foster 52.

STARKEY & WINTERS, Wholesale and Retail Druggists, Owego.

TOWN OF SPENCER.

Vincent Henry G., (Harford Mills, Cort. Co.) r 10, farmer, leases of Delia Vincent 142.
Vunk J. Frank, carpenter, h Main.
Walker Albert, (Berkshire) r 45, farmer 86.
Walker Lyman M., r 43, farmer 130.
Walker Orrin, r 40, farmer 196.
WATKINS AMOS G., justice of the peace and dealer in horses, cattle, sheep and swine, also farmer 400, and with James L. Watson estate 195, h Main.
Watkins Eugene, (Harford, Cort. Co.) r 23, farmer 31.
Welch Luther H., (Caroline, Tomp. Co.) off r 23, farmer 84.
Welch Rufus H., (Caroline, Tomp. Co.) off r 23, carpenter and farmer 130.
Westcott Matthew, conductor Southern Central R. R., h Main.
Wheaton Mason S., (Harford, Cort. Co.) r. 29, farmer 67.
Wightman George W., r 43, farmer.
Wilbur James F., prop. grist mill at Harford and dealer in flour, meal and feed.
Wilcox Frederick, off r 18, laborer.
Wilcox Gardner, (Harford Mills, Cort. Co.) r 9, farmer 160.
Wilcox John, (Harford Mills, Cort. Co.) r 8 cor. 21, farmer 95.
Wilcox Justin, (Harford Mills, Cort. Co.) r 9, farmer.
Wilcox Smith, r 10, farmer 10, and leases of Ransom Sexton 160.
Williams Cyrel, (Harford Mills, Cortland Co.) r 12, farmer 52.
Williamson James, r 50, farmer 43.
Wilson Josiah, r 50, farmer 44.
Witter Daniel P., r 44, dairy 14 cows, farmer 143.
Woodard Edgar, r 10, laborer.
Woodard Elijah, r 10, laborer.
Woodard John, r 33, farmer 54.
Woodard John P., r 33, farmer 50.
Woods Elisha B., r 40, contractor and builder, and dealer in apples and all kinds of furs and hides.
YAPLE DELOSS, teaming, h Main.
YAPLE O. A., wife of Deloss, dealer in millinery and fancy goods Main.
Yaple Philip H., r 25 cor. 26, farmer 100.
Zee Franklin, r 33, farmer 28.
Zee Horner, r 50, farmer.
Zimmer Hiram, r 17, laborer.

SPENCER.

(*For explanations, etc., see page 3, part second.*)

(Postoffice address is Spencer, unless otherwise designated in parenthesis.)

Abbey Lizzie, millinery, Main, h do.
Abbott Andrew, (North Spencer) r 1, farmer 100.
Abbott Reuben, cartman, h Brooklyn.
Abbott Solomon, drug clerk, h Academy.

STARKEY & WINTERS, promptly fill Mail and Telephone Orders.

Ackerman Riley, farm laborer, h Main.
Ackerman Roscoe E., r 34, farmer, leases of Samuel Eastham 40.
Ackles Lewis, (North Spencer) r 22, laborer.
Ackles Truman, r 29, farmer.
Adams Frank W., (North Spencer) r 19, justice of the peace, and farmer 120.
Adams William, r 48, farmer.
Aldred Cynthia, widow Robert B., resident, h Park.
Allen Jerome, r 8, laborer.
Allen Olive, widow Joel, resident, bds. Main.
Ammerman Daniel, r 43, retired farmer.
Armstrong Dennison B., laborer, h Liberty.
Armstrong William H., emp. Seely's Mill, h Van Etten.
Bacorn Darius, r 27, farmer, leases of Dr. Davis 40.
Bailey Oliver P., r 48, farmer 50.
Baker Emily, widow Epaphras, resident, h Van Etten.
BAKER L. E., prop. Spencer Marble Works, h Academy.
Barber Adeline, off r 41, widow of Stockholm, farmer 50.
Barber Charles, r 61, laborer.
Barber Fred C., off r 41, farmer.
Bartley Larow, farmer, h Mill.
Bartrom John P., (Halsey Valley), r 54, farmer 50.
Batz Jacob, retired, h North ave.
Beadle Edward G., laborer, bds. Liberty.
Beadle George, resident, h Liberty.
Bell Alfred F., r 17, farmer.
Bellis Elizabeth Miss, laundress, h Academy.
Benedict William H., emp. Seely's Mill, h Liberty.
Benton Harry, r 13, farmer.
Benton James, r 14, farmer 103.
Benton William, r 13, farmer 10.
Berry Nathaniel, (North Spencer) r 19, farmer 8.
Besley Reuben D., emp. Seely's Mill, h Laurel.
Bidlack Ranson, r 54, farmer 177.
BINGHAM I. AUGUSTUS, r 10, farmer 250.
Bingham Seth H., r 10, farmer.
Blanch Maria, widow David, resident, h Brooklyn.
Bliven Charles, resident, h Main.
Bliven Luther, r 33, farmer 92.
Bliven Samuel G., retired, h Van Etten.
Boda Charles, r 11, farmer 150.
Boda Frederick C., breeder and dealer in horses and cattle, and farmer 50.
Boda George, r 10½, farmer 50.
Bogart John J., r 42, laborer.
Bogert Clarence, r 53, laborer.
Bogert Franklin, r 33, laborer.
Bogert Orlando W., r 33, laborer.
Bogert William W., r 49, farmer 50, and leases of Jane Williams 128.
Bosley Asa, r 27, dairy 30 cows, farmer, leases of Seymour Seeley 360.
Bowen James G., r 28, laborer.
Bower Brothers, (Philip and Levi) furniture and undertaking, Main.
Bower Philip A., (Bower Bros.) h Main.
Bower Levi, (Bower Bros.) bds. at Van Ettenville.
Bowen Samuel, r 24, laborer.
Bowen Seth, groceries, Academy, bds. do.

Bradley Calvin W., retired, h Main.
Bradley Charles E., merchant, Main, h do.
Brearley Arthur J., r 43, brickmaker.
Brearley Willie J., r 43, laborer.
Breese Frank, r 42, farmer, leases of L. Emmons 80.
Breese Fred P., r 43, emp. brickyard.
Brock Clinton, r 18, farmer 50.
Brock Estella, teacher, bds. Academy.
Brock Ethel, farmer, h Academy.
BROCK JOHN, r 42, dealer in cattle and breeder of sheep and lambs, also wool-buyer, and farmer 280.
Brock John A., r 34, farmer, leases of Ethel Brock 150.
Brooks Daniel, r 26, farmer 85.
Brooks Daniel C., agricultural implements, and farmer 145, h Maple ave.
BROOKS GEORGE, r 45, justice of the peace, and farmer 55.
Brooks Leonard, r 15, clerk.
Brooks Victor W., r 45, farmer 47.
Brown Frederick R., r 33, farmer 50 in Candor, and leases of J. Thompson, of Candor, 250.
Brown Lee A., r 43, laborer.
Brown William, r 18, cooper.
BRUNDAGE DeWITT C., carriage, wagon, and sleigh manuf., VanEtten, h. do.
Brundage Jay C., wagon-maker, bds. VanEtten.
Buckley Frank A., r 43, laborer.
Bunnell Charles, r 37, farmer 53.
Burchard Stephen, r 34, farmer 16.
Burdick Peter, r 42, stone mason.
Burhyte Andrew, r 43, farmer 147.
Burtless James, (North Spencer) r 2, basket-maker.
Buttles Morden U., (VanEttenville, Chemung Co.) r 43, farmer 75.
Butts Andrew P., retired tanner, h Main.
Butts Celestia, widow Hyatt, resident.
Butts Charles E., justice of the peace, and farmer 127, h Main.
Butts Charles E., Jr., carpenter, bds. Main.
Butts Fred G., farmer with his father Charles E., bds. Main.
Butts Harvey, laborer, bds. Main.
Canfield Edgar E., teamster, h VanEtten.
Canfield Fred U., miller, h Liberty.
Card Albert J., street commissioner, and farmer 52, h VanEtten.
CARD ALVIN D., r 43, farmer 94.
Card Charles B., r 43, cider-mill.
Carter Frank E., barber, Main, h Water.
Cashady Guy, meat-market, Main, h Brooklyn.
Cashady John, (Halsey Valley) r 54, farmer 133.
Cashman William H., r 37, farmer.
Cavanaugh Edwin, (North Spencer) r 21, farmer 50.
Chadrick Lewis, r 41, farmer 97.
Chapman Samuel, lumberman, h Main.
Chapman Willard E., (North Spencer) r 2, laborer.
Clapp John W., miller, h VanEtten.
Clapp Walker G., photographer, VanEtten, h do.
Clarey Dennis, emp. L. V. R. R., h Liberty.

TOWN OF SPENCER.

Clark Howard, carpenter, h Brooklyn.
Clark John S., upholsterer, bds. Brooklyn.
Clark Lewis, r 34, blacksmith, and farmer 90, and leases of James Bishop, of Candor, 100.
Clark Samuel, (Halsey Valley) r 59.
Clark Shepard B., medical student, bds. Brooklyn.
Clark Sylvenus B., r 38, blacksmith and farmer, works for Lewis Clark 90.
Clark Theodore A., r 9, farmer 215.
Clark William A., (Halsey Valley) r 59, farmer 12.
Clay John, r 26, farmer 85.
Coggin George E., r 15, farmer 100.
COMPTON SILAS, (West Candor) r 37, general blacksmith and wagon-maker, horse-shoeing a specialty, served in Co. F, 76th N. Y. Vols.
Coney Frank G., emp. Seely's mill, h Liberty.
Coney Irving M., r 28, lumberman.
Congdon V. B., r 51, farmer 56.
Converse Lottie, r 41, widow Theodore, farmer 160.
Cook Almon, (North Spencer) r 1, resident.
Cook Anderson B., (North Spencer) station agent and telegraph operator, also machinist.
Cornell Charles S., r 43, grain threshing, and farmer 100.
Cortright Albert, r 48, farmer 8, and leases of A. S. Emmons 120.
Cortright Ayres D., (Halsey Valley) r 54, mason and farmer.
Cortright David, (Halsey Valley) r 54, farmer 16.
Cowell Alvah, (North Spencer) r 19, farmer.
Cowell Betsey, (North Spencer) r 1, widow Lewis, farm 45.
Cowell Charles, (North Spencer) r 1, farmer 150.
Cowell Edward, (North Spencer) r 19, farmer 150.
Cowell Eliza, (North Spencer) r 19, widow James, resident.
Cowell Eva S., teacher, bds. Maple ave.
Cowell Mariette, (North Spencer) r 1, widow John A., farm 19.
Cowell Mary A., widow John, resident, h Main.
Cowles Aaron, (North Spencer) r 1, farmer, leases of A. Abbott 100.
Cowles Almiron, (North Spencer) r 1, farmer 50, and leases of D. Randall of Etna 50.
Cowles Ebenezer, emp. Seely's Mill, h Liberty.
Cowles Jason, r 24, farmer 50.
Cowles John S., (North Spencer) r 2, farmer, leases of Almiron Cowles 50.
Cowles Marcus E., (North Spencer) r 2, lumberman, and farmer 127.
Cowles Mary L., (North Spencer) r 2, owns with Edgar D. Sabin of Candor 107.
Cowles Sylvester, (North Spencer) r 2, carpenter.
Crafts Calvin B., student, bds. Main.
Crane John, r 27, farmer 22.
Crum Peter, r 48, farmer 50.
Cummings Albert, r 40, lumberman and farmer, leases of Jerome Thompson of Candor 180.
Cummings Andrew, r 61, laborer.
Cummings Jacob W., r 42½, farmer 12.
Cummings Williams P., (Van Ettenville) r 43, musician and farmer.
Daughty Robert, laborer, bds. Liberty.
Davenport Arthur V., r 66, farmer.
Davenport John S., clerk, bds. Main.

DAVENPORT SHERMAN, r 66, farmer 50.
Davis Cornelius W., farmer, h Academy.
DAVIS GEORGE W., physician and surgeon, Main, h do.
Davis Isaac S., r 38, laborer.
DAVIS JEROME S., manuf. of all kinds mowing machine knives, and Buckeye hand cornplanters. also all kinds of machine job work, Cedar, bds. do.
Dawson Chester, r 32, farmer 173.
Dawson John, peddler, h Liberty.
Dawson Mary E., widow Myron, resident, bds. Main.
Dawson Nelson, retired, h Main.
Dawson Seth W., r 32, farmer, leases of Chester 173.
Dawson Sidney A., r 32, threshing, and farmer 65.
DAY CYRENUS N., general merchant, h North ave.
DAY JOHN & SON, (Cyrenus N.) hardware, stoves and tinware, groceries and provisions, boots and shoes, and agricultural implements, Main.
DAY JOHN, general merchant, h Maple.
Day William S., r 28, blacksmith, and farmer 78.
DEAN EDWARD E·, atty. at law, Main, h do.
Dean Mary, r 47, widow Casper, farm 16.
Dean Orrin F., farmer 54, h Main.
Decker Andrew, r 61, laborer.
Decker William, emp. Bower Bros., h at Van Ettenville.
Deming Augustus C., r 61, farmer 192.
Deming Joseph B., r 61, farmer.
Deming William H., r 63, stump-pulling and farmer 36.
Denniston Chester B., asst. station agt. G. I. & S. R. R. and telegraph opp. h Liberty.
De Remer Enos, (West Candor) r 36, carpenter.
De Remer Olan, (West Candor) r 36, farmer 75.
Devereaux Seymour, r 61, laborer.
Dewey Charles, r 11, farmer.
Deyo Chauncey, r 33, mason.
Deyo Harry, r 33, mason.
Dickens Robert E., emp. Seely's mill, h off Liberty.
Dikeman George, r 59, farmer 103.
Dodge Alvin, retired, h Myrtle.
Dodge Anthony, r 49, lumberman.
Dodge Sarah A., r 18, widow Edwin, saw-mill and farm 190.
Dorn Abram, r 32, farmer 60, and leases of Nelson Dawson 107.
Doty Asa T., r 26, farmer 109.
Douglass James, r 26, farmer, leases of Edward Cowell 100.
Downey Frank, laborer, h Academy.
Downey Robert L., sawyer, h Academy.
Drake Charles W., farmer 35, h Van Etten.
Dresser Jacob S., clerk for S. A. Seely, h Railroad ave.
Dumond Harry, watchmaker and jeweler Main, h Center.
Dutton James, r 45, laborer.
Eastham John, (West Candor) farmer 40.
Eastham Lucy A., (West Candor) r 39, widow of Edmund, farm 59.
Eastham Peter, farmer 50.
EASTHAM SAMUEL, (West Candor) r 37, prop. saw-mill and manf. and dealer in hemlock lumber, lath and wood, also shipper of baled hay and straw, and farmer 165, and works for Maggie Eastham 100.

TOWN OF SPENCER.

Eastham Thomas, (West Candor) r 39, farmer 106.
Eastham Thomas J., farmer 80.
Eaton Harris, (North Spencer) r 22, farmer 2.
Edwards Clarissa, widow Philo, resident, h Liberty.
Edwards George, r 28, laborer.
Elbrooks Charles, clerk, bds. Main.
Elbrooks Elmore L., clerk, h Main.
Ellis Edwin R., lumberman, h Van Etten.
Embody Isaac, laborer, h Main.
Emery David, r 32, farmer 90.
Emery James C., r 13, prop. saw-mill and farmer 33.
EMMONS ALFRED S., general merchant and farmer 260, Van Et ten, h do.
EMMONS LUCIUS E., drugs, books and stationery, Main, h do.
English Minor W., (Van Ettenville, Chemung Co.) r 64, farmer 150.
Ennis Aldis F., farmer, h Academy.
Ennis Samuel, farmer, h Academy.
Esmay Claude H., drug clerk, bds. Main.
Eveland Samuel, r 53, laborer.
Fanning Andrew J., r 41, laborer.
FARMERS' AND MERCHANTS' BANK OF SPENCER, (Thomas Brock, pres't; O. P. Dimon, vice-pres't; M. D. Fisher, cashier; M. B. Ferris, ass't cashier, Main.
Farnsworth Edgar, farmer, h Main.
Farnsworth George, laborer, h Cedar.
Farnsworth James, r 45, farmer 26.
Farnsworth Marcellus, r 24, laborer.
Ferguson George N., shoemaker, Main, h do.
Ferris Andrew P., laborer, h Laurel.
Ferris S. Arthur, r 49, farmer.
Ferris Charles, (Halsey Valley) r 53, farmer 50.
Ferris Cornelia, widow George H., resident, h Main.
Ferris Cyrus B., r 49, farmer 82.
Ferris Daniel, (Halsey Valley) r 53, farmer 63.
Ferris David A., r 63, carpenter and farmer, works for Electa A. Ferris 30.
Ferris Edmund r 53, farmer 127.
Ferris Gabriel, off r 41, farmer.
FERRIS GEORGE C., (West Candor) r 35, apiarist 50 colonies, and farmer 100.
Ferris James, off r 41, farmer 50.
Ferris John, r 40, farmer 90.
Ferris Harvey, r 53, farmer.
Ferris Louisa, widow Joshua H., resident, Main.
Ferris Moses, r 49, farmer 50.
Ferris Myron, (West Candor) r 36, laborer.
FERRIS MYRON B., ass't cashier Farmers' and Merchants' Bank, also fire and life insurance, h Main.
Ferris Willis C., r 57, farmer, leases of D. B. Hadorn 120.
Field Henry E., farmer, h Main.
Fields Noah, farmer 50, h Main.
FISHER BERT F., (Fisher Bros.) r 19, musician.
FISHER BROTHERS, (B. F. and S. J. F.) r 19, dairy 20 cows, farmers, lease of J. P. Fisher 190.
Fisher Charles, (Halsey Valley) r 59, farmer 25.

Fisher Charles A., r 28, farmer, leases of Harriet L. Fisher 80.
Fisher Charles J., drugs and medicines, Main, h do.
Fisher Clarence, (Halsey Valley) r 59, laborer.
Fisher Fred M., laborer, h Main.
Fisher Joseph T., r 17, farmer.
Fisher Leonard, farmer, h Liberty.
FISHER MARVIN D., postmaster, and general merchant, Main, h do.
Fisher Philip J., farmer, h Main.
Fisher Robert H., r 17, dairy 30 cows, farmer 375.
FISHER STEPHEN J., (Fisher Bros.) r 19.
Fisher Susan, widow Thomas, resident, h Main.
Fisher William H., physician and surgeon, Main, h do.
Fleming William H., farmer 280, h Academy.
Forsyth Augustus, r 33, laborer.
Forsyth Henry, r 37, farmer 77.
Forsyth Henry B., (Halsey Valley) r 59, farmer 60.
Forsyth Hettie, resident, bds. North ave.
Forsyth Nelson A., r 40, apiarist, and dealer in bee-keeper's supplies, also farmer 25.
Forsyth Perry, r 13, laborer.
Forsyth Rumsey, (Halsey Valley) r 59, farmer 50.
Forsyth Wallace, r 40, laborer.
Fox John, (North Spencer) r 2, leases of Bethaney Hill 50.
Frisbie Lucinda, widow Charles, resident, h Academy.
Fulton Frederic, r 66, farmer 50.
Fulton Maria, r 47, wife of Frederic, farm 45.
Furman Horace, (North Spencer) off r 19, farmer 80.
Gallagher Patrick, emp. Seeley's mill, h off Liberty.
Galpin George R., r 34, farmer.
Galpin James, r 34, farmer 60.
Galpin Orrin B., r 34, farmer.
Garatt Elmore, r 38, farmer with Harriet 218.
Garatt Harriet, r 38, widow Corinth, farmer with Elmore 218.
Garatt S. C., widow Amasa, milliner, Van Etten, h do.
Garey Abram L., wagon-maker, h Brooklyn.
Garey Daniel, (North Spencer) r 2, shoemaker.
Gay Patrick, (West Candor) r 37, farmer 150.
GEORGIA D. LAMONT, supt. Spencer creamery, h Liberty.
Georgia Mary M., widow Nathan S., resident, h Liberty.
Georgia William W., emp. Spencer creamery, h Liberty.
Gilbert Burdett, r 42, laborer.
Gilbert Norman A., barber, Brooklyn cor. Main, h Creek.
Giles Mary, r 41, farm 75.
Gilkie Riley, r 61, farmer 3.
GOEHNER LOUIS G., r 54, cigar manuf. and farmer.
Goodrich Austin L., foreman Seeley's mill, h Liberty.
Goodrich Calvin E., r 61, farmer 30.
Goodrich Calvin J., r 61, stone mason, h Myrtle.
Goodsell Rebecca A., widow Jared H., resident, bds. Liberty.
Green Anson, (North Spencer) r 2, farmer.
Green John B., resident, h Park.
Green Wheeler C., (Halsey Valley) r 54, farmer 105.
Greer Charlotte, r 61, farm 24.

TOWN OF SPENCER.

Griffin James A., carpenter and builder, Park, h do.
Griffith Absalom, r 14, blacksmith and farmer 60.
Griffith Frederick D., clerk, h Center.
Grinnell Daniel P., r 13, laborer.
GROVE HOTEL, C. J. Rice, manager, opp. G. I. & S. depot.
GUINNIP DEMPSTER N., painter, paper-hanger, Brooklyn, h North ave.
GUINNIP GEORGE, painter and paper-hanger, Brooklyn, h North ave.
HAGADORN DAVID B., r 57, feed-mill, and farmer 193.
Hall Cornelia L., r 38 cor. 41, wife of H. S., farm in Ulysses, Tomp. Co. 95.
Hall Harvey Smith, r 38 cor. 41, manuf. and dealer in lumber and shingles, and farmer 600.
Hall Leonard F., r 38, wagon-maker.
Hallock Emily, widow John, resident, h Main.
Hallock William M., farmer 138, h Main.
Hanson Charles, tinsmith, h Main.
Harding Ella Mrs., resident, h Main.
Hart Morris, r 8, farmer 50.
Haskins Charles, laborer, h Brooklyn.
Hawkins Albert, r 49, farmer.
Hawley Edward, laborer, h Myrtle.
Hawley Edward, r 18, farmer.
Head Bradford, r 47, laborer.
Head Theron, r 47, tobacco-grower and farmer, leases of A. J. Card 21.
Hedges Frank L., emp. Seely's mill, h Academy.
Hedges Laton N., resident, h Aurora.
Hess John. (Halsey Valley) r 53, farmer, leases of Daniel Ferris 63.
Hevland William H., r 45, laborer.
Hiers Theodore, laborer, h Main.
Hike W. Harvey, mason, h Academy.
Hill Bethaney, (North Spencer) r 2, widow Luther, farm 50.
Hilligas Joshua, life insurance, h Tompkins ave.
Hinds James H., (Halsey Valley) r 54, laborer.
Hinds William H.,(Halsey Valley) r 54, farmer leases of Joshua Tompkins 110.
Holdridge Amos, r 41, with William A., farmer 217.
HOLDRIDGE WILLIAM A., r 41, apiarist, and with Amos farmer 217.
Hollister Warren L., (West Candor) off r 39, farmer 90.
Homiston Ezra W., physician and surgeon, Main, h do.
Hover Elisha, (West Candor) r 39, farmer.
House George W.,(North Spencer) r 1, farmer 107.
House John P., mason, h Academy.
House Lewis M., (North Spencer) r 22, farmer 175.
Howard Alvin, (West Candor) laborer.
Howard Henry, off r 66, laborer.
Howard Loring P. Rev., pastor M. E. church, h Van Etten.
Howell Charles, r 47, laborer.
Howell Frank C., book-keeper Bachelor's endowment association, h Main.
Howell Henry H., r 61, farmer 50.
Howell Ira M., farmer 45, h Van Etten.
Howell James K., r 47, farmer 5.
Howell John, r 47, farmer 27.
Howell Myron P., station agt. G. I. & S. R. R., h Park.
Howell Norman J., r 61, brickmaker.

STARKEY & WINTERS, Wholesale and Retail Druggists, Owego.

TOWN OF SPENCER.

Hubbell Ira, r 27, laborer.
Hugg Horace A., carpenter, h Liberty.
Hugg Luman H., r 28, farmer 119,
Hulburt Luther J., (North Spencer) r 20, farmer 130.
Hulet George, r 26, farmer.
Hull Eben, blacksmith, Cedar, h Main.
Hull James B., r 30 cor. 54, farmer 125.
Hull Loring W., farmer 100, h Main.
Hunt Isaiah, retired, h Main.
Hunt James O., off r 51, farmer, leases of Isaiah Hunt 87.
Hutchings Eli M., carpenter, h Laurel.
Hyatt William, farmer 14, h Main.
Johnson Allen, off r 66, laborer.
Johnston Chauncey, (North Spencer) r 2, farmer.
Johnston David, (North Spencer) r 2, farmer 140.
Johnston Ira, (North Spencer) r 2, farmer.
Joy Abel, off r 13, farmer.
Joy Alvah, r 10, farmer 50.
Joy Daniel, r 42½, tobacco grower, and farmer 70.
Joyce Joseph, resident, h Academy.
Kellogg Mahlon A., (North Spencer) postmaster, and general merchant.
Kelsey Charles, r 23, farmer 100.
Kelsey Lewis, off r 24, farmer 50.
Kelsey Walter, r 61, farmer.
Kelsh John G., laborer, h Brooklyn.
Ketcham Henry, r 33, laborer.
Keyes Nathan, r 23, resident.
King Duane C., clerk, h North ave.
Kinner Asa, emp. Seely's mill, h Van Etten.
Kirk Charles, (Halsey Valley) r 59, carpenter, and farmer 33.
Kirk Charles N., (Halsey Valley) r 59, blacksmith, and farmer 40.
Kirk Fred G., (Halsey Valley) r 59, farmer.
Kirk Henry P., (West Candor) off r 39, farmer 75.
Kirk Stephen, (Halsey Valley) r 59, farmer 64.
Knapp Elias, r 53, farmer, leases of Franklin Poole of Barton 75.
Knapp Isaac, (Halsey Valley) r 53, farmer 30.
Knupenburg Frank, r 28, laborer.
Knupenburg Myron, (North Spencer) r 2, laborer.
Lake Fred W., (North Spencer) r 2, farmer 99.
Lake George W., (North Spencer), r 19, farmer 150.
Lake Harvey, (North Spencer) r 19, farmer 10.
Lake Orlando, (North Spencer) r 19, farmer 15.
Lane Oscar, (West Candor) r 39, farmer 40.
Lang Charles F., blacksmith Brooklyn, h Maple.
Lange Frederick W., r 10½, farmer 175.
Lange Parker P., r 10½, farmer.
Lange William H., blacksmith and horse-shoer, h Water.
Larne James C., r 8, farmer 75.
Lawrence Ernest, butcher, h Van Etten.
Lawrence Sevellan F., off r 17, laborer.
Leonard John, r 31, farmer.
Leonard Michael, r 31, farmer 94.

STARKEY & WINTERS, Druggists, Owego. Close Prices to Dealers.

Leonard Sarah J., teacher, bds. Main.
Leonard William J., butcher, h Main.
Lewis Benjamin F., r 28, farmer 300.
Lewis Fred, r 28, farmer.
Livermore Albert Rev., pastor Presbyterian Church, h Aurora.
Loomis Herman, r 56, farmer 80.
Lotz Hartman, (North Spencer) r 2, farmer 56.
Lyke Stanley, r 3, farmer.
Lott Benjamin, carpenter, h Laurel.
Lott Isaac M., clerk, h Water.
LOUSHAY ADELBERT E., fireman N. Y. L. E. & W. R. R., bds. Liberty.
Loushay Julia A., widow Henry, h Liberty.
Mabee Clarence, r 11, farmer.
Mabee Daniel, blacksmith Van Etten, h do.
Mabee Franklin H., (Halsey Valley) r 54, farmer 103.
Mabee John B., r 43, farmer 40.
Mabee Theodore, r 11, farmer 258.
Maine Ira L., r $42\frac{1}{2}$, farmer 57.
Maine William F., painter and paper-hanger, h North ave.
Manning Frank D., (Halsey Valley) r 53, farmer 100.
Manning Robert, (Halsey Valley) r 53, farmer.
Manning William H., r 13, farmer 170.
Marsh William, r 61, laborer.
Martin Charles, laborer, h Main.
Martin Frank A., r 17, farmer, leases 105.
Martin Jane B., r 17, widow Ira, farm 85.
Martin Olive C., r 17, farm 50.
Matteson George E., dentist, Main, h Center.
McFall Dorus H., farmer, h Tompkins ave.
McKee George R., carpenter, h Van Etten.
McKoon Patrick, (West Candor) r 34, laborer.
McMaster James O., manf. and dealer in lumber, lath and wood, with Jeremiah T.
McMaster Jeremiah T., r 53, prop. saw-mill, dealer in lumber, lath and wood, also farmer 550.
McMaster Susan Mrs., bds. Van Etten.
Mead John, (North Spencer) r 2, farmer 50.
Mead Lewis, (North Spencer) r 2, laborer.
Messenger Chauncey P., emp. Seely's mill, h off Liberty.
Middaugh John, r 61, farmer.
Miller Edmund, emp. A. Seely, h Liberty.
Miller Sherman, laborer, h Main.
Mills Henry C., station agent E. C. & N. R. R., also National Express agent, h Brooklyn.
Montgomery George, expressman, bds. Academy.
Montgomery John, expressman, h Academy.
Montgomery William, shoemaker, Brooklyn, h Maple.
Moody Charles E., r 42, milk dealer, market gardener and farmer, leases of Charles Moody 95.
Morse Dana, peddler, h Van Etten.
Morse Mary M., resident, h Van Etten.
Mosher Stephen G., stationary engineer, h Park.
Mosher William G., emp. Seely's mill, h Liberty.

Mosier Bartley L., r 13, farmer 32.
Mowers Jacob Henry, (North Spencer) r 20½, prop. saw-mill, and farmer 60.
Nelson William B., emp. Seely's mill, h Academy.
Newman Daniel, mason, h Main.
Newman Henry, r 48, farmer 50.
Newman William H., r 48, cabinet-maker and farmer, leases of Henry Newman 50.
News Gabriel P., off r 41, farmer 97.
News Jane, resident, h Cedar.
Nichols Charles, porter Grove Hotel, bds. do.
Nichols David A., groceries and provisions, Main, h Liberty.
Nichols Jane, widow John A., resident, h Academy.
NORRIS ALONZO, M. D., physician and surgeon, also farm 550.
O'Connor Jerry, R. R. section foreman, h North ave.
Odell Marcellus C., billiards, pool-room and restaurant Main, h do.
Odell William H., r 40, farmer 83.
Osborn John, meat market, h Van Etten.
Osborn John C., r 43, carpenter.
Ostrander Jerome, retired, bds. Aurora.
Ostrander Mary J., widow William, h Aurora.
Owen Fidelia, widow Elijah, resident, h Liberty.
PALMER HEMAN L., (J. H. Palmer & Son), also telegraph opp. h Main.
PALMER J. H. & SON, (Heman L.) undertakers, Main.
PALMER JOHN H., (J. H. Palmer & Son) also farmer 45.
Parks Anthony, farm laborer, h Main.
Parlett Robert, Jr., bakery Academy, h Railroad.
Patrick Alva T., clerk, h Liberty.
Patty Jasper, r 66, farmer 105.
Pelan James, r 18, laborer.
Perrin Alexander, r 31, farmer 60.
Perrin Daniel, r 31, farmer.
Perrin William, r 13, blacksmith, and farmer 73.
Personius Ester, widow Jacob, housekeeper, Maple ave.
Personius Myron C., (North Spencer) off r 19, section hand, and farmer 50.
PERT ELLEN P., widow Rev. Luther B., resident, h Liberty.
Pierson George, carpenter and builder, h Academy.
Post Catherine, widow Thomas L., resident, h Main.
Post Thomas, r 3, farmer 280.
Post William, resident, h Van Etten.
Pritchard Pratt A., blacksmith, h Academy.
Puff Charles H., buyer for S. A. Seely, h Park.
Quick Elmer, (West Candor) r 37, farmer 50.
Radeline Sarah A., r 6, farmer 40.
RANSOM WILLIAM, r 41, farmer 124.
Raub Henry S., r 50, farmer 150, and in Tomp. Co., '18.
Raub Robert J., r 50, farmer.
Reeve Aaron D., carpenter, h Liberty.
RICE CHARLES J., manager Grove Hotel, bds. do.
Richardson & Campbell, r 43, contractors and builders, also manuf. of Spencer brick, residence in Ithaca.
Richardson Sherman, r 32, farmer, works for Milton Dawson estate 100.
Riker Captain L., r 34, carpenter, and farmer, works for Mrs. C. L. Riker 48.
Riker Charles F., r 38, farmer 50.

13

TOWN OF SPENCER.

Riker Eugene, r 38, farmer, works for Anthony Riker estate.
Riker James L. Rev., (local M. E.) retired, h Main.
Riker Oliver P., r 38, farmer 50.
Riker William H., r 38, carpenter.
Ritchie George, r 24, farmer.
Ritter Charles W., emp. Seely's mill, bds. Academy.
Ritzler Charles C., r 48, photographer, and farmer 22.
Robinson Clarissa, widow Dana, resident, bds. North ave.
Robinson Fletcher O., carpenter and builder, h Maple ave.
Roe William W., r 38, carpenter.
Rogers Benjamin F., emp. Seely's mill, h Liberty.
Rogers John F., resident, h VanEtten.
Rolfe Leonard, r 40, farmer 50.
Rumsey Johnson, (Halsey Valley) r 58, farmer 73.
Rumsey Nelson, laborer, h Maple ave.
Ryant Daniel J., (North Spencer) r 20, blacksmith.
RYANT JAMES P., (North Spencer) r 20, with Ransom steam threshing, and farmer 100.
RYANT RANSOM, (North Spencer) r 20, with James P., steam threshing, and farmer 100.
Ryder Thena J., widow James, resident, h Laurel.
Sabin Otis L., r 42½, with William P., farmer 160.
Sabin Seth O., r 42½, blacksmith.
Sabin William P., r 42½, farmer with Otis L., 160.
Sager Cornelius, (Halsey Valley) off r 58, farmer 52.
Sager Douglass C., (Halsey Valley) off r 58, farmer 80.
Sager Willard J., jeweler, Main, h Creek.
Sammons Matthew, (West Candor) r 37, farmer.
Sandford James, traveling salesman, h Brooklyn.
Sawyer Carrie C., teacher, bds. Academy.
Sawyer Ezra O., contractor and builder, Academy, h do.
Sawyer Viola M., teacher, bds. Academy.
Sayles Charles E., (North Spencer) r 1, farmer 56.
Schutt Charles, (Halsey Valley) r 58, farmer 78.
Schutt Lemuel H., (Halsey Valley) r 58, farmer 25.
Scofield Albert L., r 32, farmer.
Scofield Horace, r 32, farmer 111.
SCOFIELD WALLACE L., r 15, farmer 115.
Seely David N., book-keeper for S. A. Seely, h Railroad ave.
SEELY FRANCIS S., miller, h Mill.
Seely Fred, emp. Seely's mill, h Mill.
Seely Myron, off r 45, farmer 70.
SEELY S. ALFRED, general merchant, saw and grist-mill, creamery, blacksmith shop, and farmer 140, h head of Academy.
Seely Seymour, farmer, h Mill.
Seely Seymour A., resident, bds. Maple ave.
SHAW GEORGE E., r 40, apiarist 70 swarms, and farmer 25.
Shaw Henry C., r 56, farmer 90.
Shaw Henry W., r 57, farmer 71.
Shaw John W., (West Candor) r 39, carpenter and farmer 54.
SHAW JOSEPH B., (West Candor) r 39, farmer 100, served in Co. G, 1st N. Y. Veteran Cavalry.
Shaw Silas H., r 40, farmer 60.

Shaw William, r 54, mason and farmer 87.
Shepard George T., r 28 cor. 30, live stock dealer and farmer with J. Q. Shepard.
Shepard Goodrich C., r 33, farmer 107.
Shepard Hattie F., teacher, bds. Liberty.
Shepard Heth H., r 43, laborer.
Shepard John Q., r 28 cor. 30, dealer in cattle and sheep, and farmer 255.
Shepard La Grange S., r 6, farmer 106.
Shepard Lewis A., clerk, bds. Main.
Shepard Myra A., widow Sylvester, resident, h Liberty.
SHEPARD SYLVENUS, general merchant, Van Etten, h do.
Signer Adonijah, (North Spencer) r 2, lumberman and farmer.
Signer Albert, (North Spencer) r 2, prop. saw-mill and farmer 519.
Signer Edward, r 28, farmer 4.
Silke Louisa, clerk, h Railroad ave.
SILKE JAMES, supt. Seely's mill, h Railroad.
Simms John C., (Van Ettenville, Chemung Co.) r 43, carpenter, farmer 50.
Simms William R., (Van Ettenville, Chemung Co.) farmer.
Sincepaugh William, farm laborer, h Main.
Sipley Sidney W., r 49, traveling salesman and farmer 50.
Skinner Oliver, farmer, h Main.
Smith Edmund, off r 47, farmer 140.
Smith Leroy, (North Spencer) r 22, farmer.
Smith Schuyler F., (Halsey Valley) r 59, farmer 40.
Smith William H., (North Spencer) r 1, leases of F. B. Clark 46.
Sniffin William A., general merchant, Main, h Liberty.
SNOOK DAVID L., apiarist 75 swarms, and harness-maker, Main, h do.
Snook Esther, widow Peter, resident, bds. Main.
Snyder Sely, r 40, farmer 130.
Southern Tier Bachelors' Endowment Association, (W. H. Fisher, M. D., prest.; W. R. Swartout, secy.; M. P. Howell, treas.) Academy.
Spaulding Adelbert, r 47, laborer.
Spaulding Frances, r 43, wife of G. S., farm 100.
Spaulding John J., r 47, farmer 128.
Spaulding John P., r 47, laborer.
Spaulding John S., r 43, farmer, works 100.
Spaulding Maria, widow Joseph, resident, h Main.
Spaulding Phineas E., traveling salesman, h Liberty.
SPENCER CREAMERY, (S. A. Seely, prop., D. La M. Georgia, supt.) Liberty.
*SPENCER HERALD, (Van Gelder & Son, publishers) Main.
Spencer Hezekiah, r 65, farmer 55.
SPENCER MARBLE WORKS, L. E. Baker, prop., Academy.
Stage Eliab, clerk, bds. Liberty.
Stage Philip A., (North Spencer) r 21, farmer 92.
Stanclift Elizabeth, teacher, bds. Main.
Stanclift Isaac S., general merchant, Van Etten, h do.
Starkes Charles, laborer.
Stebbins Frederick, farm laborer, h Liberty.
STEENBURG ALBION L., r 13, with Francis E., prop. Spencer Springs farm 119.
Steenburg Asa H., r 13, farmer.

STEENBURG FRANCIS E., r 13, with Albion L., prop. Spencer Springs farm 119.
Stevens Charles N., (North Spencer) r 1, farmer 64.
Stevens David, r 11, farmer 75.
Stevens Harmon, r 13 cor. 10½, farmer 158.
Stevens Jacob, r 33, farmer 59, and in Candor 75.
Stevens John, (West Candor) r 36, laborer.
Stevens Seneca, r 65, carpenter and farmer 30.
Stevens Thomas J., (North Spencer) r 1, farmer 50.
Stevens William H., r 41, basket-maker.
Stewart Ira, (North Spencer) r 20½, farmer 80.
Stilson Dianna, (West Candor) widow of James L., farm 37, and with N. T. Stilson 60.
Stilson James L., (West Candor) off r 39, farmer 97.
STILSON NELSON T., (West Candor) off r 39, farmer 100, and with Diana 60.
Stone Silas, (West Candor) r 37, farmer, leases of Patrick Gay 150.
Stow John M., turning and sawing, North ave., h do.
Strait David, r 37, laborer.
Stubbs William A., r 43, farmer 42, served in Co. C, 76th N. Y. Vols.
Sutton Charles A., emp. Seely's mill, h off Liberty.
Sutton William W., emp. Seely's mill, h Liberty.
Swartout James, (North Spencer) r 22, farmer.
Swartout Lewis, (North Spencer) r 22, farmer 28.
SWARTOUT MARCUS L., (M. L. Swartout & Son) h Ithaca.
SWARTOUT M. L. & SON, (William R.) produce dealers, Academy.
SWARTOUT WILLIAM R., (M. L. Swartout & Son) also secretary Southern Tier Bachelors Endowment Association, h Academy.
Tanner J. Henry, laborer, bds. Centre.
Tanner John H., physician and surgeon, h Centre.
Taylor Simeon, r 43, engineer.
Thornton Fred V., emp. Seely's mill, bds. Van Etten.
Thornton George, (West Candor) r 37, carpenter.
Thornton John J., emp. Seely's mill, h Van Etten.
Thornton Mary, (North Spencer) r 19, widow of Charles, resident.
Tollman Ansel B., r 27, farmer 20.
Tompkins James, r 37, farmer 217.
Tompkins James B., r 37, farmer, leases of James Tompkins 217.
TOMPKINS JOSHUA, farmer, h Tompkins ave.
Tucker William, r 42, farmer 53.
Tuckerman Hector, laborer.
Turk Charles M., resident, bds. Maple ave.
Turk Charles, blacksmith, h Myrtle.
Turk David, blacksmith, Academy, h Main.
Turk Stephen D., blacksmith and constable, Academy, h Main.
Tuttle Benjamin F., emp. Seely's mill, h Liberty.
Tyler George, r 51, farmer 56.
Tyler Henry E., r 59, farmer 101.
Tyler James, off r 66, laborer.
Valentine Adrian A., r 54, farmer.
Valentine Electa J., r 54, widow William, farm 104.
Valentine Elvin, (West Candor) r 35, farmer 30.
Valentine Fred, (West Candor) r 35, farmer 50.

Valentine Jacob E., r 54, teacher.
Vallentine William O., r 54, teacher.
Van Duyn William C., emp. Seely's Mill, h Liberty.
VAN GELDER & SON, (Phineas C. and Charles J.) publishers of Spencer *Herald*, Main.
VAN GELDER CHARLES J. (Van Gelder & Son) h Park.
VAN GELDER PHINEAS C., (Van Gelder & Son) h Park.
Van Gelder William, emp. A. Seely, h Railroad.
Van Gorder Lafayette, r 50, farmer 28.
Van Marter Aaron, resident, h North ave.
Van Marter Amos, r 41, apiarist 42 colonies, farmer 58, and leases of Silas Shaw 60.
Van Marter Enos T., (West Candor) r 35, dealer in groceries, and farmer 5.
VAN MARTER HOUSE, Jacob Van Kuren, prop., Main.
Van Marter Jared, (Halsey Valley) r 54, saw-mill.
Van Marter Nelson, (West Candor) farmer.
Van Natta Edwin, r 66, farmer 85, and leases of W. H. Fleming 275.
Van Natta Fred, r 47, carpenter, and farmer 111.
Van Natta John, r 52, farmer 107.
Vankleek Jesse B., r 63, carpenter, and farmer 16.
VAN KUREN BEN S., clerk Van Marter House, bds. do.
VAN KUREN JACOB, prop. Van Marter House, Main.
Van Natta John D., r 47, butcher.
Van Norman Cassius M., emp. Seely's mill, h Railroad.
Van Norton John, r 65, laborer.
Van Norton Warren, r 65, laborer.
Van Ostrand Peter, off r 47, farmer 30.
Van Ostrand Truman, off r 47, laborer.
VAN WOERT LEWIS J., r 7, assessor, and farmer 175.
Van Woert Maria E., r 13, wife of Samuel, farm 25.
VAN WOERT WILLIAM G., r 15, auctioneer, and farmer 65.
Vorhis A. Louisa, widow Rev. Stephen, resident, h Aurora.
Vorhis James W., mason, h Brooklyn.
Vorhis John W., retired, bds. North ave.
Vorhis J. Wallace, mason, h North ave.
Vorhis Mary H., teacher, bds. Aurora.
Vorhis Mead, cartman, h Main.
Vorhis Rebecca, (North Spencer) r 19, widow Jacob, farm 50.
Vorhis Truman, (North Spencer) r 19, manuf. washing machines, and farmer 43.
Vose Ephriam, r 38, carpenter and manuf. of lumber.
Vose George H., r 66, farmer, leases of George Pierson 95.
Vose Lavina, (West Candor) r 37, widow Alfred.
Vose O. Sumner, r 11, farmer 75.
Vose Othniel J., r 11, farmer.
Vose Samuel, r 10½, farmer 50.
Vose Sylvenus, r 15, farmer 85, and leases of E. S. Willet, 75.
Vose Sylvester S., r 6, farmer 82.
Wait George, r 13, farmer 104.
Waggett John, r 13, miner.
Walden Charles, r 17, laborer.
Warner William W., r 48, farmer 100.
Washburn Charles, (West Candor) r 36, laborer.

Watkins David, r 13, farmer 113.
WEEKS JOSHUA P., livery, Water, bds. Van Marter House.
Weeks Stephen M., r 41, farmer 100.
Weeks William W., r 38, carpenter.
Wells Josiah, blacksmith, Main, h do.
West Marshall C., contractor and builder, h Railroad.
Westbrook Arthur, carpenter, bds. Main.
Westervelt Leslie, r 65, farmer.
Wetzel Elmer, marble-cutter, bds. Academy.
Whalen Edmund, (West Candor) r 36, laborer.
Wheeler Frank E., emp. Spencer Creamery, bds. Liberty.
Wheeler Frank R., laborer, h Maple ave.
Wheeler Jesse, r 31, farmer 103.
Wheeler William C., r 31, farmer.
White George G., r 13, farmer 70.
White Squire, r 49, laborer.
Whitlock Ramer, r 42½, laborer.
Wild Joseph, laborer.
Willett Edward S., dealer in hides, and farmer 75, h Maple.
Williams Ziba, laborer, h Main.
Wilson Peter, r 41, laborer.
Winchell James N., (Halsey Valley) r 59, farmer 56.
Witherall Henry, r 47, farmer 40.
Wood William H., wagon and sleigh manuf., Brooklyn, h Maple.
Woodford Harriet, r 33, farmer 185.
Woodruff George, r 61, farmer 31.
Woodruff S. Delevan, r 28, farmer.
WOODRUFF THOMAS, r 28, farmer 80.

TIOGA.

(For explanations, etc., see page 3, part second.)

Ackley Nathan G., (Smithboro) prop. pool-room.
Ahart Albert, (Strait's Corners) r 6, farmer with his father George.
Ahart George, Strait's Corners) r 66, farmer 45.
Allen George, (Smithboro) r 58, farmer 50.
Anderson Ezra F., (Owego) r 12, farmer 125.
ANDERSON JAMES M., (Owego) r 10, farmer 200, and in Candor 100.
Anderson John J., (Owego) r 10, dentist.
Anderson Willis D., (Owego) r 12, farmer, works on shares for his brother James M. 74.
Andrus Peter J., (Smithboro) off r 61, farmer 77.
Armstrong James R., (Smithboro) r 73, resident.
Armstrong William, (Owego) r 12, farmer, works for his brother Fred 50.
Ayers Angelo, (Owego) r 12, farmer.

STARKEY & WINTERS, Wholesale and Retail Druggists, Owego.

TOWN OF TIOGA.

Badger Celia, (Owego) r 18, widow Lucius, farm 100.
Badger Luke, (Tioga Center) farmer.
Badger Noah, (Tioga Center) r 40, farmer 50.
Bailey Eugene, (Smithboro) trackman.
Bailey Lucy, (Smithboro) widow, resident.
Ballou Charles, (Owego) r 28, laborer.
Banfield Elmer, (Tioga Center) r 57, farm laborer.
Barber Ami W., (Halsey Valley) general merchant.
Barden A. E., (Smithboro) carpenter.
Barnes Charles E., (Owego) r 34, farmer 20, and in Pa. 80.
Bartron Alonzo, (Smithboro) r 58, farmer with his father Moses.
Bartron Moses, (Smithboro) r 58, farmer 75.
Bates William, (Halsey Valley) r 21, prop. blacksmith shop.
Bauer Adam, (Strait's Corners) r 5, farmer 100.
Bauer Christian, (Strait's Corners) r 17, farmer 130.
Bauer George W., (Strait's Corners) r 5, farmer.
Bauer Martin, (Strait's Corners) r 5, tanner.
BAUER MARTIN L., (Strait's Corners) (Ford & Bauer) r 5.
Bauer Simon, (Strait's Corners) r 5, farmer.
Beddell Mary G., (Smithboro) widow Bently F., farm 100.
Bedell Charles M., (Smithboro) r 40, farmer 50.
Bedell William H., (Smithboro) r 40, farmer 100.
Beilis William L., (Smithboro) station agt. Erie R. R.
Bennett Sabrina, (Tioga Center) r 51, widow Chester, resident.
Bentley Webster, (Halsey Valley) r 22, farmer.
Best Charles, (Tioga Center) r 36, farmer 60.
Best Jay, (Tioga Center) r 36, farmer.
Best Jay C., (Tioga Center) r 36, farmer 100.
Best William H., (Tioga Center) r 58, farmer 55.
Blake John, (Tioga Center) currier, h Main.
BLAKE WILLIAM, (Tioga Center) drugs and medicines, Main, h do.
Bogart Almon, (Owego) r 33, farmer 35, and works for Oliver P. Ford 60.
Bogart David R., (Halsey Valley) carpenter.
BOGART EUGENE D., (Owego) r 14, farmer with his father Henry.
BOGART HENRY, (Owego) r 14, farmer 51.
Bogart Peter V., (Smithboro) r 66, farmer 150.
Bogart William, (Strait's Corners) r 3, farmer.
BONHAM CHARLES H., (Tioga Center) general merchant, Main, h do.
Bonham Morris, (Tioga Center) retired merchant, h Main.
Booth Ann E., (Owego) r 48, resident.
Bowman Ann, (Smithboro) r 73, widow Zebulon, resident.
Bowman Charles, (Smithboro) r 73, teamster.
Bowman Isaac, (Smithboro) resident.
Bowman John A., (Smithboro) rector of Emanuel Church.
Bradley Andrew, (Smithboro) farm laborer.
Bradley Edward (Tioga Center) farm laborer.
Bradley Mariette Miss, (Smithboro) resident.
Brearley John W., (Tioga Center) r 57, farmer 100.
Briggs David, (Smithboro) r 69, farmer, works for George Eckert 60.
Brink Amos, (Owego) r 25, farmer.
Brink Edward, (Tioga Center) r 43, laborer.
Brink Frederick, (Strait's Corners) r 19, farm laborer.

STARKEY & WINTERS, promptly fill Mail and Telephone Orders.

Brink George, (Halsey Valley) r 37, farmer 20.
Brink Joseph, (Owego) r 33, farmer 90.
Brink William, (Tioga Center) laborer.
Brooks Benjamin J., (Tioga Center) r 52, farmer.
Brooks Charles, (Tioga Center) off r 40, farmer 50.
Brooks Cornelius, (Tioga Center) r 43, farmer 40.
Brooks Frank, (Smithboro) off r 58, farmer for his father William.
Brooks George H., (Tioga Center) r 52, farm laborer.
Brooks Lot M., (Tioga Center) r 51, bridge carpenter.
Brooks Nicholas, (Tioga Center) r 36, farmer 100.
Brooks William, (Tioga Center) farmer 100.
Brown Alvah S., (Halsey Valley) shoemaker.
Brown David L., (Tioga Center) drug clerk, bds. Main.
Brown John B., (Owego) r 44, farmer 48.
Brown William H., (Tioga Center) r 19, farmer, works for C. D. Hoff 76.
Brundage Matthias, (Owego) off r 6, farmer 35.
Buchanan James H., (Halsey Valley) farmer 58.
Burlington Ephraim, (Owego) r 30, farmer 61.
Burlington Hugh W., (Owego) r 30, farmer 100.
BURLINGTON JOHN A., (Owego) r 8, farmer 125.
Burlington Joseph, (Owego) r 8, farmer 58.
Burnham Elizabeth Mrs., (Smithboro) resident.
Burns Robert, (Owego) r 31, farmer 60.
Burns Willie J., (Owego) r 31, farmer for his father Robert.
Butler William, (Tioga Center) trackman.
Cable Silas, (Owego) r 32, farmer, works for Mrs. John Taylor 100.
Campbell Alexander, (Owego) r 48, laborer.
Campbell Bert, (Owego) r 28, farmer.
Campbell Fred, (Halsey Valley) r 21, farmer for L. B. West.
Campbell Jacob, (Halsey Valley) r 21, farmer for L. B. West.
Campbell Orlando, (Owego) off r 12, farmer.
Canfield Alfred, (Smithboro) r 71, farmer, works for his father Amos 160.
Canfield Amos, (Smithboro), r 71. farmer 170.
Caple John, (Owego) r 7, farmer 50.
CAPLE PHILIP, (Catatonk) r 7, farmer 100.
Carlisle William, (Tioga Center) r 22, laborer.
Carmer Amasa, (Halsey Valley) off r 2, farmer 140.
Carns John A., (Owego) r 12, farm laborer.
Carpenter Charles E., (Smithboro) r 60, farmer with his father Peter R.
Carpenter Jesse C., (Tioga Center) r 53, farmer 200.
Carpenter Peter R., (Smithboro) r 60, farmer 75.
Casterline Stephen B., (Tioga Center) r 40, farmer 54.
Casterline Warren, (Smithboro) r 60, farmer 50.
Catlin Andrew R., (Tioga Center) off r 40, farmer, works for George Truman 150.
Catlin Benjamin F., (Owego) r 25, farmer 110.
Catlin Charles, (Owego) r 18, farmer 123.
Catlin Edmund S., (Tioga Center) r 43, carpenter, and farmer 51.
Catlin Emeline, (Owego) r 32, widow Jonathan, farmer 42.
CATLIN FRANK H., (Owego) r 45, produce dealer, and farmer.
Catlin Frederick H., r 33, farmer 42.
Catlin George, (Tioga Center) r 52, wagon-maker.
Catlin Jacob, (Tioga Center) r 43, farmer 55.

TOWN OF TIOGA.

CATLIN JAMES H., (Tioga Center) r 43, physician, and farmer 50.
Catlin Laverne, (Owego) r 33, farm laborer.
Catlin Mary J., (Owego) r 33, widow Nathaniel, farmer 27.
Catlin Mead, (Owego) r 47, emp. foundry.
Catlin Nathan S., (Tioga Center) r 56, farmer 80.
CATLIN NATHANIEL, (Owego) r 33, farmer 38.
Catlin Sarah E. Mrs., (Owego) r 34, farm 20.
Catlin William, (Owego) r 44, farm laborer.
Catlin Willis E., (Owego) r 25, farmer with his father Benjamin F.
Chamberlain Oscar C., (Owego) r 12, farmer.
Chandler Horace, (Owego) r 12, laborer.
Chew Clark, (Owego) r 11, farmer.
Chew Guy, (Owego) r 11, farmer 167.
Clune James, (Smithboro) r 61, farmer 50.
Coburn & Van Norstran, (Tioga Center) (C. S. B. & G. Van N.) r 51, tin and iron roofing, and manuf. eve spouting.
Coburn C. Sidney,(Tioga Center) (Coburn & Van Norstran) r 51. also tin shop.
Coburn Eliza, (Tioga Center) r 51,widow Charles R., resident.
Coffin Milton, (Owego) r 45, farmer.
Cole Alfred, (Owego) r 31, farmer, leases of James Taylor 30.
COLE AUSTIN R., (Smithboro) r 73, farmer 50.
Cole Benjamin F., (Smithboro) r 71, farmer.
Cole Daniel H., (Tioga Center) r 51, retired farmer.
Cole Frank, (Smithboro) off r 58, farmer 100.
Cole Frank, (Smithboro) r 40, farm laborer.
Cole Horace, (Owego) r 48, farmer.
COLE SAMUEL E., (Smithboro) r 73, farmer 50.
Cole William, (Halsey Valley) r 22, farmer.
Coleman Isaac, (Tioga Center) r 52, bridge carpenter.
Coleman Jackson, (Halsey Valley) r 22, farmer 116.
Coleman James, (Tioga Center) r 52, carpenter.
Coleman John P., (Tioga Center) r 41, farmer 180.
Coleman William D., (Tioga Center) r 52, carpenter.
Congdon Harry,(Tioga Center) r 36, farmer, leases of Mrs. Mary Munnohan 12.
Conklin Elizabeth, (Owego) r 30, widow John, resident.
Conklin Sylvenas, (Owego) r 18, farmer, works on shares for Alexander Duncan 110.
Conway John, (Smithboro) r 55, farmer 50.
Cook DeWitt C., (Halsey Valley) r 2, farmer 53.
Cook Esther, (Strait's Corners) r 20, widow Samuel, farmer 100.
Cook Florence, (Strait's Corners) r 20, farmer for his mother Esther.
Coon Walter, (Strait's Corners) r 18, farmer 104.
Coons Arthur, (Tioga Center) r 22, farmer with his father Johnson.
Coons Daniel, (Strait's Corners) r 4, farmer 100.
Coons George B., (Tioga Center) r 58, farmer, works for Mrs. Perry Ward 75.
Coons Hiram, (Strait's Corners) r 4, farmer.
Coons John, (Tioga Center) r 22, farmer with his father Johnson.
Coons Johnson, (Tioga Center) r 22, farmer 200.
Coons Lemuel, (Tioga Center) r 22, farmer 50.
Cooper Frank A., (Halsey Valley) r 2, farmer 50.
Corsin William, (Owego) r 47, farm laborer.
Cortright Alfred, (Tioga Center) r 43, laborer.
Cortright Charles, (Tioga Center) farm laborer.

TOWN OF TIOGA.

Cortright James, (Tioga Center) farm laborer.
Cortright John, (Tioga Center) farm laborer.
Cortright Richard, (Tioga Center) farm laborer.
Crandall Benjamin, (Tioga Center) off r 40 farmer 50.
Crandall Daniel, (Smithboro) r 66, farmer, works for Mrs. M. Richards 117.
Crawford Absalom, (Smithboro) laborer.
Crawford Abram, (Tioga Center) r 40, farmer 95.
Croft Michael, (Smithboro) trackman.
Crum Henry, (Owego) r 28, resident.
Cunningham Daniel, (Owego) r 32, farmer 33.
Curkendoll Cornelius, (Smithboro) prop. Erie Hotel.
Curkendoll Prudence Mrs., (Smithboro) resident.
DAILY DANIEL, (Barton) r 64, farmer 380.
DAILY EUGENE E., (Barton) r 64, farmer 150.
DAILY FRED C., (Barton) r 64, dealer in agricultural implements, wagons, etc., and farmer 75.
Davenport Adelbert, (Halsey Valley) r 39, farmer 50.
Davenport Alvin M., (Smithboro) r 71, works on shares for Henry Light 73.
Davenport Emmet J., (Smithboro) r 71, farmer with his father Alvin M.
Davenport George, (Smithboro) r 71, section-hand.
Davenport Henry, (Strait's Corners) r 4, farmer 70.
Davenport Jackson, (Smithboro) r 59, farmer 50.
Davenport Judson, (Barton) r 64, farmer, works for James J. Green 73.
Davis Albert J., (Tioga Center) r 40, farmer 82.
Davis Nathaniel W., (Owego) r 45, farmer 117.
DAY GEORGE H., (Owego) r 12, farmer, works for Herbert Farnham 65.
Day Marvin G., (Owego) r 29, farmer.
Dean Franklin S., (Smithboro) resident.
Decker Alexander D., (Tioga Center) Methodist minister, h Main.
DeCaytor Ralph, (Owego) r 16, farm laborer.
DeHart Sanda, (Tioga Center) laborer, h Main.
DeHart Thomas, (Owego) r 45, laborer.
Delano Charles, (Owego) r 28, mason.
Delano Sarah, (Owego) r 28, widow Reuben, resident.
Densmore Samuel, (Owego) r 26, farmer, works on shares for A. J. Goodrich 240.
Deyo Charles, (Tioga Center) r 53, farmer, works for Joseph DuBois 220.
Deyo Chauncey (Owego) r 47, farmer.
Deyo Elijah W., (Tioga Center) r 41, miller.
Dinehart John, (Tioga Center) r 41, farm laborer.
Dinehart Robert, (Smithboro) farm laborer.
Doane Jane Mrs., (Smithboro) resident.
Doane Leroy, (Smithboro) laborer.
Doane Timothy, (Strait's Corners) r 3, prop. saw-mill and farmer.
Doane William H., (Smithboro) r 59, farmer 50.
Dorn David, (Halsey Valley) r 20, farmer 160.
Dorn Willis, (Halsey Valley) r 20, farmer for his father David.
Dorwin Asa F., (Owego) r 46, farmer.
DORWIN WILLIAM E., (Owego) (Dorwin, Rich & Stone) r 46, also railroad contractor and farmer 235.
DRAKE C. SIDNEY, (Smithboro) (W. J. Drake & Son) h Main.
Drake Ezra P., (Halsey Valley) r 39, farmer 100.
Drake George P., (Smithboro) tinsmith.

DRAKE WILLIAM J., (Smithboro) (W. J. Drake & Son) postmaster, h Main.
DRAKE W. J. & SON, (Smithboro) (C. S. Drake) general merchants, hardware and tinshop and dealers in agt. imp., coal, lime, plaster and cement, Main.
DuBois John E., (Tioga Center) lumberman, h in DuBois, Pa.
DuBois Lucy, (Tioga Center) resident, h Main.
DuBois William, (Tioga Center) r 53, farmer, works for Charles Poole 234.
Duff Alexander, (Strait's Corners) r 19, farmer 150.
Duff Andrew, (Strait's Corners) r 19, farmer.
Duff Harry, (Strait's Corners) r 19, farmer with his father Alexander.
Duff James, (Owego) r 25, farmer 90.
Duff Millie, (Tioga Center) r 36, widow Moses, resident.
Duff Robert H., (Tioga Center) r 36, farmer 206.
Duff Thomas, (Strait's Corners) r 2, farmer 75.
DUNCAN ALEXANDER, (Owego) r 29, farmer 150.
Duncan James, (Owego) r 30, farmer 30.
Earll David, (Tioga Center) r 49, retired physician and farmer 28.
Easton Frances M., (Catatonk) r 9, resident.
EATON AMBROSE P., lawyer, office at Waverly.
Eaton Daniel B., (Smithboro) cooper.
Eckert George F., (Smithboro) r 71, manf. eave-spouts.
Eckert Maria J., (Smithboro) r 71, widow Alexander B., resident.
Edwards Christopher, (Halsey Valley) laborer.
Edwards Samuel, (Owego) r 9, meat and grocery peddler.
Ehle George, (Strait's Corners) r 3, laborer.
Elliot Sarah A., (Smithboro) widow, resident.
EVELIEN ALFRED, (Tioga Center) hay and potato dealer, and farmer in Candor 97, h Main.
Evelien Christopher, (Tioga Center) farmer 100.
Evlin John, (Strait's Corners) r 3, farmer.
Emerson Charles, (Strait's Corners) r 4, farmer 160, and in Candor 40.
Emerson David B.,(Strait's Corners) r 24, farmer 96.
Emerson Frank, (Strait's Corners) r 4, farmer 108.
Emerson George, (Strait's Corners) off r 34, farmer 50.
Emerson Lot S., (Strait's Corners) r 5, farmer for his father William.
Emerson Luther, (Halsey Valley) r 37, farmer.
Emerson Mary, (Owego) r 18, widow Jonathan, resident.
Emerson Robert H., (Strait's Corners) r 4, farmer.
EMERSON SAMUEL H., (Owego) r 24, farmer 200.
Emerson Walter, (Strait's Corners) r 4, farmer.
Emerson William, (Strait's Corners) r 5, farmer 70.
Erie Hotel, (Smithboro) Cornelius Curkendoll, prop.
Estep Jacob, (Tioga Center) r 58, farmer 45.
Estep Loren, (Tioga Center) r 51, blacksmith and wagon-maker, h do.
FARNHAM AGNES L., (Owego) off r 12, widow Frederick A., resident.
FARNHAM ENOS S., (Owego) r 13, commercial traveler and farmer 80.
FARNHAM GEORGE A., (Owego) r 12. farmer 65.
FARNHAM HERBERT A., (Owego) off r 12, wool-carding, wood-turning, cider-mill and farmer 250.
FARNHAM JOEL S., (Owego) off r 12, farmer 40.
Farnham Orin, (Smithboro) blacksmith.
Farnham Roland B., (Owego) r 12, farmer with his father George A.

Farnham Sylvester J., (Owego) off r 12, farmer 7.
Fassett Alonzo, (Tioga Center) r 22, farmer 25.
Fenderson Althier, (Tioga Center) r 41, widow Isaiah, resident.
Fenderson Ely, (Tioga Center) r 41, carpenter.
Finch Herbert, (Owego) r 48, farm laborer.
Finn William H., (Owego) r 8, sup't Campbell farm 230.
Finnegan Barney, (Owego) r 27, farmer 30.
Fisher Frank, (Strait's Corners) r 5, laborer.
FOOTE JARED A., (Owego) r 13, farmer 13.
Foote Jared H., (Owego) r 28, traveling salesman.
Foote Lyman C., (Owego) r 28, farmer 12.
FORD & BAUER, (Strait's Corners) (L. F. and M. L. B.) r 5, contractors and builders.
Ford Lucius, (Strait's Corners) (Ford & Bauer,) r 5.
Ford Zera T., (Tioga Center) r 52, farm laborer.
Forsyth W. Henry, (Halsey Valley) r 21, cooper.
Franklin Burton B., (Tioga Center) r 52, prop. grist-mill.
Franklin Ransom J., (Tioga Center) r 52, miller.
French Jeremiah, (Tioga Center) shoemaker, and farmer 13.
Fox Henry, (Owego) r 47, carpenter.
Frister Noah, (Smithboro) r 70, farmer.
Garber John, (Tioga Center) r 40, resident.
Gardner Frederick, (Tioga Center) nurseryman, h Main.
Gasier William H., (Tioga Center) r 19, laborer.
Gavin Michael, (Tioga Center) trackman.
Geer Rezin J., (Strait's Corners) r 19, farmer 83.
Genung Adam S., (Smithboro) wagon-maker.
Gile Adelbert, (Tioga Center) r 24, farm laborer.
Gile George, (Tioga Center) r 24, farmer for his father Leonard.
Gile Joseph, (Halsey Valley) r 39, farmer for his father William W.
Gile Leonard, (Tioga Center) r 24, farmer 63.
Gile Samuel, (Tioga Center) r 23, farmer 25.
Gile William W., (Halsey Valley) r 39, farmer 100.
Gile Willis. (Tioga Center) r 24, farm laborer.
Giles Cyrus, (Halsey Valley) r 22, farmer.
Giles Daniel, (Strait's Corners) r 3, farmer.
Giles George, (Tioga Center) r 22, laborer.
Giles George, (Strait's Corners) r 3, invalid.
Giles Rufus, (Strait's Corners) r 3, laborer.
Giles Rufus D., (Strait's Corners) r 3, farmer 60.
Giles Sophia Mrs., (Smithboro) resident.
Giles Waterman, (Halsey Valley) r 22, farmer 100.
Gilkey Martha M., (Halsey Valley) r 1, widow Peter P., farm 60.
Gilkey Samuel G., (Halsey Valley) off r 2, farmer 102.
Gillson Nathan S., (Owego) r 34, farmer 38.
Giltner William, (Barton) r 63, farmer 100.
GOODENOUGH CHANCEY J., (Tioga Center) shoe-shop, and grape grower, Main, h do.
GOODRICH ANDREW J., (Owego) r 48, farmer 1,150.
GOODRICH CHARLES P., (Owego) r 12, farmer 44.
Goodrich Charles T., (Owego) r 48, farmer 100.
GOODRICH EPHRAIM, r 48, farmer 160.
Goodrich George L., (Owego) r 45, farmer 170.

GOODRICH HIRAM E., (Owego) r 47, farmer 85.
Goodrich Jairus T., (Owego) r 45, farmer 27.
Goodrich Louisa, (Owego) r 45, resident.
GOODRICH NOAH, (Owego) r 48, justice of the peace, and farmer 25.
Goodrich Sarah, (Owego) r 48, widow Herman, resident.
Goodrich Sarah, (Owego) r 46, farm 12.
GOODRICH STEPHEN S., (Owego) r 46, apiarist 15 swarms, poultry raiser, and farmer 60.
Goodwin William H., (Halsey Valley) r 1, farmer.
Gould Charles, (Halsey Valley) r 21, farm laborer.
Gould William, (Halsey Valley) r 39, farmer 50.
Green James J., (Barton) r 64, farmer 73.
Green James L., (Halsey Valley) r 39, farmer 50.
Groat Ira, (Owego) r 25, farmer 70.
Gulden Henry J., (Owego) r 30, works for A. J. Goodrich 230.
Gulden John, (Owego) r 31, farmer.
Guyles Charles P., (Strait's Corners) r 32, farmer, works for James Taylor 50.
Haddock Andrew J., (Tioga Center) r 41, farmer 96.
Haddock Lamont, (Tioga Center) r 41, farmer with his father Andrew J.
Halsey Valley House, (Halsey Valley) Mrs. Jane P. Higgins, prop.
Hamilton Charles, (Tioga Center) r 22, carpenter.
Hamilton George, (Halsey Valley) harness-maker.
Hamilton Henry, (Halsey Valley) teamster.
Hamilton Sarah Miss, (Smithboro) school teacher.
Hamilton Thomas A., (Halsey Valley), farmer.
Hanbury Adam, Jr., (Owego) r 6, farmer 105.
Hanbury Ezra, (Strait's Corners) r 17, farmer 58.
Hanmer George W., (Catatonk) r 9, telegrah operator.
Hanna John, (Smithboro) trackman.
Harding Adna, (Owego) r 13, farm laborer.
Harding Alonzo, (Owego) r 9, farm laborer.
Hardman John, (Owego) r 47, retired tanner.
Hardman John, (Owego) r 16, farm laborer.
Hardman John F., (Owego) r 47, drug clerk.
Hardman Patrick, (Owego) r 16, farmer 100.
Hardy Lizzie, (Smithboro) r 68, widow John, farmer 60.
Harford Edward, (Smithboro) r 54, farmer 70.
Harlin Lott, (Strait's Corners) r 4, farmer.
Harlin William, (Strait's Corners) r 4, farmer 120.
Heath Rebecca, (Halsey Valley) widow.
Hermberger Adam, (Strait's Corners) r 5, farmer 42.
Hess William, (Strait's Corners) r 3, laborer.
Hevland Douglass (Owego) r 28, cooper.
Higbee Augusta, (Tioga Center) r 51, widow Forman S., resident.
Higby James, (Tioga Center) laborer.
Higgins Jane P. Mrs., (Halsey Valley) prop. Halsey Valley House.
HILL ABNER G., (Tioga Center) r 51, justice of the peace and sawyer.
Hill Ward, (Smithboro) r 71, trackman.
Hoaglin Peter, (Owego) r 45 laborer.
Hobler Peter, (Owego) r 18, farmer 50.
Hodge Adelia, (Owego) r 29, widow Andrew C., resident.
Hoff Cornelius, (Strait's Corners) r 19, farmer 75.
Hoff Hiram, (Tioga Center) r 19, farmer 100.

HOLLENBECK CHARLES E., (Halsey Valley) r 21, physician and surgeon, and farmer 90.
Hollister William H., (Halsey Valley) r 22, farmer 95.
Holloway John, (Tioga Center) r 52, farm laborer.
Holmes John C., (Tioga Center) r 36, farmer 23.
Holt C. Edgar, (Tioga Center) r 52, farmer 96.
Holt William, (Smithboro) r 73, farmer 70.
Hoover Benjamin, (Smithboro) r66, farmer with his father Smith F.
Hoover Smith F., (Smithboro) r 66, farmer 73.
HORTON ABRAM, (Owego) r 48, farmer 220.
Horton Ada F., (Owego) r 28, farm 25.
Horton Charles, (Owego) r 32, farmer 90.
Horton George M., (Smithboro) r 70, carpenter, and farmer 12.
Horton Gurdon, (Owego) r 48, farmer 100.
Horton Hannah, (Owego) r 48, widow George C., resident.
Horton Isaac S., (Owego) r 48, farmer 100.
HORTON JOHN, (Owego) r 28, farmer 105.
Horton Julia A., (Owego) r 28, widow Daniel B., farmer 25.
HORTON THEODORE, (Owego) r 49, agricultural implements, and farmer 100.
Houghtaling William, (Owego) r 8, farmer 14.
Housten George, (Owego) r 6, farmer 5.
Howard Bishop, (Owego) r 6, farmer 25.
Hoyt Fred D., (Halsey Valley) general merchant.
HOYT IRA, (Halsey Valley) r 21, prop. cooper shop, and farmer 95.
Hoyt LaGrange, (Tioga Center) r 43, laborer.
Hunt Theodore, (Catatonk) r 9, farmer 34.
Hurlburt Henry, (Owego) r 9, farm laborer.
Hurlburt Perrine, (Owego) r 13, farmer.
Hyatt John D., (Owego) r 14, retired farmer.
Hyatt John M., (Owego) r 14, farmer 121.
Hyde Gordon, (Owego) r 12, cooper.
Hyres Charles, (Halsey Valley) cooper.
Ide Irwin N., (Smithboro) r 70, small fruits, and farmer 52.
Ide Jacob A., (Smithboro) r 69, berry raiser, and farmer 25.
Ingersoll Susan, (Tioga Center) widow Ebenezer, resident.
JEWETT CHARLES F., (Catatonk) r 9, lumberman, and farmer 120.
Jewett Harris, (Catatonk) r 9, farmer 110.
Jewett Henry, (Catatonk) r 9, farmer 87.
Johnson Abigail Mrs., (Smithsboro) resident.
Johnson Jay, (Halsey Valley) r 22, farmer 100.
Johnson J. Edward, (Smithboro) undertaker and carpenter.
Johnson Julius, (Barton) r 63, farmer 100.
Johnson Peter M., (Tioga Center) r 53, carpenter, and farmer 18.
Johnson Thomas, (Tioga Center) r 52, farmer, works for William Ransom 96.
Johnson Warren, (Smithboro) r 55, carpenter.
Johnson William H., (Smithboro) r 58, farmer 100.
Johnson William W., (Tioga Center) farmer.
Jones Anna, (Owego) r 28, widow Horton, resident.
Jones Horace, (Owego) r 28, farmer 60.
Jones Levi J., (Owego) r 29, farmer, works for Mrs. Beers 60.

STARKEY & WINTERS, Wholesale and Retail Druggists, Owego.

JONES STEPHEN W., (Owego) r 9, saw and grist-mill, turning shop, plaining-mill, etc., and farmer 10.
Kane John, (Smithboro) trackman.
KEELER EGBERT, (Owego) r 29, miller for Shaw & Dean, h 2½.
Kelly Johanna Mrs. (Smithboro) resident.
Kelly John, (Tioga Center) watchman.
Ketchum Ruth M., (Barton) r 63, widow Seymour, resident.
Ketchum Seymour C., (Barton) r 63, farmer 50, and works for Daniel Daily 50.
King Adam, (Owego) r 6, farmer 185.
King Charles C., (Barton) r 64, farmer 45.
King Ezra, (Owego) r 7, farmer, works for his father Adam 53.
King Frank, (Owego) r 17, farmer 50.
King George, (Owego) farmer with his father Adam.
Kinney Amzi, (Smithboro) resident.
Kline Philip, (Tioga Center) r 51, tanner.
KIRK CHARLES N., (Halsey Valley) blacksmith, and farmer 52.
KNAPP FREDERICK J., (Smithboro) boots & shoes, barber, Main, h do.
Knapp Sylvester, (Smithboro) physician.
Knowlton William, (Tioga Center) farm laborer.
Krum Dillen, (Owego) r 14, farmer 25.
KURKENDALL SAMUEL, (Tioga Center) r 53, farmer 37.
Lamberson Jedusen, (Halsey Valley) r 39, farmer 100.
La Monte Allen D., (Tioga Center) r 36, farmer with his father Seth D.
LA MONTE SETH D., (Tioga Center) r 36, horse farrier and farmer 60.
Landers William, (Owego) r 25, farmer 100.
Lane Charles, (Owego) r 31, farmer, works for Thomas Dundon 50.
LATIMER JONATHAN C., (Tioga Center) assemblyman for Tioga Co., lumberman and farmer 1,300.
Lawler John, (Owego) r 25, farmer with his brother Patrick 110.
Lawler Patrick, (Owego) r 25, farmer with his brother John 110.
Leach Stephen W., (Owego) r 28, prop. "Leach's Mills" grist-mill.
Leach William H., (Owego) r 28, farmer 30.
Leonard Elbridge, (Tioga Center) r 40, farmer 42.
Leonard George, (Tioga Center) r 51, mason and farmer 50.
Levett Edward, (Tioga Center) laborer.
Lewis David, (Owego) r 45, farmer 15 and works for Gilbert Truman 126.
Lewis Martin V., (Owego) r 30, farmer 75.
Light Mary, (Smithboro) r 71, widow Ely S., farm 160.
Link Joseph, (Tioga Center) r 51, laborer.
Lockwood Charles, (Tioga Center) peddler.
Lollis Mercy Mrs., (Smithboro) resident.
Lollis Samuel C., (Smithboro) general merchant, Main, h do.
Longley James F., (Owego) resident.
Lounsberry Amos L , (Smithboro) r 71, farmer 100.
Lounsberry Benjamin, 2d, (Smithboro) r 71, farmer 109, and in Nichols 52.
Lounsberry Robert L., (Smithboro) r 71, medical student.
Lounsbury Amy F., (Tioga Center) r 36, school teacher.
LOUNSBURY ANSON B., (Tioga Center) r 36, farmer with his mother Mary.
LOUNSBURY CLARK, (Tioga Center) r 36, farmer 32.
LOUNSBURY CORNELIA H., (Tioga Center) r 36, school teacher.
LOUNSBURY HARRIET A., (Tioga Center) r 36, school teacher.
LOUNSBURY JOHN L., (Tioga Center) r 36, farmer with his mother Mary.

STARKEY & WINTERS, Druggists, Owego. Close Prices to Dealers.

LOUNSBURY MARY, (Tioga Center) r 36, widow Lewis, farm 150.
Lounsbury Sheldon, (Smithboro) r 61, apiarist 52 swarms and farmer 129.
Loveless James J., (Smithboro) r 40, farmer 25.
Lovell House, (Smithboro) O. E. Lovell, prop.
Lovell Oliver E., (Smithboro) prop. Lovell House.
Luce Parmelia P., (Smithboro) r 40, widow Lot, farmer 75.
Luddington James A., (Smithboro) r 58, farmer 85.
Luddington Joseph, (Smithboro) r 58, farmer.
Lunger Alvin, (Owego) r 49, laborer.
Lyons Marvin, (Tioga Center) r 52, laborer.
Mack Anthony, (Smithboro) section boss.
Madden John, (Smithboro) trackwalker.
Madden Martin, (Smithboro) retired.
Mallery George, (Smithboro) mason.
Mallery Henry, (Smithboro) mason.
Manchester Henry H., (Owego) r 47, life insurance.
Manley Frank N., (Halsey Valley) farmer.
Manley George S., (Halsey Valley) farmer 50.
Mapes Lewis, (Owego) r 28, blacksmith, bds. do.
Martin Fred, (Tioga Center) general merchant, Main, h do.
Martin Jay H., (Tioga Center) r 51, retired merchant, and farmer 113.
Mastin Julia Mrs., (Smithboro) resident.
MATTESON FAYETTE A., (Smithboro) r 71, Baptist clergyman.
Matteson Frank, (Smithboro) r 71, divinity student.
Matteson George M., (Tioga Center) r 53, laborer.
McBride John, (Tioga Center) tanner, Main.
McCormick Elias, (Smithboro) laborer.
McDermott Michael, (Catatonk) r 9, fireman N. T. Co.
McDonald Charles H., (Smithboro) r 68, physician and surgeon.
McDonald Edward, (Tioga Center) trackman.
McDuffee Nathaniel J., (Smithboro) r 68, farmer.
McNeal Jane, (Smithboro) r 70, widow George, resident.
McNeil ———, (Smithboro) r 70, works for L. B. Pearsall 160.
McWhorter DeForest, (Tioga Center) clerk, bds. 1 Main.
MEAD JAMES R., (Owego) r 25, farmer 100.
Meder Paul, (Owego) r 7, farmer 25.
Meeker Jane, (Smithboro) r 53, resident.
Merritt John, (Tioga Center) r 52, laborer.
Mespell Joshua, (Owego) r 6, farmer 40.
Mespell Willis, (Owego) r 6, farmer.
Middaugh Jacob, (Owego) r 13, resident.
Middaugh Lorenzo T., (Smithboro) r 73, carpenter, and farmer.
Miller C. Henry, (Smithboro) r 53, farmer 400.
Miller George, (Tioga Center) tanner.
Miller Julia A., (Smithboro) r 53, widow Henry, resident.
Morris Caroline D., (Tioga Center) widow Almon, h Main.
Mortz George, (Tioga Center) tanner, bds. Main.
Mortz William, (Tioga Center) tanner, bds. Main.
Mulligan Thomas, (Owego) r 11, farmer 42.
Mulock Chancy, (Smithboro) farmer.
Mulock David, (Smithboro) farmer.
Mulock Edwin, (Smithboro) r 71, carpenter.
Munnahun Charles, (Tioga Center) r 52, farm laborer.

Munnahun Mary, (Tioga Center) r 36, widow Martin, farm 12.
Munson Frederick, (Owego) r 28, farmer.
Munson Heman, (Owego) r 28, farmer.
Myers Alford, (Owego) r 33, farmer, leases of Charles Catlin 40.
Nelson George, (Owego) r 32, farmer.
Nelson James J., (Owego) r 12, farmer 20.
Nelson Winslow, (Owego) r 26, farmer 50.
Nichols Addie R. Mrs., (Smithboro) r 58, resident.
Northrop James B., (Tioga Center) r 57, farmer, works for Dr. J. Wilson 200.
Oakley Joshua, (Smithboro) r 59, farmer 50.
O'Connor James, (Owego) r 30, invalid.
O'Connor John, (Owego) r 30, farmer.
O'Connor Joseph, (Owego) r 30, gardener.
O'Hara John, (Smithboro) trackman.
Ohart Moses, (Tioga Center) prop. Tioga Center Hotel, Main.
O'Hern William, (Smithboro) trackman.
Osborn Joseph, (Strait's Corners) r 3, farmer 50.
Ott Frank U., (Owego) r 14, farmer for his father Nicholas.
Ott George D., (Owego) r 14, farmer for his father Nicholas.
Ott Nicholas, (Owego) r 14, farmer 159.
Ott Sophia, (Owego), r 14, widow Nicholas, Sr., resident.
Pace John, (Tioga Center) r 43, trackman.
Park Dunham, (Barton) r 65, farmer 200.
Parmentier Franklin M., (Owego) r 28, butcher.
Pearsall John C., (Smithboro) r 71, carpenter.
Pease William (Owego) r 14, farmer, leases Mrs. Sisson 20.
Pelham Charles (Owego) r 44, carpenter and farmer.
PEMBLETON JOHN E., (Tioga Center) lumberman, farmer 350 and wild land 318.
Pepper Jackson S., (Smithboro) r 60, farmer 50.
Pepper John F., (Smithboro) r 68, grain and potato dealer, and farmer 100.
PERRY ALBERT A., (Smithboro) carpenter and joiner.
Perry Leonard, (Smithboro) farmer 45, h Main.
Perry Milo M., (Smithboro) hostler.
Piche Gasper Mrs., (Tioga Center) r 51, resident.
Pickering Joseph, (Smithboro) resident.
Pilkington Charles (Catatonk) r 9, telegraph operator.
Platt Houston, (Smithboro) r 71, farmer 10.
Poole Charles F., (Tioga Center) r 53, farmer 234.
Poole Edward V., (Smithboro) retired merchant.
Poole Murray, (Smithboro) lawyer.
Post Albert W., (Tioga Center) r 51, physician and surgeon, and farmer 160.
Pressure George, (Tioga Center) laborer.
Preston Frederick, (Owego) r 48, farm laborer.
Preston Louis, (Owego) r 48, farmer, works for A. J. Goodrich 100.
Preston Silas, (Owego) r 48, farmer.
Price John, (Owego) r 26, farm laborer.
Pudbuagh John, (Tioga Center) r 23, farm laborer.
Quirin Charles M., (J. G. Quirin & Co.) (Tioga Center) h Main.
Quirin Edward, (Tioga Center) r 49, tanner.
Quirin Emil J. F., (Tioga Center) tanner, h Main.
Quirin Emil F., (J. G. Quirin & Co.) (Tioga Center) h Main.
Quirin George L. A., (Tioga Center) tanner, Main.

Quirin J. G. & Co., (W. C. A., E. P. and C. H. N. Quirin) (Tioga Center) tanners, Main.
Quirin John G., (J. G. Quirin & Co.) (Tioga Center) also farmer 137, h Main.
Quirin William, (Tioga Center) tanner, h Main.
Quirin William C. A., (J. G. Quirin & Co.) (Tioga Center) h Main.
Ragan Daniel, (Owego) r 9, laborer.
Randall Walter C., (Smithboro) justice of the peace and farmer.
Ransom Warren W., (Tioga Center) r 49, farmer 130.
RAUCH GEORGE, (Strait's Corners) r 5, farmer, 117.
Rauch Henry E., (Strait's Corners) r 5, farmer.
Rauch John M., (Strait's Corners) r 5, farmer.
Rauch Peter A., (Strait's Corners) r 5, farmer.
Rauch Wesley, (Owego) r 16, farmer, works for Rev. S. Evans 115.
Reed Maria, (Catatonk) r 9, widow George, house-keeper.
Rice Chauncey, (Owego) r 18, farmer, leases of James Anderson 125.
Rice Rachel, (Owego) r 9, widow Merrick, resident.
Richards Benjamin, (Smithboro) r 68, farmer 168.
Richards Eugene, (Tioga Center) clerk, bds. Main.
Rider Amos L., (Strait's Corners) r 4, farmer 96.
Rider Dana B., (Halsey Valley) r 22, farmer 90.
Rider David, (Strait's Corners) r 24, farmer 100.
Rider Elethere, (Strait's Corners) r 19, resident.
Rider George T., (Halsey Valley), bartender Halsey Valley House.
Rider Isaac, (Halsey Valley) r 22, farmer 80.
Rider Jacob S., (Tioga Center) r 23, thresher and farmer 105.
Rider Seymour, (Halsey Valley) 22, farmer with his father Dana B.
Rider Stephen J., (Strait's Corners) r 19, farmer 98.
Rider William, (Halsey Valley) mason.
Ring Jesse B., (Owego) off r 12, resident.
Ring Theron S., (Owego) off r 12, farmer.
Roberts James A., (Smithboro) painter.
Robinson Duncan, (Owego) r 26, farm laborer.
Robinson Joel, (Owego) r 45, farmer, works for Henry Young 150.
Romine Hannah, (Owego) r 47, widow Samuel, resident.
Romine William, (Owego) r 47, tailor.
Root Oris L., (Halsey Valley) billiard and pool room and farmer in Barton 36.
Ross John W., (Smithboro) r 58, farmer 300.
Rousier Charles, (Owego) r 8, farmer 30.
Rumsey James, (Halsey Valley) r 1, farmer, works for Fred Taylor 150.
Russell Holmes W., (Owego) r 14, farmer 160.
Sanderson P. W. N., (Tioga Center) station and express agt. and telegraph op. Erie R. R., h Main.
Sargent Alvin, (Smithboro) carpenter.
Schoonover Ambrose L., (Barton) r 73, farmer 117.
Schoonover Eliza, (Tioga Center) r 53, widow Smith, farm 16.
Schoonover Eugene S., (Tioga Center) r 53, farmer with his father Nicholas.
Schoonover Jackson J. F., (Tioga Center) 35, farmer 63.
Schoonover James M., (Tioga Center) r 35, lumberman.
Schoonover Jerome J., (Tioga Center) r 53, farmer with his father Nicholas.
Schoonover Nicholas, (Tioga Center) r 53, farmer 200.
Schoonover Nicholas M., (Barton) r 73, resident.
Schoonover Simeon L., (Barton) r 73, farmer 170.
Scott Wilson, (Owego) r 48, gardener.

Searles Martha, (Owego) r 28, widow John, farmer 80.
Severn George W., (Smithboro) resident.
Sexsmith Thomas, (Tioga Center) section foreman.
Sharp Samuel, (Tioga Center) r 41, farm laborer.
Sharp William, (Smithboro) r 73, farmer 65.
SHAW W. HULSE, (Owego) r 28, prest. Tioga Co. Agr'l Society, breeder of Holstein cattle and fine horses, and farmer 133.
Sherman John, (Owego) r 14, farmer 5.
Sherwood William, (Tioga Center) laborer, h Main.
SHIFFER GEORGE B., (Owego) r 13, farmer.
Shipman George, (Halsey Valley) laborer.
Signor Charles, (Tioga Center) r 36, prop. saw mill and farmer with his son George H. 100.
Signor George H., (Tioga Center) r 36, wagon-maker and farmer 10, and with his father Charles 100.
Sly John M., (Smithboro) resident.
Smith & Truesdail, (Owego) (H. K. Smith & George Truesdail) r 44, props. of hay press and threshing machine.
Smith Cornelius D., (Tioga Center) r 51, farmer 100.
Smith David T., (Tioga Center) r 50, farmer 100.
Smith Frank, (Tioga Center) r 51, farmer 87.
Smith George, (Tioga Center) r 36, farmer 240.
Smith George A., (Owego) r 12, farm laborer.
Smith Harry J., (Tioga Center) r 36, farmer with his father George.
Smith Horace K., (Tioga Center) r 36, agrl. implements and farmer 50.
Smith James E., (Smithboro) r 40, steam thresher and farmer 150.
Smith John E., (Smithboro) r 40, farmer 125.
Smith John J., (Tioga Center) r 36, farmer with his father Horace K.
Smith John Y., (Smithboro) r 40, resident.
Smith Losey M., (Smithboro) r 68, farmer 100.
Smith Michael, (Smithboro) farmer 125.
Smith Spencer E., (Owego) r 34, farmer 35.
Snyder Adam, (Strait's Corners) r 17, farmer 113.
Snyder Charles, (Owego) r 6, carpenter.
Snyder Frank, (Strait's Corners) r 5, laborer.
Snyder George, (Strait's Corners) r 4, farm laborer.
Snyder Henry A., (Strait's Corners) r 5, prop. saw-mill, and farmer 57.
Snyder Nicholas, (Owego) r 6, farmer 100.
Snyder Nicholas N., (Strait's Corners) r 4, carpenter.
Snyder Peter, (Owego) r 14, laborer.
Snyder Samuel, (Owego) r 6, farmer with his father Nicholas.
Southwick Mary J. Mrs., (Halsey Valley) general merchant.
Speer Irwin L., (Strait's Corners) r 24, farm laborer.
Speer Tunis, (Strait's Corners) r 24, farmer 32.
Spencer Albert O., (Tioga Center) r 36, laborer.
Spencer Alvah, (Owego) off r 34, farmer 122.
Spencer Ambrose G., (Owego) r 31, farmer.
Spencer Charles (Owego) r 34, farmer 76.
Spencer Charles, (Owego) r 25, farmer 50.
Spencer Elijah C., (Tioga Center) mail messenger.
Spencer John, (Owego) off r 34, farmer.
Spendley Araminta, (Nichols) r 53 widow Anderson.
Spendley Robert H., (Nichols) r 53, farmer 100.

Spicer Harry, (Halsey Valley) r 22, laborer.
Springstead Alfred, (Halsey Valley), r 37, farmer for J. C. Latimer.
Springstead Daniel P., (Tioga Center) r 51, farm laborer.
Starks James, (Strait's Corners) r 4, farmer 260.
Starks William, (Strait's Corners) r 4, farmer for his father James.
STEELE FRED C., (Owego) farmer 65.
Steele James, (Owego) r 31, farmer 212.
STEELE JANE Miss, (Smithboro) resident.
Sterling John, (Smithboro) laborer.
Stetler Charles J., (Tioga Center) r 35, farmer 126.
Stetler Irving F., (Tioga Center) r 35, school teacher.
Stetler Stokes, (Tioga Center) r 35, farmer.
Stetler William, (Tioga Center) r 35, farmer with his father Stokes.
Steward John, (Smithboro) off r 66, farmer 100.
Stewart Delos, (Owego) off r 12, mason.
STEWART EDWARD, (Owego) off r 12, mason and farmer.
STEWART EMILY A., (Owego) off r 12, dressmaker.
STILES FRED H., (Stiles & Sibley) (Owego) r 47, farmer.
STILES GEORGE B., (Owego) r 46, farmer.
STILES RHODA, (Owego) r 46, widow Benjamin C., farmer 15.
Stimpson Charles, (Smithboro) cooper.
Stimson Henry (Smithboro) station agent Southern Central R. R.
Stone Edward F., (Tioga Center) drug clerk.
Stone William, (Owego) r 28, laborer.
STOWELL CORNELL S., (Smithboro) r 73, lumberman, and farmer 236.
Strait Alvinza, (Strait's Corners) r 4, postmaster and farmer.
Strait Aretus A., (Strait's Corners) r 4, hay-dealer and farmer 66.
Streibel Peter, (Tioga Center) tanner.
Stutler Andrew, (Tioga Center) r 36, laborer.
Sullivan Thomas, (Smithboro) section boss.
Swartwood Charles, (Halsey Valley) r 37, farmer.
Swartwood Edwin, (Owego) r 30, farmer 100.
Swartwood Eugene, (Owego) r 30, farmer.
Swartwood Frank, (Strait's Corners) r 3, farm laborer.
Taylor Addison J., (Owego) r 44, farmer 50.
Taylor Charles D., (Owego) r 29, farmer.
Taylor Cynthia, (Owego) r 32, widow John T., farmer 113.
Taylor Frank E., (Owego) r 32, farmer with his mother Cynthia.
Taylor John E., (Owego) r 26, farmer, leases of Abram Vermilyea 50.
Taylor John H., (Owego) r 47, painter.
Taylor John M., (Owego) r 28, farmer 22.
Taylor John T., (Owego) farmer, works for Abram Vermilyea 50.
Taylor Norman, (Owego) r 32, farmer 50.
Taylor Rodney, (Smithboro) r 58, farmer 50.
Tewilleger Jay, (Strait's Corners) r 4, farm laborer.
Thomas David B., (Owego) r 13, farmer 53.
Thomas Delos H., (Owego) r 13, farmer with his father David B.
Thomas Frank, (Owego) r 13, keeper at Binghamton asylum.
Thomas George, (Halsey Valley) r 2, farmer 27.
Thomas John D., (Smithboro) r 71, millwright, and farmer 4.
Thorn Warren, (Owego) r 31, farmer.
Tiffany Austin, (Owego) r 28, farmer $6\frac{1}{2}$.
Tilden Alanson Rev., (Tioga Center) pastor Baptist church.

TOWN OF TIOGA. 213

Tioga Center Hotel, (Tioga Center) Moses Ohart, prop., Main.
Toff William, (Tioga Center) r 35, laborer.
TOFT ISAAC, (Owego) r 18, farmer 153.
Towner Andrew J., (Smithboro) r 60, farmer 50.
Traynor Mary, (Owego) r 48, widow Edward.
TRIBE CHARLES H., (Tioga Center) carpenter and joiner, and prop. saw and plaining-mill, Railroad cor. Alden.
Tribe Frank B., (Tioga Center) r 52, farmer 50.
Tribe James P., (Halsey Valley) r 38, farmer 104.
Tribe John, (Halsey Valley) off r 2, farmer 56.
Tripp Seymour, (Smithboro) jeweler at Nichols.
Trowbridge E. Owen, (Smithboro) school teacher.
Truesdail David S., (Owego) r 44, farmer 57.
Truesdail Frank J., (Owego) r 44, farmer.
Truesdail George, (Owego) (Smith & Truesdail) r 44, thresher.
Truesdail Jeremiah, (Owego) r 44, farmer 60.
Truesdail John, (Tioga Center) r 43, laborer.
Truesdail William, (Owego) r 44, carpenter, and farmer 36.
Truesdell Alvin, (Owego) r 47, laborer.
Tuff Sarah, (Tioga Center) r 41, widow Thomas, resident.
Turner Cornelius, (Tioga Center) trackman.
Turner Peter, (Strait's Corners) r 3, justice of the peace, and farmer 200.
Tuthill Joseph M., (Smithboro) groceries, provisions and drugs, Main.
Tyler Luzerne, (Halsey Valley) invalid.
Ulrick George, (Owego) r 7, farmer for Adam King.
Ulrick John, (Owego) r 6, farmer 150.
Ulrick John, Jr., (Owego) r 15, farmer 7.
Valentine Louisa, (Strait's Corners) r 8, resident.
Van Dermark John, (Smithboro) r 40, farmer 50.
Van Dermark Mary, (Smithboro) r 40, widow Henry, resident.
Van Dermark Selinda, (Smithboro) r 73, widow George, farmer 50.
Van Duser Frank, (Catatonk) r 9, farm laborer.
VAN DUSER GILBERT, (Catatonk) r 9, laborer.
Van Duser Henry, (Catatonk) r 9, laborer.
Van Etten Alonzo, (Smithboro) r 58, farm laborer.
Van Etten Lorenzo, (Halsey Valley), r 37, farmer 50.
Van Leven Elias, (Strait's Corners) r 4, butcher and farmer 32, and in Candor 52.
Van Luven John B., (Halsey Valley) stock-buyer and farmer.
Van Norstran Arthur G., (Smithboro) r 55, farmer for his father James.
Van Norstran Charles C., (Tioga Center) r 53, farmer 125.
Van Norstran George, (Tioga Center) (Coburn & Van Norstran) r 51, also farmer 16.
Van Norstran James, (Tioga Center) r 58, farmer 30.
Van Norstran James, (Smithboro) r 55, farmer 30.
Van Riper George W., (Halsey Valley) r 38, farmer 90.
Van Tyl Anthony W., (Tioga Center) r 36, farmer, works for Henry Wiggins 40.
Vincent Colvin, (Barton) r 65, farmer 50.
Vosburgh Henry P., (Halsey Valley) physician and surgeon, and farmer 285.
Vroman Moses, (Owego) r 30, farm laborer.
Walden Joseph, (Halsey Valley) r 21, laborer.
Wallace David B., (Owego) r 48, farmer for his mother Rachel.

Wallace Rachel, (Owego) r 48, widow David, farm 140.
Wallace William, (Tioga Center) r 40, farmer 100.
Wallis Harry C., (Owego) r 48, farmer.
Walworth Seymour E., (Owego) M. E. clergyman and farmer 17.
Ward Lewis J., (Smithboro) r 70, farmer, works for Judson Winters 260.
Ward Perry C., (Tioga Center) r 41, carpenter and farmer 40.
Waterman Oren, (Owego) r 48, farmer, works on shares for Lottie A. Horton 100.
WATERMAN WILLIAM P., (Tioga Center) r 54, farmer, works for C. H. Van Norstran 50.
Watkins Charles H., (Catatonk) r 9, engineer N. T. Co.
Watkins Elizabeth Mrs., (Tioga Center) r 53, resident.
Watkins John, (Smithboro) stone mason.
Watkins Thomas, (Smithboro) r 54, farmer 50.
Watkins William H., (Tioga Center) meat market in Binghamton.
Weber George, (Owego) r 7, farmer 63.
Weber Philip, (Owego) r 7, farmer.
Weber Philip, Jr., (Owego) r 7, carpenter and farmer 55.
Weiss Sebastian, (Owego) r 16, farmer 100.
West Andrew L., (Halsey Valley) r 1, farmer 140.
West Charles, (Halsey Valley) r 22, farmer.
West Grant M., (Halsey Valley) r 21, postmaster and assistant to his father Luther B.
WEST LUTHER B., (Halsey Valley) r 21, retired merchant, lumberman, dairyman and farmer 530, and in Newark Valley 181.
Wheeler John N., (Strait's Corners) r 4, general merchant.
Whitcomb Benjamin R., (Smithboro) r 68, farmer 55.
Whitcomb John M., (Smithboro) r 59, farmer 50.
White Dudley, (Owego) farmer 35.
White Jerome, (Smithboro) r 54, farmer, works on shares for Henry Miller 50.
White Leon, (Halsey Valley) physician and surgeon.
White Lewis, (Smithboro) r 73, farmer 95.
White Lorenzo, (Catatonk) r 9, laboror.
Whipple Fernando, (Tioga Center) r 50, farmer 50.
Whitley Emily, (Owego) r 13, widow Joel S., farm 141.
Whitmarsh Abram, (Owego) r 28, farmer 74.
WHITMARSH AVERY, (Owego) r 9, sawyer and farmer 5.
Whitmarsh Harvey, (Owego) r 28, sawyer.
Whitmarsh Herrick, (Tioga Center) r 52, farmer.
Whitmarsh Sidney D., (Tioga Center) r 52, farm laborer.
Whitney Isaac N., (Owego) r 33, farm laborer.
Wiggins Eliza, (Tioga Center) widow George.
Wiggins Henry, (Tioga Center) r 36, farmer 40.
Wiggins Silas, (Tioga Center) r 36, blacksmith, h do.
Wilbur Frederick, (Halsey Valley) laborer.
Williams Charles, (Tioga Center) off r 57, farm laborer.
Willis Sylvester, (Halsey Valley) r 22, farmer 75.
Willmott George W., (Owego) r 14, farmer 133.
WILLMOTT JAMES R., (Owego) r 28, prop. saw and plaster-mill, and ice-dealer.
Wilson William, (Owego) r 34, resident.
Winfield James, (Owego) r 28, retired farmer.
Winner James F., (Owego) r 47, cartman.

Winter Byron L., (Tioga Center) law student, bds. Main.
Winters Harry B., (Tioga Center) clerk, bds. Main.
Winters Joseph, (Tioga Center) postmaster and grocery, and farmer 159, h Main.
Winters Thomas, (Tioga Center) laborer.
Wolcott George B., (Smithboro) r 58, farmer 60.
Wood Edward, (Tioga Center) r 53, laborer.
Wood Elmer, (Tioga Center) r 53, farm laborer.
Wood George, (Strait's Corners) r 3, farmer 50.
Wood James, (Strait's Corners) farmer 50.
Wood Joseph, (Strait's Corners) r 3, farmer 100.
Wood Spencer (Halsey Valley) r 39, farmer 90.
Woodburn Clarence, (Tioga Center) r 36, laborer.
Woodburn David P., (Tioga Center) farmer.
Woodburn Henry Q., (Tioga Center) laborer.
Woodcox Richard, (Tioga Center) trackman, h Main.
Wright William, (Tioga Center) stone mason and carpenter.
Yaples Charles, (Owego) r 31, carpenter.
Yearsley Frank, (Smithboro) r 54, farmer with his father John.
Yearsley John, (Smithboro) r 54, farmer, works for Henry Miller 250.
Yontz Chloe, (Smithboro) r 71, widow John, resident.
Young Franklin H., (Owego) r 48, farmer with his father Henry.
Young Henry, (Owego), r 48, speculator, dairy 14 cows and farmer 200.
Zorn Charles, (Owego) r 14, farmer 27.
Zorn Christopher, (Owego) r 17, farmer 15.
Zorn George, (Owego) r 17, farmer 39.
Zorn Jacob, (Owego) r 14, farmer 27.

THE OWEGO GAZETTE.

ESTABLISHED NOVEMBER 23, 1800.

The * Only * Democratic * Paper

PUBLISHED IN TIOGA COUNTY.

A GOOD ADVERTISING MEDIUM.

Sample·Copies·Sent·on·Application.

THE FINEST JOB PRINTING

Neatly and Promptly Done, and at Low Prices.

STARKEY & WINTERS, Wholesale and Retail Druggists, Owego.

TIOGA COUNTY
CLASSIFIED BUSINESS DIRECTORY

EXPLANATION.

The towns are alphabetically arranged at the end of the line, under the business classifications. The postoffice address of each individual or firm follows after the name, except in cases where the name of the postoffice and the township is the same. In the villages the name of the street is generally given, and precedes that of the postoffice. The classification of farmers is omitted in this list, as they can readily be found in the general list, by noting the figures at the end of the line, which indicate the number of acres owned or leased by each. Road numbers signify the same as in the general list.

Agents Railroad.
See Railroad Agents.

Agents Ticket.
See Railroad Agents.

Agricultural Implements.
(See also Hardware, also General Merchants.)
COLEMAN CHARLES H., (dealer) Lockwood, Barton
Guyer H. E., Broad cor. Clark st., Waverly, "
Sneffin & Scott. Broad st., Waverly, "
BRAINARD CHARLES E., Berkshire
Higgins John, r 18, Speedsville, Tomp. Co., "
Judd John N., r 6, "
WITTER F. A. & CO., "
Courtright Henry A., (dealer) West Newark, Candor
HART LEWIS A., (dealer) Main st., "
HEATH HENRY D., (dealer) Main st., "
Van Debogart Peter, Main st., "
Woodford E. Jerome, (dealer) r 62, "
GAGER ULYSSES S., r 45, (Champion drills) Newark Valley
Kenyon Charles E., r 53, "
ADAMS S. B., r 5, (harvesters) Hoopers' Valley, Nichols
EDSALL JOHN R., (dealer) Main st., "
GERE, TRUMAN, PLATT & CO., (manuf.) Central ave., Owego
Like George W., r 106, Apalachin, "

Pitcher Leroy H., r 65, Owego
THOMAS MOSES H., (dealer) 64 Temple st., "
Wood Charles E., r 40, Flemingville, "
MILLER WILLIAM F., Main st., Richford
THELEMAN HIRAM W., "
Brooks Daniel C., Maple ave., Spencer
DAVIS JEROME S., Cedar st., "
DAY JOHN & SON, Main st., "
HORTON THEODORE, r 49, Owego st., Tioga
Smith Horace K., r 36, Tioga Center, "

Apiarists.
Andre John, Lockwood, Barton
BESEMER DANIEL V., North Barton, "
Church Franklin L., r 46, Lockwood, "
CRANS FRANK, Lockwood, "
Edgcomb George G., Factoryville, "
Hanford Clark, Factoryville, "
Holt Charles B., r 53, "
Lent W. Nelson, Lincoln st., Waverly, "
MANNING ELI D., Halsey Valley, "
SHIPMAN RUFUS T., r 43, Waverly, "
Walker Loren A., Waverly, "
Clark Sanford H., r 36, Berkshire
Houk Daniel, Wilson Creek, r 35, "
Scott Charles & Edward F., r 22 cor. 41, "
Shepard James, r 3, "
WILLIAMS & WALDO, "
Williams George, "
Anderson Joel, r 125, Owego, Candor
Houck Israel, r 95, "

STARKEY & WINTERS, promptly fill Mail and Telephone Orders.

ESTABLISHED IN 1835.

THE FARMERS' FAVORITE!

THE OWEGO TIMES

The largest and best weekly paper published in Tioga county, and contains more reading matter. The TIMES is the paper for the Farmer, Mechanic, Merchant, Laboring Man, in fact, for all classes to take. Correspondence from every Town in the County. The TIMES has the largest circulation by many hundreds of any paper published in Tioga county, consequently it is the BEST ADVERTISING MEDIUM.

SEND FOR A SAMPLE COPY.

―――――FOR―――――

FINE JOB WORK

Of all kinds, from the smallest Visiting Card to the Mammoth Poster, go to the Times Office. Our Jobbing Facilities are unequaled in the Southern Tier.

BOOK-BINDING.

Book-binding, in all its branches, neatly, cheaply and promptly done. Paper Ruling in every conceivable style and form. Especial attention given to, and best facilities for, manufacturing Blank Books, Ledgers, Hotel Registers, &c. Pamphlets, Magazines and Old Books skillfully and neatly rebound. Persons wishing anything pertaining to this business will do well to call at the Owego Times Bindery.

WM. SMYTH & SON, Propietors.

193 Main St., opposite Lake St., - Owego, Tioga Co., N. Y

APIARISTS—BLACKSMITHS AND HORSESHOERS.

HOFTALING JOHN, R. R. ave. Candor
MASTEN GEORGE W., "
MOREY ARCHIE E., r 71, "
Osburn William, r 18, Speedsville, "
ROE EUGENE F., r 5, "
Roe William F., r 25, "
Taylor William J., r 86, Weltonville, "
Burchard Harvey J., r 9, Ketchumville, Newark Valley
Councilman Edwin W., r 35, "
STEVENS HENRY W., r 42, "
DEAN NATHAN S., r 1, Nichols
HERRICK WILLIAM, r 1, "
Lane David J., r 17, "
Matthews Hiram P., r 38, "
Sherwood Wesley W., r 10, "
WATERMAN ALONZO C., r 8, "
WHITE WILLIAM W., r 21, "
BROWN L. & G., off North ave., (near S. C. R. R. Round house, Owego
Fox Charles, off r 91, "
Gage Miner, r 37, "
Gage Walter, r 37, "
GILES JOHN S., r 87, Apalachin, "
Nichols Washington, r 102½, Apalachin, "
Noteware Wallace R., r 110, South Apalachin, "
TALCOTT CHARLES, r 40, "
Talcott George B., r 40, "
Ferris George C., r 35, West Candor, Spencer
Forsyth Nelson A., r 40, "
Holdridge William A., r 41, "
SHAW GEORGE E., r 30, "
SNOOK DAVID L., Main st., "
Van Marter, r 41, "
GOODRICH STEPHEN S., r 46, Owego, Tioga

Apothecaries.
See Drugs and Medicines.

Architects and Builders.
(See also Carpenters and Builders, and Masons and Builders.)

Utter John, 120 Howard st., Waverly, Barton

Artists, Portrait, Landscape, etc:
(See also Photographers.)

Comstock A. B. Mrs., 126 Waverly st., Waverly, Barton
Stanley Belle, (teacher) 101 Penn. ave., Waverly, "
HAIGHT EDITH J., (teacher) Glen st., Berkshire
SUTTON GEORGE B., r 41, Newark Valley
MITCHELL IDA A., Cady ave., Nichols
MITCHELL MARY J., Cady ave., "
CAMP MARY L., MRS., 259 Erie st., Owego
*HARGRAVE, W. G., 38 and 40 Lake st., "
Kimball Helen Mrs., 425 Main st., "
MOREHOUSE ALLIE, Spencer ave., "
SMITH HATTIE A., 443 Main st., "

Bakers and Confectioners.
(See also Confectionery, Fruits, etc.)

Clark Charles H., 121 Broad st., Waverly, Barton
HANFORD & LORD, 222, Broad st., Waverly, "
PILGRIM FREDERIC, 241 Broad st., Waverly, "
JACKSON DWIGHT P., Main st., Candor
Stannard Hiram R., Newark Valley
Bonham Emma, 3 Park st., Owego
Burton Nathaniel T., 61 North ave., "

NYE BROTHERS, 44 Lake st., Owego
PARLETT ROBERT JR., Academy st., Spencer

Bands.
(In Societies, See Contents.)

Banks.
FIRST NATIONAL, Broad cor. Fulton st., Waverly, Barton
THE CITIZENS' BANK, 214 Broad st., Waverly, "
FIRST NAT. BANK, Main st., Candor
FIRST NATIONAL BANK, 179 Front st., Owego
OWEGO NATIONAL BANK, 6 Lake st., "
TIOGA NATIONAL BANK OF OWEGO, 199 Front st., "
FARMERS' & MERCHANTS', Main st., Spencer

Barbers and Hair-Dressers.
Gibson Robert W., 213 Broad st., Waverly, Barton
Hancock Irving, 225 Broad st., Waverly, "
Henry Edward, 209 Broad st. Waverly, "
Lockerby Wallace H., 12 Fulton st., Waverly, "
Woodburn James L., Fulton st., Waverly, "
ROCKEFELLER CHARLES H., Main st., Berkshire
Stewart Charles, Main st., Candor
SANDWICK JOHN R., Newark Valley
Mallory William W., Main st., Nichols
Williams George F., Main st., "
Butler James, 65 North ave., Owego
Flamer Isaiah, 154 Front st., "
Foster & Hampton, 129 North ave., "
Hollensworth Jeremiah M., 22 Lake st., "
Horrigan William, 152 North ave., "
Hubbard Thomas, Lake st., "
King Charles H., Ah-wa-ga House, "
Lee Albert S., 109 North ave., "
Spaulding Enoch R , 47 Lake st., "
Carter Frank E., Main st., Spencer
Gilbert Norman A., "

Basket Makers.
Stevens James M., Willseyville, r 1, Candor
Thornton James J., r 93, "
Neff Asel, Newark Valley
Crandall William, r 10, Nichols
Thornton Jeremiah, 32 W. Main st., Owego
Thornton Thomas, r 27, "
Burtless James, r 2, North Spencer, Spencer
Stevens William H., r 1, "

Bee Keepers.
See Apiarists.

Blacksmiths and Horseshoers.
Boyce Lyman, Halsey Valley, Barton
COLEMAN CHAS. H., Lockwood, "
Crans Ard F., Factoryville, "
Edgarton Willis, Lockwood, "
Gillan Ben. R., Main st., Factoryville, "
Kinsman & Young, 3 Penn. ave., Waverly, "
Leonard Charles, r 55, "
Mapes Milton C., Factoryville, "
McArdle Bernard, 302 Broad st., Waverly, "
Murray William, W. Factoryville, "
Poole Frank, Halsey Valley, "
Quinly Elmer, Broad st., Waverly, "
Simpson Elliot, Elizabeth st., Waverly, "
Simpson Isaac, Broad st., Waverly, "
SIMPSON WILLIAM H., 301 Broad st., Waverly, "

220   BLACKSMITHS AND HORSESHOERS—BOTTLING WORKS.

BUFFINGTON CALVIN A. Railroad st., Berkshire
Whiting Frank S., Speedsville, Tomp. Co.,
Baylor Charles T., Main st., Candor
Bolton Clarence S., Main st., "
CARPENTER WILLIAM L., Railroad ave., "
Casterline Romeo W., Strait's Corners, "
DRAPER MENZ V., Catatonk, "
Eiklor George I., r 8, "
Holden Dallas, r 120, Weltonville, "
Houck George E., r 95, "
Hover Leander, r 88, "
Kirk Richard, r 63, "
Kyle Enos J., r 22, Speedsville, Tomp. Co., "
Mix Emory C., Willseyville, r 30, "
QUIMLY ELMINA E., Owego st., "
Slawson James G., Foundry st., "
Smullen George B., Weltonville, r 120, "
Smullen Patrick, r 120, Weltonville, "
Terwilliger Solomon E., r 133, Catatonk, "
Woodard Elias H., r 82, Weltonville, "
Belden Uriah L., Newark Valley
Belden William H., r 22, West Newark, "
Buffington Chancey L., r 11, Ketchumville, "
Mix Eugene P., "
Nowlan & Abbott, "
Sharp Robert B., r 11, Ketchumville, "
Smullen Charles M., r 1, Jenksville, "
Sweet Charles E., r 13, Ketchumville, "
Riley William, r 13, Ketchumville, "
DeGroat William, r 16, Owego, Nichols
Miller Edmund S., Main st., "
Smith Oliver P., Hooper's Valley, "
WATERMAN & METTLER, Main st., "
WATERMAN JOHN G., r 8, "
Dye Ansel M., r 17 cor. 11, Richford
Marshall Charles, r 31, "
Moreland George D., "
Owens Levi, r 31 cor. 18, "
Connant Simeon, r 117, Owego
Cornell Henry, r 56, "
Edward Edward, r 54, Campville, "
Gould Adam C., 16 Temple st., "
Howell & Tracy, Apalachin, "
Johnson Stillman, r 40, "
McCaslin Alexander, Apalachin, "
Meachan Erastus, 221 North ave., "
Reed James, L., r 4, Flemingville, "
Rhinevault Myron, 81 North ave., "
Riley & Gillett, 140 Front st., "
Riley James, 81 North ave., "
Severson George, r 51, Campville, "
SMITH LEWIS, 168 North ave., "
Terbush Lancelott B., r 16, Flemingville, "
Wood George H., North ave., "
Clark Lewis, r 34, Spencer
Clark Sylvenus B., r 38, "
COMPTON SILAS, r 37, West Candor, "
Day William S , r 28, "
Griffith Absalom, r 14, "
Hull Eben, "
Kirk Charles N., r 59, Halsey Valley, "
Lang Charles F., "
Lange William H., "
Mabee Daniel, "
Perrin William, r 13, "
Pritchard Pratt A., "
Ryant Daniel J., r 20, North Spencer "
Sabin Seth O., r 42½, "
SEELY S. ALFRED, (prop.) "
Turk David, Academy st., "
Turk Stephen D., Spencer
Wells Josiah, Main st., "
Bates William, Halsey Valley, r 21, Tioga
Estep Loren, r 51 Tioga Center, "
Farnham Orin, Smithboro, "
KIRK CHARLES N., Halsey Valley, "
Mapes Lewis, r 28, Owego, "
Wiggins Silas, r 36 Tioga Center, "

Boarding Houses.

Boyce Genevieve, Factoryville, Barton
Hinman Eliza A., 114 Chemung st., Waverly, "
Seely Edmund, 12 Park ave., Waverly, "
Hamilton Elliott, r 6, Berkshire
COOLEY BENJAMIN F., Newark Valley
Winship Charles B., "
Dunham Hannah, 118 Temple st., Owego
Dutton Mortimer E., r 69, Apalachin, "
Freehill Maria, 64 South Depot st., "
Lawheed Joseph W., 118 Temple st., "
Seely Lewis, 133 North ave., "
Sykes Maria B. 313 Main st., "

Book Binderies.

OWEGO TIMES, W. Smyth & Son, props., 193 Main, "

Books and Stationery.

Tracy John L., 204 Broad st., Waverly, Barton
COBURN & STRAIT, 17 Lake st., Owego
Decker Phoebe Mrs., 186 Main st., "
Pinney Hammon D., 45 Lake st., "
EMMONS LUCIUS E., Main st., Spencer

Boots and Shoes, Dealers and Shoemakers.

(See also General Merchants.)
Baldwin Albert B., 6 Fulton st., Waverly, Barton
BUNN ALBERT R., 73 Broad st., Waverly, "
Demorest Clarence L., 247 Broad st., Waverly, "
Hildebrand Andrew, 225 Broad st., Waverly, "
Racklyeft John, 267 Broad st., Waverly, "
Spencer Charles F., 226 Broad st., Waverly, "
Conant Luther, Main st., Nichols
Goodenough Delos, Main st., "
DANA CHARLES, (custom) 65 North ave., Owego
Greenwood James (custom) 188 Front st., "
HARDER EMMOTT, 23 Lake st., "
Chamberlain L. N. & Son, Lake st., "
Lounsbury William H., 63 North ave., "
Lyon & Ripley, 188 Front st., "
MORTON LEVI, Apalachin, "
SWEET BROTHERS, 54 North ave., "
WALL & CO., 200 Front st., "
Wilbur William E., 182 Main st., "
DAY JOHN & SON, Main st., Spencer
KNAPP FREDERICK J., Main st., Smithboro, Tioga

Bottling Works.

MILLS & O'BRIEN, Elizabeth st., Waverly, Barton
Sheahan Michael, Broad cor. Loder st., Waverly, "
Cronk W. D., r 90, Candor
Hulslander John H., r 24, Newark Valley

STARKEY & WINTERS, Wholesale and Retail Druggists, Owego.

BOTTLING WORKS—CARPENTERS AND BUILDERS. 221

COBWEB BOTTLING WORKS, P. Maloney, prop., Fox st., Owego

Cabinet Makers.

(See also Furniture Dealers and Manufacturers.)

Barr John C., Elizabeth st, Waverly, Barton
Hart Selem M., (Speedsville, Tomp. Co.) r 18, Berkshire
FESSENDEN W. L. & SON, Candor
Johnson Leonard A., Church st., "
Ross Leonard B., Main st., Nichols
Corchran John T., 51, George st., Owego
Hibbard Ralph W., 112 Franklin st., "
Newell Friend G., 17 Lake st., "
Wood Charles H., r 60, "
Newman William H., r 48, Spencer

Carpenters and Builders.

(See also Architects and Builders, Masons and Builders, Contractors and Builders.)

BALDWIN HUGH, Broad n Penn. ave., Waverly, Barton
Barr John C., Jr., Waverly, "
BURKE OSCAR F., Waverly, "
Casterline Coe, Factoryville, "
Courtwright M. V. B., "
Davenport Miles, r 39, "
Drake George C., Waverly, "
Filkins Cornelius, Factoryville, "
Hamilton Simeon, off r 60, Waverly, "
HARDING CHARLES E., Ithaca st., Factoryville, "
Harris George V., Factoryville, "
Giltner Dexter E., Waverly, "
Parker Charles P., Factoryville, "
Rhodes Isaac, Factoryville, "
Ross Frank, 10 Pine st., Waverly, "
Rowland William A., Waverly, "
Skillings Giles, r 9, Halsy Valley, "
SOLOMON JOHN V., Waverly, "
Swarthout Charles B., Factoryville, "
Westfall Harry, Factoryville, "
Yaple Amos S., r 39, "
Brown Abraham, Main st., Berkshire
Brown Myron, r 38, "
Church Orris, r 29, "
Crawford James H., "
Hart Arthur L., r 18, Speedsville, Tomp. Co., "
Hart Samuel L., r 18, Speedsville, Tomp. Co., "
Hart Selem, r 18, Speedsville, Tomp. Co., "
Hayden Patsey W., Glen st., "
Hubbard Howard M., r 20, "
Legg Reuben T., r 18, Speedsville, Tomp. Co., "
McCoy Oliver A., r18, Speedsville, Tomp. Co., "
Northrup Frank L., r 18, Speedsville, Tomp. Co., "
Payne Henry A., "
Sherman James W., r 27, "
Young Edward W., "
Abbey William, r 112, Candor
Allen James M., r 29, "
Allen William D., r 29, "
Ayers Willis, Wilseyville, "
Barden Robert S., r 24, "
BARROTT VAN NESS W., r 84, Weltonville, "
Burleigh Eben, r 39, "
Carl Peter, Owego st., "
CORTRIGHT JOSEPH J., Weltonville, "

Eiklor George I., r 8, Candor
Elmendorf Clarence, "
Farley Eli J., r 14, Speedsville, Tomp. Co., "
Frank Fred, r 134, Catatonk, "
Flack Thomas W., r 133, Catatonk, "
Galpin Edward, r 85, Weltonville, "
German Frederick E., "
Gransbury Edward, r 102, "
Gridley Demorn, r 63, "
Harding Sherman, "
Hatch Parker, r 85, Weltonville, "
Herdic Peter, r 139, Strait's Corners, "
Howes Oscar, "
Katell Marshall R., r 90, "
Keeler Ethelbert B., r 94, "
Leet Julius C., r 22, Speedsville, "
Leet Samuel, Speedsville, "
Lewis Theodore H., Owego st., "
Lynch Ira. Royal st., "
Manning Robert P., r 31, South Danby, "
Mead Russel J., Weltonville, "
Merchant Gideon, r 32, Willseyville, "
Orcott David, r 95, "
OWEN ABEL, C., r 109, "
Robinson Murtillow A., "
Sarson Samuel T., r 3, "
Sewell John, r 78, Weltonville, "
Smith John J., "
Smith Davelle, r 37, "
Smith Lucius, r 95, "
Smith William R., r 37, "
Starkweather Joel, Pond st., "
Tacey Alexander, "
Tubbs Charles N., r 41, "
Tubbs Ebenezer, r 41, "
Turk Levi, "
TURNER GEORGE C., r 143, Strait's Corners, "
Van Debogart Lawrence, r 30, Willseyville, "
Woodford Elbert C., r 62, West Candor, "
Abbey Reuben, r 16, Newark Valley
Barber Virgil C., "
BERKLEY CHARLES E., r 53, "
Bishop La Mont, "
Davison D. Henry, r 22, West Newark, "
Fellows William A., "
Gaskill Levi C., r 41, "
HAMMOND ADELBERT C., r 16, "
Hammond Melville F., r 6, "
Hover Marvin L., r 22, West Newark, "
Jackson O. Lester, "
Keith Lucius A., r 1, Jenksville, "
Legg Melville M., "
Luck Ozias F., r 35, "
Miller Daniel H., r 5, "
Nolton William, "
Pease Henry F., r 12, Ketchumville, "
Riley Andrew B., "
Saddlemire Alexander, r 31, "
Sherman Hiram L., "
Walter Clarence S., r 41, "
Williams Theodore, "
Bixby Charles R., Nichols
Bixby Chester, "
Curkendoll William, r 10, "
Dunham Benjamin, r 36, Owego, "
Edsall Benjamin F., "
Ellis George, Jr., Hooper's Valley, "
Ellsworth Henry N., "
Laning Charles P., "
Loveland Seth H., Waverly, "
Mallery John L., r 23, Owego, "
Merrill Albert S., "

STARKEY & WINTERS, Druggists, Owego. Close Prices to Dealers.

THE·OWEGO·RECORD

DAILY AND WEEKLY.

172 FRONT STREET, - OWEGO, N. Y.

THE ❋ DAILY ❋ RECORD.

The *Only Daily Paper in the County*, published every evening and sent to any address for $4.50 per year; 40 cents per month; or 10 cents per week. Full telegraph, county and local news. Acknowledged as the best advertising medium in Owego.

THE
Tioga County Record

Published every Friday. Contains more general, local and county news than any other paper in the county. Full market reports, court proceedings, and reports of all real estate transfers in the county published every week. Correspondents from every important place in the county.

TERMS—$1.50 PER YEAR.

THE BEST ADVERTISING MEDIUM IN THE COUNTY.

❧———JOB WORK———❧

Of all kinds done in the best of style. In its Job Rooms the Record has the leading trade in town.

SCOTT & WATROS,   -   Publishers.

CARPENTERS AND BUILDERS. 223

Mosher Edwin, Nichols
Newland Samuel, r 18, Owego, "
Turner G. M. Dallas, "
Waterman James H., r 8, "
Wiggins George, r 8, "
Abel Alonzo, 84 McMaster st., Owego
Becker Fayette A., Fifth ave., "
Beers Edwin W., South Side, "
Case Ellis L., 216 East Temple st., "
Cheeks Moulton, 508 Main st., "
Cole Smith B., 40 Adaline st., "
Conant Frank L., 122 Franklin st. "
Crans Egbert, 67 Central ave., "
Decker John S., Apalachin, "
Dexter Edwin J., r 54, Campville, "
Diamond Irving, 126 McMaster st., "
Duncan Stephen, 85 Paige st., "
Durfee Edgar S., 137 North ave., "
Durkee Charles R., 32 Main st., "
Edson George, over 107 North ave., "
Evans Josiah R., 4 William st., "
Evans Truman, r 54 Campville, "
FERGUSON T. JEFFERSON, 151 Talcott st.
Finch Smith, 170 West ave., "
Ford Charles H., r 35 Gaskills Corners, "
Ford Lucius, 607 Main st., "
Forgason Charles, 19 Lake st., "
Frank Walker, r 27, "
Genung Abram C., 118 Franklin st., "
GILLSON WILLIAM H., 116 West ave., "
Hall Granville W., Cortright House, "
Haner Addison L., r 96. "
Hemstrought Abram V., 198 E. Temple st., "
Holes George, 7 Park st., "
Hooker Archie S., 113 Franklin st., "
Hooker Warren, George st., "
Howard Orville, 7 Spruce st., "
Hutchinson James, 232 E. Temple st., "
Jones Edward, r 84, Apalachin, "
JONES JAMES E., 191 McMaster st., "
Jones Pardon, Apalachin, "
Kaley Adam I., r 4, "
Kaley William H., 177 Main st., "
Kellogg Ulysses P., 22 Fulton st., "
Knight Milton W., 56 Forsyth st., "
Lainhart Thomas, r 30 Union, Broome Co., "
Leasure George, r 123 South Owego, "
Leonard Allen, Water st., "
Lindsley Hiram, r 40, "
LOCKE REUBEN B., 241 Erie st., "
Male William, 22 William st., "
Manning William H., 113 Main st., "
McLean Ezra, 172 Talcott st., "
MEACHAM CHARLES D., 99 Talcott st., "
Middaugh Augustus B., 32 Adaline st., "
Newell Frank, 117 Central ave., "
Noble Asa S., 12 Adaline st., "
Noonan David E., 96 Franklin st., "
Orford Charles F., Apalachin, "
Park George W., 74 Fox st., "
Perkins Frederick, 21 Fulton st., "
Perry William H., South Side, "
Potter Isaac L., 100 Chestnut st., "
Randall Frank, 607 Main st., "
Relyea Andrew, 26 Fulton st., "
Reynolds Peter, 27 North ave., "
Richardson Wesley L., 557 Front st., "
Rightmier Charles H., 17 George st., "
Robinson Alvin T., Adaline st., "
Robinson George, 115 Temple st., "
Russell Minor, r 108 South Apalachin, "
Savey Edmund G., Apalachin, "
Savey William, Apalachin, "
Saxton Edward, 96 Liberty st., Owego
Searles Lot, 97 Central ave., "
Shepard W. Henry, Main st. "
Sisson William D., 18 Fulton st., "
Somers Daniel T., 130 Talcott st., "
Storm John C., 42 George st., "
Strong Lewis, 258 North ave., "
SYKES THEODORE P., 52 Liberty st., "
Upham Marcus K., 5 Temple st., "
VanBrunt Henry, 20 Temple st., "
VanOver Jacob, River st., "
Vermilyea Abram, 39 West ave., "
Wade Charles M., 119 West ave., "
Walker Amos, Adaline st., "
Walker Rial H., Buckbee Block, "
Walter Franklin A., r 25, Gaskill's Corners, "
Way William E., 174 North ave., "
Welch Charles, Adaline st., "
White John, 26 William st., "
Whittemore John, r 27, "
Williams Chester D., 59 West ave., "
Williams Edward W., 119 Main st., "
Yerks William A., 246 E. Temple st., "
Zimmer Albert, 66 Adaline st., "
Abbey Edward B., r 25, Richford
Allen Elmer, r 42, "
Barden Edward, r 18, "
Genung Orrin L., r 45½, "
HEATH NATHANIEL, r 40, "
HOWLAND HARRISON r 36, Center Lisle, Broome Co., "
Hutchinson Wesley J., Railroad st., "
King William W., r 10, Harford Mills, "
MEACHAM ORRIN N., r 37, "
Morton William, r 10, "
Robinson Isaac N., r 21, "
Vunk J. Frank, Main st., "
Welch Rufus H., Caroline, Tomp. Co., off r 23, "
Butts Charles E., Jr., Spencer
Clark Howard, "
Cowles Sylvester, r 2, North Spencer, "
De Remer Enos, r 36, West Candor, "
Ferris David A., r 63, "
Griffin James A., "
Hugg Horace A., "
Hutchings Eli M., "
Kirk Charles, r 59, Halsey Valley, "
Lott Benjamin, "
McKee George R., "
Osborn John C., r 43. "
Pierson George, "
Reeve Aaron D., "
Riker C. L., r 34, "
Riker William H., r 38, "
Robinson Fletcher O., "
Roe William W., r 38, "
Shaw John W., r 39, West Candor, "
Simms John C., r 43, Van Etten st., "
Stevens Seneca, r 65, "
Thornton George, r 37, West Candor, "
Van Kleek Jesse B., r 63, "
Van Natta Fred, r 47. "
VOSE EPHRAIM, r 38, "
Westbrook Arthur, "
Weeks William W., r 38, "
Barden A. E., Smithboro, Tioga
Bogart David R., Halsey Valley, "
Coleman James, r 52, Tioga Center, "
Coleman William D., r 52, Tioga Center, "
Fenderson Ely, r 41, Tioga Center, "
Fox Henry, r 47, Owego, "
Hamilton Charles, r 22, Tioga Center, "
Horton George M., r 70, Smithboro, "

CARPENTERS, BUILDERS—CLOTHIERS, MERCHANT TAILORS.

Johnson J. Edward, Smithboro, Tioga
Johnson Peter M., r 53, Tioga Center, "
Johnson Warren, r 55, Smithboro, "
Middaugh Lorenzo T., r 73, Smithboro, "
Mulock Edwin, r 71, Smithboro, "
Pearsall John C., r 71, Smithboro, "
Pelham Charles, r 44, Owego, "
PERRY ALBERT A., Smithboro, "
Sargent Alvin, Smithboro, "
Snyder Charles, r 6, Owego, "
Snyder Nicholas N., r 4, Strait's Corners, "
TRIBE CHARLES H., Tioga Center, "
Truesdail William, r 44, Owego, "
Ward Perry C., r 41, Tioga Center, "
Weber Philip, jr., r 7, Owego, "
Wright William, Tioga Center, "
Yaples Charles, r 31, Owego, "

Carpet Weavers.

Price N. W. Mrs., 5 Pine st., Waverly, Barton
HART SARAH E., Speedsville, Tomp. Co., r 18, Berkshire
Emerson Charity, r 128, Strait's Corners, Candor
Hover Lucinda A., r 38, Newark Valley
LAWRENCE SARAH A., r 61, "
Wright Nancy W., r 8, Nichols
Lewis Maria Mrs., r 56, Owego
Locke Mary E., 91 Fox st., "
Yerks Clarissa, 31 Adaline st., "

Carriage, Wagon and Sleigh Manufacturers, and Wheelwrights.

COLEMAN CHARLES H., Lockwood, Barton
Dunham James J., Broad st., Waverly, "
Ellas A. Clark, Main st., "
Finch Amasa, Factoryville, "
Guyer H. E., Broad c. Clark st, Waverly, "
Rowland John R., 242 Broad st., Waverly, "
VanAmburgh Abdial B., 304 Broad st., Waverly, "
BRAINARD CHARLES E., Berkshire
BUFFINGTON CALVIN A., Railroad st., "
Houghtaling Burt, "
HOUGHTALING WILLIAM M., Main st., "
Humphreys Erastus E., Speedsville, Tomp. Co., r 19 cor. 17, "
Judd John N., r 6, "
PRATT MARSHALL D., "
CARPENTER WILLIAM L., Candor
Curtis William, r 5, "
Embody Jacob, "
Holden Dallas, r 120, Weltonville, "
PARMELE FREDERICK, (dealer) Main st., "
Searles George M., Main st., "
Chambers Charles, Newark Valley
Riley Andrew B., (dealer) "
WHITING BROS., "
Turner Harvey, off Main st., Nichols
Ballou Hartwell M., r 12, Owego
Hemstrought James, r 54, Campville, "
Hill Charles O., 89 Central ave., "
Kellum Ambrose, Apalachin, "
Moore & Ross, 146 North ave., "
Raymond & Emery, Central ave., cor. Temple st. "
Russell Minor, r 108, South Apalachin, "
Stratton Richard, r 20, "
Terbush Lancelot B., r 16, Flemingville, "
Genung Orrin L., r 45½, Richford
PERRY EDWIN A., r 43, "
Smith Julius C., "
BRUNDAGE DeWITT C., VanEtten st., Spencer
CAMPTON SILAS, r 37, West Candor, "

Garey Abram L., Spencer
Hall Leonard F., r 28, "
Wood William H., "
Catlin George, r 52, Tioga Center, Tioga
Genung Adam S., Smithboro, "
Signor George H., r 36, Tioga Center, "

Cider Mills.

Manning Fred B., Halsey Valley, Barton
Mercereau & Co., Broad st., Waverly, "
Akins Henry S., r 18, Speedsville, Tomp. Co., Berkshire
Cooper & Thornton, r 62, West Candor, Candor
DU MOND DAVID, "
Snyder DeWitt M., r 1, Willseyville, "
Wheeler Abram T., "
FARNHAM OSCAR E., r 49½, Nichols
MATTHEWS ISAIAH, r 38, "
Rounds Simeon, r 83, Apalachin, Owego
Smith Orville, r 54, Campville, "
Card Charles P., r 43, Spencer
FARNHAM HERBERT, off r 12, Owego, Tioga

Clergymen.

Bowen George N., (Episcopal) Waverly, Barton
Cooper David H., (Baptist) Waverly, "
Evans Ziba, (M. E.) Lockwood, "
McShane Edward, (R. C.) 103 Clark st., Waverly, "
Peck Luther, (M. E.) "
Pendell John R., (Bapt.) Waverly, "
Salmon Franklin J,, (Bapt.) "
Taylor John L., (Pres.) Waverly, "
Woodruff James O., (M. E.) Waverly, "
Hough Joel J., (Cong.) Berkshire
Cronk Byron E., (Bapt.) Candor
Jacobs Hiram C., (Bapt.) r 75, "
Osburn Arthur, (M. E.) r 116, "
Williston Horace, (M. E.) Owego st., "
Angell Thomas, (retired M. E.) "
Ketchumville, Newark Valley
Gale Hiram, (reform Meth.) Ketchumville, "
Leach Daniel F., (Bapt.) "
Treible Wilson, (M. E.) "
Van Deusen H. Newton, (M. E.) Nichols
Wilson James M., M. D. (Pres.) "
Barnes Newton W., (M. E.) Apalachin, Owego
Burton Reuben E., (Bapt.) 19 Ross st., "
Dickinson Ira W., (M. E.) r 73, Campville, "
Fessenden Nelson, (W. Meth.) Apalachin, "
Howe Olin R., (Cong.) 290 Main st., "
Johnson Thomas D. (R. C.) Main st., "
Ketchum La Fayette F., (reform Meth.) 92 Franklin st., "
Kidder James H., (P. E.) 100 Main st., "
McKenzie Alexander, (Pres.) 321 Front, "
Sandford William, (African M. E.) bds. 106 Paige st.. "
Shepard Charles D., (M. E.) r 40 Flemingville, "
Tyler Edward, (Christian) Harford Mills, Richford
Howard Loring P., (M. E.) Spencer
Livermore Albert, (Pres.) "
Matteson Fayette A., (Bapt.) r 71, Smithboro, Tioga
Tilden Alanson, Tioga Center, "

Clothiers, Merchant Tailors, and Tailors.

(See also General Merchants.)

Betowski W. Leon, 123 Broad st., Waverly, Barton

STARKEY & WINTERS, Wholesale and Retail Druggists, Owego.

CLOTHIERS, MERCHANT TAILORS, TAILORS—CREAMERIES. 225

Mott Amasa S., 222 Broad st., Waverly, Barton
PERKINS FRED. C., 208 Main st., Waverly, "
Salonsky Isaac, 224 Broad st., Waverly, "
Smitt Antoni B., 10 Fulton st., Waverly, "
Unger Adolph, Waverly, "
Unger Solomon, 230 Broad st., Waverly, "
Van Velsor & Co., 212 Broad st., Waverly, "
Cross James O., Berkshire
Goldstein Bros., "
BANDLER ROBERT, 19 and 21 Lake st., Owego
Berger Andrew F. F., Lake st., "
Coleman Juliette, 9 and 11 Lake st., "
Dwelle & Link, Front st., "
Whitson Isidor, 201 Front st., "

Coal and Wood Dealers, also Lime and Cement.

Gray DeWitt C., Erie st., Waverly, Barton
Guyer H. E., Broad cor. Clark st., Waverly, "
HAGADORN DeWITT C., Lockwood, "
Kane Edward M., "
Scott Charles, 256 Broad st., Waverly, "
Sneffin & Scott, Broad st., Waverly, "
Gridley William C., West Candor, Candor
HEATH FRANK L., Main st., "
DIMMICK & YOUNG, Newark Valley,
Williams Lucius E., "
*HOUSE EPHRAIM H., cor. West ave. and McMaster, Owego
KEELER ALBERT H., Temple cor. Central ave., "
Morse Newell, 133 Temple, "
STEDMAN WHEELER, r 40, Flemingville, "
Smith W. C. & Co., Richford

Confectioners, Fruits, Ice Cream, Etc.
(See also Bakers and Confectioners, also Grocers)

Frauenthal Isedore E., 244 Broad st., Waverly, Barton
Horton Emma E. Mrs., 210 Broad st., "
Larnard Asolph S., 3 Elizabeth st., "
Turney William E., 239 Broad st., Waverly, "
JACKSON DWIGHT P., Main st., Candor
Johnson Silas W., r 88, "
Westbrook Levi, Main st., Nichols
Beers Frank J., 55 North ave., Owego
CLARK HERMAN C., 68 North ave., "
Cuneo Pietro, 181 Front st., "
Graves Henry A., 49 Lake st., "
Groat Abram W., 115 North ave, "
McArthur John, 107 North ave., "
Tillotson James E., 86 North ave., "

Contractors and Builders.
(See also Architects and Builders, Carpenters and Builders, and Masons and Builders.)

Blossom Jason B., 16 Chemung st., Waverly, Barton
BROOKS AUGUSTUS. Lockwood, "
Doane Gabriel P., 138 Chemung st., Waverly, "
GENUNG SHERMAN A., Fulton st., Waverly, "
Hess Nirum J., Fulton st., Waverly, "
LARNARD A. WARREN, Lyman ave., Waverly, "
LENT CLARENCE A., Lincoln cor. Spring st., Waverly, "
ROGERS CHARLES H., 413 Chemung st., Waverly, "

Seacord John, 27 Lincoln st., Waverly, Barton
Simcoe Eli, Waverly, "
VanAtta Azariah, 111 Penn. ave., Waverly "
Vibbert Charles M., 148 Waverly st., Waverly
WALLACE ALFRED H., 150 Waverly st., Waverly, Barton
Brooks George T., Owego st., Candor
Cronk Byron E., "
ELMENDORF CYRENUS, Main st., "
German Cyrus B., "
STOWELL ALMOND F., Railroad st., "
VOSE ENOCH, West Candor, r 108, "
Ackerman Cornelius R., Jenksville, Newark Valley
Angell Elworth J., "
Chapman Canfield, "
Chapman George M., "
BIXBY SMITH R., River st., Nichols
Evans Elijah K., r 8, "
WIGGINS CLOYD B., r 8, "
Woods Elisha B., r 40, Richford
Corchrane & Conant, 62 Temple st., Owego
Dean James A., Spencer ave., "
Fox William S., Apalachin, "
Groesbeck George S., r 61, "
Hamilton Joel A., 3 Front st., "
Johnson Andrew J., r 104, Apalachin, "
KEELER ALBERT H., Temple cor. Central ave., "
Kellogg Charles T., 262 Prospect st., "
Sullivan James, 58 Liberty st., "
Terrill L. Fontenell, 100 Franklin st., "
WARNER FRANK H., Fox st., "
WELCH DAVID A., 243 Prospect st., "
Welch William H., 267 Prospect st., "
Richardson & Campbell, r 43, Spencer
Sawyer Ezra O., "
West Marshall C., "
FORD & BAUER, Strait's Corners, Tioga

Coopers.

Manning Judson, r 9, Halsey Valley, Barton
Skellenger Daniel J., Speedsville, Tomp. Co., Berkshire
Ahlers Dedrick G., Gould st., Candor
Barber Hiram, r 139, "
Reasor James B., r 44, "
Strong Eugene B., Willseyville, r 3, "
Wolverton Charles A., r 131, "
Golden Augustus H., r 22, West Newark, Newark Valley
Golden Prentis E., r 22, West Newark, "
Moon Levi B., "
Campbell Amos B., Owego, Nichols
Hyde William, r 20, Owego
Ingersoll Eugene F., r 46, "
Vincent Dexter C., r 46, "
Thompson Benjamin, r 44, Richford
Brown William, r 18, Spencer
Eaton Daniel B., Smithboro. Tioga
Forsyth W. Henry, r 21, Halsey Valley, "
Hevland Douglass, r 28, Owego, "
HOYT IRA, r 21, Halsey Valley, "
Hyde Gordon, r 12, Owego, "
Hynes Charles, Halsey Valley, "
Stimpson Charles, Smithboro, "

Country Stores.
(See General Merchants.)

Creameries.

CAYUTA CREAMERY, Schuyler & Harding, props., Factoryville, Barton
GILLETT & DECKER CREAMERY, W. E. Gillett and A. I. Decker, props., Reniff, "

STARKEY & WINTERS, promptly fill Mail and Telephone Orders.

15

THE
Waverly ✻ Advocate.

FRANK!
LOYAL!
EARNEST!

The Oldest, Largest and Best Paper Published in

WAVERLY, NEW YORK.

Republican to the Core!
  True to Friends and Fair to Foes!
    Full of News!
      Bristling with Sense!
        Complete in Every Department!

→ The Largest Circulation in Waverly and Still Climbing Up. ←

ITS MOTTO - "STRAIGHT AHEAD."

TERMS, - $1.00 IN ADVANCE.

A Complete Job Department

In the hands of Thoroughly Competent Workmen.

EDGAR L. VINCENT, Proprietor.

GEO. D. GENUNG, Local Editor and Manager.

CREAMERIES—EGGS AND POULTRY. 227

Higgins & Rounsevell, Speedsville, Tomp. Co., Berkshire
BAKER BROS., Nichols
SPENCER CREAMERY, S. A. Seely, prop.; D. La M. Georgia, sup't; Liberty st., Spencer

Crockery and Glassware.

FARLEY & SANDERS, 231 Broad st., Waverly, Barton
HIBBARD GEORGE R., 84 Front st., Owego

Dentists.

Nelson Elmer, 251 Broad st., Waverly, Barton
Snook Frederick M., 231 Broad st., Waverly, "
VanDERLIP CHARLES T., 201 Broad st., Waverly, "
House Willard E., Main st., Candor
Fellows Russell S., Newark Valley
DOWNS EDWIN D., 192 Front st., Owego
HILL BROTHERS, Front st., "
Jackson John, 12 Lake st., "
MAYOR WILLIAM E., over 173 Front st., "
Walker Ransom, over 200 and 202 Front st., "
Rawley George W., Main st., Richford
Matteson George E., Main st., Spencer
Anderson John J., r 12, Tioga

Dressmakers.

Aikins Jane, 118 Clark st., Waverly, Barton
Beardslee Mary Mrs., 2 Ithaca st., Waverly, "
Beekman Emma, 127 Chemung st., Waverly, "
Brooks Lizzie D., 12 Waverly st., Waverly, "
Cooley Hattie J., North Barton, "
Dollason Frances H., "
Falsey Sarah A., Clark st., Waverly, "
French Carrie, 314 Broad st., Waverly, "
Miller Cassandra B., 482 Chemung st., Waverly, "
Minnick J. H. Mrs., 28 Loder st., Waverly, "
Murray Mary L., Pine st., Waverly, "
Osterhout Katie, 23 Broad st., Waverly, "
Sargeant J. C. Mrs., 28 Orange st., Waverly, "
Shaw Hulda J., 9 Waverly st., Waverly, "
SHIPMAN PERLIE E., r 34, Waverly, "
Shulenburg Sarah, 304 Cherry st., Waverly, "
Smith D. S. Mrs., 21 Fulton st., Waverly, "
Strause Huldah, 218 Broad st., Waverly, "
Sullivan Anna. 105 Chemung st., Waverly, "
Sullivan Etta, 315 Broad st., Waverly, "
Terry E. H. Mrs., 5 Penn. ave., Waverly, "
Tompkins Mary A., Factoryville, "
VanDerlip Sisters, 24 Park ave., Waverly, "
Williams Addie, 20 Clark st., Waverly, "
Brown Sarah J., Candor
Brown Mary A., Newark Valley
Flannigan Susie, "
Sears Lizzie M., "
Reeves Ella, River st., Nichols
Scott Sisters, Cady ave. "
Bauer Elizabeth, 26 Adaline st., Owego
Bowen Abby A., over Owego Nat. Bank, "
Bryan Esther C., Spencer Blk. Lake st., "
Catlin Sarah E., 75 Talcott st., "
Catlin Mary E., 75 Talcott st., "
Cortright John Mrs., 201 E. Temple st., "
Cole Ida M., 261 Erie st., "
Donovan Mary A., 102 Paige st., "
Dorsey Alma J., 207 E. Temple st., "
Dowd Anna E., 5 Park st., "
Earsley Belle Mrs., Commerce st., "

Edwards Susie, r 83, Apalachin, Owego
Greenwood Lizzie M., 80 William st., "
Hickey Lizzie C., 399 Main st. "
Hoagland Emma D., Buckbee Blk., "
Hodge Ella A., 86 Temple st., "
Hogan Catherine M., 60 Delphine st., "
Horgan Katie, 56 Delphine st., "
Kelly Julia F., 246 E. Temple st., "
Kingcade Charles Mrs., 90 Paige st., "
Laird George H. Mrs., Apalachin, "
Ross Allie M.. 42 William st., "
Rowe M. & G., 192 Front st., "
Skellenger Emma E., 51 Forsyth st., "
Stever Amanda E. Mrs., over 78 North ave., "
Wade L. N. Mrs., 175 North ave., "
Whipple Sisters, 139 Main st.. "
Wood Lydia, 76 Talcott st., "
STEWART EMILY A., off r 12, Owego, Tioga

Drugs and Medicines.

Bennet Stephen, Broad st., Waverly, Barton
Hayes H. H. & Son, 236 Broad st., Waverly, "
Mullock Bros., 229 Broad st., Waverly, "
SLAUGHTER & VAN ATTA, 233 Broad st., Waverly, "
Tracy Edward G., 228 Broad st., Waverly "
HOLCOMB WALLACE, Berkshire
Jennings James H., Front st., Candor
Ross M. L. & Son, Main st., "
Smith William B., Main st., "
SMITH L. M. & SON, Newark Valley
Latham & Cady, Main st., Nichols
BEACH & PARMELEE, Main cor. North ave., Owego
Beaumont John H., 135 North ave., "
HOPKINS LANCY N., Apalachin, "
JANSEN J. W. & Co., 60 North ave., "
Kenyon Joel C., 5 Lake st., "
*STARKEY & WINTERS, cor. Front and Lake sts., "
WHITE & HUMISTON, 194 Front st., "
Rawley Hiram B., Richford
Fisher Charles J., Main st., Spencer
EMMONS LUCIUS E., Main st., "
Blake William, Tioga Center, Tioga

Dry Goods.

KNAPP JOSEPH W., 203 Broad st., Waverly, Barton
Murdoch E. N. & Co., 222 Broad st., Waverly, "
STOWELL HOLLIS R., 237 Broad st., Waverly, "
WATROS BROS., 227 Broad st., Waverly, "
Wilcox H. M. & Co., 218 Broad st., Waverly, "
JOSLYN EDWARD, Main st.. Nichols
BUCKBEE, PETERSON, WOOD & CO., 190 and 192 Front st., Owego
GOODRICH & CO., 196 Front st., "
Hall George H., 122 Main st., "
HASTINGS & STRATTON, 186 Front st., "
Hulslander Levi S., 59 North ave. "
Hyde Earl Mrs., Main st., "
Newman Bros., 31 and 33 Lake st., "
Tuck Isaac, 198 Front st., "
Taylor Robert J., 377 Front st., "

Eggs and Poultry.

(See also Fancy Fowls, etc., Poultry Dealers.)

ROBERTS JOHN O., (wholesale) Newark Valley

EXPRESS AGENTS—GRIST, FLOURING MILLS AND DEALERS.

Express Agents.
HAGADORN DeWITT C., Lockwood, Barton
Kane Edward M.,
Murdoch John K., (U. S.) Waverly, "
BROWN FRANK W., West Candor, Candor
HEATH FRANK L., Main st., "
Rockwood Lorenzo F., (U. S.) Newark Valley
KIRBY ALLEN B., Nichols
Hutchins Frank F., (U. S. Ex.) 34 Lake st., Owego
Mabee Foster N., (Erie Ex. Co.) 18 Lake st. "
STEELE AARON, Apalachin, "
Rich Lucien D., Richford
Mills Henry C., Spencer
Sanderson P. W. N., Tioga Center, Tioga

Fertilizers.
Bushnell William B., Berkshire
HART LEWIS A., Main st., Candor
CAMPBELL ARBA, Talcott st., Owego
KEELER ALBERT H., Temple cor. Central ave., "

Florists and Seedsmen.
(See also Seedsmen.)
Angell Mary L., 472 Chemung st., Waverly, Barton
Dingee John T., 116 Lincoln st., Waverly, "
THOMAS ALEXANDER J., Main st., Owego

Furniture Dealers.
HALL & LYON, 356 Broad st., Waverly, Barton
Slawson Andrew A., Waverly, "
Sweet C. W., Broad st., Waverly, "
WITTER F. A. & CO., Berkshire
Frost John O., Main st., Candor
CARGILL WILLIAM, Newark Valley
Neal N. E., Cady ave., Nichols
HUBBARD & KING, 29 Lake st., Owego
Matson John L., 183 Front st., "
PIERCE WALLACE C., Richford
Bower Bros., Spencer

Gents' Furnishing Goods.
(See also Clothing, also Dry Goods, also General Merchants.)
McDONALD SARAH C. Mrs., 265 Broad st., Waverly, Barton
PERKINS FRED C., 208 Main st., Waverly, "
Salonsky Isaac, 224 Broad st., Waverly, "
Goldstein Bros., Berkshire
BANDLER ROBERT, 19 and 21 Lake st., Owego
Berger Andrew F. F., Lake st., "
Fairchild Samuel F., 27 Lake st., "

General Merchants.
(Who keep a general assortment of Dry Goods, Groceries, Hardware, etc. See also Dry Goods, also Groceries.)
BINGHAM BROS., Lockwood, Barton
Cornell William, "
Evarts Andrew J., Factoryville, "
GILLETT WILLIS E., Reniff, "
Gridley T. E. & Son, Main st., Factoryville, "
VAIL A. V. C. & CO., Lockwood, "
WOOD JAMES C., Main st., Factoryville, "
Wright & Cary, Main st., "
Clark Horatio, Main cor. Depot sts., Berkshire
DEWEY & DARBONNIE, "
Eldrige E. O. & Co., Main st., "

Andrews William H., Front st., Candor
Booth & Williams, Front st., "
Cooper Fred B., Strait's Corners, "
Knapp Burr D., Weltonville, "
McCARTHY & THOMPSON, Main st., "
MEAD CHARLES, r 75, Weltonville, "
Minor Christopher, r 30, Willseyville, "
Orcutt William C., Owego st., "
Owen William, r 29, "
Sawyer Luther, r 62, West Candor, "
Smith H. A., Catatonk, r 133, "
VanDebogart Frank L., Main st., "
Byington Alphonso, Newark Valley
ELWELL WILLIAM, "
Finch Charles, Ketchumville, "
FORD ALBERT N., "
Nixon John G., r 1, Jenksville, "
RANDALL OSCAR S., "
ROYS & TODD, "
Bliven Cranston, Main st., Nichols
EDSALL JOHN R., Main st., "
Sherwood Casper I., Main st., "
Kinney & Gray, Apalachin, Owego
KNAPP CHARLES R., Apalachin, "
SLEEPER & WHITTAKER, Apalachin, "
Rawley Hiram B., Richford
Smith W. C. & Co., "
Bradley Chas. E., Main st., Spencer
DAY JOHN & SON, Main st., "
EMMONS ALFRED S., Van Etten st., "
FISHER MARVIN D., Main st., "
Kellogg Mahlon A., North Spencer, "
SEELY S. ALFRED, Academy st., "
SHEPARD SYLVENES, Van Etten st., "
Sniffin William A., Main st., "
Stanclift Isaac S., Van Etten st., "
Barber Ami W., Halsey Valley, Tioga
Bonham Charles H., Main st., "
Drake W. J. & Son, Main st., Smithboro, "
Hoyt Fred. D., Halsey Valley, "
Lollis Samuel C., Smithboro, "
Martin Fred, Main st., Tioga Center, "
Southwick Mary J. Mrs., Halsey Valley, "
Wheeler John N., Strait's Corners, "

Grain Threshers.
Albright Adam, North Barton, "
Hoover William, r 41, Barton
Cooper & Thornton, r 62 West Candor, Candor
Coon A. H. & W. L., Strait's Corners, "
DU MOND DAVID, "
Hulslander Sylvester, r 101, "
MEAD WILLIS A., r 70, "
Mix John C., Willseyville, r 1, "
BURCH & WELLS, Newark Valley
Nichols John E., East Nichols, Nichols
BLOW FRANK L., r 95, Owego
Camp Orin, r 54, "
RYANT R. & J. P., r 20. North Spencer, Spencer
Smith & Truesdail, r 44, Owego, Tioga

Grist and Flouring Mills and Dealers.
BINGHAM BRO'S, Lockwood, Barton
Manning Fred. B., Halsey Valley, "
Waverly Steam Flouring Mills, (J. C. Shear prop.) 300 Broad st., Waverly, "
BERKSHIRE FLOURING MILLS, Berkshire
Bushnell William B., "
Hart Samuel L., (grist) Speedsville Tomp. Co., r 18, "
BARROTT SAMUEL R., r 82, Weltonville, Candor
Candor Mill, A. Beebe prop. Main st. "

GRIST, FLOURING MILLS AND DEALERS—HARNESS, TRUNKS. 229

Hoff Lewis R., Main st., Candor
HUBBARD WILLIAM H., r 98, "
JENKSVILLE STEAM MILL, C. D. Nixon, prop., Jenksville, Newark Valley
Moses Philander P., (custom) "
White George W., (custom) Jenksville, "
Williams Lucius E., (feed) "
Dunham's Mills, Caleb Wright, prop., r 8, Nichols
HUNT ADONIJAH. r 37, Owego, "
NICHOLS STEAM FLOUR MILLS, John Fenderson, prop., "
Beeman Horace W., (feed) r 116, Owego
Curtis Harmon, r 35, Gaskill Corners, "
DORWIN, RICH & STONE, office 177 Front st., "
Ellis Nathan H., r 40, "
FOSTER LEONARD, (feed) r 27, "
Kile George O., (feed) r 95, "
Terbush Lancelott B., (feed) r 16, Flemingville, "
Weed J. D. & G. W., (Custom) "
Bliss Franklin, Richford
HARFORD MILLS, Granger Francis & Son, props., "
PERRY EDWIN A., r 43, "
Wilbur James F., "
HAGADORN DAVID B., r 57, Spencer
SEELY S. ALFRED, "
Franklin Burton B., r 52, Tioga Center, Tioga
JONES STEPHEN W., r 9, Owego, "
Leach Stephen W., Owego, "
Tuthill Joseph M., Smithboro. "

Groceries and Provisions.

(See also General Merchants.
BARNES & MILLER, 227 Broad st., Waverly, Barton
FARLEY & SANDERS, 231 Broad st., Waverly, "
Gerould B. & Co., 111 Broad st., Waverly, "
Gibbons James S., 246 Broad st., Waverly, "
Hallet & Son, 245 Broad st., Waverly, "
HANFORD & LORD, 222 Broad st., Waverly, "
Hart Brothers, 205 Broad st., Waverly, "
Hern John, 117 Broad st., Waverly, "
Parsons & Freestone, 207 Broad st., Waverly, "
Persons E. Delos, 206 Broad st., Waverly, "
Quigley Michael, 263 Broad st., Waverly, "
Sager & Munn, 234 Broad st., Waverly, "
SEELY WILLIAM F., 257 Broad st., Waverly, "
SWAIN LESTER, Fulton st., Waverly, "
Stevens Samuel, r 46, Lockwood, "
WALKER LEANDER, 253 Broad st., "
WALKER T. S. & Son, 250 and 252 Broad st., Waverly, "
WAVERLY CASH STORE, 227 Broad st., Waverly, "
HOLCOMB WALLACE, Berkshire
Bush Abram R. Willseyville, Candor
Fister John W., Main st., "
JACKSON DWIGHT P., Main st. "
O'Brien Thomas, r 30, Willseyville, "
Wardwell & Cooper, r 62, West Candor. "
White Morgan A., Willseyville. "
Woodard Mary G., r 82, Weltonville, "
BENTON WILLIS S., r 1, Jenksville, Newark Valley
Chapman Lyman F., "
ROBERTS JOHN O., "
ANTHONY FLOYD H., Main st., Nichols

Van Ness Belle H. Mrs., Main st., Nichols
Cornell H. W. & Son, 405 Main st., Owego
Cortright Albert, North ave. "
Cortright Theodore, 64 North ave. "
Curtis Harmon, r 35, Gaskell's Corners, "
Dickinson McKenzie, r 54, Campville, "
DUGAN JOHN, 173 Front st., "
GREEN A. L. & R. D. r 25, Gaskell's Corners, "
Hyde & Winters, Front cor. Court sts., "
Johnson Edward J., 100 North ave. "
KNAPP WILBUR F., Apalachin, "
Lake Thomas B., 119 North ave., "
Leach Benjamin C., North ave., "
Leahy Patrick & Son, Main cor North ave., "
Maroney John F., 56 North ave. "
MILLREA BROTHERS, 178 Front st., "
Olmstead Seth, r 40, "
Raymond Mary F., 199 Main st., "
Searles J. F. & Son, 136 North ave., "
Shays Jonas, 72 North ave., "
Shaw & Ringrose, Lake cor. Main sts., "
Sheldon & Yates, 131 North ave., "
SMITH CHARLES F., 172 Front st., "
Steele G. Odell, 177 Front st., "
Thurston Chester P., 176 Front st., "
Thurston Frederick G., 130 North ave., "
Truman Benjamin L., 182 Front st., "
Wade George N., West ave., "
Wheeler John, r 54, Campville, "
MILLER WILLIAM F., Main st., Richford
Bowen Seth, Spencer
DAY JOHN & SON, Main st., "
Nichols David A., Main st., "
Van Marter Enos T., r 35, "

Hair Goods.

PELLUM MARGARET H., 459 Main st., Owego
Yost Mary E. Mrs., over Owego National Bank, "

Hardware, Stoves and Tinware.

(See also General Merchants.)
CLARK JAMES A., 217 Broad st., Waverly, Barton
EATON D. H. & SONS, Factoryville, "
MERRIAM BROS., 235 Broad st., Waverly, "
WITTER F. A. & CO., Berkshire
CHIDSEY JOHN R., Candor
DeGraw John, Main st., "
HEATH HENRY D., Main st., "
CHAPMAN EDGAR E., Newark Valley
HUTCHINSON HORACE W., "
Coleman & Horton, Main st., Nichols
Everitt Fred M., "
HOUK JONATHAN S., 184 Main st., Owego
KNAPP FRANK J., Apalachin, "
STANBROUGH JOHN B., 180 Front st., "
STORRS, CHATFIELD & CO., Front cor. Lake st., "
Swift Charles H., Main st., Richford
DAY JOHN & SON, Main st., Spencer

Harness, Trunks, etc.

Deuel Amos E., 250 Broad st., Waverly, Barton
Nelson Phineas, 127 Broad st., Waverly, "
ROLLEY HIRAM, Berkshire
Humiston Morris, Railroad st., Candor
PIERSON CHARLES O. Newark Valley
Smead David J., 150 Front st., Owego
Williams John E., Apalachin, "
Wyman William. 112 North ave., "
BARNES GRANT W., Richford

THE WAVERLY FREE PRESS

ESTABLISHED OCTOBER 15, 1887.

WAVERLY, TIOGA COUNTY, N. Y.

JAMES B. BRAY, Editor and Proprietor.

Published + Every + Saturday + at + 50 + Cents + per + Year.

The Best and Cheapest Paper in Tioga County,

And is the only home-printed paper in Waverly.

HAS THE LARGEST CIRCULATION,

Therefore is the Best Advertising Medium. Sample Copies and Rates of Advertising furnished on application.

Fine Job Printing a Specialty

Excelled by none in Southern New York.

✦FULL LINE OF STATIONERY✦

HARNESS, TRUNKS, ETC.—JEWELRY, WATCHES, ETC.

SNOOK DAVID L., Main st., Spencer
Hamilton George, Halsey Valley, Tioga

Hats, Caps and Furs.
(See Clothiers, also General Merchants.)
PERKINS FRED C., 208 Main st., Waverly, Barton
BANDLER ROBERT, 19 and 21 Lake st., Owego
Fairchild Samuel F., 27 Lake st., "
Smith James L., 8 Lake st., "

Hay and Grain.
Barnum & Personius, 264 Broad st., Waverly, Barton
BAILEY W. H. & CO., 164 North ave., Owego
SPEERS WILLIAM S., 207 North ave., "
STEDMAN WHEELER, r 40, Flemingville, "

Hotels.
American House, A. P. Head, prop., 260 Broad st., Waverly, Barton
Central House, F. D. Tooker, prop., Factoryville, "
Christie House, W. H. Goldsmith, prop., Fulton st., Waverly, "
Commercial Hotel, D. S. Kennedy, prop., Fulton cor. Elizabeth sts., Waverly, "
Gilbert House, Mrs. Eva J. Gilbert, prop., Lockwood, "
HOTEL WARFORD, Wadsworth & Kelsey, props., Broad cor. Fulton, Waverly, "
Jackson House, A. Jackson, prop., Factoryville, "
Johnson House, E. J. Johnson, prop., Main st., "
Temperance Hotel, Miles Forman, prop., "
TIOGA HOTEL, Ackley & Bailey, props., Fulton Cor. Elizabeth, Waverly "
BERKSHIRE HOUSE, Ira Crawford, prop., Berkshire
ALLEN HOUSE, Iddo Vergason, prop., Main st., "
ASHLAND HOUSE, Frank J. Norton, prop., Main st., Candor
DIMMICK HOUSE, Dimmick & Young, props., Newark Valley
Ketchum's Hotel, Seneca Ketchum, prop., r 12, Ketchumville, Newark Valley
NICHOLS HOTEL, J. Platt, prop., River st., Nichols
AH-WA-GA HOUSE, B. J. Davis, prop., Front cor. Church sts., Owego
Central House, Alanson Goodenow, prop., Apalachin, "
CENTRAL HOUSE, W. G. Gardner, mgr., Main cor. Lake sts., "
CORTRIGHT HOUSE, J. A. Cortright & Son, props., 157 North ave., "
DUGAN HOUSE, Charles B. Dugan, prop., 139-145 Front st., "
EUROPEAN HOUSE, John Hayes, prop., 151 North ave., "
EXCHANGE HOTEL, John S. Ryan, prop., Apalachin, "
FLEMINGVILLE HOTEL, Mrs. Eunice E. Hall, prop., r 40, Flemingville, "
Hiawatha House, (summer) Hiawatha Island, "
Lackawanna House, Ira J. VanDemark, prop., 176 River, South Side, "
Park Hotel, Nichols & Huber, props.; 161 Main st., "
Thomas Samuel H., 54 South Depot st., "
RICHFORD HOTEL, H. W. Theleman, prop., Richford
GROVE HOTEL, C. J. Rice, manager, opp. G. I. & S. depot, Spencer
VAN MARTER HOUSE, J. Van Keuren, prop., Main st., "
Erie Hotel, Cornelius Curkendoll, prop., Smithboro, Tioga
Halsey Valley House, Mrs. Jane P. Higgins, prop., Halsey Valley, "
Lovell House, Smithboro, "
Tioga Center Hotel, Moses Ohart, prop., Main st., Tioga Center, "

Insurance Agents.
BROOKS CHARLES C., 201 Broad st., Waverly, Barton
Excelsior Mutual Benefit Association, 201 Broad st., Waverly, "
FAIRCHILD & THOMAS, First Nat. Bank Bld'g, Waverly, "
Hallett Joseph E., 409 Chemung st., Waverly, "
Lemon Israel G., (fire and life) 245 Broad st., Waverly, "
LUM DANIEL J., Waverly st., Waverly, "
Tew William E., 214 Broad st., Waverly, "
Johnson Eugene F., agt. r 6, Berkshire
Bishop James (fire and life) Main st., Candor
BOOTH HORACE F., Main st., "
KETCHUM WILLIAM P., Kinney st., "
ROBINSON ALDICE A., (fire and life) Main st., "
Royal Morris B., Owego st., "
SPAULDING U. P., (fire and life) Main st., "
HUNT LEWIS, Newark Valley
FAY GEORGE W., 203 Front st., Owego
HOSKINS WATSON L., 185 Front st., "
Laird George H., Apalachin, "
LEONARD GEORGE S., 209 Front st., "
Snyder George, (life) over 63 North ave., "
STEBBINS BARNEY M., 34 Lake st., "
VAN KLEECK JOHN J., Court House, "
Hilligas Joshua, (life) Tompkins ave., Spencer
Manchester Henry H., (life) r 47, Owego, Tioga

Iron Founders and Machinists.
LEMON JAMES, Broad st., Waverly, Barton
CANDOR IRON WORKS, H. F. Booth prop., Candor
*CAULDWELL & GRAY, (engines, boilers, castings, &c.,) McMaster cor. Delphine, Owego

Jewelry, Watches, Etc.
Harris George L., 2 Fulton st., Waverly, Barton
Knapp David D., 211 Broad st., Waverly, "
Mandeville Mahlon H., 228 Broad st., Waverly, "
Hartwell Warren T., Main st., Candor
FRANK CHARLES, Newark Valley
Tripp Seymour C., Main st., Nichols
COMFORT MELVILLE L., 25 Lake st', Owego
DURUSSEL & SON, 35 Lake st., "
HOSKINS WATSON L., 185 Front st., "
STARR CHARLES P., 15 Lake st., "
Rawley George W., Main st., Richford
Dumond Harry, Main st., Spencer
Sagar Willard J., Main st., "

232 LAUNDRIES—LUMBER MANUFACTURERS AND DEALERS.

Laundries.
Tioga Laundry, Geo. B. Witter prop. 113 Broad st., Waverly, Barton
Bing Wah, (Chinese Laundry) 71 North ave., Owego
Casey Thomas F., 210 Front st., "
CITY STEAM LAUNDRY, 83 North ave., "

Lawyers.
ALLEN ADOLPHUS G., 203 Broad st., Waverly, Barton
Allen D. Wellington, Waverly, "
EATON AMBROSE P., Exchange Blk., Main st., Waverly, "
Floyd Jacob B., Broad st., Waverly, "
SHOEMAKER JUDGE F., 214 Broad st., Waverly, "
WARNER WILLIAM F., Waverly, "
Scott Elbert O., Main st., Candor
BIEBER ROMAINE F., Newark Valley
ANDREWS GEORGE F., 214 Front st., Owego
CAMP GEORGE SIDNEY, 132 Front st., "
CLARK C. A. & H. A., Academy Bldg., Court st., "
EASTON DAVID T., over 168 Front st., "
GLEZEN OSCAR B., Academy Bldg., Court, st., "
GROSS JERRY S., 178 Main st., "
Hill Fred C., Court House, "
Lynch Martin T., Lake cor. Main st., "
MEAD & DARROW, Main cor. North ave., "
NIXON CHARLES D., Front cor. Court st. "
Oakley Timothy B., 214 Front st., "
O'HART S. JAY, Academy Bldg., Court, "
PARKER CHARLES E., Court House, "
SEARS JOHN G., Lake cor. Main st., "
SETTEL LYMAN L., Post-Office Bldg., "
TAYLOR JOHN J., Front cor. Court st., "
Watkins Charles D., over 168 Front st., "
ROBINSON CALVIN J., Richford
DEAN EDWARD E., Main st., Spencer
Poole Murray, Smithboro, Tioga

Livery Stables.
Atwater DeWitt C., Clark st., Waverly, Barton
Bentley Abram W., Broad st., Waverly, "
Hagadorn Henry, 2 Broad st., Waverly, "
LASSLY ELIJAH M., Clark cor. Broad st., Waverly, "
Tozer John F., Fulton st., Waverly, "
ROCKFELLER CHARLES H., Main st., Berkshire
CHIDSEY GEORGE C., Main st., Candor
GRIFFIN N. W., Main st., "
HOLLISTER WARREN L., Main st., "
ANTHONY FLOYD H., Main st., Nichols
DEAN CALVIN B., Church st., Owego
COYLE WILLIAM, 73 North ave., "
FORGASON THADDEUS, Central ave., "
Ford Lewis, 132 North ave., "
WEEKS JOSHUA P., Water st., Spencer

Live Stock Breeders and Dealers.
Coleman Jedediah D., (dealer) Barton
BLACKMAN ABRAM, (dealer) Berkshire
Brown Robert C., (breeder) r 38, "
CROSS LOUIS J., (horse breeder) "
Kimball & Stannard, (horse breeders) r 35, "
LEGG ERASMUS D., Speedsville, Tomp. Co., (breeder) "
Lynch Theodore, (dealer) "
MAYOR THEODORE & SONS, (dealers and breeders) r 38, "
PATCH HENRY W., (dealer in horses) r 39, "

ROYCE GEORGE C., (breeder of horses) Main st., Berkshire
SHAW WILLIAM T., (breeder) r 5, "
Shepard James, r 3, (breeder of horses) "
SIMMONS WILLIAM E., (breeder of horses) Jenksville, r 41, "
BARROTT AMMIEL W., (breeder and dealer) r 120, Candor
Holmes John, (dealer) "
HOWARD HIRAM O., (horse breeder) r 118, "
McCay Edwin C., Jenksville, r 49, (dealer) "
Miller Fred, Weltonville, (dealer) r 120, "
PETERS CHARLES G., (breeder and dealer) r 65, "
Schofield Truman, West Candor, (dealer) r 62, "
SEAMAN LeGRAND, (dealer) r 89, "
Stinard Sylvester, Jenksville, r 50, (breeder) "
Ward Oswald J., (dealer) "
Webster Edwin, (breeder and dealer) r 132, Owego, "
Whitney Joseph S., (dealer) "
Bieber Philip, (dealer) r 42, Newark Valley
Holmes Jerome D., (horse dealer) "
SMITH ALFRED, (horse breeder) r 51, Jenksville, "
Briggs Herman I., (dealer) off r 9, Nichols
INGERSOLL GEORGE A., r 10, (breeder) "
LOWMAN FREDERIC C., (breeder) r 3, "
CAMP GURDON H., (horse) Apalachin, Owego
Delavan Irving J., (dealer) Front st., "
HOLMES BROS., (horses) Apalachin, "
LaMonte David M., (horse breeder) r 68, "
MARSHLAND STOCK FARMS, B. F. Tracy & Son, prop., (breeders) r 69, Apalachin, "
McCofferty Anthony C., (horses) European House, "
Sherwood George J., (breeder) r 106, Apalachin, "
Town William P., (horses) r 122, South Owego, "
Tracy Harvey J., (breeder) r 83, Apalachin, "
Clark Charles A., (horses) Richford
Curtis Charles F., (breeder and dealer) r 39, "
FINCH CHARLES R., (breeder) horses, "
Finch Philander W., (dealer) "
GOODRICH WILLIAM S., "
Jennings Henry A., (breeder and dealer) r 35, "
Meloy Frank P., (breeder and dealer) r 33, "
Sears James M., (breeder and dealer) r 16, "
Smith Ralph P., (breeder and dealer) r 35, "
WATKINS AMOS G., (dealer) "
Roda Frederick C., r 9, Spencer
BROCK JOHN, r 42, "
Shepard J. Q. & G. T., r 28, "
SHAW W. HULSE, (breeder Holstein) r 28, Owego, Tioga

Lumber Manufacturers and Dealers.
(See also Saw Mills.)

ANDRE ABRAM T., (contractor) Lockwood, Barton
BALDWIN HUGH, Broad n Penn. ave., Waverly, "
Dodge Ira G., Waverly, "
HAGADORN DeWITT C., (fence-posts and R. R. ties) Lockwood, "

STARKEY & WINTERS, Wholesale and Retail Druggists, Owego.

LUMBER MFG'RS AND DEALERS—MEAT MARKETS, BUTCHERS. 233

Ball John, Berkshire
JAPHET MILO G., "
Williams George, "
Booth Brothers, (manufrs. and dealers)
  r 56, Candor
Little William L., Main st., "
RYAN JOHN, Mill st., "
VAN DEUSER H. & M., r 133, Catatonk, "
Van Vleet Theodore, (dealer) Main st., "
VERGASON SOLOMAN, (dealer) r 112, "
CLINTON ROYAL W., Newark Valley
Williams Lucius E., "
CLAPP SAMUEL, River st., Nichols
Hill Charles O., 89, Central ave., Owego
*HOUSE E. H., 299, McMaster st., "
*OWEGO CRUCIFORM CASKET CO.,
  42, 44 and 46 Delphine st., "
STEDMAN WHEELER, r 40, Flemingville, "
ALLEN J. W., r 18, Richford
FINCH H. S. & C. W., "
EASTMAN SAMUEL, r 37, West Candor,
  Spencer
Hall H. S., r 38, "
McMaster J. O. & J. T., "

Marble and Granite Workers and Dealers.

DONLEY BROS., Newark Valley
HAYWOOD CHARLES M., 80 North
  ave., Owego, and 107 Broad st.,
  Waverly, Barton
SPENCER MARBLE WORKS, L. E.
  Baker, prop., Academy st., Spencer

Masons and Builders.

(See also Architects and Builders, also Carpenters and Builders, and Contractors and Builders.)

Curran Horace H., Waverly, Barton
Curran John J., Waverly, "
DAILEY WILLIAM E., Spring st.,
  Waverly, "
ISLEY & SONS, 36 Waverly st., Waverly, "
Jones George, off r 60, Factoryville, "
McINTYRE ALBERT J., Lincoln st.,
  Waverly, "
MORGAN FRED S., Clark st., Waverly, "
MORGAN JOHN W., 112 Lincoln st.,
  Waverly, "
SHERMAN CHARLES W., 428 Chemung
  st., Waverly, "
Sherman James, r 64, Waverly, "
Sherman John H., r 64, Waverly, "
SMEATON THOMAS, 152 Clark st.,
  Waverly, "
CHURCH ORRIS, r 29, Berkshire
Smith Emory J., Railroad st., "
Braman Jesse H., Candor
Cortright Franklin, Weltonville, "
COWLES JAMES C., r 91, "
FIELD RICHARD, Mountain ave., "
Gibbons Frank, "
Keeler Ethelbert B., r 94, "
Markle David, r 91, "
Merrick Abner, r 13, Speedsville, Tomp.Co., "
Perrine Daniel H., r 134, "
GOODFELLOW HEZEKIAH, r 40½,
  Newark Valley
HILLIGAS LORENZO D., "
Neal Harvey, (stone) "
Perry George, (stone) "
Searles Ezra, r 61, "
THORNTON C. FRANK, (stone) "
Keech Miles W., r 46, Nichols
Sullivan Dennis O., "

Williams Stephen, r 8, Nichols
Conklin Lewis D., r 60, Owego
Cragan John, Apalachin, "
Eckler Marvin, (stone) 188 West ave., "
Howe Rufus C., Main st., "
Kaley William H., 177 Main st., "
Keeler Charles P., 68 Paige st., "
Lillie William, r 108, Apalachin, "
Lynch Michael, 7 Fulton st., "
McDonald John, 18 W. Main st., "
Mott Israel D., r 54, "
Noonan Daniel, Paige st., "
Rulison George P., Apalachin, "
Schopp Francis A., River Road, South
  Side, "
Schopp Peter, River Road, South Side, "
Searles George, r 4, Flemingville, "
Searles Nathan P., r 16½, Flemingville, "
Shehan Timothy, 105 Paige st., "
Skillman David, 219 North ave., "
Van Fleet James, "
Vincelett John, 79 Forsyth st., "
Ward Ezra, South Side, "
White Davis, 154 Front st., "
Nigus Judson, (stone) r 7, Richford
Morton William, r 10, "
MEACHAM JAMES W., (brick) r 37, "
MEACHAM ORRIN W., r 37, "
Burdick Peter, r 42, Spencer
Cortright Ayres D., r 54, Halsey Valley, "
Deyo Chauncey, r 33, "
Goodrich Calvin J., "
Hike W. Harvey, "
House John P., "
Newman Daniel, "
Shaw William, r 54, "
Vorhis J. Wallace, "
Delano Charles, r 28, Owego, Tioga
Leonard George, r 51, Tioga Center, "
Mallery George, Smithboro, "
Mallery Henry, Smithboro, "
Stewart Delos, off r 12, Owego, "
STEWART EDWARD, off r 12, Owego, "
Watkins John, Smithboro, "
Wright William, Tioga Center, "

Meat Markets and Butchers.

Boda & Dimmick, 231 Broad st., Waverly,
  Barton
Carr & Teachman, 119 Broad st., Waverly, "
Dorsett & Faulkner, 215 Broad st., Waverly, "
Hanna Lorentes J., Main st., Factoryville, "
Miller Samuel W., 248 Broad st., Waverly, "
Pike Grove N., 109 Broad st., Waverly, "
PUFF & WILLIAMS, Fulton st., Waverly, "
Stevens Samuel, r 46, Lockwood, "
WILCOX & BARROWS, 271 Broad st.,
  Waverly, "
PRENTICE NORMAN A., (fish) Main st.,
  Berkshire
MILKS WILLIAM J., Spencer st., Candor
BYINGTON SHERMAN W., Newark Valley
JAYNE & BALL, "
Waterman Walter S., Main st., Nichols
Lake Thomas B., 119 North ave., Owego
MILLREA BROTHERS, 178 Front st., "
Shays George, 82 North ave., "
STEVER PETER, 74 North ave., "
WEBSTER GILBERT E., 133 North ave., "
White Charles, 36 Lake st., "
Cashaday Guy, Main st., Spencer
Osborn John, "
Watkins William H., Tioga Center, Tioga.

STARKEY & WINTERS, Druggists, Owego. Close Prices to Dealers.

TIOGA COUNTY HERALD

PUBLISHED WEEKLY AT

NEWARK VALLEY, N. Y.

CHARLES L. NOBLE —— AND —— **G. E. PURPLE,**

PUBLISHERS AND PROPRIETORS.

AN INDEPENDENT FAMILY NEWSPAPER, DEVOTED TO HOME INTERESTS AND GENERAL NEWS.

SUBSCRIPTION PRICE, - - $1.25 PER YEAR

IF PAID IN ADVANCE.

JOB ✶ PRINTING

Of all kinds done in the Best Style and at the Lowest Prices.

Milk Dealers.

ALLEN JOHN, Waverly, Barton
BUCK LYMAN, Waverly, "
Hoyt Joseph N., Waverly, "
Warner John A., r 65, Waverly, Barton
Roper Frank H., r 18, Owego, Nichols
SMITH JOHN JR., r 18, Owego, "
Moody Chas. E., r 42, Spencer

Milliners, Millinery and Fancy Goods.

Delaney Josie E., 211 Broad st., Waverly, Barton
Manning E. W. Mrs., 249 Broad st., Waverly, "
Morgan George Mrs., 16 Johnson st., Waverly, "
TANNERY IDA, 233 Broad st., Waverly, "
Walsh Maggie, 232 Broad st., Waverly, "
Ward & Van Vleet Misses, Candor
Brougham (Helen & Sarah) Newark Valley
Holladay Anna M., "
JOSLYN EDWARD, Main st., Nichols
Van Demark Emma Mrs., Main st., "
Brown Della, 67 North ave., Owego
BUCKBEE, PETERSON, WOOD & CO., 190 & 192 Front st., "
Gilman N. M. Mrs., 204 Front st., "
Manning Caroline M., 206 Front st., "
Newman Brothers, 31 and 33 Lake st., "
YAPLE O. A. MRS., Main st., Richford
Abbey Lizzie, Main st., Spencer
Garatt S. C., Van Etten st., "

Millwrights.

Houghtaling Burt, Berkshire
Cleveland George M., r 1, Willseyville, Candor
Starkweather Joel, Pond st., "
Stevens Aaron C., r 41, Newark Valley
Wiggins George, r 8, Nichols
Leonard John B., r 35, Richford
Smith Julius C., "
Thomas John D., r 71, Smithboro, Tioga

Music and Musical Instruments.

BROWN CHARLES E., 267 Broad st., Waverly, Barton
Slawson Jeremiah M., 202 Broad st., Waverly, "
BACON GEORGE G., dealer, r 65, Candor
DeGroat J. DeWitt, (pianos) r 67, Owego
Leach Benjamin C., North ave., "
SIGNOR ALBERT, 207 Front st., "
SPENCER WILLIAM H., 220 E. Temple st., "
Thompson John M., 107 North ave., "
HOAGLIN MARVIN A., r 43, Richford

Music Teachers.

Speh Charles Prof., Waverly, Barton
Pendell Mary E. O., Waverly, "
BACON GEORGE G., r 65, Candor
Caple Adam, r 104, "
Humiston John H., Main st., "
Locey Charles E., "
Ballou Wendell D., r 56 1-2, Owego
Benner Louise E., Apalachin, "
Druckenmiller Charles Prof., 73 Liberty, "
JOHNSON FRANCES M., 459 Main st., "
Leach Tillie C., North ave., "
Pultz Griffin, jr., 51 Fox st., "
Purdy Emma D., 147 Main st., "
Putman Louis H., 425 Main st., "
Perry Frank, r 44, Richford

Painters and Paper Hangers.
(See also Artists.)

Bostwick Silas W., Waverly st., Waverly, Barton
Keeler Thomas, Broad st., Waverly, "
Lyon Alonzo, Waverly, "
Salisbury Thomas L., 130 Waverly st., Waverly, "
Sliter Warren, Factoryville, "
Smith S. Charles, Broad c. Pine, Waverly, "
Stuart Will E., Main st., "
Toppen Henry, 114 Waverly st., Waverly, "
CROSS LEWIS J., Berkshire
HAY HENRY L., "
Carpenter Harry L., (house) Weltonville, Candor
Sarson John C. F., (house) r 3, "
Stevens Andrew T., r 3, "
Hooker Charles B., Newark Valley
Howard Urial A., "
Sturtevant David M., (carriage) "
Ellsworth Elwin T., Nichols
JOHNSON HORACE A., 52 George st., Owego
ROMINE CHARLES F., 121 Erie st., "
Romine Clarence W., 119 Chestnut st., "
ROMINE EDWIN B., (house and decorative) Opera House Block, "
ROMINE PERCIVAL H., (house and ornamental) 81 Fox st., "
WEBSTER GEORGE H., 242 E. Temple st., "
Hopkins Daniel H., Main st., Richford
GUINNIP DEMPSTER N., Brooklyn st., Spencer
GUINNIP GEORGE, Brooklyn st., "
Maine William F., "
Roberts James A., Smithboro, Tioga

Patent Medicine Manufacturers.

Butts Henry S., 204 Penn ave., Waverly, Barton
Carey Daniel G., Broad st., Waverly, "

Peddlers.

Bently George, off r 39, Barton
Stanton Elisha W., Speedsville. Tomp. Co., r 18, Berkshire
Phipps George, r 12, Ketchumville, Newark Valley
Bush James L., Constines Lane, Owego
Hayes Michael J., 185 E. Temple st., "
Perkins Barney, r 89½, Apalachin, "
Reynolds Smith, 133 North ave., "
Damson John, Liberty st., Spencer
Morse Dana, "
Edwards Samuel, r 9, Owego, Tioga
Lockwood Charles, Tioga Center, "

Photographers.

Comstock A. B., 208 Broad st., Waverly, Barton
Mead Tabatha J. Mrs., 204 Broad st., Waverly, ".."
*HARGRAVE WILLIAM G., 38 and 40 Lake st., Owego
Jackson John T., 12 Lake st., "
Lovejoy Charles L., Front cor. Court sts., "
Clapp Walker G., Van Etten st., Spencer
Ritzler Charles C., r 48, "

Piano Manufactures.

SPORER, CARLSON & BERRY, 58 North ave., Owego

Piano Tuners.

Carlson John M., 63 Paige st., Owego
VICKERY CHARLES S., 84 Paige st., "

Physicians and Surgeons.

Beach Eliza J., 208 Penn. ave., Waverly,
CANFIELD EZRA, Lockwood, Barton
Cook Daniel, r 55, "
Harnden Daniel D., 7 Waverly st., Waverly, "
Harnden Rufus S., 31 Fulton st., Waverly, "
Johnson Parmeous A., 14 Pennsylvania ave., Waverly, "
JOHNSON WILLIAM E., Waverly st., Waverly, "
Tucker John T., Waverly, "
Tyrrell Augustus, 222 Broad st., Waverly, "
Vosburgh Henry P., Halsey Valley, "
Vreeland Isaac S., 229 Broad st., Waverly, "
EASTMAN RALPH D., Main st., Berkshire
Gay Isaac W., Main st., "
Walter Joseph S., r 27 cor. 11, "
Chidester Chauncey W., Weltonville, Candor
DIXON JOHN C., Main st., "
HARRIS ALGERNON J., Main st. "
Miller Daniel S., Main st., "
Osburn Arthur, r 116, "
ROPER WILLIAM E., Owego st., "
BISHOP FRANCIS M., Newark Valley
BURR WILLIAM J., "
ROGERS CORNELIUS R., "
Tappan Revere C., "
Cady George M., River st., Nichols
CADY GEORGE P., River st., "
Allen Lucius H., 140 Main st., Owego
AYER WARREN L., 207 E. Main st., "
Ayers Charles, r 94, "
BARRETT JAMES M., Main c. North ave., "
Beach George W., Apalachin, "
Briggs Mary L., 5 Park st., "
CRANS ABRAM F., 126 North ave., "
DUTCHER MERRITT T., over 15 Lake st., "
FRANK JOHN, 115 Main, "
GREENLEAF JOHN T., 101 Main st., "
HEATON CARLTON R., Park cor. Main, "
Jansen Jesse W., 60 North ave., "
LEWIS GEORGE B., Lake cor. Main, "
LEWIS ISAAC W., r 314, Apalachin, "
*NEWGEON MARY F., 295 Main st., "
PEARSALL ANDREW T., Taylor Blk., Main cor. Spencer ave., "
STEARNS PHINEHAS S., "
*WILSON JAMES, 295 Main st., "
Allen James, Main st., Richford
DAVIS GEORGE W., Main st., Spencer
Fisher William H., Main st., "
Homiston Ezra W., Main st. "
NORRIS ALONZO, "
Tanner John H., Center st., "
CATLIN JAMES H., r 43, Tioga Center, Tioga
HOLLENBACK CHARLES E., r 21, Halsey Valley, "
Knapp Sylvester, Smithboro, "
McDonald Charles H., r 68, Smithboro, "
Post Albert W., r 51, Tioga Center, "
White Leon, Halsey Valley, "

Planing Mills.

BINGHAM BROS., Lockwood, Barton
GILLETT W. E., Reniff. "
VAIL A. V. C. & CO., Lockwood, "
GRIDLEY S. EGBERT, Candor
BURCH & WELLS, Newark Valley
FENDERSON JOHN, Nichols
CAMPBELL & LAMPHERE, Apalachin, Owego
Weed J. D. & G. W., "

JONES STEPHEN W., r 9, Owego, Tioga
TRIBE CHARLES H., Tioga Center, "

Poultry Dealers and Raisers.

(See also Produce Dealers.)

Councilman Edwin W., r 35, (breeder)
NOBLE LYMAN B., (dealer) "
STEVENS HENRY W., r 42, (raiser) "
GOODRICH STEPHEN S., r 46, Owego, "

Printing Offices.

*FREE PRESS, James B. Bray, prop., 15 Fulton st., Waverly, Barton
*THE WAVERLY ADVOCATE, E. L. Vincent, prop., 4 Elizabeth, Waverly, "
*WAVERLY TRIBUNE, Noble & Noble, props., Elizabeth st., Waverly, "
*TIOGA COUNTY HERALD, Noble & Purple, props., Newark Valley
BROCKWAY LEON L., 34 Lake st., Owego
*OWEGO GAZETTE, L. W., Kingman, prop., 28 Lake st., "
*OWEGO RECORD, Scott & Watros, props., 172 Front st., "
*OWEGO TIMES, W. Smyth & Son, props., 193 Main st., "
SLATER FRANK B., 75 Paige cor. Temple sts., "
*SPENCER HERALD, VanGelder & Son, props., Main st., Spencer

Produce (Country) Dealers.

(See also General Merchants.)

Jones John R., 268 Broad st., Waverly, Barton
Ball George P., (buyer) Berkshire
COLLINS JUNIUS, (dealer) "
Lynch Eugene F., "
Manning Alexander D., (buyer) "
Waldo Elijah B., William st., "
WILLIAMS MORRIS, A., (potatoes) "
BARROTT AMMIEL W., Weltonville, Candor
HART LEWIS A., Main st., "
Kyle S. F. & Co., Catatonk, "
Strong Joel H., r 98, "
DIMMICK & YOUNG, (shippers) Newark Valley
JAYNE & BALL, "
Bliven Cranston, Main st., Nichols
DUNHAM EBENEZER, Main st., "
Harris, DeGroat & Co., Main st., "
BARTON ISAAC W & CO., 114 Front st., Owego
Barton William, Apalachin, "
Delavan Irving J., Front st., "
Hover Robert, (buyer) 274 North ave., "
Jewett Charles, r 104, Apalachin, "
RODMAN CHARLES, Front st., "
Rodman Edward D., Main cor. Court st., "
SLEEPER & WHITTAKER, Apalachin, "
SPEERS WILLIAM S., 207 North ave., "
SMITH FRED W., 38 Lake st., "
Stedman Wheeler, r 40, Flemingville, "
STILES & SIBLEY, "
TRUMAN G., SONS & CO., 174 Front st., "
Finch Philander W., Richford
MILLER WILLIAM F., Main st., "
Moore Charles H., (butter and eggs) "
SWARTOUT M. L & SON, Academy st., Spencer
EVELIEN ALFRED, Tioga Center, Tioga
Pepper Jackson S., r 60, Smithboro, "

Real Estate.

Parshall Luther, Waverly, Barton
Tew William E., 214 Broad st., Waverly, "
SPAULDING U. P., Main st., Candor
NIXON CHARLES D., Front cor. Court, Owego
Pumpelly James F., South Side, "
Stebbins Barney M., 34 Lake st.. "

Restaurants.

(See also Hotels.)
Head Richard, 252 Broad st., Waverly,
SWAIN LESTER, Fulton st., Waverly, Barton
WEBBS DINING HALL, (Henry A. Webb, prop.) 216 Broad st., Waverly. "
Griner John N., Depot st., Berkshire
Wilbur William E., 182 Main st., Owego

Saw Mills.

(See also Lumber Manufacturers and Dealers.)
Ackley Alex. W., Lockwood, Barton
BINGHAM BROS., Lockwood, "
Bogart John, Waverly, "
Cornell William, "
GILLETT W. E., Reniff, "
HANNA CHARLES F., off r 66, Factoryville, "
Lott George W., r 1, Van Ettenville, Chem, Co., "
VAIL A. V. C. & CO., Lockwood, "
Akins Henry S., r 18, Speedsville, Tomp. Co., Berkshire
Ball John, "
JAPHET MILO G., "
Williams George, "
BARROTT SAMUEL R., r 82, Weltonville, Candor
Hoose & Hasbrouck, Willseyville, "
HUBBARD WILLIAM H., r 98, "
Snyder Dewitt M., Willseyville, r 1, "
Mayo Hiram, r 29, "
VAN DEUSER H & M., Catatonk, r 133, "
White Morgan A., Willseyville, "
BURCH & WELLS, Newark Valley
CLINTON & BURROUGHS, r 9, "
Davis Franklin, r 25, "
White George W., "
Williams Lucius E., "
HUNT ADONIJAH, r 37, Owego, Nichols
Lounsberry John, r 21, "
Loveland Seth H., Waverly, "
NICHOLS STEAM SAW MILL, John Fenderson, prop., "
PEARSALL L. BURR, r 5, Hooper's Valley, "
CAMPBELL & LAMPHERE, Apalachin, Owego
Curtis Harmon, r 35, Gaskill's Corners, "
FOSTER LEONARD, r 27, "
Kile George O., r 95, "
Rounds Simeon, r 83 Apalachin, "
Searles Homer, r 16½, Flemingville, "
Tobey James D., r 83, Apalachin, "
Weed J. D. & G. W., "
ALLEN J. W., r 18, Richford
Cooper Ephraim A., r 3, Slaterville, Tomp. Co., "
FINCH H. S. & C. W., "
HARFORD MILLS, Francis Granger & Son, prop., "
Tobey Josiah G., r 26, "

TUBBS GAMALIEL C., Center Lisle, Broome Co., r 36, Richford
EASTHAM SAMUEL, r 37, W. Candor, Spencer
Emery James C., r 13, "
Mowers Jacob H., r 20 1-2, North Spencer, "
SEELY S. ALFRED, "
Signer Albert, r 2, North Spencer, "
Doane Timothy, r 3, Strait's Corners, Tioga
JONES STEPHEN W., r 9, Owego, "
Signor Charles, r 36, Tioga Center, "
Snyder Henry A., r 5, Strait's Corners, "
TRIBE CHARLES H., Tioga Center, "
WILLMOT JAMES R., r 28, Owego, "

Seedsmen.

(See also General Merchants, also Hardware.)

Barnum & Personius, 264 Broad st., Waverly, Barton
Corwin Oliver B., 270 Broad st., Waverly, "
Sneffin & Scott, Broad st., Waverly, "

Sewing Machines.

Slawson Jeremiah M., 202 Broad st., Waverly,
Sherwood Warren D., Newark Valley
Lewis John A., r 95, Candor

Shoemakers.

(See also Boots and Shoes.)

Corwin Lewis, Broad st., Waverly, Barton
Donnelly Owen, 218 Erie st., Waverly, "
Hanford Clark, Factoryville, "
Hill George W., 127 Broad st., Waverly, "
Mahoney John, Broad st., Waverly, "
Root Ransom R., Main st., "
Houk Daniel, r 35, Wilson Creek, Berkshire
Cornish Albert A., r 95, Candor
Graham Andrew J., Weltonville, "
Legg Stillman J., Main st., "
Benton Lyman C., r 1, Jenksville, Newark Valley
Hall Sheridan G., r 22, Jenksville, "
HAVENS GEORGE, "
Holdridge Ira J., r 11, Ketchumville, "
WOOD HENRY A., "
VanNess William W., Main st., Nichols
Basford James, 150 River st., South Side, Owego
Bennett Nathaniel, Fox st., "
Branch Andrew, r 54, Campville, "
Collins William, Lake st., "
Courtright Herbert N., r 106, Apalachin, "
MORTON LEVI, Apalachin, "
Pease George, 160 North ave., "
Shupp Lawrence, 18 Lake st., "
Thornton Thomas, r 27, "
AYERS JAMES W., Richford
Bell Augustus E., Main st., "
Garey Daniel, r 2, North Spencer, Spencer
Montgomery Wm., "
Brown Alvah S., Halsey Valley, Tioga
French Jeremiah, Tioga Center, "
Goodenough Chauncey J., Main st., Tioga Center, "

Soap Manufactories.

Beseler C. William, cor. Temple and Liberty sts., Owego
Excelsior Soap Factory, 37 Temple st., "
EMPIRE SOAP WORKS, office 83 North ave., "

P. C. VanGelder.   C. J. VanGelder.

THE SPENCER HERALD

A Five Column Quarto Weekly Newspaper, Eight Pages, Forty Columns.

VAN GELDER & SON,   **P. C. VAN GELDER,**
Publishers.   Editor and Proprietor.

SPENCER, TIOGA COUNTY, N. Y.

It has a large and growing circulation, is an outspoken independent journal, and has a liberal local advertising patronage.

The office is located in the extreme northwest corner of Tioga County, N. Y., and adjoining Tompkins and Chemung Counties. Two railroads run through the place—the E. C. & N. and the G. I. & S.,—which make it invaluable to local advertisers.

Sporting Goods.

Bennet Stephen, Broad st., Waverly, Barton
Waring Norman K., (fly rod manuf.) Newark Valley
Beach D. & Co., 197 Main st., Owego
PIERCE WALLACE C., Richford

Station Agents.

Atwood Wm. W., (D. L. & W.,) Waverly, Barton
Clock C. E., (G. I. & S.,) Factoryville, "
Hubbell Nelson, (Erie R. R.,) Waverly, "
Kane Edward M., "
HAGADORN DEWITT C., Lockwood, "
Waldo Elijah B., William st., Berkshire
BROWN FRANK W., West Candor, Candor
HEATH FRANK L., Main st., "
Smith H. A., r 133, Catatonk, "
Rockwood Lorenzo F., (S. C. R. R.) Newark Valley
KIRBY ALLEN B., (D. L. & W. R. R.) Nichols
DEAN CAMERON B., (N. Y. L. E. & W.) Owego
Corey William H., (D. L. & W.) "
Gale William E., (S. C. R. R.) "
STEELE AARON, (D. L. & W.) Apalachin, "
Rich Lucien D., Richford
Cook Anderson B., North Spencer, Spencer
Howell Myron P., (G. I. & S.) "
Mills Henry C., (E. C. & N.) "
Bellis William L., (Erie R. R.) Smithboro, Tioga
Sanderson P. W. N., Tioga Center, "
Stimpson Henry, (S. C. R. R.) Smithboro, "

Tanners.

DECKER TANNERY, A. I. Decker, prop., Factoryville, Barton
DAVIDGE, HORTON & CO., Berkshire
Hulmboldt Tannery, Candor
DAVIDGE, LANDFIELD & CO., Newark Valley
CAMPBELL ARBA, Talcott st., Owego
DEAN H. N. & SON, North ave., "
Quirin J. G. & Co., Tioga Center, Tioga

Telegraph Operators.

Beach Arthur N., Waverly, Barton
Bixby Fred, Waverly, "
Corey Leonel C., Factoryville, "
HAGADORN DEWITT C., Lockwood, "
Kane Edward M., "
Kinney F. Eloise, Waverly, "
Scanlon Martin, Waverly, "
SMITH JAMES H., Factoryville, "
Steele Edward J., Waverly, "
Patch Robert C., Main st., Berkshire
BROWN FRANK W., West Candor, Candor
German Edward C., "
Merrill Nellie, Willseyville, "
Joslin Joseph D., r 41, Newark Valley
Rockwood Lorenzo F., "
Kennedy John M., Nichols
Barnes Katie, 73 Liberty st., Owego
Billings John, 73 Liberty st., "
BROWN PATRICK, 182 River, South Side, "
Dee James, 313 Main st., "
Fox Lewis L., Apalachin, "
Gale William E., (S. C. R. R.) "
Pert William, 31 Front st., "
Yothers Horace, "
Lacy Louis V., Richford

Robinson James, Richford
Robinson Fred J., "
Cook Anderson B., North Spencer Spencer
Denniston Chester B., "
PALMER HEMAN L., "
Hanmer George W., r 9, Catatonk, Tioga
Pilkington Charles, r 9, Catatonk, "

Tobacco and Cigars.

Clark & Ralyea, 275 Broad st., Waverly, Barton
Ferguson Hartwell M. & Co., 200 Broad st., Waverly, "
Myers Charles K., 201 Broad st., Waverly, "
NICHOLS HURLEY L., 213, Broad st., Waverly, "
Ziegler Benjamin F., Johnson st., Waverly, "
Hart Colden H., r 34, Wilson Creek, Berkshire
MATTHEWS ISAIAH, r 38, (manuf.) Nichols
Barton George W., 191, Main st., Owego
Gavell Edward, 169, Main st., "
Ogden Aaron, 7 Lake st., "

Toy Manufacturers.

Crandall Charles M., Broad st., Waverly, Barton

Undertakers.

Fessenden Harvey G., Waverly, "
Slawson Andrew A., Waverly, "
Sweet C. W., 243 Broad st., Waverly, "
CARGILL WILLIAM, Newark Valley
HUBBARD & KING, 29 Lake st., Owego
Matson John L., 183 Front st., "
PIERCE WALLACE C., Richford
PALMER J. H. & SON, Main st., Spencer

Variety Stores.

Brewster Curtis, Broad st., Waverly, Barton
ENGLEMAN GUS, 131 Broad st., Waverly, "
McDONALD DUNCAN J., 247, Broad st., Waverly, "
BALL JOHN P., 170 Front st., Owego
Lainhart George, 212 Front st., "
SLATER FRANK B., 75 Paige cor. Temple sts., "
Straus Julius L., 43 Lake st., "

Veterinary Surgeons.

Sherry J. Robert, 6 Pine st., Waverly, Barton
PRATT MARSHALL D., Berkshire
Heath James H., r 30, Wilseyville, Candor
MILKS WILLIAM J., Spencer st., "
Burr William H., Newark Valley
FORGASON THADDEUS, Central ave., Owego

Wood Turning.

BROOKS AUGUSTUS, Lockwood, Barton
COLEMAN CHARLES H., Lockwood, "
FARNHAM OSCAR E., r 49½, Nichols
FARNHAM HERBERT, off r 12, Owego, Tioga
JONES STEPHEN W., r 9, Owego, "

Wool Carding.

FARNHAM HERBERT, off r 12, Owego, Tioga

Wool Dealers.

COLLINS JUNIUS, Berkshire
Bliss, Thompson & Co., 174 Front st. Owego
PITCHER DANIEL M., 175 Front st., "

Woolen Mill.

BARAGER CHARLES F., Candor

THE
Waverly
Tribune

A LIVE LOCAL NEWSPAPER.

GIVES ALL THE LOCAL, COUNTY AND NEAR-BY HAPPENINGS.

FIRST IN THE WEEK,

IS ALWAYS FREE FROM VULGARITY.

IS A GOOD FAMILY NEWSPAPER THAT WE SHOULD GET $2.00 A YEAR FOR, BUT WE LET YOU HAVE IT FOR $1.50, ON ACCOUNT OF LOCAL CUSTOM.

ADVERTISERS LIKE IT,

BECAUSE THE READER HAS CONFIDENCE IN IT, AND BEING EIGHT-PAGE THERE ARE MORE CHOICE LOCATIONS FOR THEM.

ADVERTISEMENTS—RATES GIVEN ON APPLICATION.

SOCIETIES.

Masonic Fraternity.

BARTON.—Waverly Lodge, No. 407, F. & A. M., meets first, third and fifth Monday evenings of each month, in Masonic Hall.

Cayuga Chapter, No. 245, R. A. M., Waverly, meets second and fourth Monday evenings of each month.

NEWARK VALLEY.—Newark Valley Lodge, No. 614, F. & A. M., meets in Davidge, Landfield & Co.'s Hall, second and fourth Monday evenings of each month; E. G. Nowlan, W. M.

NICHOLS.—Westbrook Lodge, No. 333, F. & A. M., meets the Wednesday evening on or after the full moon in each month; Samuel Clapp, W. M.; E. Coleman, S. W.; Dr. George P. Cady, Sec.

OWEGO.—Friendship Lodge, No. 153, F. & A. M., meets on the first Wednesday evening after the first Monday in each month; B. J. Davis, W. M.; C. S. Carmichael, Sec.

New Jerusalem Chapter, No. 47, R. A. M., meets at Masonic Hall, first and third Mondays of each month; F. M. Mabee, H.P.; M. B. Watkins, Sec.

Owego Chapter, No. 510, R. M. R., meets at Masonic Hall, monthly, C. M. Haywood, M. W.; N. A. Steevens, Sec.

Ahwaga Lodge, No. 587, F. & A. M., meets at Masonic Hall, first and third Tuesdays after the first Monday in each month; N. A. Steevens, W. M.; George H. Thompson, Sec.

Evening Star Lodge, No. 19, F. & A. M., meets first and third Monday evenings of each month, opposite Ahwaga House; J. W. Barrett, W. M.; A. Sample, Sec.

SPENCER.—Spencer Lodge, No. 290, F. & A. M., meets first and third Tuesday evenings of each month; Charles Riker, W. M.; I. S. Stancliff, Sec.

TIOGA.—Tioga Lodge, No. 534, F. & A. M., was organized at Smithboro, 1863; William J. Drake, W. M.; John P. Swartwood, Sec.

Temperance Societies.

NEWARK VALLEY.—North Star Lodge, No. 21, P. of T., Jenksville, meets every Saturday evening; Monroe Barrett, W.S., Frank Keith, Sec.

OWEGO.—Apalachin Lodge, No. 564, I. O. G. T., Apalachin; S. M. Rulison, C.T., Carrie Rulison, Sec.

Union Council, No. 47, R. T. of T., meets at Odd Fellows' Hall, the second Wednesday evening of each month; F. S. Hodge, S.C., H. C. Brainard, Sec.

SPENCER. -Spencer Council, No. 181, R. T. of T., meets second and fourth Tuesday evenings of each month; William Swartout, S.C., David Seely, Sec.

Grand Army of the Republic.

BARTON.—Stebbins Post, G. A. R., No. 361, Lockwood, meets first an third Thursday evenings of each month; Richard Andrus, Com., G. W. Brink, Adj.

CANDOR.—Candor Post, No. 383, meets at Grand Army Hall, first and third Tuesday evenings of each month; B. E. Cronk, Com., S. J. Legg, Adj.

NEWARK VALLEY.—Williams Post, No. 245, G. A. R., meets second and fourth Saturday evenings of each month, in Roys Block Hall; Harvey Neal, Com., B. S. Harvard, Adj.

NICHOLS.—Warwick Post, No. 259, G. A. R., meets second and fourth Tuesday evenings of each month; William Herrick, Com., L. B. Ross, Adj.

OWEGO.—Babcock Post, No. 59, G. A. R., meets every Wednesday evening, at Grand Army Hall; D. S. Legg, Com., O. L. Newell, Adj.

Tracy Post, No. 613, G. A. R., Apalachin; J. S. Giles, Com., H. J. Cooper, Adj.

RICHFORD.—Belden Post, No. 342, G. A. R., meets every Saturday evening; F. Hutchinson, Com., N. Heath, Adj.

SPENCER.—Dawson Post, No. 464, G. A. R., meets second and fourth Saturday evenings of each month; W. A. Stubbs, Com., L. Brooks, Adj.

Patrons of Husbandry.

BARTON.—North Barton Grange, No. 45, P. of H., meets every Saturday evening; C. S. Nichols, W. M., John F. Hoyt, Sec.

Sullivan Grange, No. 217, P. of H., meets every Saturday evening at Grange Hall, Shepard's Creek; H. Bunnell, W. M., T. Hulett, Sec.

Acme Grange, P. of H., meets weekly; R. R. Cooley, W. M., H. Stebbins, Sec.

CANDOR.—Candor Grange, No. 203, P. of H., meets at Grange Hall, first and third Fridays of each month; Epenetus Howe, W. M., G. H. Hart, Sec.

 Weltonville Grange, P. of H., meets every Thursday evening; W. R. Mead, W. M., H. E. Reese, Sec.

 Strait's Corners Grange, No. 453, P. of H., meets on the first and third Saturdays of each month; A. L. Rider, W. M., S. Hammond, Sec.

NEWARK VALLEY.—Newark Valley Grange, No. 476, P. of H., meets Friday evening of each week; W. F. Prentice, W. M., Mrs. C. S. Shaffer, Sec.

NICHOLS.—Wappasening Grange, No. 522, P. of H., meets on the first and third Saturday evenings of each month; F. C. Lowman, W. M., Robert P. Coryell, Sec.

OWEGO.—Pomona Grange, a county organization, made up of members of subordinate Granges, meets regularly at Owego every three months; O. H. Van Atta of Barton, W. M., Mrs. B. J. Brooks of Barton, Sec.

 Gaskill Corners Grange, No. 403, P. of H., meets every Saturday evening; George W. Hull, W. M., Mrs. G. W. Hull, Sec.

RICHFORD.—Eureka Grange, No. 345, P. of H., meets every Friday evening; Mrs. Emma Jayne, Sec.

Knights of Honor.

BARTON.—Waverly Lodge, No. 293, K. of H., meets every Friday evening in K. of H. Hall.

CANDOR.—Candor Lodge, No. 542, K. of H., meets first and third Tuesdays of each month; Richard Fields, Dic., J. O. Frost, Rep.

NICHOLS.—Susquehanna Lodge, K. & L. of H., meets on the first and third Wednesday evenings of each month; Rev. H. N. Van Deusen, Prot., Sarah A. Ketcham, Sec.

OWEGO.—Owego Lodge, No. 54, K. of H., meets at Odd Fellows' Hall, second and fourth Tuesday evenings of each month; G. Strang, Dic., F. A. Darrow, Rep.

 Diamond Lodge, No. 76, K. and L. of H., meets at Odd Fellows' Hall the first and third Tuesday of each month; S. Goodrich, Prot., M. H. Tuch, Rep.

TIOGA.—Tioga Lodge, No. 263, K. of H., organized at Tioga Center in 1880.

 Emerald Lodge, No. 384, K. & L. of H., organized at Tioga Center in 1881.

Independent Order of Odd Fellows.

BARTON.—Manoca Lodge, No. 219, I. O. of O. F., Waverly, meets every Tuesday evening, in Odd Fellows' Hall.

 Spanish Hill Encampment, No. 52, I. O. of O. F., Waverly, meets first, third and fifth Friday evenings of each month, in Odd Fellows' Hall.

 Cayuta Lodge, I. O. of O. F., No. 159, Lockwood, meets every Friday evening; G. W. Bingham, N. G., D. C. Hagadorn, Sec.

OWEGO.—Tioga Lodge, No. 335, I. O. of O. F., meets every Friday evening; W. L. Stewart, N. G., W. H. Thomas, Sec.

Order of the Iron Hall.

BARTON.—Local Branch, No. 23, O. of I. H., Waverly, meets Monday evenings at K. of H. Hall.

NEWARK VALLEY.—Local Branch, No. 281, O. of I. H., meets the first and third Monday evening of each month; Robert Donley, C. J., D. C. Hand, Acct.

OWEGO.—Branch No. 256, meets first and third Saturday evenings of each month; E. Kimball, C. J., A. S. Hooker, Acct.

 Branch No. 306, Apalachin, J. S. Giles, C. J., C. L. Barton, Acct.

Improved Order of Red Men.

BARTON.—Iroquois Tribe, No. 42, I. O. of R. M., Waverly, meets every Thursday sleep at eight run.

NEWARK VALLEY.—Council fire the first and third Tuesday's sleep, each moon, in Masonic Hall; M. A. Howard, Sachem, H. Leonard, C. of R.

OWEGO.—Ahwaga Tribe, No. 40, I. O. of R. M., meets at the Wigwam, every Friday's sleep; James T. Rogers, Sachem, C. H. Keeler, C. of R.

SPENCER.—Mascawa Tribe, No. 88, I. O. of R. M., meets on the second and fourth Friday's sleep of each moon; J. M. Stowe, Sachem, E. L. Brooks, C. of R.

Miscellaneous Societies.

BARTON.—Cayuga Lodge, No. 35, A. O. U. W., Waverly, meets every Wednesday evening, in Select Knights' Hall.

Schoeffeld Legion, No. 19, Select Knights of A. O. U. W., Waverly, meets every Friday evening in Select Knights' Hall.

Tioga Lodge, No. 101, K. of P., Waverly, meets at Mott's Hall every Wednesday evening.

Equitable Aid Union, No. 417, Factoryville, meets every Thursday evening; J. C. Wood, Dis. Dep. Supreme Pres., F. A. Squires, Pres., Fred Brewster, Sec.

CANDOR.—Candor Council, Royal Arcanum, No. 928; H. P. Potter, Reg., F. S. Woodford, Sec.

OWEGO.—Progressive Assembly, No. 3147, K. of L., meets every Tuesday evening; M. J. Murrey, M. W., J. A. Dodge, R. S.

Star Lodge, No. 91, A. O. U. W., meets on the second and fourth Monday evenings of each month; E. Fitzgerald, M. W., C. Dana, Rec.

SPENCER.— The Tioga County Patron's Fire Relief Association; S. Alfred Seely, Pres., L. W. Hull, Sec.

Markell & Butts orchestra, four pieces.

Robinson Cornet Band, twelve pieces, F. O. Robinson, leader.

TIOGA.—Lodge No. 106, A. O. U. W., meets on the second and third Mondays of each month; Edward M. Forman, M. W., Robert H. Spendley, Recorder.

THE RATES OF POSTAGE.

Postal cards one cent each, to all parts of the United States and Canada.

FIRST-CLASS MATTER—TWO CENTS PER OUNCE OR FRACTION THEREOF.

Letters and all other mailable matter of other classes subject to letter postage by reason of a violation of the postal laws, two cents per ounce to all parts of the United States and Canada.

REGISTRATION, DROP LETTERS, ETC.

On registered domestic letters and third and fourth-class matter an additional fee of ten cents is required.

Local, or "Drop" letters, that is for the city or town where deposited, two cents if delivered by carriers, and one cent if there is no carrier system, per ounce.

Manuscript for publication in books, (except when accompanied by proof-sheets), newspapers and magazines chargeable as letters.

FREE.

Newspapers, to each actual subscriber in the county, where published, free of charge.

SECOND-CLASS MATTER—ONE CENT PER POUND.

Newspapers and periodicals, transient excepted, to be prepaid, at the office of publication at one cent per pound, or fraction thereof.

THIRD-CLASS MATTER—ONE CENT FOR TWO OUNCES.

(Must not be sealed.)

Mail matter of the third-class embraces printed books, (except transient newspapers, four ounces for one cent,) and periodicals, circulars, proof-sheets and corrected proof-sheets, manuscript copy accompanying the same, and all matter of the same general character, as above enumerated, the printing upon which is designed to instruct, amuse, cultivate the mind or taste, or impart general information, and postage shall be paid thereon at the rate of one cent for each two ounces or fractional part thereof.

FOURTH-CLASS MATTER—ONE CENT FOR EACH OUNCE.

Mail matter of the fourth-class embraces labels, patterns, photographs, playing cards, visiting cards, address tags, paper sacks, wrapping paper and blotting pads with or without printed address thereon, ornamented paper, and all other matter of the same general character, the printing upon which is not designed to instruct, amuse, cultivate the mind or taste, or impart general information. This class also includes merchandise, and samples of merchandise, models, samples of ores, metals, minerals, seeds, &c., and any other matter not included in the first, second or third-class, and which is not in its form or nature liable to destroy, deface or otherwise damage the contents of the mail-bag, or harm the person of any one engaged in the postal service. Postage rate thereon, one cent for each ounce or fractional part thereof.

Packages of mail-matter must not exceed four pounds each in weight, except in cases of single volumes of books.

Undelivered letters and postal cards can be re-sent to a new address without additional charge. Senders may write their names on transient newspapers, books or any package in either class, preceded by the word "from."

Stamps cut from the stamped envelopes are rejected by the postoffice.

Stamped envelopes and wrappers, postal cards, and stamps of different denominations for sale at the postoffices.

Stamped envelopes accidentally spoiled redeemed at the postoffice where bought.

POSTOFFICES AND POSTMASTERS.

POSTOFFICES.	TOWNS.	POSTMASTERS.
Apalachin,	Owego,	Frank J. Knapp.
Barton,	Barton,	John B. Coleman.
Berkshire,	Berkshire,	John R. Ford.
Campville,	Owego,	McKenzie Dickinson.
*Candor,	Candor,	John R. Chidsey.
Catatonk,	Candor,	Alanson H. Smith.
Connecticut,	Newark Valley,	James DeGaramo.
East Nichols,	Nichols,	Elizabeth A. White.
Factoryville,	Barton,	Clarence E. Clock.
Flemingsville,	Owego,	Charles E. Truman.
Gaskill's Corners,	Owego,	Harmon Curtis.
Halsey Valley,	Tioga,	Grant M. West.
Hooper's Valley,	Nichols,	Lucas T. Field.
Jenksville,	Newark Valley,	Samuel M. Avery.
Ketchumville,	Newark Valley,	Charles Finch.
Lockwood,	Barton,	George D. Brock.
*Newark Valley,	Newark Valley,	Sherman W. Byington.
Nichols,	Nichols,	Emmet Coleman.
North Barton,	Barton,	Edmund H. Hoyt.
North Spencer,	Spencer,	Mahlon A. Kellogg.
*Owego,	Owego,	Frederick O. Cable.
Reniff,	Barton,	Willis E. Gillett.
Richford,	Richford,	Charles A. Clark.
Smithsboro.	Tioga,	William J. Drake.
South Apalachin,	Owego,	Alonzo Bills.
South Owego,	Owego,	Lyman B. Truman.
*Spencer,	Spencer,	Marvin D. Fisher.
Strait's Corners,	Tioga,	Alvinza Strait.
Tioga Center,	Tioga,	Joseph Winters.
*Waverly,	Barton,	Andrew A. Slawson.
Weltonville,	Candor,	Andrew J. Graham.
West Candor,	Candor,	Charles F. Gridley.
West Newark,	Newark Valley,	Willis E. Hover.
Willseyville,	Candor,	Emory C. Mix.
Wilson Creek,	Berkshire.	Colden N. Hart.

Rate of Commission Charged for Money Orders.

On orders not exceeding $10, eight cents; over $10, and not exceeding $15, ten cents; over $15, and not exceeding $30, fifteen cents: over $30, and not exceeding $40, twenty cents; over $40, and not exceeding $50, twenty-five cents; over $50, and not exceeding $60, thirty cents; over $60, and not exceeding $70, thirty-five cents; over $70, and not exceeding $80, forty cents; over $80, and not exceeding $100, forty-five cents. No single order issued for a greater sum than $100.

*Money order offices.

ERRATA.

PART FIRST.

In seventh line, second paragraph, page 192, read 1851, for "1857."
In eighth line from bottom, page 192, read Hull for "Hall."
In tenth line from bottom, page 383, read 1876, for "1776."
In ninth line, second paragraph, page 387, read Mrs. Lovejoy for "Mr. Lovejoy."
In second line, second paragraph, page 388, read comprise for "confine."
In fifth line, second paragraph, page 391, read Wheeler H. for "George W."
With reference to Mr. LeRoy W. Kingman's history of the town of Owego, we wish to make an explanation, fearing that we have left some points ambiguous. On page 361, we say: "This completes the biographical sketches furnished by Mr. Kingman," etc., and, "We add the following additional sketches." The latter sketches end with the heading, "Business Centers," on page 383, and Mr. Kingman's sketch continues, the remainder of the history being his matter, except an interpolation of a brief sketch of the "present business interests," page 391, and "physicians," page 393, by the Publishers. We make this explanation to justly relieve Mr. Kingman from the responsibility of authorship of any facts we may have inserted in his sketch.

PART SECOND.

In the town of Spencer, page 185, should have been inserted the following: Brock Thomas, president Farmers' and Merchants' Bank, stock dealer, farmer 50, in Chemung county 450, and in Tompkins county 50, h VanEtten.

GENERAL CONTENTS.

	PAGE
Business Directory, by towns	3
Classified Business Directory	217
Errata	245
Gazetteer of County, Part I	5
Gazetteer of Towns, Part I	70
Map of Tioga County	inside of back cover
Postal Rates and Regulations	243
Postoffices and Postmasters	244
Societies	241

INDEX TO ILLUSTRATIONS.

Barager Charles F	172
Camp George Sidney	330
Campbell Arba	374
Clark Charles A	360
Clinton Royal W	260
Dorwin William E	472
Elmer Howard	94
Elmer Richard A	964
Haywood Charles M	380
Hill James	384
Latimer Jonathan C	468
Parker Charles E	350
Parker James M	346
Platt Thomas C	334
Smyth William	354
Taylor John J	348
Thompson Clarence A	392
Tracy Benjamin F	400
Truman Lyman	342
VanKleeck John J	358
West Luther B	484

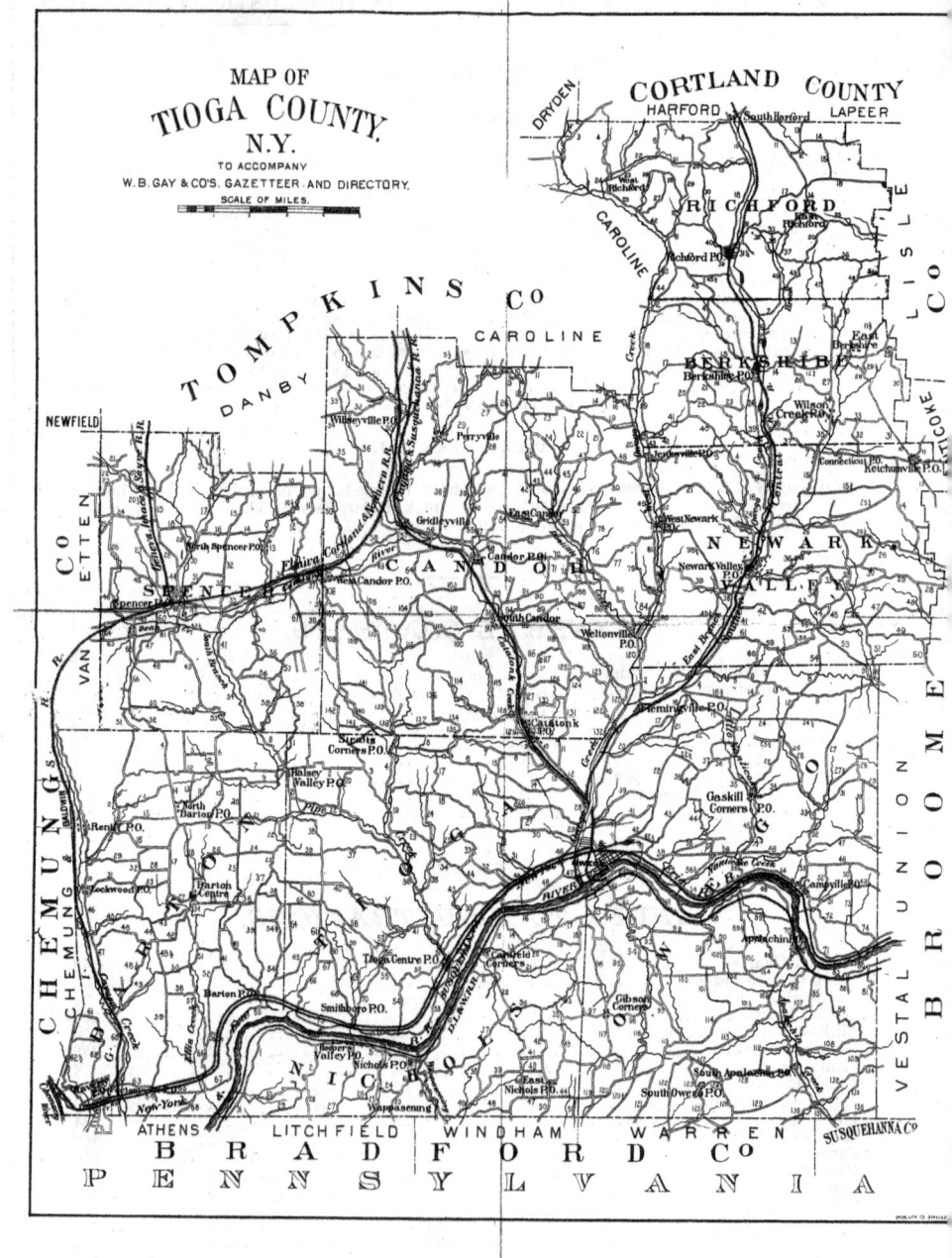

www.ingramcontent.com/pod-product-compliance
Lightning Source LLC
Chambersburg PA
CBHW071429150426
43191CB00008B/1085